MW00887238

World's Fastest Neurosurgeon

World's Fastest Neurosurgeon by Dr. Jim Lowe

Published by Dr. Jim Lowe
1233 Valley Road
Villanova, PA 19085

www.WorldsFastestNeurosurgeon.com

Cover by Roger Garbow

ISBN: 978-1975941352

Dr. Jim Lowe

World's Fastest Neurosurgeon

For Ginny and Aidan,
without whom there would be no story worth telling.

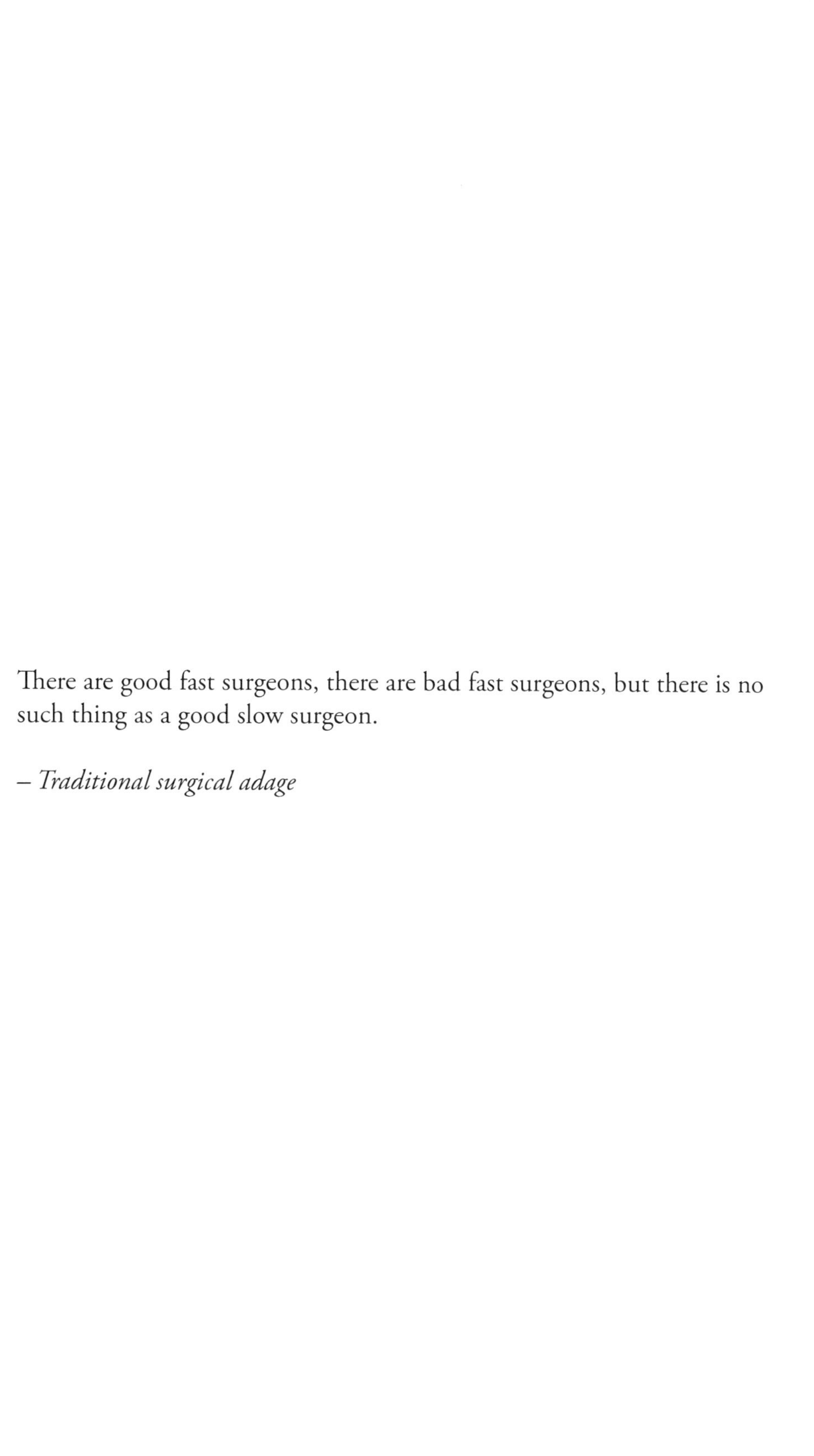

There are good fast surgeons, there are bad fast surgeons, but there is no such thing as a good slow surgeon.

– *Traditional surgical adage*

1

Chapter One

I was flat-out at maximum rpm in sixth gear screaming down the front straight at Daytona, my right foot pressed firmly to the floor of the brand-spanking-new Porsche, when the car directly in front of me blew up in a cloud of gray-white smoke. I was positioned roughly 100 feet behind the Daytona Prototype racer, which equated to a gap of about four-tenths of a second at the 180 mph-plus speed we were traveling. Not willing to waste any more time checking my math, I stomped on the brakes hard—hard enough to lock up all four discs, stopping my wheels from spinning instantly. The unfortunate result of this panic action was to blow out all four of the racing slicks on the Porsche, sending my car blindly spinning out of control down toward Daytona's first turn and the concrete wall next to it.

This of course occurred in full view of the entire Grand-Am contingent gathered for that day's practice in preparation for the Rolex 24 Hours of Daytona race later that month. Despite their good seats along pit lane, they, like me, were not able to see much through the thick smoke that both cars were generating. In fact, when a crash like this occurs, seemingly for all to witness, there often isn't much to see in "real time." Mostly, when involved as a spectator, you do what all other drivers and crew do—you listen for the big bang at the end and silently give thanks it isn't you in the seat. Trust me, it's much more entertaining to be a seemingly disinterested observer than the guy in the spinning racecar.

Disappointing as it might seem, there was no moment of epiphany, no sense of enlightenment, and certainly no "life flashing before my eyes" experience while I was spinning down the track at Daytona. I wasn't reflecting on a life well lived, or any such esoteric bullshit; I was in fact worried about killing the guy in the car in front of me—and trying not to wreck a perfectly good new car two weeks before the biggest race of the season. I did, however, manage to pay some attention to what was happening outside the car, but mostly out of a perverse interest in when I was going to hit the wall or, worse yet, the decelerating prototype somewhere out there in the cloud of smoke. But I was no longer in anything resembling control of my racecar. Once the car starts to spin, you're a passenger—you may as well order another cocktail, this thing's going down whether you like it or not. Put "both feet in"—one hard on the brake, the other depressing the clutch pedal—and hope your wife's not paying attention.

While I waited patiently for the inevitable big crunch, an amazing thing happened. My Porsche came to a smoky stop in the middle of the pavement of turn one—no impact, no big bang, no respectful memorial service. Nothing. I looked around tentatively, astonished to be apparently safe and sound in the cockpit of my unharmed race car. I tore off one racing glove and checked my carotid pulse, just to be sure.

My tachycardia was interrupted by my engineer, Steve Bunkhall, checking in on the radio.

"Talk to me, Jim. You OK?"

I keyed the mike. "Yeah, had a bit of a spin just now."

"Uh, yeah, I know, we all saw it. A bit of excitement.... So, how's the car?" A natural and appropriate question since, once the driver is deemed capable of talking on the radio, all attention turns to the condition of the racecar.

"Believe it or not, I didn't hit a damn thing, but I blew out all four tires."

Roger Reis, crew chief and den mother, chimed in. "I'll send a guy down with four new slicks. Just sit tight for now. Do you need anything else?"

"Copy that, four new tires. And maybe a fresh change of underwear?"

On exiting the racecar, I found that I had come to a stop about fifteen feet from the guilty prototype, whose driver was standing just off to the side after extracting himself from his mostly intact vehicle. Intact except for the missing bodywork on the rear of the car, which had rather spectacularly disintegrated when his right rear tire blew.

Once again, the classic question: "You OK?"

He held out his arms just a bit, as if to demonstrate. "No problem, I'm still in one piece. Thanks for not hitting me."

We stood there together, staring at our racecars, holding our untouched helmets and scratching our heads, waiting for our heart rates to return to normal and the wreckers to arrive. We both probably looked the same—sweaty, smelly, breathing heavily, and both wearing that stunned look familiar to guys who find that the parachute, in fact, works as advertised.

Fifteen minutes later, we gathered around the car in our assigned Daytona garage stall, accepting congratulatory hugs and receiving respectful stares from a large contingent of drivers and crew from various teams, all wanting a quick glimpse of the car's reportedly intact condition. I spoke with more than one fellow driver, including the paddock's only other physician-driver, Dr. Michael Gomez. He also expressed admiration of my handling of the spinning Porsche, but I chalked that up to his skewed sense of normalcy, given his chosen field of psychiatry.

As the crew began to examine the cooling car, Roger directed my attention to the Porsche's two rear wheels, highlighting the flat-spotted rims that would later serve as great table bases in my garage at home. Co-drivers Tim Sugden and Johannes van Overbeek arrived from the pits via golf cart and quickly confirmed my more-alive-than-dead status. We then packed it in early so the crew could get a jump on preparing the car for the next day's practice. After all, I would need to get back on the horse tomorrow—and do so quickly in order to avoid any new hesitation about driving flat-out.

Monday morning I gratefully awoke in my bed at the hotel, acutely aware that I was lucky not to be part of some trauma intern's "to do" list that day. Following the script prepared by mentor Jim Pace, I ran early and often in the Porsche, ultimately setting down my personal best lap in the last session of the day. I focused on braking later into turn one and tried not to peek at my own personal set of looping skid marks laid down the day before.

Eighteen hours later I was scrubbed and gowned in the OR, bent over a freshly-fractured spine. I had long since grown accustomed to that day-after-racing surreal feeling of being back at work in the real world, but this was extra-sweet, extra-special, somehow. Days later, I was still buzzing, still amped, and ultimately more focused than ever. I joked with my partner as we operated, told endlessly repetitive tall tales to unsuspecting new nurses, and thought a lot about when I'd next be back behind the wheel of the racecar.

One thing I didn't think too long about, though, was crashing at Daytona.

2

Chapter Two

A completely natural and appropriate question at this point would be, "Why the hell did a neurosurgeon get behind the wheel of a racecar in the first place?" And it is, in fact, the same question I ask myself often. After all, being a racecar driver wasn't what I originally set out to be. But it turns out that racing is yet another "test" I've subjected myself to—including more than a few that, in retrospect, were unnecessary. Years of high school and college football (including being on a Harvard team that never lost to Yale) resulted in numerous dislocations and breaks, but those had far less impact than the psychological challenges that I experienced in the process. As a twenty-year-old college student, I joined the Marines, escaping Officer's Candidate School at Quantico with an honorable discharge and a great deal of respect for short but nasty drill sergeants. I survived my collegiate pre-med experience despite my chemistry professor's distaste of all things athletic, and my med school experience was an out-of-focus blur. Internship and my subsequent neurosurgery residency training were grueling endurance runs, harsh but unforgettable; I emerged from both in one piece, and stronger for it. In fact, whether it was heliboarding in British Columbia, surfing big waves in Portugal, or lugging an M-16 through the Virginia mud, I've walked away mostly intact from more than a few tests over the years. But nothing, not one of those other activities and challenges consumed me with the intensity and thrill that racing would.

But that doesn't answer the question. To do that, I need to start at the beginning: Christmas 1969.

***

My brother and I sat side by side at the top of the stairs, impatiently waiting for the "OK" from our parents. We had awakened before dawn, and whispered to each other excitedly as we waited for light to come through the windows. After two unsuccessful trips into my parent's bedroom, we finally convinced my mom to get out of bed, put on her nightgown, and elbow my dad awake.

"You boys can go and sit on the steps, but don't go downstairs until your dad's up and everybody's ready."

Rick and I nodded eagerly, and got into position on the stairs, sitting as far down as we dared without spoiling the view into the living room. I risked a quick look around the edge of the wall, and spotted something bright yellow, alongside the many wrapped presents under the Christmas tree. "Hey, no peeking!" my younger brother scolded. "Mom said we have to wait!"

"Shhh, I wasn't peeking, but there's something down there…."

Moments later, my four older sisters were gathered on the stairs behind us, with my mom close behind. As the youngest, Rick and I got prime positions at the front of the pack, but collectively, the six Lowe kids vibrated with a single energy as we waited for my dad to emerge and Christmas to officially begin.

After what felt like forever, my dad appeared at the top of the steps, and before he could finish saying "OK, you can go down now," Rick and I were tearing down the stairs at full speed. Rick pretty much dove into the pile of presents, and I made a beeline straight for the toy I had only glimpsed a few minutes before.

It was, without a doubt, the greatest Christmas present ever. Sitting off to one side of the Lowe family tree that morning was a fully-assembled Johnny Lightning L.M. 500 Race Set. Easily the coolest gift a six-year-old race fan could possibly receive back then, the toy was manufactured by Topper, a small New Jersey company that competed directly with the likes of Mattel's Hot Wheels. In a stroke of marketing genius or just plain luck, Topper would later sponsor Al Unser, who promptly won both the 1970 and '71 Indianapolis 500. But a full five months before that, Johnny Lightning became a fixture in the Lowe household when Bob Lowe picked out the perfect gift for his sons. And, knowing his overeager boys well enough, my dad had taken time away from his other Santa duties to get it up and running so that my brother and I could begin racing moments after we arrived on the scene that morning.

The design of the Johnny Lightning set was genius, and perfectly suitable both for six-year-old boys and forty-six-year-old dads. The plastic black and yellow two-lane track was oval shaped, but with an uphill section just past start/finish. That section was covered with a clear plastic roof, intended to keep the cars from taking flight as they accelerated up the hill. The "lightening motion" propulsion of the cars was accomplished simply enough: a movable knob was attached to a hook that engaged a loop on the bottom of each car; each player would try to time it so that he slid the knob forward exactly as the car went by. With practice, a semi-coordinated six-year-old could time it perfectly to create a near-perpetual motion race, until mom, church, or fatigue put an end to that particular contest.

Johnny Lightning L.M. 500 Race set

When it comes to race cars, young boys like to see things crashing, so Rick and I quickly learned how to get the cars airborne. We mastered the fine art of catapulting the cars off the track's ramp, resulting in a few choice plaster divots in the living room walls that remain visible today. Even though we quickly created a "keep your wits about you" situation for the rest of the family, I distinctly recall my dad launching more than a few of those projectiles, right before we were carted off to church in the Lowe family pink '59 DeSoto.

Rick and I both slept with our Johnny Lightning cars that night; I recall my younger brother grabbing his favorite blue car, which was fine with me, since that left the red A.J. Foyt Indy Special for me. Sharing a small room in our parent's three-bedroom house, we whispered and fidgeted in our beds until dad's "Knock it off and go to sleep!" call shut us down for the day. But once it got quiet enough, I could hear the unmistakable sounds coming from the living room, where my dad was perfecting his runs through turns two and three, trying to get a jump on his boys for the next day's rematch.

***

Earlier that summer, I had joined my parents and siblings in front of our black-and-white TV while fuzzy images relayed from the moon allowed us to witness history live as Neil Armstrong made his giant leap. I realized then, with all eight Lowe's huddled in the basement, that we were watching something special; I recall my dad's ultimate compliment – "that's really great" – but didn't quite realize the enormity of the event. Still, for weeks afterward, Rick and I played astronauts in the front yard, stepping out of the tree/lunar module and mimicking Armstrong's words. (To this day, I suspect that my brother remains a bit subconsciously annoyed that he always had to be Aldrin.)

The crew of Apollo 11 became early icons of the Jim Lowe heroes club, but they weren't alone back then. Like much of the sports fan world, I had enjoyed watching the '68 winter Olympics when French skier Jean Claude Killy dominated the downhill events. I was so enthralled with his daring and fearlessness that I insisted afterward that everyone call me "Jean Claude," which certainly beat the hell out of my then-current nickname of "Tubby." May had brought the annual Indy 500 viewing to our house, during which dad and I saw a diminutive Italian-American named Andretti win. It would be four more years before I was introduced to the sobering reality of auto racing, when Swede Savage's racecar blew apart and burst into flames in front of a live TV audience in the '73 Indy 500. But the race in 1969 was most memorable, probably because it's the first one I remembered—and was the start of my long history as a racing fan. It didn't have the global impact that the moon landing had, of course, but from the perspective of my small world, all of these events seemed giant and worthy of celebration.

To be sure, a replica plastic gray lunar module kit and a pair of wooden skis (seriously ill-equipped with springs for binders) shared space with the Johnny Lightning racetrack under the Lowe tree that December, but my attention was definitely more focused on names such as Jim Clark, Al Unser, and Jackie Stewart. Given my dad's interest in spectator sports, and his obvious enjoyment of watching sports of virtually any kind with his two boys (frequently combined with a Schaefer pony beer or two), it was a short transition for me to become an avid fan of pretty much any televised competition. While football and baseball cemented their places as mainstays of American sporting events worth viewing, I was always on the lookout for the rarely televised racing, both from US venues and more exotic locales in Europe.

With the increased visibility of racing events on TV in the late sixties and early seventies, my awareness of the concept of the racecar driver as hero grew rapidly. The Indy 500 and Daytona 500 races first came into the Lowe home courtesy of announcer Jim McKay and Sunday TV programming in the form of ABC's Wide World of Sports. Learning about Jackie Stewart's first Formula One World Championship in 1969 took a search beyond the local papers, but after he won two more F1 titles, Jackie then became an auto racing mainstay at Wide World of Sports. His Scottish accent still remains a visceral memory of my early years watching fast cars crash spectacularly. My own attempt to imitate Jackie ("This is Jockey Stoowart, calming to yew live from the straits of Monaco!") was always good for a laugh, although admittedly few kids in my neighborhood realized exactly who he was, or why he was on that show that started with the crashing ski-jumper. There was no reasonable way that I could have known then, from the perspective of a six-year-old, that Jackie Stewart and his crusade for safety at the track would have a far bigger influence on my life decades later, when I changed roles from fascinated spectator to that of an actual racecar driver.

***

F. Scott Fitzgerald advised us, "Show me a hero and I will write you a tragedy." I was oblivious to this idea as a young racing fan, but racing was a painful example of this concept many times in those early years. Drivers routinely risked their lives, race promoters shrugged that same risk off as part of the deal, and fans came to accept the inevitability of losing drivers every season. Unthinkable now, the deaths of racecar drivers were likened to those of ancient gladiators: somehow perceived as noble, the huge risks were allowed as some necessary part of the entertainment, simply the price paid for the spoils available. But as the death toll mounted, TV exposure, and especially sponsor involvement, demanded changes. A new type of hero was needed. Nearly a tragedy himself, Jackie Stewart indeed stepped forward.

There's an incredible racetrack in Belgium known as the Circuit de Spa-Francorchamps or, more commonly, "Spa." It's a marvelous relic of a track that was built in 1921 and that initially included some nine miles of twisting public roads in the classic "road course" style typical of the period. Situated in the Ardennes, the layout has hills and valleys spread widely enough that it frequently rains on one end of the forest circuit while the other might remain dry. Although the current track is a more manageable and modern four-mile course, in 1966 it consisted of what amounted to country roads without barriers, unless you counted the roadside farmhouses sprinkled throughout the thirteen-turn lap. Despite its intimidating design, the annual Formula One race there was a favorite of many drivers and was thought to favor those with good cars and better courage. That year, the grid for the Grand Prix of Belgium held John Surtees on pole, with Stewart starting third, in front of British Racing Motors teammates Graham Hill in fourth, and Bob Bondurant in eleventh.

Jackie Stewart's wrecked F1 car. Spa, 1966

The race started in heavy rain, with seven cars crashing on the first lap—including all three of the BRM pilots. Midway through the first lap, Jackie slid off at a turn called the Masta kink and landed upside down in a ditch adjacent to a barn. Trapped in his car, Stewart was saturated with leaking fuel while awaiting rescue. He was finally freed—by his own teammates who borrowed a spectator's tools to remove the car's steering wheel before moving Stewart to safety. It then took over thirty minutes for an ambulance to arrive at the scene of the crash, after which Jackie was taken to the track's poorly equipped first aid center. Upon the realization that Stewart was badly injured with shoulder and rib fractures, a second ambulance was called to transport him to the local hospital. Adding further drama to the situation, the second van's driver got lost en route, resulting in a further delay before Jackie finally received the medical attention he needed.

Stewart's Belgian Grand Prix experience occurred during a particularly deadly period in Formula One's history. No fewer than nine drivers had been killed in the period between the beginning of the decade and the 1966 Belgian GP; ultimately, ten more would die while racing before Stewart's retirement in 1973. The final blow for Jackie would come when his teammate Francois Cevert was killed during qualifying for the Watkins Glen Grand Prix in 1973. Having already clinched his third championship, Stewart reluctantly ran the race and retired shortly afterward, one race shy of his one-hundredth Grand Prix.

For the racing community in that period, the most shocking event was surely the death of Stewart's compatriot Jim Clark in a Formula 2 race at Hockenheim in April 1968. Then, as now, Clark was widely considered the world's best driver; his fatal accident was proof positive that no one was safe—even the more skilled drivers. Clearly changes were needed urgently.

Jackie Stewart's close call in Belgium, combined with his unique status among racing's elite class, positioned him perfectly to take on the role of safety advocate. Stewart quickly became an outspoken campaigner for new safety measures in auto racing. He thereafter always used seatbelts, a full-face helmet, and a fireproof suit. He also demanded many changes be made to update circuits with purpose-built barriers, remove dangerous objects close to the racing surface, and provide better medical facilities with ambulances on standby at all events. When race promoters balked at the cost involved in these provisions, Stewart threatened to withdraw from events, with other drivers willing to follow his lead. Ultimately, Jackie's clout won out and his demands were met, with immediate improvements seen. In the next twenty years of Formula One racing, only seven more drivers would die behind the wheel. Although efforts to protect racing drivers, crew, and spectators continue to evolve as our understanding of the risks and dangers of the sport expands, we certainly have Jackie Stewart to thank for creating the culture of safety that now protects the modern driver so well.

***

Mario Andretti's win in the '69 Indy 500, followed by ABC's Wide World of Sports Athlete of the Year honors, propelled him to instantly recognizable celebrity in the United States. Decades before first-name-only monikers became the sports hero norm, "Mario" was an instantly recognizable name attached to many kids my age deemed to be doing any activity too fast. Whether I was running in the house or pedaling my Schwinn with the red banana seat wildly down Edgewood Drive, "Slow down, Mario!" was a frequent warning yelled by my parents and various frustrated neighbors tired of my occasional detours into flower beds and, on one occasion, fresh concrete.

Given that I had no access to motorized machinery back then, my personal need for speed had to be met through self-powered means, usually while navigating bikes or skateboards. Conveniently, our house was situated on a long, steeply inclined circular street, with even steeper sections on the curving back side road called Glendale Circle. At the bottom of my street, Edgewood drive, there was a right-handed turn, gentle enough for the average young bike rider to make without drama, providing that speed was controlled and the runoff area grass wasn't too wet (in case of the all-too-common understeer situation). By 1969, negotiating that corner on my bike at moderate speeds had become rather uneventful, so I naturally hatched a plan to do it from the top of the hill, adding a significant component of speed.

Perhaps I didn't examine the running surface thoroughly enough, but I was at least aware that my neighbors' lawns had some well-manicured grass gutters bordering the sidewalk, ideally positioned to catch an unsuspecting bike rider's wheels. I knew about these course obstacles but simply planned on ignoring them. Besides, if you stayed on the hardtop, and didn't venture off into the grass, it was a nonissue. Why plan for failure when there's glory in the offing?

Starting at the very top of the street, my only goal was to max out my entry speed into the turn far below—basically the same concept that racers the world over strive for—without overcooking the corner. A simple enough idea, even for a six-year-old brain with zero racing experience and little genetic propensity for speed. Pedaling furiously down the hill, I focused first on the driveways intersecting the sidewalk— I knew that an errant Buick would ruin my run and that I would probably never get out of the doghouse if I dented a neighbor's car. Midway down the hill, at terminal Schwinn velocity, I made the mistake of taking a quick peek at the sidewalk gutters. As any racer will tell you, the vehicle will tend to follow your eyes—in this case, off to my left and into the thin gutter at the edge of Mrs. Edwards' lawn. At full speed my front tire found the trough, caught up abruptly, and launched me over the handlebars before I even realized that making the corner was no longer a priority. I landed on the pavement squarely on my unhelmeted head, awakening a few minutes later to my own howling and the anxious face of Mr. Edwards. Blood streamed down from a gash on the growing egg on my forehead, and seemingly every exposed inch of skin (I was wearing the road rash special: shorts and a tank top) was abraded. My neighbor walked me to see my mom, who was calm enough given that I was standing up, talking, and apparently OK. A later doctor visit ("Bette, the boy should probably stay off the bike for a while.") confirmed that I would live to fight another day, but for some time after that, the Edgewood Drive speed record attempts were curtailed.

Edgewood Drive was also a busy place when it came to after-school pick-up games. Depending on the season, and how the local sports teams were faring in the standings and collective psyche of the neighborhood, games of football, street hockey, and baseball were ever present. Each afternoon, I would rush though homework, struggle through piano practice, and head outside to play. However, the "to play" part was sadly misleading, as it suggests action of some sort. I ran out the door with eager anticipation that I'd get to join the other kids, but each time my enthusiasm would come face to face with reality. Whether it was my overweight and non-athletic physique, or simple shortcomings in the bravery department, I normally ended up sitting on the curb. When the older kids chose sides for games, the less athletic kids always had to wait until the end to be picked. But instead of being picked last, I wasn't picked at all, a veritable no-show in the neighborhood pecking order. Despite this, I showed up every day, painful as it was. As much as I wanted to play and hated being excluded, I loathed staying indoors, away from the action. And if I was out there watching, there was at least a chance; if I stayed inside, well, there wasn't even that. So, from the safety of the curb, I watched the big kids, who in reality were probably still preteens, playing right out there in front of my house or in the park around the corner. As I watched, I fantasized that one of the players would pull up lame, and the team would suddenly need a super sub. In my imagination, a finger would be pointed at me, and after confirming that it was in fact me they wanted, I would feign nonchalance, step in, and promptly hit the buzzer-beater or home run for the win. But at least for a while longer, I would simply sit, arms around my knees, and wait to someday play also.

By the time I was ten, my mother had already experienced several of the assuredly frightening events that raising two active boys entailed. Being a stay-at-home mom, Bette Lowe got to be first on the scene for many of the Lowe boys' traumas, dealing with scrapes, sprains, and abrasions well before my dad arrived home from work. Despite being a first responder, my mother was somehow able to put forth a calm demeanor, all the while quietly fearing for our safety. Perhaps this was a byproduct of her immense faith, exhibited in her daily prayers to protect her kids. I'm pretty sure that Rick and I occupied, then and now, a disproportionate amount of "Please God" space in my mom's private moments.

Despite her well-founded fears, and in spite of my demonstrated ability to land successfully on my head at high speed, my mother finally broke down and allowed me to buy my first skateboard in 1974. I somehow managed this feat through a carefully orchestrated assault on Bette Lowe's usually airtight sensibilities. First I showed her my friend's benign-looking skateboard; then I demonstrated how we were only doing a few tricks, such as popping wheelies or trying to spin 360 degrees, and finally I promised that I would never do the dangerous run down Edgewood Drive. What I hadn't promised, though, was that I wouldn't do an attempt at Glendale Circle, the Mt. Everest of our 1970's neighborhood high-speed runs.

Unlike the makeable turn at the bottom of Edgewood Drive, the right-hander at the bottom of Glendale circle was a 90-degree off-camber horror for which my low-grip polyurethane skateboard wheels were no match. With my friend and chief accomplice, Danny Devine, I walked the run from top to track-out, debating wildly the possibility of actually surviving the run. Ultimately, Danny convinced me that it was doable, but his good judgment took advantage of my adrenaline rush when he convinced me to go first.

Equipped with the requisite summer outfit—Chuckie T's with shorts and tank top again—I set off down the hill, wobbling just a bit with the few mid-course corrections required for the gently curving upper section, and braced myself for the final right turn at the bottom. Fully committed, I passed on the last bail-out chance just before corner entry, firmly believing that gravity, grip, and determination would beat the wicked geometry of the turn.

I was wrong. Big.

Leaning into the right-hander at full speed, I initially turned in—but realized in an instant that I was in no way going to come out at the exit unscathed. I tried a frantic mid-turn correction, only to immediately lose traction just before the apex. What I hadn't planned on was a car appearing at the intersection just as I was in need of runoff area. Danny screamed from his pre-planned vantage point at the exit of the turn, and I tried leaning in further in a last-ditch attempt to regain control. The car's brakes screeched and tires squealed as I exited the pavement, crossed airborne over the grass boundary, and bounced firmly off the right front fender of Mrs. Cope's skidding car. (Ironically enough, she was in a Dodge, but I digress).

I jumped up, more scared than hurt, a bit unnerved by the sound of Mrs. Cope's yelling and the sight of the Coronet's tire so close to my head. There were some requisite scrapes, a distinct ringing in my ears, and a curious amount of instant swelling from my right elbow (which still bears the scars today). However, I was most worried about the sting of retribution once my mom found out about our adventure. Danny was nowhere to be found, having taken off at a sprint once Mrs. Cope had stopped her car, and it was a full day later before he had the guts to reappear and corroborate my story of having fallen out of a tree. Although Mrs. Cope later supplied my mom with the correct version, I did enjoy a brief delay and cooling-down period that lessened somewhat the eventual punishment resulting from yet another confirmation of my parents' suspicion about my apparent poor judgment.

To this day, whenever I visit my parents, I take a long look at the right-hander at the end of Glendale Circle on my way by. I swear I could make it, with just a little more grip and a better line through the corner.

3

Chapter Three

Growing up in the 1960s and '70s Philadelphia suburb that was Springfield was not necessarily a kinder and gentler experience. Although my mother endlessly taught the concept of "acting like a gentleman," other kids in my neighborhood didn't necessarily get the same message. The direct result of this is that I ended up getting my ass kicked a lot. Two especially willing participants in this activity were my neighbors, Anthony and Sammy Marcozzi. Practitioners of the fine art of name-calling and taunting, Anthony and Sammy spotted in me a reluctance to participate, and decided that the best way to address the situation was to beat me up. I often found myself struggling on the ground, getting alternating views of pavement/lawn/curbing while avoiding blows from above and simultaneously trying to figure out what a "faggot!" was. Many such fights were concluded when the ever-vigilant Bette Lowe—restrained from uttering any non-church sanctioned expletives—pulled Anthony or Sammy (or occasionally both) off of me.

Even though fighting wasn't especially common for me, I definitely learned that there were risks involved in not being one of the "cool" kids. I recognized early on that kids who were acknowledged as cool rarely suffered the same schoolyard or front yard confrontations. I also quickly realized that one way to shortcut the whole process was to participate in sports—and to participate well. This insight ultimately got me out of my designated seat as a timid spectator and into the action when the opportunity arose. I firmly believed that if I could become one of the guys on the court or running down the field, I would be insulated from the ambushes of the Sammys and Anthonys of the world. It became obvious to me that if you hit the ball far, evaded tacklers, or sank the baseline shot, nobody much cared if you were actually a bit of a dork in real life. Becoming an accepted member of a team also counteracted somewhat the perception that I was an "egghead" because I happened to get straight A's in school. Latching onto this fact, I spent considerable focused effort in trying to become the best athlete I could— mostly out of a desperate sense of self preservation.

Once I realized that there was safety, acceptance, and adolescent salvation in athletic participation, I embraced the concept whole-heartedly. I was also lucky enough to go through a few growth spurts during my later grade school years, which had the bonus effect of further diminishing the frequency of Anthony's and Sammy's bullying. And what happened next was something completely unexpected: by eighth grade, I was one of the bigger kids in the class, and that size combined with some element of inner determination helped enormously to put me squarely at the top of the football player pecking-order. After spending years riding the pine, I suddenly blossomed into a star running back and linebacker, finally enjoying success at the upper-level 120-pound Springfield team. My coach, the remarkably-named Nick Nicholas, taught me to hit hard, cut on a dime, and curse like a sailor, much to the dismay of Bette. In the process I achieved a semblance of very-local stardom, enhanced further when I scored my first touchdown. Sweeter still was the fact that the TD came on an interception of Barry Blundin's pass, which I somehow managed to not drop on my way into the opposite endzone. Barry was the acknowledged best athlete in my school, so I had long since been in awe of his physical gifts and resultant status among my schoolmates. But when I scored off of him during that game between Springfield and Kedron, it was a moment that overwhelmingly reinforced my theory of sports and acceptance: it felt not just good, it felt great. Even better, the high lasted well past my return to school, where the event hadn't gone unnoticed. It was a guilty pleasure, but being recognized as a good football player easily outdid getting beat up any day of the week.

Springfield Lions, 1975

The next step up, playing for the freshman football team at Cardinal O'Hara High School, was a big one. I knew this would be a huge jump in terms of player skill, speed, and size; I had overheard my dad talking to other dads about the team with a hushed reverence. Over one-hundred kids tried out for the team, and many arrived at the first practice with advance press, big reputations, and more confidence than I would ever have the right to feel. All I wanted was to quietly gain acceptance. And while I readily made a few friends, it always seemed as the outsider requesting permission to join, rather than as an insider sharing a mutual connection.

However, once I started playing, there was a perceptible change in attitude—mine and also that of the other players. I felt more comfortable out on the field—playing hard and being part of the team—than virtually anywhere else in school. I kept my head down, literally and figuratively, and only later realized that I had established myself as a solid player worthy of some recognition based on game performance, which unexpectedly (to me, at least), was good. A few touchdowns here and there, and next thing you know, no one's stealing your lunch money.

All that was well and good, for playing on the freshman team at O'Hara was demanding in several special ways. The most obvious was simply the change in time management demands from grade school to the high school level. All at once, I was spending thirty hours a week playing ball while trying to comprehend biology late into the night. Beyond that was the pressure put on the players to perform: that first year was more than an introduction, it was a showcase for the big team the following year. The reputation of the varsity team was large and mighty, and we all knew that playing there someday would be a visible payoff for a lot of miles run and weights lifted.

To add to the stress, the freshman team hadn't lost a game in years and the varsity players never passed up a chance to remind us that losing was not an option.

"You idiots lose, we're going to shave all your heads!"

I cringed a bit as we tried to make our way past the gauntlet of varsity studs taking a breather during their practice There was no hiding from their collective gaze as we approached the field for our first game.

Gerry Feehery, only four years separated from being drafted by the Eagles, stood up directly in our path. There was no way around the 6' 3" 250-pound senior lineman, and I certainly didn't want to show the fear I felt by breaking into a sprint.

"No kidding, you worthless Frosh, we never lost even once. You guys blow this one, and we're going to make you all pay."

"Better believe it," added Jimmy McAllister, "Don't fuck up our record."

Our little group stood there meekly, staring at the ground silently until Gerry and Jimmy lost interest.

"Let's go, these guys don't stand a chance," they laughed as they returned to the assembly of their teammates. "We'll be watching!" they warned over their shoulders as the rest of the guys smirked in agreement.

Appropriately motivated, we went out and went 6-0 that season. I scored eight TD's in those six games, including one long run where the varsity coach, Bob Ewing, happened to be watching from the end zone as I arrived.

"Nice going, kid," coach said while patting me on the shoulder as I trotted up to him.

"Thanks, coach," I managed, in between gasps after the long sprint.

"We'll be on the lookout for you next year, son," Ewing added.

I couldn't believe my luck, having that chance to show off a bit before the big man—a legend in the high school football community.

"Did you see that, Bette?" my dad beamed on the way home in the car. "Ewing congratulated him and shook his hand, right there in front of everybody!" My dad sounded like I had just met the president or something. For my part, I settled into the good vibe, enjoying the warmth of my dad's proud moment and knowing it would go well for me at school for at least another week or so.

I made it through that first season, and my freshman year at O'Hara, with a work pattern that has stayed with me even today. Basically I worked my butt off once I made up my mind that I wanted to be successful. Coming home exhausted each night after practice, I then sat down to a few hours of studying Latin, calculus, or some other similarly obtuse subject. I juggled the schoolwork with the football practices, and without really noticing, I had made the team, earned a starting job at running back, and somehow managed straight A's.

What I did notice, however, was that no one was bullying me. I had groups of friends who were acknowledged geeks and others who were big and popular jocks. I wasn't sure what category was made for me and, frankly, didn't care. I just realized that I had a sort of safe haven in more than one clique of fellow students, and no one had yet asked me to leave. In a way, I was a bit of an anomaly—I studied and practiced hard, and ended up performing well both in and out of the classroom. While that might not have gone unnoticed among my teachers and friends, I was simply satisfied to be accepted, for whatever reason. I also recognized that competition, in any sport but especially football, was rewarding in a visceral way. Although an admitted "smart kid," I wasn't really interested in making it very obvious, and academics didn't seem so much competitive as simply demanding of my time and modest effort. I knew I was close to Joe Diguisseppe, the number one ranked kid in the class, but didn't give it any more thought beyond what was required to keep me ahead of the curve academically. For me, football was the more valuable asset—one that gave me access, friendship, a sense of achievement, and a reason to get my nose out of a textbook. The ultimate goal of academics would be attained later in life.

As I continued working hard enough and late enough, I was rewarded by good grades and a high class rank. It's hard to describe, but most of my early success was unanticipated and really a pleasant surprise. I worked hard because, well, there didn't seem to be any reason not to, and it was far easier every day to arrive prepared and with none of the stresses associated with missed or incomplete assignments. It wasn't really some conscious effort to perform, at least not initially. Eventually, though, I became aware of the direct result of focused effort. When I applied myself, I was capable of outperforming academically nearly all of my peers. This fact wasn't a matter of pride, it was simply a concept I relied on as a comfort when schoolwork became more challenging than usual. Anxieties about uncontrollable factors interfering with my grand plans (such as engines blowing up at Daytona) were not yet part of the equation. Instead there emerged an easily recognizable pattern: work hard and success is just part of the completed package.

It was at that point that a theme emerged, beginning a process that continues to mature to this day. I found some aspects of my life easier—such as academic performance—and therefore discounted them to some degree, as there was less of a challenge involved. On the other hand, activities that were atypical and non-conforming for the kid labeled as smart were simply enticing. I wanted to be different—recognized as unusual in my participation and dedication to apparently incongruous activities—not because I stood out as a typical A-student.

For sure, the balance required to do this was the real challenge. Knocking heads on the football field was pretty diametrically opposite to doing Math Club problems, but I managed to find a fit in both places. And in both the classroom and the locker room, I really wanted to be "just one of the guys." In some sense, my varied and unusual participation probably diminished that possibility in each instance, so that by trying to fit in, I probably stood out even more. But I was happier and less anxious about myself and my peers' opinion of me when I occupied safe space in whatever group I was part of at the moment.

To be included was critical. I had spent more than enough time sitting on the curb as a kid, watching the other kids play and secretly wishing to be invited in. Back then, I wasn't being excluded—there was no deliberate barring of me by those already playing—but I lacked the assertiveness to dive in unsolicited. Why I didn't think to ask in, I still don't know; perhaps the acute understanding of the cautious role of an outsider was present even then. As a result, I sat there and watched, fantasizing about scoring the goal or hitting the home run, all while I silently observed other kids acting out my dreams. In that fashion, my mind equated the possession of the courage to actually participate with success and acceptance, regardless of the actual level of performance. You had to get in and be in, in order to belong. As that concept became more concrete in my adolescent mind, I forced myself to participate, joining teams, entering schoolyard and backyard games, and generally actively trying to be, well, just one of the guys.

***

It was in the midst of that developing pattern that I decided to try out for track and field in the spring of my freshman year at O'Hara. Because the track season ran counter to football, it was a great way of staying in shape and keeping the football players together and off the streets until the fall. It was here that I would find yet another test of perseverance and intestinal fortitude.

Not content to simply sign up for various sprints (and unwilling to torture my body with distance running of any sort), I figured that running hurdles would be pretty cool. Without really understanding exactly what was involved, I somehow decided that it had to be that event—another way to be just a bit more challenged, a bit more intense. Not just sprinting, but jumping over obstacles in the process, hurdling was a natural activity expressed rather unnaturally in several different events. I expected to run the high-hurdle short-distance sprints, but was drafted into also running the longer intermediate hurdle events. The latter would be the event, the animal, the gut-buster that I dreaded but couldn't quit.

In those days, the intermediate hurdle event was a 300-meter affair, which was a medium-demand sprint distance for me, at least when done without hurdles. Add hurdles to the equation and you have a true bitch of an event. My coach actually introduced me to the event only moments before the scheduled start of my first track meet. He grabbed me by the elbow, pointed at the shortish-hurdle, and informed me that I was signed up for the next race. I shrugged, guessing that it was just part of the deal in order to be allowed to run the more glamorous high-hurdle event later.

I warmed up with a few tentative hops over the intermediate-height hurdle, which sure seemed easier to clear than the higher barriers I was used to in the 110-meter event. No big deal, I figured. (Eventually, I'd learn that when something seems to be "No Big Deal" at first glance, alarms should be going off, but back then, I was pleasantly clueless). I trotted over to where my dad was positioned on the sidelines and mentioned that I was going to do the 300-meter hurdles.

"Have you done that one before?"

"Nope. But it doesn't look too hard. Coach wants me to do the 300 hurdles if I want any chance to run the high hurdles later."

"Well, OK, but maybe you should practice first."

I was frustrated by my dad's apparent lack of confidence in me and his failure to understand the importance of my first varsity track meet. "Dad, there's no time to practice. Besides, (lowering my voice), the other guys will see me."

Consistent with his firm belief in the school of hard knocks, my dad backed off on offering any more useful tips, and as I headed for the starter's area, he made his way up the hill for a better view of the carnage about to happen.

I assumed the sprinter's four-point stance at the start line and waited for the starter's pistol to begin the race. No big deal, right? You sprint some, you jump in between, all over in less than a minute. How hard could it be?

I fired out of the blocks, running full speed toward the first hurdle. I hadn't bothered to count steps the way I had been coached to for the high hurdles event, since I didn't know how many steps I'd need anyway. Why worry about details when the race is on? As a result, I arrived at the first hurdle awkwardly, realizing that I needed to stretch my last step, and do something resembling a long-jump, to make it over the hurdle. Hesitating for just a split-second, I failed to clear the top of the hurdle, striking the cross bar hard enough to slam the hurdle against the ground. I tumbled over the hurdle, sprawling onto the asphalt track, landing on hands, then knees, then rolling onto my head and back. Stunned, I barrel-rolled over and popped up, partially facing the wrong direction. I was peripherally aware of the yelling of my coach and the other kids but more aware of the need to get going again in the proper direction.

I stood up and started running again, arriving at the next hurdle with more determination to clear the obstacle. My lead foot hit the crossbar, but this time I simply knocked over the hurdle as I ran through it. Stumbling briefly, I kept on going forward. Two down, only seven more to go.

The third hurdle treated me much like the first, conspiring to pull me over with it as I hit it in mid-stride. Again I hit the hard track, this time allowing the hurdle to impact me directly in the crotch as I added to my collection of abrasions. I'm relatively sure I heard the laughing of my teammates then, although it's altogether possible that they only laughed afterwards upon the retelling—my recollection is understandably a bit fuzzy on that detail.

Righting myself once more, I started running again, now desperate to just get the thing over with, and then be allowed to limp on home. Managing to clear the next five hurdles, I dully thought that the worst might actually be over. Instead, the ghost of Jim Thorpe had not yet had his fill of me. My legs by this point were feeling leaden, and my sprinting strides were much more of a stagger. I attempted one last clumsy leap, but instead crashed into the final hurdle, sprawled onto the ground beyond, and came to a rest on my back. I blankly looked up at a few clouds silently floating by and wondered how they kept marching on, ignorant of my plight down below. Unable now to ignore the hurt that came rushing at me simultaneously from multiple origins, and feeling every bump and crack in the asphalt at my back, I considered staying right there. Or I could crawl off to the outside of the track where the grass was more comfortable, and I could possibly start digging a hole big enough to fit into.

Instead, I got up. Slowly, as I wasn't sure whether my injuries might have resulted in the inability to stand, let alone run any further. Hands and knees first, and then trotting again, I felt my legs protest the strain of flexing and extending abraded skin over painful joints. I looked awkwardly downward, not ahead, and made it finally over the finish line. Instead of stopping there, I continued a few more steps off onto the grassy infield, sat down hard, and assumed the plane-crash position with my head between my knees. Looking up briefly, I noticed my coach approaching from further down the track. I hoped that he was simply planning on throwing a tarp over me, but he was apparently intent on talking.

He started with the standard question that people have been asking me for various reasons over the decades: "Are you OK?"

I gave a silent head nod, wincing as I waited for a public rebuke.

"Pretty tough race, huh? Always good to get the first one out of the way though."

Huh? The first one? As if there would be more, really?

"Better shake it off. You have the high hurdles in about fifteen minutes."

What, no courtesy ambulance ride? No last rites? "OK coach, but I'm going to need a minute here."

My dad arrived next on the scene, with his unexpectedly blunt observation. "Way to go out there, Jimmy; you just kept getting up"—a pause here for effect – "I was waiting for you to stop, but you didn't quit. No matter how many times you fell, I saw you keep on getting up. I couldn't believe you kept going!"

I looked up at my dad, expecting his face to betray sarcasm, and prepared myself to admit that I was once again foolish to have not taken his advice. Admitting ignorance on top of defeat on top of pain was a tough combination to work with, but I knew it was my lot at that particular moment.

Instead, I saw a rare expression on my dad's face. He smiled with a mixture of kindness, concern, and pride all at once. No criticism in there, no reminder of how I had blown him off earlier. As I wondered who had switched dads with me, he extended a hand.

"Can you get up? Easy does it, now. Let's go walk a bit so we can get you ready for the next race, OK?"

We walked slowly around the track's perimeter, my dad with his arm draped over my bloody shoulder, silently bonding over the moment when I first fully realized that he could be proud of something I had done. I had won nothing but his respect; instead of pity, embarrassment, or regret, I experienced an emotion with him that I couldn't have purchased by winning a race, then or ever.

***

Born in 1923, Bob Lowe was in every way a product of the Great Depression during which he was raised. The oldest son of a German mother and English/Irish father, my dad's nature easily co-existed with the nurturing of very frugal, conservative, and demanding parents. To this day, he doesn't tolerate nonsense, and my father was always quick to pronounce a wide variety of activities and sentiments as "happy horseshit." As in, "Cut the happy horseshit, I'm trying to watch the news in peace down here."

The oldest of three boys, my dad was athletic and fit, but he readily describes his brothers as having been more successful at sports. Never one to point out his own virtues, it's apparent to me now that Bob Lowe had bigger fish to fry – working through the Depression and enlisting in the Navy – than participating in sports. But he certainly grew up a fan of all things athletic, and much of that interest later rubbed off on his two boys.

My father's stoicism was demonstrated daily as he dealt with the challenges of raising six kids on a government worker's income. He happilywent to off to work each day, as he once admitted, because it was a peaceful respite where he felt comfortable and more than capably in control. At home, he was subject to the demands of maintaining broken-down cars, corralling misbehaving kids, and keeping a small roof intact over a large raucous family. And on a daily basis, for sure, Bob Lowe worried for his kids that life only be somehow better for them, and less stressful and demanding.

Bob Lowe, circa 1942

Charles and Clara Lowe were surely parents who disciplined Bob and his two brothers with classically physical incentives to behave properly. This was ultimately passed on to my dad as the only way he knew for sure to raise a child properly. As a result, my father was an active and demanding disciplinarian, who didn't tolerate well any deviations from what he perceived as correct behavior. I certainly feared my father at times, and coincidentally, those times were always predictably based on having recently done something wrong—though the thought of getting punished was always worse than the actual occurrence. And to this day, the hair on the back of my neck still stands up at the sound of coins or keys jingling in someone's pockets – the very sound I would hear as I ran from my dad up the stairs in an attempt to get to the safety of my bedroom. Still, that the memory is so vivid is testimony to the effectiveness of that technique. Dad kept us in line and demanded respect, and we rarely had any misunderstanding of what would occur should we cross the line. While there was little physical discipline for my four older sisters, my brother Rick and I were targets of tough love on many occasions, and rarely stepped far out of line as a result.

In the context of those memories, I recall much more strongly the moments when I would finally have my dad's full attention. With five siblings, there were demands on his emotional time exceeding what his non-working hours would permit. Still, the occasion to sit in his lap and watch Lassie or even the more-rare later invites to chip golf balls in the backyard were priceless opportunities to experience another side of my father altogether. When he showed me how to throw a knuckleball, I felt like I had been given a private gift that would remain mine forever.

Competing with my sibs for the already rationed attention of my father, I found sports to have yet more value, for my dad wanted to be there watching his oldest son whenever he could. His work schedule demanded much travel, and more than a few games were missed while dad was busy engineering tank weapons in South Korea, but when he was home, the time was mine if I had a game.

Given that Bob Lowe rarely had the opportunity to relax, with cars to keep running, and six busy kids to keep running after, holiday time took on special meaning. I treasured the chance to find one-on-one time with my dad, and even enjoyed it when we could fit Rick into the equation. The window of opportunity was small, and closed quickly, but we seized on any chance to get time with my dad. And somewhere in there, Bob Lowe introduced me to car racing, in the form of watching the Indy 500 on Memorial Day.

Over the years, I looked forward to the annual event that was the world's greatest auto race, even when I was later away from home and watching without my dad. The event, and even the setting—the storied track in Indianapolis—took on special meaning as I always felt closest to my dad while that race was front and center.

Once I was old enough to participate in organized sports, my dad would often attend games and even practices when he could get away. However, in those early days, before I matured some, I was pretty much a scrub and rarely saw playing time. My goal was to make a team, even if it meant securing only a spot on the bench. Grateful to be involved at all, I was initially unaware of the distress this lack of playing time caused my father. While I wore my often spotless uniforms proudly while taking my place on the Little League or the seventy-five pound football team roster, my dad privately seethed over the fact that I was typically a non-participant when it came to actually playing in the games. My goals were simple—make the team, be one of the guys, and fit in, somehow, anyhow. My father certainly never understood how those goals could be acceptably met when one wasn't actually playing during games, but we were both guilty of examining different parts of the same elephant. What worked for the son, allowing me to harvest some kernels of self-esteem, was at the same time a puzzling and frustrating experience for the father.

Perhaps Bob Lowe was unprepared or just ill-equipped to manage the emotions of watching his son ride the bench, but much of his anger at my coaches was vented during many a long car ride home from the non-playing fields. Sitting silently in the dark front seat of the Chrysler, helmet or glove in my lap, I squirmed while dad voiced emotions too complex for my twelve-year-old psyche to absorb and understand. I knew only that it was me at fault, that I was failing my dad with each inactive inning/quarter, and that he'd be happier if only I played better, and of course, therefore more. I'm fully aware now that his anger was not for his son, and that he never intended for me to be its primary recipient, but still, the air in the Chrysler was always thick with expletives and remorse on those rides home.

Later, as I grew bigger and stronger, there was a natural progression for both of us: my skill level and size caught up with my desire to perform, and my dad's pleasure with his son's choice to play various sports improved immensely. I might not have noticed, but eventually discussions with my dad skewed more towards advice and encouragement, rather than the previously familiar disappointments aired.

Either way, I sought his attention through sports, and I enjoyed the opportunity to have him to myself in that small universe when the occasion arose. Whether the interactions with him in those circumstances were immediately pleasant or not, it was one-on-one time, valued as something rare and not taken for granted. For in those moments, good or bad, he was there, not elsewhere, and tangibly part of my world and my life.

***

I ran a great deal many more hurdles races over the next four years, but never fell again in the intermediate event. I did manage to get a little better at it but always pretty much felt that it was something to be endured rather than enjoyed. The shorter high-hurdles races were much more to my liking, although I was in no way a star there either. I was typically a mid-pack competitor, lacking the top-end speed and sweet stride that the front-runners exhibited. However, through some form of perseverance combined with attrition, I ultimately become at least competitive in most of the events I entered. What I wasn't though, was the guy who won medals.

To earn a varsity letter in track, one had to win or come in second in at least one of the events during the season, and by senior year, I had come close but never accomplished that feat. With the end of the season came my last chance to win a medal; without a top result, I'd have nothing but scarred kneecaps to show for my four-year effort. Getting a letter wasn't some lifelong goal or dream or anything like that; rather, it seemed like the only fair ending after several long seasons dedicated to getting just a bit faster.

I competed that last day in the morning high hurdles race, finishing fourth, respectably behind a few guys that had been smoking me all year in the same event. The intermediate hurdles though, were another story altogether. For some forgotten reason, the league champ had already dropped out of the event, leaving me with maybe two or three guys to beat if I wanted that red and blue "CO'H." I qualified third and spent the next half hour imagining all the possible combinations of who to beat, how, and in what order to win or place. By the time we were organized at the start line, I looked around at the others and realized that everyone had gone through a similar mental process, and most were counting on me to be behind them at the finish.

I sprinted out of the blocks at the gun, running strongly over the first few hurdles with good, measured steps. From my vantage point in the third lane, I could see almost the whole field stretched out in front of me. I caught and passed the first five runners early, and then evened up to the sixth guy halfway through. The leader was just ahead, but I guessed him to be out of reach for all of us. It would be a battle for second all the way home.

Sucking wind hard, feeling the bear on my back, I approached the last hurdle side-by-side with the West Catholic High runner. Leaping for one last time, I glanced to my right to see the guy tumbling down in a heap, rolling off to the outside of the track. I glanced up towards the finish, seeing my coach and a few of my teammates jumping and waving. I felt a surge of adrenaline as I pushed over the line, then coasted to a stop a few steps later. Hands on knees, I scratched for fresh air and fought down an urge to vomit. My coach arrived to give me the standard "Way to go," but it wasn't until my dad made his way over to my side that I received the ultimate compliment.

Still bent over and gasping, I felt a hand on my shoulder. I recognized the pants and shoes, and felt just a little bit stronger. "Hey dad," was all that I could muster as I straightened up.

Dad cleared his throat and smiled that rare smile. "That's pretty great, Jimmy."

Those words, to the boy wanting desperately to be accepted not just by friends and teammates, but also by his father, were like oxygen to me. My dad unfailingly demonstrated love always in his own way, but it wasn't often a way that I appreciated or even understood. Back then I wanted to please him so that he willingly responded—acknowledging that I had in fact done something, anything, good in his eyes. Those were the eyes that mattered, and his observation, I knew, was unflinching.

Chapter Four

Having performed well enough to gain acceptance and recognition at the freshman football program at O'Hara, I anticipated a doable, although much tougher, challenge at the varsity level. I worked out daily in preparation for the rigors of my first two-a-day camp, endured the hazing rituals suffered by the initiates that summer, and managed to run and scramble my way onto the varsity squad as a sophomore. I didn't expect to see much playing time, as I was clearly in the second- or third-string slot on all of the depth charts, but I was happy nonetheless to dress for the first varsity game of the season.

That Sunday morning, I donned the Cardinal O'Hara Lions' game jersey and pants for the first time and immediately felt a sense of personal accomplishment, a feeling of arrival that, for me, is intimately associated with donning a uniform. I still remember the bright white fabric, clunky shoulder pads, and every other detail of the uniform that allowed me to stand with my teammates as part of something special. It was an entry into a closed society, permission to claim ownership and membership, and a ticket to the inner workings of the group. That sensation was palpable then and has been present for me with virtually every uniform since: my Harvard football jersey, USMC combat fatigues, OR scrubs, and of course, various fire suits over the years. Even if the outfit does not, in fact, make the man, the inner satisfaction that I still feel pulling on the special clothing of inclusion in a group is strong and fulfilling. Even when torn, bloodied, stained, or reeking of burnt rubber, wearing a uniform is a tactile event that always takes me back to that first experience with the varsity football jersey over thirty years ago.

Wearing "away" whites for that first varsity game, I watched all four quarters from the sidelines as we beat a tough team from Cardinal Dougherty High School. My uniform stayed pristine since I didn't get on the field, but I was still satisfied to be a part of it all. Joining the fray on the field would have been that much sweeter, but the victory of being there in the first place was sufficient. Besides, as a sophomore, I was expected to prove my mettle further in the junior varsity game that always followed on Monday.

I started in the JV game at Dougherty the next afternoon and got off a few good runs into their mostly-bigger-than-me defense. Ultimately though, whatever results I had managed were erased before the end of the first half when I made, what turned out to be, my final play of the year.

Diving into the slot just off the right tackle's inside shoulder, I spied a crack of daylight and cut over a step, off balance for a split-second. At that moment, the Dougherty inside linebacker launched at me, slamming into me just as I shifted my weight from one foot to the other. The impact, combined with his seventy-five pound weight advantage, sent me straight backwards onto my head and shoulders, bearing his bulk all the way—a clean, all-pro hit that drove me into the turf, at which point my right shoulder exploded in pain. As I gasped for air and tried to understand what had just happened, he reached down and grabbed my right hand to help me up. Reflexively, I extended my hand and felt searing pain in my shoulder as he pulled me to my feet. I choked back a scream and stumbled to the sidelines, bent over and holding my right arm cradled in my left. My day, and in fact my whole season, was over, all on one play.

The diagnosis was a broken clavicle, made only after a painful ride to the ER, followed by four hours of waiting for the overworked orthopedic resident to show up in order to reduce the displaced fracture. I was placed in a figure-of-eight splint and sent home to figure out how to sleep flat on my back. Hurting and depressed, I left the hospital struggling to cope with the pain and the realization that I was sidelined for the year. Ultimately, the loss of the football season was at least an academic advantage, as I was able to focus more time on schoolwork—and did more of my studying during daylight hours without the constant background of exhaustion. I also adopted the misfortune of injury as a motivator in my workouts while preparing for my junior season. I ran and lifted weights as soon as I was cleared to do so by the surgeon, I rehabbed my shoulder as much as I could bear, and I dreamt about getting a second chance to perform against the big boys.

Most of my rehab was done in a solitary fashion. I became a frequent visitor to the gym, learning the proper weightlifting techniques while pushing myself harder and harder in and out of the weight room. I ran daily, early morning or late at night, in rain, bitter cold, and even in the snow on occasion. Each session was marked by singular thoughts: next season, next season, next season. I focused on getting stronger and faster, drawing strength from thoughts of playing with the varsity boys and performing well in front of teammates who wanted me to be out there with them. My family would be there, and my dad—well, I imagined he would always be there watching, observing, and approving of my success.

Summer two-a-days as a high school junior weren't nearly as intimidating as my first go-round. I was less anxious and better prepared for the routine and the rigors of camp, and I headed for the concluding scrimmage of the summer penciled in as a starting running back. The first half of the contest went as hoped: I ran well, picked up yards in bunches, and felt great. Deep into the third offensive series of the day, I took a pitch-out wide around the right end and sprinted eighty yards untouched for a score. The joy I felt then was pure and undiluted. I celebrated with my teammates in the end zone as energy surged through me with every ounce of adrenaline seemingly squeezed out at once. I was high and loving the sensation, made all the more intoxicating after spending a year dreaming of just such a moment.

Seeing an opportunity to practice some of the rarer offensive plays, coach Ewing then called for a two-point conversion play, giving me the ball off center in a short lunge up the middle. I squeaked through the small gap cleared by the center and right guard, and fell over the goal line, where the defense converged upon me as I went down. As I bounced on the ground sideways, it suddenly felt as if I had stepped on a land mine. A defensive lineman had fallen backwards onto my right foot, fracturing three bones and introducing me to my first pair of crutches.

During the four weeks that I was recovering from the broken foot, the two other running backs stepped up to perform well enough that there was no job waiting for me when I was finally cleared to play. Nonetheless, the moment I was allowed to jog, I taped up my foot and ran. The moment I was freed to play, I dressed and appeared in the locker room, ready to go. Despite the pain, I wanted desperately to play, but the year was already lost to me: I was a step slower and mired on the bench, resigned once again to mostly spectator status.

Instead of surrendering, I again found inspiration in adversity and worked out incessantly in anticipation of my last-gasp senior season. Arriving for my last football camp well prepared and in shape, I earned my way back to the top of the depth chart. With my foot and clavicle injuries distant memories, I was looking forward to getting through the last part of camp and the requisite scrimmage, and finally getting on with a championship season. On one of our last requisite scrimmage plays, I outsprinted the defensive end around the corner and juked around the cornerback, only to be hit sideways by the safety who was coming over hard to help his fellow defensive back. As I rolled over, I felt a "pop" and an odd sensation of dull pain in my right shoulder. I was tempted to play on, as it didn't hurt too badly (and certainly wasn't nearly as severe as my prior injuries, I thought). However, when I couldn't lift my arm past vertical, I knew my day, plus some, was over. The team orthopod, who by now had a boat named after me, diagnosed a separated shoulder. The verdict was three to four weeks out of action. I resigned myself to the shorter sentence and set about running wind sprints with a brace on my shoulder. No way was I going to miss my last chance to play, last chance to feel that adrenaline rush again.

Three weeks to the day, I dressed for practice and, three days later, won back my starting job. My shoulder still hurt and I wore larger, bulkier shoulder pads, but I was ready to play for the season opener at St. Marks. Just in case, I took maybe a dozen extra-strength Tylenol right before the game, hoping to somehow control any pain I might have with the first few hits.

I immersed myself in the game, enjoying every moment—the huddle, the noise of the band and the crowd, the organized chaos on the sidelines. It was all bright, different, exciting, and more than a bit nauseating. Actually, my progressive nausea was Tylenol-induced, but I had long since forgotten any concerns about shoulder pain by the second quarter.

Stuck down in the St. Mark's end of the field, quarterback Chris Cassidy called my favorite play, a pitchout and end sweep. I took off for the far sideline, ball tucked in my elbow, and head on a swivel. Fullback Johnny Bauer made the last key block on the cornerback, and I was free and clear down the sidelines, running the remaining seventy yards as if there were a K9 dog on my tail. I crossed into the end zone and held the ball high in a modest celebration, remembering to act as if I had been there before. I was spent, still nauseated, and out of breath and energy.

I jogged over to the sidelines as things settled down for the extra point kick. I bent over, hands on my knees, fighting the nausea and feeling like I had just been rescued at sea.

Coach Ewing, who sported a pronounced stutter which was amplified when he got excited, found me and clapped me on the shoulder pads. "JJJJimmy LLLowe, you sssshoulda sssseen it! You had a bbbbblue ffffflame out your ass (holding his arms wide apart) thththththisss llllllong!"

I looked up as everybody erupted in laughter, and said, "Thanks, coach. It felt great." I then promptly vomited my entire stomach contents all over his Adidas sneakers. "Ah," I managed, "that feels even better."

Jim and his dad pose before an O'Hara game, 1980

We celebrated on the bus ride that evening, yelling, cheering, singing, and enjoying the opening season win with a juvenile lack of restraint. I was serenaded with the ritual "Jimmy Lowe, Jimmy Lowe, Jimmy Lowe, is a horse's ass!" chorus, and savored the intense feeling for the rest of the ride home. This time, I happily participated front and center during the after-game party, enjoying those festivities well past the midnight hour. Beer was present but unnecessary; I could have floated home, riding only the good vibe of the night.

I woke up Sunday morning to the phone ringing. My mom answered and quickly roused me from my pleasant dreams, telling me that Johnny Bauer was waiting to talk to me. Looking concerned, my mom handed me the phone as I stumbled into the kitchen. "There's some bad news from John, about coach Ewing," she said.

John was clearly upset. "Ewing had a massive heart attack last night. I just talked to Hoot, who got the call this morning from coach's son. He's alive, but just barely. They operated for, like, ten hours or something."

"Shit, what happened?"

"He just passed out at home right after the game. Mrs. Ewing called the ambulance, I guess. Bobby said he almost died on the ride there."

"Wow. What now? Who's going to be coach now?"

"Well, we're both screwed. Sparky is taking over, and you know he hates both of us. My guess is, we're out, probably soon, unless by some miracle Ewing recovers. Don't get your hopes up."

I hung up, feeling a bit guilty for being selfish about football when a guy was hanging on for dear life, but I couldn't help but feel frustrated. Damn, just when I thought it was all pointed the right way.

It took another game before Sparky benched both Johnny and me, despite the fact that I was leading the team in rushing at the time. I played on through the rest of the season, filling in well and scoring a few more times, but never starting again. Coach Ewing recovered enough to attend a few games toward the end of the year, but he never came back to coach. The player who took my spot went on to marry one of the coaches' daughters, and I found my way to Harvard, despite some questionable interviewing skills. The outcome was certainly better in the long run than it looked back then on that fateful Sunday morning, but to this day, I still wish that Bob Ewing had had a stress test and an angioplasty long before I puked on his shoes.

***

Early on in my high school career, it became evident that I was a competitive student. While I was not particularly cognizant of the fact, my memory gift—what amounted to some version of a photographic memory—enabled me to consistently score well on standardized tests and to maintain high-level grades all through primary and secondary school. I was aware that I was a strong student, but my good grades seemed to be mostly evidence of my ability to not draw unwanted attention to myself from the sisters of St. Francis. That technique later came in handy when trying to avoid the wrath of drill sergeants at Quantico, some of whom bore a frightening resemblance, both in demeanor and countenance, to Sister Helen

Alouise. Having set the bar high, I continued to perform well despite modest effort, graced with the ability to identify specific times when I needed to accelerate my effort in order to succeed. That trait continues to come in handy even today, although it's been awhile since I was last officially ranked at anything not resembling a qualifying grid.

By my junior year, I was beginning to hear from a wide variety of colleges regarding possible academic scholarships, although most of the unsolicited notices were from obscure institutions that seemed a bit overeager to have me "enjoy all the benefits we offer at our private college in East Dakota." However, on one of those cards was a name that was easily recognizable. Buried in the usual pile of solicitations, and nearly thrown out with the rest of the junk mail, was an offer for me to attend Harvard's summer school program. My mother, who measured the merit of many such things thusly, noted that "The Kennedy's went there," neglecting to mention that Harvard also had the good sense to throw Ted Kennedy out.

At my mother's urging, I applied, more out of curiosity than anything else, and was accepted for the 1980 summer program. I elected to study introductory biology as a suitable preparation for my planned pre-med major in college and eagerly awaited my eight-week introduction to near-total independence and the world of preppie academics. My mother and sister Michelle drove me to Cambridge—in a typical and recurring theme of my youth, our car broke down on the way—and I was deposited in my dorm with $160 cash and instructions to call home Sunday nights to verify my alive and well status. Although I was initially pretty uncomfortable—maybe even scared—with my sudden independence, I trusted the judgment and support of my mom. She wouldn't have OK'd this first-time-away-from-home deal without giving it critical thought, and her consent was definitely required before any Lowe kid packed up and headed anywhere, even to Harvard.

For my part, I had recognized that this was another test—a leap of faith was again required—but I had examined the opportunity from a few different angles, spotted some potential value, and made the commitment. I thought I would be up for the challenge, but I also realized it might just as easily end up as a regrettable experience. However, once there, I settled surprisingly easily into a routine of two hours of classwork daily, with more than a bit of textbook study to fill the rest of the day schedule. More unsettling were the uncontrolled nights, where I experienced only slight supervision and seemingly no real rules or restrictions for the first time ever. Yet I somehow survived the experience, despite my still-developing knack for questionable decision-making. Academically, the memory gift once again came in handy, and I departed with two semester's credits in biology and B+'s for the transcript. The other thing I left with was a strong desire to go to Harvard for my undergraduate studies.

To get accepted to Harvard, I first needed to undergo an alumnus interview sometime in the winter of my senior year at O'Hara. During summer school, I had heard that some undergrads had had difficult interview experiences, but no one seemed truly disturbed by the concept—after all, the source of description had always been a current Harvard student. My Harvard interview was assigned to one Mr. Hall, a resident of the Main Line—Philadelphia's ultimate high-rent suburb—literally and figuratively across the tracks from my 1950s development of middle-class Edgewood Drive. To present my best, my mom bought me an interview suit, carefully selecting something that I could also wear to school, graduation, college, and my first accounting job if necessary. Looking pretty spiffy, I jumped into my sister's Volkswagen Rabbit, and headed off to the interview. I managed to get about ten blocks from home before the right rear tire went flat, requiring an in-the-dark, side-of-the-road, don't-mess-your-suit-up tire change. Not a big deal, but I finally arrived at Mr. Hall's mansion spotted with grease and about twenty minutes late for the appointment.

Terrified as I was, Mr. Hall did absolutely nothing to assuage my anxiety. If central casting had called down for someone to play the part of intimidating prick, they need have looked no further. While I sat there, sweating out the process and stifling the urge to vomit on his musty Indian rug, Mr. Hall stuffily proceeded to brag about his success getting all the great students from the Haverford School admitted each year. When I meekly confirmed that no one from O'Hara had ever gone to Harvard, he smugly assured me, "Don't worry, there're lots of good schools you could probably get into." More than a bit shaken, and already hating those Main Line kids from an expensive private school I had never heard of, I stuttered and mumbled my way through the interview, wondering if the admissions committee would frown upon my request for a second chance. Finally, Mr. You're Just an Unfortunate Kid Without A Chance finished the interrogation and escorted me to the door; on my way out, he again reassured me that I'd "get into some good school somewhere." I stifled the urge to cry all the way home, but at least made it without another tire change. More than a bit distressed by the whole experience, I reassured my parents that at least East Dakota State was offering a full ride.

When I received my acceptance letter from Harvard two days before Christmas, I wasn't totally shocked, but I assumed that the interview report from Mr. Hall must have not yet made its way to the committee. I didn't give it any further thought, though, excited as I was about getting the early Christmas present from Cambridge. My mom and I had a brief celebration, and I allowed myself a "Whoo-hoo!" or two before settling in to the day's homework. As I sat down to study, my mom made sure to place the letter on top of the pile of mail awaiting my dad's arrival from work.

When my dad came home a few hours later, my mother and I waited patiently as he took off his coat and made his way to the stack of letters. He looked down at the pile and spied the letter with the Harvard logo.

"What's this?"

I was pretty sure he knew what it was, but couldn't wait any longer for him to open it. "Dad, I got into Harvard!" I blurted out. My mom smiled broadly beside me as we waited for his reaction.

My dad's reaction was hard to gauge, since, well, there was none. Shrugging, he said, "Well, what did you expect?"

The grin slid off my face, and I heard my mom softly say, "Oh, Bob…"

My dad looked back down at the letter, tossed it in the "done" pile, and then got back to sorting his mail. I retreated to my room, where I laid on the bed, staring at the ceiling, unable to bridge the gap between my anticipations and the reality of my dad's reaction. A few minutes later, my mom appeared and tried her best to explain my dad's response, but at the time I wasn't able to grasp the concept. It took me many years, but I later understood that my dad actually thought he was giving his son a compliment—"Why, of course they would accept you, what did you expect?" Instead, I was hurt because my expectations were entirely different from what was actually said, and my dad—well, he was just being the son of strict parents who didn't suffer fools gladly. He had tried to connect in the way most comfortable to him, completely consistent with his every other move, and he was surely puzzled when I seemed unappreciative. But my seventeen-year-old psyche wasn't well-equipped to see the problem. Instead of feeling congratulated, I was hurt, and the man whose approval I most wanted was simultaneously wondering what the hell was wrong with his son just then.

Now, when gaps appear between my expectation and someone else's response—particularly when trying to connect with my son—I try to at least consider the possibility that there's something lost in translation, and maybe we ought to try again. And I've pretty much eliminated the phrase "What did you expect?" from my list of potential responses.

Having had only modest success playing football at the high school level certainly eliminated my chances of fulfilling a boyhood fantasy of being USC's tailback in the Rose Bowl, but my Ivy League alternatives were still viable. I had the good fortune of also getting an acceptance letter from Yale and even spent a recruiting weekend there, courtesy of coach Carm Cozza and the Yale team. After a wild weekend, during which the academic strengths of Yale were never discussed, I seriously had changed my mind about college choice. I didn't want to pass up the opportunity for that much fun and, especially, having that fun while playing for what was then the best team in the Ivies.

Mulling over the decision until the last possible moment, and seriously considering choosing Yale because they had better bars in New Haven, I stared at the admissions documents late into the night before final answers were due. My dad happened into the kitchen and looked over my shoulder as I shuffled the papers back and forth, unable to settle on either choice without second thoughts.

"I'm seriously thinking it's gonna be Yale, dad."

"Well, if you're hell-bent on that, fine. But nobody in their right mind turns down Harvard."

Without further comment, he turned around and left, leaving me alone with that last bit of wisdom, combined uniquely with a warning so classically typical of my dad's way of dispensing advice.

I checked the "yes" box on Harvard's form letter, unwilling to risk a chance at screwing a Harvard education just to be obstinate towards my dad.

While settling in at Harvard, I had mostly forgotten the interview experience I had with Mr. Hall until, during my sophomore year, my resident advisor pulled me aside down at the Admissions office.

"Ever see your application file?" he asked with a smirk.

I was momentarily alarmed. "No—uh, Nope, why? Is there some problem?" My default thought was ooops, did they finally find some mistake, and now I'm being sent home?

He laughed as he handed me a thick packet. "Be sure to check out that interview report."

I pulled out the flagged report page, which was, at best, two paragraphs long. The concluding sentence from Mr. Hall was a memorable gem: "This student has the personality of a wet dishrag."

I've been conducting interviews for Harvard applicants for over ten years now, and always start each interview with that story. The rest of each interview always seems to go much more smoothly than what I can recall of my evening with Mr. Hall. And I have yet to come across the second wet dishrag in Harvard's long, storied history deserving of admittance.

***

Despite playing on two Ivy League title-winning teams at Harvard, my college football career was notable really only for my continued penchant for getting injured. I suffered multiple concussions, including two requiring hospitalization, tore ligaments in both knees, dislocated a few fingers (not the best way for a future surgeon to get hurt), and generally got the shit beat out of me by much bigger and better players. I was definitely punching above weight, but I kept working at it, mainly because that was the only way I knew. Well defined as primarily a special-teams player, I enjoyed little of the collegiate football experience and found progressively less reward for all the pain and intensity of preparation it demanded. I had brief moments of success when opportunities arose, including a few fun runs in front of a big crowd at the Harvard-Yale game, but by senior year I was pretty disenchanted with the whole deal. I was focusing then on the pre-med curriculum, which demanded much of my waking time when not working out or drinking beer. More and more, there was no joy in Saturdays and even less so in the weeks of practice before the games.

When I reinjured my knee early during senior season summer camp, I knew it was time to talk turkey with the running back coach, Larry Glueck. I had been mired down at second and sometimes third string on the depth chart and feared it would be a lost season if I couldn't play through my injury.

I made my way into coach Glueck's office, depositing my crutches on the floor next to the hot seat in front of his desk. I sat down with some reservation, as the coach had already made it clear over the past three years that, whatever amount of talent and brand of effort I might have had, he found it all lacking. I wasn't ever his guy, I wasn't ever going to be, and he and I both knew that I knew it.

Jim's official Harvard uniform photo, 1984

"Coach, the doc says I'm out for at least three weeks with this knee. It looks like I'll miss the scrimmage this Saturday. I'm worried about the season and where that will leave me when I get back."

Coach Glueck barely looked up at me. "Well, you're right to worry. At this point, I'm not sure if you fit into our plans this season. But if you don't play in the scrimmage, I can't evaluate you in time to make a roster decision. You better find a way to get out there Saturday or there's nothing much more I can tell you about the rest of the season." With that, he swiveled his chair away from me, picking up the phone and dialing, just to make extra sure I knew the meeting was over.

I found the trainer in the medical area of the locker room. We talked briefly, and I arranged to get a brace made and planned an extra tape job for the knee so that I could survive the scrimmage. I had only a partial medial collateral ligament tear, so I was hopeful that the knee would hold up long enough for the coach to get the on-field look he demanded. I then spent the next few days avoiding the team doctor, who I knew would never give me clearance to play.

That Saturday, I played several series with the second string offense. Since the first teams never go against each other, I was facing the first team defense all afternoon. Gritting my teeth with each step, I returned two kicks for good yardage and scored two TD's on short runs. I didn't drop anything thrown in my direction, and while I was hurting when we finished, I was satisfied that I had won back my job. Whatever the ultimate outcome, I knew that I had left it all out there, on the grass at Harvard's Soldier Field, the only way I knew how.

At the conclusion of Monday's pre-practice running backs' meeting, coach Glueck revealed the roster for the upcoming game against Army. My name wasn't on the posted blackboard list, which coach displayed just before the meeting broke up.

I hesitated a beat as the group scuffled for the exit.

"Coach, I noticed I wasn't on the roster. I thought I played well enough Saturday to earn a spot, like we talked about."

"Sorry, Lowe, I was up in the press box and didn't see you play. I know you were in there, but I missed it."

"There's film, right?" I was a bit panicked, knowing it was a loss already. "You can watch the film, right? Like you said, I went out there, and I played well. I scored twice. You saw all that, right?"

"Didn't see anything, and I don't have any time to watch film now. Look, go on out there, and we'll talk about this another time. But the lineup is what it is."

Stunned, I got up and limped out of the meeting room, leaving coach shuffling through some more important papers and probably wondering what the hell I was so upset about.

I slumped on the stool in front of my locker, wondering why I couldn't have foreseen this scenario more clearly. As the final stragglers dressed and then left for practice, I remained seated, staring at my jersey and helmet as if they belonged to some alien player. My knee ached, and my chest felt heavy. "Fifteen years?" I thought. "Fifteen years of this, and it ends now?

Because of that asshole? Shit!"

All the pain, all the sweat, it had all been so important to me for so long, I just didn't understand how it could be over, even if it had been over in reality for some time already. I couldn't process the concept well enough to make sense of it. It just seemed so foreign and unfair, an indigestible truth that had never been on the list of options to consider.

I perched on my stool, trying once again to motivate myself to simply put on the pads, lace up the shoes, and go out to the fields. I had done it before, I could do it again.

"I know what you're thinking, but don't do it, don't throw it all away now." Steve Abbott, team captain and a tight end who was also an off-season work-out partner, stood behind me, dressed for practice. Respected for his leadership by virtually all of his teammates, Steve was a friend with a clear head and classic sensibility. For Steve, it was "work hard, then harder, and everything will be OK." But this time, he couldn't make it OK for me.

"Man, I just can't do this anymore. That guy hates me, I'm hurting, and there's no light at the end of the tunnel that I can see."

"If you just get out there, it will be better, tomorrow will be better, it's a long season, right? Think about how hard we worked to get here. All those runs in the dark and time in the weight room. Remember that. You earned something here."

"I'm exhausted, Abs, and I can't do it anymore. I've earned nothing, and I'm just done. I know what you're trying to do, and I appreciate that you're even trying, but it's over for me. Right now. Right here. Fuck. I can't believe it."

Steve left a life raft behind before he trotted out the door. "If you change your mind, we'd all be happy to see you back out there. But if not, I understand." With that, I was alone in the locker room, sitting half-naked on a stool while my teammates warmed up for practice outside. I was numb, not knowing quite how to proceed—or if there were any real choices to make anyway.

Regardless of my inability to embrace the reality of my situation, I knew what the next steps had to be. I pulled on jeans and a t-shirt, grabbed my playbook, and left the crimson helmet and jersey hanging in place in the locker. I stopped by the office just long enough to toss my playbook on coach Glueck's chair. Most likely, he just sat on top of it when he returned after practice. On my way out the door, I didn't bother to look around much; despite the hurt, I at least could see that any worthwhile future lay ahead of me, and not back there on Harvard's playing fields.

5

Chapter Five

The combined four years of medical school and the six years of residency training that followed are now viewed in my rearview mirror as one big, amorphous lump. Shapeless in my memory, except for some highlights and lowlights inevitable during what was otherwise a "lost" decade, that time is worthy of little reflection here. Eighteen hour days of classroom and studying, and the later one-hundred-twenty hour work weeks of my residency consumed most of my time, though I did manage to shoehorn in enough extracurricular adventures to fill a book. What was completely absent was anything having to do with the racing world. My interest in fast cars was purely academic, as I was busy paying rent with student loans and then a meager in-training salary. There was no point lusting after expensive cars when neither schedule nor budget permitted experiencing one. And racing—I'm referring here only to the spectator sport—was simply not part of the schedule. My basic interest in the sport was all back there somewhere, but even the Indy 500 viewings with my dad took a backseat to my education. And the concept of actually racing cars—that was, well, not even a concept. Other guys, in some other world foreign to mine, did that.

Midway through my residency, I met Brandi Butler, and in another example of questionable judgment, married her towards the end of my training. As I barely managed the stresses and demands of a neurosurgical education, I attempted to be a good and dutiful husband to someone who was ill-prepared for marriage nonetheless. While I looked only towards the time when training was over and I could come up for air, Brandi debated from the outset the wisdom of marrying a very busy guy doing a demanding job she didn't quite understand.

With just over one year left in my training, it was time to start planning for real life and my first full-time private practice job as a neurosurgeon. Brandi was pushing pretty hard for me to set up a practice at the New Jersey Shore, preferably within reach of her parents' home in Bay City. I was blissfully unaware at the time that the person she really wanted to be within reach of was her boyfriend; I had figured only that it would be good for her to be close to home for all of those days and nights when hospital duties required me to be working late or even all night. As it were, my ninety-hour work weeks ended up being matters of fine convenience for her, but before it even got to that point, I had to pick a practice where I could start my career. That entailed finding the right fit—interviewing and visiting a practice, and guessing whether you might ultimately share a career well with guys who start out as total strangers. Recalling that most neurosurgeons are weird and by nature borderline certifiable at baseline, I should have realized that this would be tougher than it first appeared.

For most residents, the job hunting season occurs during the chief resident year, traditionally the last year of training for most physicians. However, I was spared the anxiety of making a last-minute practice decisions that year as I had an additional year of fellowship training planned, which pushed the job hunting period out another full year. As a result, I wasn't actively looking at specific practice opportunities when the first one came my way.

Late one evening midway through my chief resident year, I received an "outside line" page through the hospital operator. The caller identified himself as Barry Levin, a neurosurgeon at the Jersey Shore; he admitted that he had already heard that I was looking for a practice in his area. It turned out that one of the Jefferson OR nurses was also working part-time at the Atlantic City hospital system, and that she had clued Barry and his partner Sami Singh into the fact that I was considering a move to the Shore region. All pretty standard stuff, I assumed; I didn't realize until much later that most of the call was originally meant to be fact-finding and actually defensive. While he was more concerned about the prospect of competition from a new surgeon, I was instead initially flattered by his call. And when he offered to discuss a potential job within their practice, I readily agreed to check into whether I could get time off for a meeting and an interview.

Given that I was the sole chief resident for the Jefferson neurosurgery service, and that I was on call for the hospital 24/7, getting a weekend off would be no small feat. I cleared it with the chairman, Dr. Osterholm, and arranged coverage with one of the junior residents for what would turn out to be my only 24 hours of "vacation" all year. Hindsight being 20/20 and all that, I would have in retrospect been better off going to Tijuana on a bender, but instead Brandi and I excitedly made our plans for the big interview.

With the interview weekend about two weeks away, Brandi went about getting a new dress to wear to the dinner with spouses that would follow my initial meeting and tour of the hospital with Barry and Sami. I did my part by spending another $200 that I didn't have at Today's Man, getting a new suit, shirt, and shoes for the interview. I planned on picking up the suit on my way down to the shore on the Friday before the Saturday morning meeting with the partners; my OR and call schedule didn't allow much time if the suit didn't fit, so I crossed my fingers and hoped for the best.

Later in the week, with Brandi getting progressively more excited about the possibility of relocating nearer to those several special people that she loved, I received another outside line page, this one put through by the operator as "urgent".

"Hello, this is Dr, Lowe."

"Are you out of your mind?" It was Sami, the partner with whom I had yet to speak personally, shouting at me through the phone. "What are you thinking? Your wife's running all around town, blabbing to everyone about the fact that you're coming down here for an interview. Are you crazy?" he repeated. He had yet to say anything resembling "Hello."

"I…I…I'm sorry, what's wrong?" I stammered. I was immediately flustered, not knowing if there was a punch line coming behind the angry voice. As I would eventually learn, with Sami there was never a punch line; this was only to be my first introduction to that fact.

"Your wife and mother-in-law just got her a dress fitting or something like that, I guess, and went ahead and told the woman there all about your interview. Well, she's the wife of one of the radiologists down here, and now everyone will know. How could she be so stupid to tell everyone about this? I told Barry that this was all a big mistake." I could almost hear the spittle flying off his lips as he spat words rapid-fire into the phone.

"Look, I'm, umm…I'm really sorry if this caused a problem. We were both just really excited about this." (I thought we were supposed to be excited, but this was clearly getting less exciting by the moment, was what I wanted to say.)

"I can't have everyone knowing about you coming to the area. I told Barry this was all wrong. I'll have to talk to him about it, but for now, just keep your mouths shut, if it's not too late already." With that he hung up abruptly, leaving me staring into the receiver as if I just had a crank call from crazyland.

"Damn," I thought, this was going to be one interesting weekend and likely not going to end with me working there, but considering that Brandi was intent on me heading that way, I resigned myself to going through with the interview anyway.

Thursday afternoon, less than twenty-four hours before my first meeting with the two partners, I decided to call their office at the shore to get any final needed details about our interview. I asked for Dr. Levin and held while they hunted him down. Instead of Barry coming on the line, I heard the now-familiar voice of Dr. Singh. Except that was impossible to be sure that it was him, given the calm and quiet tone.

"Hey buddy, how are you? Ready for Saturday?"

Once again I was caught completely off guard. "Uhm, yeah, umm, I was, I was…just calling to get some information and to confirm times with you guys, I guess." I braced myself for another torrent of grief about some newly perceived misdeed.

"No problem. We'll see you about eight am, here at the office. Barry and I will talk with you, then he'll take you over to the hospital for a tour. It's the same as every other hospital, but Barry really wants to go, so just humor him, alright?"

It was so completely disarming then, talking with Sami like an actual human being. There wasn't even an inkling of our last conversation left in his voice. I immediately suspected that his med dosing had finally been titrated properly; little did I know that this was simply par for this hole. In fact, I'd eventually come to be an expert in identifying and even predicting Sami's huge range of moods and wild personality swings—a skill would help me survive the next eight years. But back then, I was perplexed, to say the least.

I forged ahead. "Thanks for your help. Brandi and I are both really looking forward to this—I'm picking up my new suit tomorrow, and will be there as soon as I can get down there, once Saturday rounds are done."

"A suit?" Sami suppressed a chuckle. "No need for that—we're pretty informal around here. After all, it's a Saturday. We like to be comfortable, especially on the weekend. I'll probably be in fishing clothes, and Barry will be casual, since he has to make rounds. He'll probably even be in scrubs, but you don't need anything other than day-to-day stuff—you know, like khakis and a button-down."

"Really?" Shit. Now I needed to get even more new clothes. "Just that? I'm OK wearing a suit, really."

Sami confirmed it. "No worries, no ties. Come casual, and you'll be fine. It'll be an easy interview, and a fun dinner later for the wives."

I hung up, and immediately called Brandi. "You won't believe this, but I just talked to Sami…yeah, the same guy, I think…I need you to go get me some more clothes—tan khakis and a blue shirt, I guess. Do I have a belt to wear? .... Well, grab one for me. Whatever things I need, please pick them up and I'll wear them Saturday morning…I know, I know, just wear the new dress, and I'll at least wear the suit to dinner. If I don't get it dirty, I might even be able to take it back."

Saturday morning, I finished rounds at 6 a m, giving me enough time to pick up Brandi and then make the hour drive to the shore in time for my meeting with Drs. Levin and Singh. I dropped Brandi at her parents' house in Bay City and then doubled back to Leeds Point to the Seashore Neurosurgeons' office building. I tried to look casual in my blue button down and khakis, but inside I was all nerves as I parked my dark red '86 Supra in front of the one-story stucco structure.

I was met at the front door by Dr. Levin, who was wearing a blue pin-striped three-piece suit, vest and all. He was a large, balding man, whose vest was a bit challenged by his girth. I noticed the suit immediately but chalked it up to our lack of direct communication about that morning's agenda.

"Dr. Lowe, I guess?" Barry offered his hand. Pleasantly enough, he held the door open for me, and ushered me inside. "Pleased to meet you. Welcome to the office. Come on in; Sami's inside waiting in the conference room."

I followed Barry through the hallway into a conference room, where Sami was starting to rise from his chair.

"Hey buddy, good to meet you!" He extended his hand, but I initially didn't notice it, and almost left the offered handshake unreturned. Instead I was temporarily immobilized, staring at Sami's silver-gray Italian-cut suit, tie, and dress loafers. I'm sure that both doctors noticed my jaw dropping as I stood there, staring down at my own blue and tan "Saturday casual" ensemble.

Sami caught my eye as I looked up, smirked, and said, "Have a seat. We just want to talk a bit. Casual, like." Emphasis on the casual. "No big deal, right?"

Once, during my partying days at Harvard, a football teammate and I got into a heated debate over a game of quarters. Fueled by beer and testosterone, we went toe to toe outside the room in the dorm hallway, pushing and shoving with open hands in what I mistakenly thought was a "friendly" tussle. Moments into the match, I was surprised when, with closed fist, my buddy clipped me on the jaw with a hard left. I slipped backward trying to avoid the punch, but landed flat on my back nonetheless. Blinking a bit, and surrounded by laughing friends as I regained my senses, I looked up at said buddy who pronounced the fight over. "What a disappointment that was," he laughed, as they all went back to the drinking game. I sat up alone, shook it off, and went home to my dorm room, wondering what had just happened to screw up a perfectly fun night. I've basically regretted ever since that I didn't go back in after him and take the opportunity to defend myself, but it's likely worked out best that I didn't pursue it then (or later).

Seeing Sami sitting there in his suit gave me instant flashbacks to the Harvard sucker-punch. Standing there in the office that Saturday triggered a flashback to the groggy kid sitting on the dorm hall floor, wondering if what I thought happened really did in fact just take place. I could feel the heat rising in my face as I stifled the urge to give them both the big "Fuck you" on the way out the door. Instead, I made a concerted effort to calm myself and regain control, assisted by my now familiar internal monologue/pep talk: "OK, this guy's an asshole, but you can do this. It's important to Brandi, and you don't have to love the guy to practice here. You can do this, just ignore him."

I swallowed hard. "Great to finally meet you too, Sami. Brandi and I are pretty excited about this opportunity" and so forth. I tried to appear at ease as we settled into a chat, mostly from Barry's perspective, about the practice and the area. Barry was thirty-eight at the time, and in his sixth year of practice; Sami was one year older than me, but in his third year of practice after completing a combined college/medical school program in just six years. Having skipped the critical social acclimatization that four years of college allowed, Sami was a bit short in the area of everyday guy skills, but I guess he at least never got cold-cocked in a dorm scuffle, so we'll call it a draw. Regardless, Sami had been Barry's junior resident at Mount Sinai's neurosurgical program in New York, where only the best residents did only the best cases while supervised by only the best attending surgeons. It was during that time that Sami apparently established his alpha-male status over Barry, a position he resumed when he later joined Barry in his practice in Leeds Point. Whenever it began, it was made clear to me by Sami that Saturday that that was the order and call at Seashore Neurosurgery.

Midway through the interview, Dr. Levin threw up the softball question: "Why don't you tell us what you think you can add to our practice if you come here to work?"

I answered with what I hoped wasn't a too-obviously prepared statement, emphasizing that I thought my fellowship training in advanced spinal surgery would be a good asset to the practice, with my contribution helping to grow the spinal surgery part of the neurosurgical practice that Barry and Sami had already so well established. I tried to be light-handed and humble, without soft pedaling it too much. Apparently, I was grossly unsuccessful in Dr. Singh's eyes.

Suddenly coming to life, Sami leaned forward in his seat for emphasis, bobbing his glasses up and down with one hand, stabbing his index finger at me with his other. "Don't you dare think" stab stab "that you're going to come down here" stab stab "and try to show us" stab stab "how to operate." He blinked rapidly while he forced out the words, a mannerism I was to become intensely familiar with over the next decade. "We"— gesturing towards Barry as he spoke—"don't need you"—he stabbed again in my direction—"to teach us anything! I don't know what you're doing up there"—with a gesture in the direction of Philadelphia—"but we're already doing just fine down here."

Barry tried weakly to deflect Sami's venom, even doing the "Calm down everybody" (everybody?) deal, as I tried to figure out how it had all gone so wrong so fast. I backtracked on my answer, apologized "if I somehow offended you" and tried to restate my answer more carefully. Sami seemed suddenly slightly calmer, evidently sated by the fresh kill in front of him. I could almost hear Marlin Perkins from Mutual of Omaha's Wild Kingdom as he narrated, "We'll watch from the safety of the helicopter as Jim tries to outrun the angry rhinoceros." I answered a few more of Barry's questions, mostly about my concept of surgical technique (drawing nary a nod from Sami), before Dr. Singh interrupted and excused himself, saying he was off to spend the rest of the day "out fishing on the bay." I stifled the urge to suggest that he change into something more casual before he baited up and, instead, confirmed that I'd see him tonight at dinner with the wives. With a skip and a wave, he was gone, leaving me with Dr. Levin.

"Well, he can be a little intense, but I think you two will get along just fine eventually." With that, we went off for the guided tour of the hospital.

I returned to my in-laws' house in the early afternoon, exhausted and depressed. Brandi greeted me with a bouncy "How did it go?!" but was cut short when she saw the look on my face. "What's wrong? What happened??" she asked, nearly bursting into tears as she did so.

I gave her the Reader's Digest version of the morning's events, sparing her the full description of Sami in mid-rant. "I'm going home. You can stay here if you want, but this guy's insane, and I don't think I can even make it through dinner tonight, let alone work with him."

"Please, please, can't we stay? I really want to live down here. Maybe it's just a first-time thing? What if it's really a good job? Please don't quit already." The pleading continued, with Brandi clearly having made up her mind about the practice despite that fact that she had no positive information or interactions whatsoever thus far.

I silently considered my options. Quit now, call Barry up and recommend a therapist for his partner, or just ignore the bullshit, and try to make the best of what appeared to be potentially a very bad situation. I had to admit that I did like the area, and the chance to work and live in a beach community was appealing to my surfer instincts, but I just couldn't be sure of anything that included Sami Singh.

"Please, please," Brandi intoned.

Thankfully, dinner was a hell of a lot less interesting than my morning.

6

Chapter Six

By the late 90s, I had only just started to re-establish a connection with my passion as a racing fan. Throughout my residency, I had been basically disconnected from anything having to do with the sport, although I had managed to read the occasional car magazine issue and fantasize about someday owning a real sports car. One-hundred-twenty-hour workweeks tend to create a degree of isolation and a distinct need to live day-to-day, seriously limiting time spent on frivolous pursuits such as watching or reading about racing. Exposure to sporting information mostly occurred passively—whatever was on the break-room TV or whatever magazine was left behind in the on-call room by the last unlucky inhabitant. Little free time or energy was left to actively indulge one's passion for anything short of blessed sleep and recovery in time for the demands of the next forty-hour stretch in the hospital.

I was in the midst of one such period during my fellowship in 1994, when Rick Armstrong, an OR nurse, turned me on to Autoweek magazine, enabling me to join the ranks of the "car guy" and fans of anything going fast. I became a religious reader, right down to the classifieds section—a great source of fantasy and entertainment—where seemingly every make and model of exotic car was right there for the taking. Although I wasn't remotely financially ready for the Bugattis, Ferraris, and Lamborghinis that graced those pages, it was certainly entertaining to compare specs, memorize vital statistics, and fantasize about which machine would look best in my very limited garage.

In the process of transitioning out of residency and fellowship training, and into a grown-up neurosurgical practice, I experienced dramatic change that resulted in hugely amplified stress, even beyond what I expected in my new world "at the Shore". My two very busy partners, who had been taking call non-stop for a number of years, decided that the junior guy was good meat for the grinder and that they deserved a much-needed rest. I was promptly penciled-in on the schedule to take call for Labor Day, Thanksgiving, Christmas (Sami explained that even though they didn't celebrate Christmas, the holiday was one "for the family, and that's the best time for us to spend with our families"), Easter (ditto), and Memorial Day. I also spent my own birthday party in the ER, evaluating a patient with a bleeding aneurysm, while Brandi and my family celebrated without me. I worked twelve-hour days on good days, and spent about every third night in the ER at one of the three hospitals we covered. I often operated until dawn, stopping home for a fresh change of scrubs before heading out for another long day.

I didn't actually notice it at first, but Brandi had grown somewhat distant over the year since we relocated to the Jersey Shore. Hell, I was distanced from just about everybody I knew at that time—which was very few people in my new surroundings—and who had time to socialize, anyway? This apparently suited Brandi just fine, since she had ample opportunity to enjoy recreational time with her boyfriend during my long absences.

I didn't give it any deep thought, but I was eventually aware that Brandi and I didn't have the closest, most loving, relationship. I chalked it up to the demanding focus required of a first-year surgeon in a brand new practice and, when I gave it any more thought, figured it would work itself out eventually as we both adjusted and things settled down at work, right?

In March 1996, I travelled out to Seattle to attend that year's American Spinal Injury Association (ASIA) conference; with me was an associate, Jerry Mello, a rehabilitation medicine doc. Jerry was working in our practice, helping treat patients with all manner of spinal and brain injuries. He was a fellow member of ASIA, and we figured we'd enjoy the week away from work while getting in plenty of continuing education credits.

Once I was settled into the hotel in Seattle, I made my way to the lobby, where I ran into one of my mentors from my training, Dr. Richard Balderston. As we stood and chatted in front of the elevators, the doors opened and out stepped Ginny Graziani. Dr. Graziani was an attending rehab doc at Jefferson, and a noted expert in Spinal Cord Injury. I had met her during my internship, only days before she finished her residency and only a week before she had eloped with a long-time boyfriend. I had harbored a not-so-secret crush since I first laid eyes on her (blue eyes, brown hair, black skirt, two-toned shoes, white coat barely hiding great legs as she walked down the hall on the ninth floor at Jefferson—yeah, I don't really remember all the details), but we had gone very separate ways since my training was completed. We had both married—as it turns out, badly—after our initial meeting, but I always felt a tingle whenever I saw her at the hospital. I enjoyed any opportunity to spend a moment around her, and knowing this, she in turn took merciless advantage of me when she needed the instant attention of the neurosurgical service at Jeff.

Ginny greeted Dr. Balderston and me with a big "Hello!" when she stepped off the elevator and punctuated my welcome with a kiss on the cheek. She slowed only a moment, promising to "catch up later" before she ran off towards the exhibit hall. Rich turned towards me, likely noticed that I was blushing, and said, "Wow."

I looked over at Rich. "Oh, no…no no, it's not…I'm…she's just…oh, never mind."

Rich laughed and pointed out, unnecessarily, "She didn't give me a kiss."

"Yeah, um, it's not like that…she's married, and well…" I trailed off, finding no good way to finish that sentence.

Rich made a really good point before leaving. "Well, she seemed awfully glad to see you, Dr. Lowe."

Later that day, Jerry and I were having a cocktail at a reception, when I again ran into Ginny. I introduced her to Jerry and we found that they had some mutual friends, since they were in the same specialty. As we shared drinks and hors d'oeuvres, we made plans to have dinner together sometime before the week was over.

The four of us met up for dinner—Jerry had invited along a friend from training who was also a rehab doc—and the night quickly morphed into a fun bit of drinking and exchanging stories about training, internship, and various other related topics. When the subject changed to more personal issues, and when the alcohol was titrated just right, Ginny loosened up enough to confess to us that she was, in fact, separated from her husband. She had kept this a closely guarded secret, not wanting to share the turbulence of her personal life with colleagues and co-workers, nor risk the unwanted attention of amorous but undeserving residents and interns. For my part, I shrugged it all off—after all, I was married, (happily, I then thought), —and the news of Ginny's availability was meaningless to my situation anyway. We finished dinner, had a nightcap, and stumbled back to the conference center, stopping at the hotel bar for only one more drink before calling it a night. I gave Ginny one last kiss—on the cheek—and retired to my room, thinking only of how much my head would hurt in the morning.

Two days later I was back home in New Jersey, operating at Atlantic City hospital until late in the day that Thursday. Afterwards, once I had settled in at home in Longport, Brandi served a nice dinner while I caught up on the TV news in the family room. As I sat on the couch, still in my scrubs, I clicked through the channels as Brandi exchanged my dinner plate for a dessert bowl. Once she had deposited the dirty plate in the kitchen sink, my wife returned to the room, and occupied a spot directly between me and the TV.

She started in a completely disarming fashion. "Umm, I have something to tell you."

I had the spoon halfway up to my mouth, stopping as I looked up at her. "OK, well, what's up?" I tried not to look past her at whatever was on the TV.

"Well, remember when I told you, before you left for Seattle, that we needed to talk?"

"Yeah, ahh…sure." I didn't really remember that part, but why quibble?

Brandi then made an announcement with the same inflection as if she were ordering a burger and fries. "Well, I'm leaving you."

The spoon still hovered in mid-air. "You're…what? Leaving? Where, like going to your parents' house?" I knew right away what she meant, but needed to have it defined for sure.

"No, you know what I mean. I'm leaving you, like, for good. I want a divorce."

I put the dripping spoon back down. "Do you want to talk about this or something? I mean, are you sure about this?"

Brandi was resolute. "I'm sure. I've been thinking about this for a long time, and waiting for the right time to tell you. I've made my decision. I'm leaving you."

Yeah, I had heard that part right. "Well, OK then." My ice cream was melting, and, what else would I say at that point?

A few days later, I finally decided to share the news with my partners and co-workers. Once I made my announcement, and the appropriate condolences were dispensed with, Jerry made his way over to me.

"Hey, you know what, you should give Ginny a call. Remember? She might be a good thing for you about now."

I waited a day or two, and then called Ginny. I didn't have a personal phone number for her, but figured it would be OK to call her at Jefferson. She picked up the outside line page after a few rings.

"Dr. Graziani. Can I help you?"

"Umm, Hi Ginny, It's Jim—Jim Lowe, from neurosurgery"—shit, that sounded dumb—"It's me, Jim, hope it's OK to call you at work."

Ginny was clearly puzzled. "Oh, yeah, OK, it's alright, I'm just making rounds. Is everything OK?"

"Oh, yeah, it's fine. Well, not so fine. I just thought I'd call—Uh, this sounds crazy, but, my wife just left me—just told me that she's leaving—just, well, my wife's leaving me."

Silence at the other end of the line.

"And, well, I know it's not what you were expecting, but I actually have a weekend off next week and was wondering if you'd like to go out to dinner or something?"

More silence. And then, "She left you?"

"Yep. She announced it right when I got home from Seattle. She hasn't moved out just yet, but she says she's looking for a place to stay."

Ginny was practical, as always. "Look, I'm sorry to hear that. Can I call you back later, when I'm done rounds?"

Ginny indeed called me later that evening. "I called my mom," she started out, "who immediately said, 'I'd check that out if I were you.'" She laughed. "I told her, 'What do I have to lose?' So, if you want to go out, let's have dinner on Saturday in Cape May."

That weekend, we had our first date, and we've been together ever since. Over the years, I've tried out various analogies fitting for the circumstances of our coming together, and the best I can come up with is this: It was like wrecking your Pinto right in front of the Ferrari dealership, tossing the keys on the seat and leaving the doors unlocked, and shortly thereafter coming home in a brand new red sports car.

When we first got together, Ginny was immediately aware of my passion for the sport of auto racing. She was tolerant of early weekend wakeups to watch F1 qualifying and races, and even helped insert racing into our honeymoon to Italy, including a three-day trip to the 1998 Formula One race at Monza. Nevertheless, racing at that time held only a peripheral position in our household—after all, I was a fan of many sports, and there were enough typical obligations each day so that the concept of further involvement in the sport wasn't present. In addition, it basically never crossed my mind that one could actually "go racing," on any level. You were supposed to join a country club, hit golf balls at the range, play 18 on rare weekends off, and fantasize about playing a pro-am with Tiger. Stick-and-ball sports at least lent themselves to casual play at the amateur level, keeping alive the weekend warrior tradition of over-30 professionals rupturing anterior cruciate ligaments while posting up at the "Y" during Thursday night adult league basketball games. Little of that concept held any attraction for me, nor did my schedule as a new private practice partner permit regular nightly participation in just about anything except answering calls in the ER.

I had managed to remain a pretty hard-core surfer after taking up the sport during my internship, but living at the Jersey Shore meant more often frustration rather than regular participation in the sport. Waves were fickle and truly good surf rare; still tougher was having any time to paddle out when the surf was up—not a thing possible to schedule. I was mostly dependent on occasional surf trips with the core group of surfer friends I had accumulated over the years—themselves a welcome departure from the usual hospital associates I worked with. Had I lived in Hawaii or Southern Cal, perhaps this would have all gone differently, as the stoke of riding waves regularly is intoxicating and addictive enough to demand an intense level of devotion. Given that that was not the case here, surfing eventually faded into the background, and with it seemingly my last participation in adrenaline sports.

I simply then wasn't aware that one could pack up the helmet and spend a weekend at the track—and if I had had some subconscious knowledge about that fact, I would have assumed that it was just a few random rich guys driving historic sports cars, about as relevant in my world at that time as sailboat racing. However, I did begin to notice ads for various racing schools in Autoweek. Initially, I remained only peripherally aware of the concept—but not with any real intention to participate. So I remained a spectator, stranded by my assumption that this was just something that other guys did—not a grown adult neurosurgeon with a job, a wife, and a call schedule. Real, active athletic participation was a thing of the past, and I assumed that the aforementioned adrenaline rush would be experienced by proxy from then on.

Nonetheless, I began to pay more attention to the ads, and at some point began to think of racing school as at least another fun diversion, and perhaps a new unique way to experience an amusement-park thrill without standing in line at Disney. The harder part, I realized, would be finding a positive way to include Ginny so that I wasn't wasting one of our truly rare vacations with a self-indulgent and selfish activity (there would plenty of that later, as it turns out).

In at least some consideration of Ginny and my newlywed status, I hatched a can't-miss plan after stumbling across a previously unnoticed ad in Autoweek in 1999: The Jim Russell Racing School had an introductory three-day school at its facility in Sonoma, California, conveniently only minutes from the best the wine country had to offer. An ideal vacation for two—romantic wine tasting, great restaurants, and just a little racing school thrown in, by the way. With this relatively easy sell, I booked my first race school experience for December 1999.

The Russell Racing School facility at Sears Point Raceway was a new, completely foreign environment for me, with its own set of rules and conventions unknown to me at the time. After years of repetition in the OR, with a familiar and comfortable routine demanded by the nature of the surgical beast, it was with a distinct feeling of unease that I settled into an unfamiliar spot in the Russell classroom. We did the standard self-descriptive introductions around the group of perhaps twenty students; I remember saying something about "hoping to someday do neurosurgery to support a racing habit," but mostly I relaxed a bit at the apparently amateur level of experience in the room. The instructors cautioned us about over-enthusiasm, dampening the spirits, I'm sure, of more than a few of the aspiring superstar F1 drivers in the room. We then had one of the few didactic sessions of the three-day school, reviewing basic car setup—right-foot-gas, left-foot-clutch type of stuff—and even a bit of "driving the line" essentials. A later session got into the foundation for race car dynamics, with a bit of the physics of car handling, balance, and mechanical grip discussed. In preparation for the school, I had read Going Faster, a fine textbook approach to driving fundamentals by Skip Barber Racing School's Carl Lopez, so I at least was hearing familiar terms and references to vehicle dynamics and the concept of the racing line around the track. However, the lectures always felt a bit like that last class before recess, when your attention seems to wander to the fun about to begin outside.

After the first chalk talk was completed, we were ushered into the equipment room and issued helmets and suits; instructions followed about proper care and feeding of the kit, but most of us rushed into the changing room like little kids with our first baseball uniform. Completing the basic outfit were shoes and gloves that I had purchased earlier that morning, adding to the sensory overload of new gear in need of some breaking-in time. I had sheepishly selected red shoes and gloves— a little guilty pleasure in homage to Ferrari's Michael Schumacher—theorizing that red was a faster color, much like the white cleats I wore on the football field twenty years prior. Besides, other than at a Village People concert, where else can a guy wear red shoes and gloves in a group of men and not stand out?

Donning my white school-issue helmet for the first time was a moment of immediate déjà vu, my first such sensation after a morning spent in unfamiliar surroundings. Having spent fifteen years playing football, I at least knew what a helmet felt like, even if the face mask had been replaced by the requisite (and somewhat nicked up) face shield, and the smell was that of fuel, not grass clippings. Helmets and fire suits on, we walked around like astronauts on the way to a shuttle launch, more than occasionally bumping into each other as we acclimated to the limited visibility of the helmet.

A tutorial followed to get us mated to the cars for the first time: step on the seat with your right foot first, avoid hitting the steering wheel and various knobs with your knees, and slide your butt down low into the seat, surprising in its lack of cushion and support. I took a moment to realize that my head stuck up well above the surrounding bodywork; I felt for the roll-hoop, and was only partially reassured by the fact that it was a bit higher than the vertex of my helmet. I decided to ignore this concern for the time being, hoping that the "roll" part of the roll hoop would never be tested in my presence.

Each of us had our belts tightened down by an instructor, for surely a novice could never anticipate the severe degree of compression of the shoulders and waist necessitated by a properly secured six-point harness. No matter how hard you pull, the belts always seem to feel too loose at the worst time—under maximum load while braking or cornering and, on at least one occasion a few years later, while upside down and airborne.

Seated low and barely able to breathe, we then traveled out on track for the first time, led by an instructor at five-tenths pace. Keeping focused on the car to my immediate front, I first viewed the world of turns, curbing, runoff areas, and elevation changes from the perspective of a guy nearly fully reclined and with his butt just a few inches off the asphalt. Just getting used to the limited visibility through tiny side mirrors, combined with a bulky helmet, was challenging enough; trying to remember brake/clutch/shift/throttle while not hitting anyone or running off the blacktop required all of my concentration. It seemed that all senses were being assaulted at once—the noise was intense, belts tight, vision a bit blurry by the vibration of the chassis against my helmet, and the smell—oh man, the smell: gasoline, hot rubber, oil, a faint whiff of sweat mixed with adrenaline, and onions from the last guy who wore my helmet in the prior class group. I made a mental note to get a new helmet of my own as soon as possible, and also to be very careful with my lunch selection that afternoon.

We took turns running close behind the leader, and gradually gained confidence in the car's stopping and turning ability, remaining all the while well below the limit of the car's true capabilities in the hands of a proper driver. Getting a sense of footwork on the pedals was the biggest task of the first session; later exercises with coned-off zones would teach threshold braking, and skidpad time would help us understand cornering loads in the school cars. However, any itch I had had to get down to wheel-to-wheel racing was scratched by the sobering fact that I needed big blocks of time just to get familiar with the sensation of being in the very different, very unfamiliar environment of a race car cockpit. The experience was somewhat akin to watching a professional hockey game, fantasizing about scoring an overtime goal, and then experiencing the crushing reality of trying to skate on ice for the first time. All of this was quite initially disturbing for a guy used to being in control, in charge, and in familiar, comfortable surroundings.

No stopwatches appeared until the second day, when we were finally allowed to run the entire track at Sears Point without a pace car, with the rev limiter turned up a bit higher with each successive session. The classmates bonded gradually, and it quickly became apparent who was in the faster group, and which particular neurosurgeon belonged in the more "cautious" group. With repetition, I did pick up pace and, by the end of the second day, had even induced my first spin, a sure sign that I was "getting on it." I also noticed one unexpected side-effect of driving the car: I was waking up sore, especially around the shoulders, and was starting to regain a sense of having been involved in a strenuous workout each time I drove. Having observed our runs from the grandstands, Ginny expressed mild surprise at the amount of muscular soreness I was experiencing, adding insult to injury when she commented, "You guys don't look like you're going very fast."

In truth, Ginny's observation then was similar to that of just about anybody watching cars race around a track from a safe distance. The violence going on in the cockpit, with the driver wrestling every bit of performance out of the vehicle while straining the laws of physics and absorbing endlessly changing g-forces, is simply not evident to the casual observer. While the pilot fights for control, the heart rate climbs to Tour de France competitor levels, all while the car dances at the edge of a loss of grip and its immediate penalty of a spin, or worse. This is the infamous "limit" of grip and maximum performance that drivers endlessly seek, with the best of them able to get there, stay there lap after lap, and somehow not exceed that point. Violate that boundary, and one likely ends up on the blooper segment of the highlight show. Add in race variables such as other cars, fatigue, rain, and darkness, and you have a prolonged and intense battle going on, without time-outs, commercial breaks, or rests between three-minute rounds.

On the third and last day, we again ran progressively faster timed group sessions, with lap times dropping as we became more familiar with the racing line around the track, and as our confidence in the basic school cars grew. We then experienced one of the smarter techniques of the school's marketing department: the head instructor informed us that "There's a chance that we might be able to try out the Advanced Open Wheel School cars (with wings, slicks, and more horsepower) after lunch," providing we didn't screw up too much in the morning session. With that incentive, we completed the last exercises of the basic school curriculum, all the while eyeing the faster machines that awaited. We then finished off the three-day school by taking careful but exhilarating laps in the advanced Russell cars, getting a blast of wind against the face shield at 120 mph and an ever stronger incentive to sign up for the next advanced course. By the time I got out of that car, I was hooked—pumped up by the adrenaline rush of the drive, anxious to tackle the next challenge, and wholly impressed by the first hint of intimidation that I had experienced in any form in years.

Jim's first run in the Russell school car, 1999

Back at home, work-related demands and accompanying stresses just seemed to accelerate and accumulate over the next few months. I dealt with the collapse of a business venture relating to the management of my larger group practice, and had increasing difficulties dealing with the bickering and personality conflicts between myself and my partners. The good buzz that Gin and I felt after our time in California was almost immediately killed by the realities of my medical practice situation and especially by the deteriorating relationship with my partners. Clearly, there was an even bigger value to just thinking and talking about my new passion of racing, which was equally clearly not understood or embraced by my partners. As quickly as possible, I made plans to return for the advanced school at Russell.

The group that assembled for the Russell School's Advanced Racing class was a bit different from the basic school group that I had joined four months prior. Although the current crowd was by no means expert or accomplished in the racing world, gone were the most casual participants of the group—those that had received the introductory school registration as a gift, those who had had a big enough thrill from the early lead-follow days, and perhaps those whose spouses had realized that the best way to cure the addiction was to stop it from growing in the first place. As the advanced school was advertised as one of the easiest paths to a Sports Car Club of America competition license, and the only path towards racing in the Formula Russell "arrive and drive" amateur race series, most of the attendees now were at least a bit more serious about continuing their racing activities and a bit more obvious about their dedication to going faster. Idle chatter among the students and instructors often included next plans for racing this car or that, in such-and-such series. There was ample "I've got big plans" talk among my fellow students, all of which went well beyond my private goal of simply not embarrassing myself in the next three days. I listened to conversations in between each driving session, always feeling that the participants had some insider knowledge about what was the best car/track/event to race. My ignorance was made even more obvious by the fact that, outside of the Russell School, I knew virtually no other racers, no other tracks, and no other racing organizations. At that point, my personal version of long-term racing goals included surviving the school with brain and ten fingers functioning properly and having a warm memory to counteract the bad vibes emanating from my current surgical practice environment.

Each day and each exercise of the advanced school brought a new level of challenge—and new excitement. My confidence grew as I realized that I was mid-pack in the student group in terms of speed, and less overwhelmed by the prospect of running nearly flat out through the many challenging turns at Sears Point. The learning curve steepened (and would remain steep for years, as it turns out), but I relaxed even more once I embraced my absolutely novice status and enjoyed the rest of the drills and exercises. Instead of trying to hide my complete lack of expertise, I surrendered to what I realized was an expected degree of ignorance—essentially the complete opposite approach to the surgical training world, where the mere admission of ignorance or inexperience is an unpardonable sin.

With this personal blank-sheet-of-paper approach, I savored even small bits of evidence of progress: a half-second faster here, a pass under braking there, and I was pleasantly surprised at the good vibe growing inside. It was both liberating to not have pre-ordained expectations of success and simultaneously intoxicating to gain progressive admittance into a world that I had only observed from outside the fences. In essence, I allowed myself the luxury of embracing a challenge, without the stress of demanding instant success. In fact, the presence of a new challenge, when recognized, was a distant if vaguely familiar feeling, one I hadn't anticipated out of subconscious surrender to the otherwise mundane cadence life had become.

I occupied the flight hours home from Sonoma with racing daydreams, experiencing for the first time the racer's quandary: "What's next, what's next?"

Chapter Seven

By the time I had finished residency and begun to practice neurosurgery, I had long since become accustomed to the emotional difficulty of resuming work after vacation periods. As an intern, we only received one week's time off, so at least that year's return-to-work experience was isolated, even if more intensely felt because of the one-time nature of the event. The two weeks of paid time off I received with Seashore Neurosurgery were similarly valued, given the call demands and other stresses placed upon me during my first year in practice. With little else to do with my free time, I went on two different surf trips during scheduled vacations, including one to Portugal that happened to have me away during what turned out to be the last anniversary of my first marriage. These at least allowed me to enjoy the freedom of wave-riding with friends while Brandi enjoyed the freedom of her cuckolded husband being out of the country.

However, the general feeling of dread and regret when returning to work was never more heart-felt than during my last year or two of practicing with Sami and Barry. Had I not then been actively planning my escape from the practice, I might have become suicidal, the intensity of my distress while working with them being so extreme. I required almost daily verbal support from Ginny, who always was able to separate the wheat from the chaff when she reassured me: "You have built a great personal practice and reputation. You don't have to love those guys to work there. Continue building something valuable. Try not to let them get in the way of your goals," and so on. Having herself joined the group practice after our marriage in 1998, Ginny had already stopped going to morning clinical reviews or evening business meetings, as she was unwilling to provide an audience to the venom and craziness of Dr. Singh and the pomposity of Dr. Levin.

As I continued to butt heads with my partners, I intensified my focus on two reassurances: the practice I was building was personally satisfying and valuable on many different levels, and my new marriage, family, and free time activities were personally rewarding enough to help me tolerate the professional bullshit created by my partners. It was against this backdrop that I made the decision to continue my racing education, and start actually entering races, in the summer of 2000.

Having completed the full training courses available through their program, I was officially qualified to compete in the Jim Russell Racing Series "arrive and drive" amateur racing program, ideally designed for new and occasional racers like myself. The concept was built around the needs of professionals and neophytes in situations similar to mine: having little understanding of exactly how to "go racing," the series allowed us to register, show up, drive, and then go back to our real lives, all without the investment and hassle of having our own car or team. Once having registered for a race weekend, we were guaranteed a seat in one of the open-wheel advanced school cars in which we had learned the craft, and assigned to a group of competing drivers of similar levels of experience and skill. I considered only briefly that I was heading into completely uncharted territory and promptly made my reservation for my first-ever race weekend in September, 2000, entered in a Formula Russell car for the race school's series at Sears Point.

Indulging my inner Walter Mitty first required that I outfit myself properly, as I wanted to experience the full effect of wearing my own race attire, along with my own helmet. I sketched out a helmet design concept, blatantly reminiscent of Michael Schumacher's red and blue design, and sent my new Bell helmet off to the painter like a kid mailing box tops to the cereal company. When the finished helmet was shipped back to me a few weeks later, I donned my new red race suit, shoes, gloves, and helmet, and sat on my couch in the living room making race car sounds, working an imaginary gear shift.

With all of the gear on, Ginny's laughter was a bit muffled, at first.

"What the hell are you doing?" she laughed. "Your beeper's going off, and you look like an ass. Hopefully no one will come to the door to see that getup."

I raised up the face shield in time to catch the last bit. "Who's at the door?"

"Nevermind, Mario. Check your beeper."

I removed the helmet before answering the call to the trauma unit at Atlantic City. Another patient with a fractured neck was awaiting in the ER. Another STAT trip that would take me away from my new helmet for the rest of the day. I bounded up the stairs, heading for my bedroom closet.

"What's up?" asked Ginny.

"There's a fresh fracture in the trauma bay at City. I'm on my way as soon as I change into scrubs."

"You'd probably get there faster if you left the red suit on."

***

I loaded my gear, new helmet mated with red suit and shoes, and flew off to Sonoma, riding out alone with my fantasies of winning my first race and impressing all those around me with my previously undiscovered talent. I envisioned running at the front of the amateur pack, trying to create mental images strong enough to counteract my fear of public failure and embarrassment. I was heading towards a new playground with new kids who already knew the game and played it well. Despite my various accomplishments, I was now again facing my old demons. I was determined not to sit this one out, watching from the curb as other guys enjoyed the competition. I had to make a good run of it.

I spent a fitful night at the Holiday Inn in Novato, fretting most about simply being able to find the track again, and the basic logistics of where do I go/who will I know/did I forget something critical? Braking later was a concern for later, only to be indulged after I had successfully gotten to the race on time with all equipment intact. That night, I dreamed perhaps the first of what would become a familiar and recurring theme: I was trying to get to the track, which always seems to be absurdly located in my hometown, on my college campus, or somewhere behind the hospital. Caught up in some other non-racing related obligation, surrounded by people who have no interest or understanding of my urgency, I unfailingly end up desperately searching for a missing shoe or my helmet, all while realizing that the race is starting without me. Struggling to get oriented, I'm hopelessly unable to even get my gear together or find my way to the unreachable paddock. I always wake sweaty and frustrated, tired from the stress and anxiety of the dream, wondering what purpose is served by my mind's unpleasant nocturnal gymnastics.

I've had similar dreams in the past about other performance-anxiety-inducing opportunities, such as playing college football (still get those) or surfing. Each and every one is clearly reflective of my not-so-subtle worries about confronting challenge and then failing, especially in any activity outside my personal comfort zone. Whether it's suiting up for a football game when gradually I realize I'm twenty years past my last game, or trying to find the path to the beach where I know the waves are breaking without me, all aspects of the dream are stereotypical: seemingly absurd and insurmountable obstacles interfere with my dogged attempts to get where I need to be. (Gin's still-favorite dream of mine is a surfing vision: During a big swell, I struggle to find a board and the beach, and finally succeed to eventually paddle out in big surf conditions. In a classic Freudian moment, my surfboard turns soft and sinks under me as soon as I get into the waves, suggesting something altogether different from anxiety about riding waves, I guess.)

It's only been recently, after a thoroughly amateur self-analysis, that I've realized that I've never once had my anxiety dream theme about operating or being in surgery. Perhaps the ultimate measure of comfort and conquering anxiety is the subconscious mind's verdict after all, but the dreams about racing haven't stopped, even today, after over ten years competing and a few hundred events.

I left the Holiday Inn at Novato fully-suited up for the day's racing: fire-retardant underwear, new red suit, red shoes, and helmet bag in hand. I had no idea what awaited me as far as basic logistics, and I worried needlessly about where to store a kit bag or where to change clothes. I decided to simply preempt all that anxiety by arriving prepared to race. Having nobody to guide my first steps, I reverted to a tried and true psychological shelter: over-prepare, check and re-check, leave nothing to chance whenever possible, and get on the road early. It was a bit uncomfortable sitting at the McDonald's eating McMuffins in a fire suit, but I really needed one less thing to worry about. Thirty minutes later, I arrived at Sears Point before the gates opened, not realizing then that it would be the last time in a great while that I came in first at a race track.

During our pre-race meeting, the chief steward outlined the format of the weekend's racing: four groups, with the fastest guys in "A" and all new drivers mixed in with the slower runners in group "D." Each group would have qualifying and two separate races on Saturday and Sunday, with group members moving up and down overnight, depending on pace and race results. Assigned to group D, I sought out a familiar instructor from the race school. "How long will I have to stay in group D? Should I be able to move up this weekend?"

"No problem, don't worry," he assured me. "You'll probably get booted up to C or even B, after they see some practice times."

Feeling confident, I suited up with the rest of the Group D drivers and started off for the first practice session. Given that it had been four months since the last time I was in a race car, I felt surprisingly at ease and comfortable in the almost-familiar cockpit of the Russell car. The good vibe continued even after I pulled my belts tight around my waist and shoulders, and accelerated down pit lane onto the track. With the instructor's words echoing in my head, I climbed through turns one and two, expecting to run quickly up to the front of the pack. I ran the familiar line into the valley of turn three, accelerating on the way down the short hill just as they had taught me in school. Forgetting my mirrors, I focused on maintaining the proper line, trying to crest the next hill in perfect position. The first real passing zone, a slightly banked right-hander, was next, and there was a car right ahead of me waiting to be overtaken.

I strained against the belts, already planning out how I would pop out into the passing zone under hard braking, replaying as I accelerated countless mental images of perfect passes executed by my racing heroes. I came up hard onto the rear wing of the slower car in front and drafted a bit to gain speed. Heart thumping away, I was just about to move to my right and thrill the crowds with my first official pass, when all of the sudden the fun disappeared.

A group of at least seven cars, two abreast, dove to my inside at the turn, zipping by with a frightening rush and forcing both me and my slightly slower leader out on the shoulder of the turn. I looked right in disbelief, not able to jump in the line for fear of getting collected by one of the faster cars passing on the inside. Abandoning all thoughts of going to the apex,

I maintained my position behind the original car and waited for a turn or two to settle myself and resume driving. I followed closely, anticipating the next hairpin and the opportunity it presented for me to finally make my first pass. Unfortunately, math being one of my weak points, I had completely forgotten to account for the additional five or six cars back there somewhere.

Turns out, there were five of them, and they all passed both of us at once going into the hairpin. This time though, I jumped on the tail of the pack as we all accelerated out of the tight turn, and finally I was free of the slower car. I drove down the curving front straight, comfortably ahead of the slower guy going into the first turn, but now hopelessly behind the rest of the pack. More than a bit disappointed, I drove on as best I could, wondering just a bit why I wasn't seeing anyone ahead or behind. I finished out the thirty minute practice nearly lapped by the fast pack; the slower guy was nowhere to be found.

When I had successfully dismounted in the pits, I turned to see a sweaty, smiling guy about my age, breathing hard and heading my way. "Did you see that? That was awesome! Those guys smoked us," he laughed, not sounding at all like I was feeling. "Wasn't that you behind me? Is this your first race? Wasn't that great?" he fired all at once.

I introduced myself as we headed together for the instructor debriefing. "Yeah, this is my first race. I thought I'd be a bit faster than that, but there's time to make up for it in qualifying, I hope."

"Never mind that, wasn't it a blast just running out there? I've never done this before either!" He assumed a bit of an apologetic tone. "I'm just a surgeon trying out a new way to have fun. What do you do in real life?"

I grinned a bit, feeling a combination of comfort at his admission, and regret that I was closer to his pace than anyone else's. "I'm a neurosurgeon, so I guess we'll need to stick together in this deal."

"Don't worry, those guys are pretty quick; we'll just have to have fun racing each other."

Racing against another surgeon wasn't exactly what I had signed up for, but there was healthy perspective to be found there. I took it for what it was worth, glad for anything at the track that was familiar and friendly at the same time.

My first-ever qualifying session was a twenty minute affair, during which I managed to push a bit and improve upon my morning practice times. Determined to make my way further towards the front of the pack, I tried to forget about the unofficial "fastest surgeon" contest. I was happy to have a colleague to run against, but I also knew that there would be no asterisk on the time sheet to excuse my lack of pace. No hiding behind inexperience or an expectation of marginal performance here—the slow guys were in the back regardless of what good reason we might have for being there.

I checked the posted qualifying sheets when I got back to the meeting room, optimistically starting at the top of the list. It took a bit of scanning, however, before I came upon my car number. I cursed under my breath as I saw my name next to P15 on the list, and then exhaled as I realized that the surgeon occupied the only place under mine, in P16. Not the Ayrton Senna-like performance I had hoped for. However, at least my lap time was a personal best thus far, so I figured there was at least still reason to run the actual race.

There was little time to debate the wisdom of picking racing as my avocation, as Group D was first up for the afternoon's races. I saddled up and took a moment to shake off the illusion that the gloved hands on the steering wheel weren't attached to me. Pulling out for the pace lap, I considered that I could simply pull into the pits before crossing the line for the rolling start, get out, and be in my car on the way back to the hotel before the first lap was over. No one would even realize I had left until the other surgeon saw that he had finished something other than last. I could make my escape back to New Jersey, where few even knew I was trying out the racing thing—and fewer still would have to know the truth of my retreat.

I listened to the sounds coming from behind my head as I ran the rpm's up and down, warming the engine. I accelerated and braked hard, warming the tires as I weaved side to side. My adrenaline surged and I could almost hear the pounding of my pulse. Focused on keeping my car lined up tight with the other rows, I passed the pit entrance with only a little regret: "Oh boy, you're really going to do this. No turning back now. Get ready, here it comes!"

The group of cars bunched up at the last hairpin, and I strained to see the starter in the flag stand well up the front straight. The noise from the engines intensified and suddenly exploded as the green flag waved. I stomped on the accelerator and started going through the gears as the pack made its way up through the flat-out first turn. I stayed tight on the backside of the car directly to my front, realizing that there was a slower turn coming up, and we would all need to brake early to allow everyone to get through.

As the cars closed up together again at the first right-hander, I saw several cars in front of me spinning off into the grass, and one off in the tire wall. Weaving to dodge cars trying to rejoin the race, I managed to stay on the blacktop, and somehow made it through the dust cloud hanging over turn two and into three. I managed a glance or two in my mirrors, realizing that there were now several cars behind me somewhere, and most of them had out-qualified me. Nothing to do but focus on what was ahead, and maintain a good pace.

I attacked each turn as best I could, braking as late as I dared, and trying to feel the car's lateral grip as I hunted for the next apex. Forgetting any semblance of "smooth" driving, I rushed my shifts, manhandled the steering wheel, and felt my forearms become fatigued almost immediately. Throughout the fifteen lap race, I pushed and sweated each turn, each straightaway, and each encounter with other cars on the track. I didn't fight off passes by the faster runners, as I was unable to be sure who was who, given that all the cars were white. I did manage to make one pass in anger, catching my surgeon friend on the second to last lap only after unwittingly letting him by in the early confusion of the race.

I spent most of the race's last laps largely alone on the track, finally enjoying the cadence of the turns and the sequence of each trip through particular sections of the track. Coming through the last hairpin, I passed two cars tangled together at the apex, feeling somewhat proud that I was at least bringing my machine home in one piece. I buzzed down the front straight and under the flag stand, eyes fixed on the waving checkered flag and feeling more like a spectator than the participant I had become.

As I decelerated into pit lane, I considered for a moment how I had disappointed myself and surely also my race school instructors. There was no way to put a good spin on this—I was pulling into the back end of the line of cars, leading only my new best-friend surgeon. Times were to be posted, results made public—all in an embarrassing exposure of my immense slowness. No way to claim that the judges were biased, that the conditions were poor, that the wind was blowing against me—the times I had run, and the race results, were official, objective, and concrete evidence behind which no one could hide. Clearly, here was an activity that required –no, demanded—that I swallow my pride and take my rightful place at the bottom rung of the ladder.

I wanted to make a break for it, and escape in my rental Ford before I was forced to witness the winner's celebration, but it was not to be. First, there would be the mandatory debriefing session with the corner instructors. One benefit of the series being based around the race school was that on-the-spot teaching and advice was available after each race. Of course, this also created an instant feedback situation, where my overall lack of pace could be cruelly dissected into small segments of failure.

I approached my first instructor, wincing a bit at his opening salvo.

"Dude, what happened to you out there?"

I shrunk a foot or two and immediately flashed back to Mr. Larkin, my little league baseball coach. All at once I was eleven years old with a bully of a coach in my face, berating me for making a poor throw, striking out, or just plain failing to meet expectations. Back then, I had been completely unable to defend myself and had managed to absorb the criticism as if it were rightfully mine. Now, standing there twenty-five years later, I had the opportunity to respond much more maturely.

"Uh, well, I, um, don't really know," I mumbled as I examined my driving shoes. "I was trying my best," I managed, almost adding, "Mr. Larkin" to my weak response.

"You went up into turn one on the first lap like a bat out of hell, and then you just slowed down! After that, you just looked lost!"

"I really was pushing, but once everyone passed me, I had no idea what my pace was."

"Well, you might have noticed the pace of all those guys who kept passing you. Maybe that was a good indicator that you needed to get on it," he observed. The instructor then took on a more nurturing tone. "Look, I know it's your first event, but you've already driven better than that, and I've seen it. Don't get psyched out by the racing—just drive your line, and work on going faster."

"Yeah, but how do I get faster? It felt fast, only it wasn't. What the hell am I doing wrong that all these guys know how to do better?" I was aware that I was whining a bit, and realized that I had now graduated to a high-school Jim Lowe, wondering why I kept tripping over the goddamn hurdles.

"Look, it's pretty simple in theory. Do you know who Juan Manuel Fangio was?"

I was familiar with the story of the famous Argentine, winner of five Formula One world championships. "Sure," I admitted, wondering how he might be able to help me now.

"Someone once asked him how he was able to drive so much faster than everybody else. His answer still works today: 'Less brake, more gas.'"

"Thanks for that gem," I replied. "At least it's an easier concept than rotating the car at speed."

"Remember, less brake, more gas," he smiled, and turned away to critique the next driver.

Before I exited through the gate at Sears Point, I slowed a moment to look a bit closer at the paddock and the cars rolling out for the other races. I truly thought it was in fact a last look for me. After that experience, I no longer felt a tingle about the prospect of racing. In fact, I felt exhausted and embarrassed. Hell, I wasn't sure they'd let me in again for the next day's racing anyway. Still dressed in my red suit, I then drove back to Novato, stopping only for drive-thru dinner at my now-favorite McDonald's.

I called Ginny from the hotel room, trying not to sound as down as I felt.

"Yeah, it was kind of fun, but it's a lot harder than I thought it would be. I basically got my butt kicked. The only guy I beat was another surgeon, the poor bastard."

"So you didn't finish last, and you did your best times in your first race?" Ginny always managed to find perspective in a way that I simply couldn't master.

"Yeah, well, when you say it that way, it doesn't sound so bad. But I still want to come home. I miss you and can't stand feeling like I'm eleven again."

"It will all look better when you've had some rest. Get some sleep, go there tomorrow, run your best—and just have fun. Forget finishing or beating someone. You went all the way to California to have fun, not to beat yourself up about it."

"Thanks honey, you always say the right things, even if you're just blowing smoke."

I hung up, gave the Quarter-Pounder a proper burial, and stretched out a moment on the bed. I replayed the race in my head, staring at the ceiling as snapshots of passing cars and spinning wrecks circulated through my brain. Details were blurred, and the whole experience started to take on a surreal air. Had I really just raced at Sears Point, jockeying for position at 120 mph? How the hell did I wind up in California? Why can't I seem to brake later? Maybe I should have picked a less visible color for my helmet?

I woke with a start, disoriented and still wearing my race suit and fireproof underwear. The room was dark, the muted TV was showing some forgettable infomercial, and the bedside clock read 1:20 am. I shed the suit and underwear, realizing that I might actually need them again in just a few hours. Skipping the shower, I washed a bit, not willing to glance in the mirror. Falling back into the bed, my last waking thought was whether it really would all be better by the light of day, as Gin had promised.

I felt a little better when the girl at the counter recognized me, or more likely, my red race suit, while ordering McMuffin number two of the weekend. Earlier that morning, I had decided that I'd rather fail there, on the track in front of strangers 3,000 miles from home, than have to retell any story that included me quitting early on something resembling a challenge. So I donned the red ensemble, winced a bit at the odors emanating from my helmet bag, and set out for Sears Point once again.

I sought out the instructor when I arrived early at the track.

"Help me, if you can. I'm a little lost—how the hell can I make up lap time?"

He looked up from his clipboard, "Now you're talkin'."

We went over a track map, isolating each turn on the Sears Point layout and then breaking down each turn into segments: braking points, apex, track out, line, gears. Each turn had its own unique geometry, its own demands that required drivers to take a similar path in order to negotiate the corner as best possible. The best drivers maximized entry speed, holding off on braking until the last possible moment, slowing just enough to make it through the turn without spinning or crashing. Acceleration at the earliest possible moment required a feel for the car underneath, with power application at the perfect moment resulting in the car surging out of the turn without looping around or falling off the outside of the corner. Every corner had an ideal theoretical line and way to get through. The fastest drivers were artists who used that canvas to express a beautiful image of speed through the turn and onto the next piece of tarmac ahead.

Although I was equipped with the same set of colors and brushes as the fast guys, I just couldn't paint very well, yet. I had to settle for a sort of paint-by-numbers approach, memorizing brake points and gears for each segment of track in a necessarily analytical but artless approach. The result was theoretically the same—I navigated my way around Sears Point in the same path as did the winner, but any critic could recognize the lack of innate talent in the result of my efforts.

I realize now what wasn't apparent then, in all my desire and hope to be fast and successful immediately. I was perhaps the only one who had expected good results right away, ignoring the rather obviously stacked odds against me. In retrospect, I can appreciate that it was rather like giving a student a few days of lessons in surgery and then throwing him into the OR environment. However, at that time it was a humbling and daunting experience to be the initiate, much less to have failure expected of me.

After studying the annotated track map, I put on my helmet and set out for race number two of my brief career. On the warm up lap, I focused on the key points of each corner and envisioned where I would brake, turn, and get on the power to maximize whatever speed I could muster. In a way, analysis made me feel a bit more in control—I was familiar with the concept of something I could dissect and attack in small organized bits. Reassured in a new way, I rounded the last turn in the pack of two cars abreast, thinking less about the green flag waving than about the anatomy of the first turn.

I drove well, considering my inexperience, and never once put a wheel off the blacktop. I passed few cars that weren't off in the tire wall or crumbled against another errant competitor, but I stayed clean. I returned the race car to the pit lane all shiny and none the worse for the wear and tear, roughly in mid-pack. Finishing up hot and breathing heavy, I sat for a moment in the cockpit before getting out to face the instructor one last time.

"Dude! Nice job!" My instructor high-fived me as I dismounted. "P10 and two seconds faster than yesterday! That's what I'm talkin' about!"

I managed a crooked smile. I hadn't really noticed that I had been moving up in the field, so intent was I on getting each turn right. "Thanks. I have to admit, that was a blast, really."

"Good job, good race. When are you racing again?"

Ah, that magic question. At least someone was asking it. At least it was out there for me to even consider, now that I had my first race weekend under my belt.

8

Chapter Eight

The second year of the new millennium was momentous for me in so many different ways that it seems artificially fabricated, as if all the possible major events were compressed into a 23-minute made-for-TV episode. Life-changing events, most by design, were evolving rapidly, and several new phases were being constructed—all seeming to happen at once. This pattern of simultaneously occurring chaotic and challenging sequences was easily a developing theme in my life, especially when viewed in retrospect. A more thoughtful pacing of the significant changes in lifestyle would have been perhaps smarter, but certainly out of character, and therefore suspect, for both Ginny and me. Instead, we found ourselves pushing head-on into several significant alterations of the status quo, setting new personal standards for challenges met.

Having already spent two years on the design and construction of our new home in New Jersey, we were finally ready to move in by February of 2001. The daily grind of construction was not remotely over then, of course, as finishing work took several more months after that. During that time, I left for work every morning just as the worker's trucks were lining up outside. Rising only slightly later, Gin was usually tasked with getting the subs pointed in the right direction before she left for the hospital or office.

However much I might have looked forward to the sanctuary that was the OR, Gin was having a progressively more unpleasant time once she arrived at the offices of her physiatry practice. Occupying a bit of space in the Seashore Neurosurgeons' offices, Gin had been struggling to develop her rehabilitation medicine outpatient practice, which would have certainly benefited from the support of the four-surgeon group to which I belonged. Instead, my three partners essentially went out of their way to minimize their support of Ginny, except when in-hospital care of their own patients was needed. Sami, Barry and Warren essentially ignored Ginny's role in the practice, refusing to refer patients to Ginny for pre-op evaluations, which would have made the later care of the patient more effective and streamlined,. There was no camaraderie expected, nor desired, on Ginny's part, but her value as an accomplished and expert physician was mostly lost on my neurosurgical partners. Much of this, I thought, was based on jealousy, as I was then the busiest surgeon in the group. I addition, there seemed to be a stubborn reluctance on the part of the other docs to contribute in any positive way to help Ginny grow her practice. Despite the fact that Gin had a curriculum vitae, a faculty teaching position, and academic recognition that dwarfed those of the surgeons (including me), she was basically a nonentity as far as my partners were concerned.

Long before Ginny left Jefferson to work in New Jersey, Sami especially had made it a vocal point that he would not support Ginny, warning me about the ramifications of having one's wife—gasp!—as a member of the practice. He took the opportunity to tell me so, in no uncertain terms, one afternoon after yet another miserable day operating with him.

"This is a big problem, and you really need to consider what'll happen if Ginny joins our practice." Sami dropped this one on me while we were changing out of our dirty scrubs in the OR locker room. He stood there in his boxers, tugging at his glasses in the way that he always did when agitated, and squared off in the aisle. "No one in our group has ever had a wife as a partner, and nobody in this practice will ever tolerate it. She brings nothing to our group but trouble." He blinked furiously as I took a deep breath and considered my response.

Staring at the floor in front of my open locker, I actively suppressed my rising anger, knowing that the satisfaction of cold-cocking the guy just wouldn't be worth the punch. "I just want to make sure I'm clear on this—tell me again, what are you saying? She's a better doc than all of the other schmucks down here combined; you should be thrilled that she's willing to work with us."

Sami just shook his head and laughed; the guy probably had a condescending look on his face while sleeping. "You just wait. It'll destroy everything I've"—he couldn't quite stop himself there—"we've worked for."

"You're kidding me, right? You'd actually try to keep her from working with us? What would you gain by that?"

By now, the volume had risen, and Sami looked around nervously, always conscious of the fact that somebody who actually referred him patients might see him during a less-than-calm moment of weakness.

"You're making a big mistake, and I'm not going to stand there and let you ruin everything."

With that, Dr. Singh stomped off, flinging open the locker room door just in time to run into one of the local orthopedists. Still shaking with anger in front of my locker, I could hear the predictable conversation across the room. "Hey, buddy," Sami soothed, "How's it going? Belinda and I had a great time at the house the other night. Thanks again for sending Mr. Carlson over—I'll let you know when we get him scheduled for surgery. Call me and we'll get together."

With that the door swung closed, and it was quiet again in the locker room. I sat a moment in front of my locker—why have so many important moments in my life occurred in front of an open locker?—and filed away yet another impression of my someday-former partner for later reference.

Paranoid people express their paranoia in many different ways; with Sami, it was often disguised as a concern for "the practice," as if his vision was the only way for a group of seven different and very educated people to act. Decisions were to be made after his consideration and with his consent only, or grave consequences would surely result. Barry's input—despite his seniority—was ignored and privately criticized by Sami, and the opinions of Warren and the rest of the partners were invisible to the man. After attending a few acrimonious practice meetings, Gin took to referring to Sami as "Chicken Little" and "the Disastricizer," so intense was this aura around him. Every challenge, every potential conflict, represented the end of the world, or at least his ability to make money, in Sami's eyes. The sky was always falling somewhere, and it was never closer than when Sami was around to bear witness.

To accommodate this pervasive attitude in the most outspoken member of the whole group, Ginny later surrendered her voting rights as a partner, in one of the finest "whitewashing the fence" tricks I've ever seen pulled. Gin happily bragged to me that it was actually demanded of her that she give up something that she never wished to partake of in the first place; for my part, I simply regretted that I hadn't thought of it first. All of this was ultimately finalized through a lunch meeting with Barry, Sami and myself, with Ginny painfully present for Sami's all-too-common ranting and finger-pointing. Over a bowl of chowder, he loudly reiterated his concern that adding Ginny to our practice was somehow the "biggest mistake we'll ever make." In that rare moment of clarity, Sami was entirely right, but for reasons altogether unknown to him, as he was hugely underestimating the damage to his practice that would occur just a few short years later when we became competitors.

After that, Ginny did what was necessary to continue her practice, keeping as wide a berth from Sami as possible, maintaining a low profile in and around the office. Since we weren't social with Sami and his wife, Belinda, (not one single invitation was ever proffered to join the Singhs for any of the many parties they threw), Ginny was able to compartmentalize things well enough to tolerate work. However, my schedule frequently required all-day interaction with Sami and the other two partners, so I wasn't able to easily escape the harshness that surrounded the damaged partnership, even in the off hours. Nonetheless, I knew that at some point the opportunity to leave the practice would present itself, and I would be ready. After all, I had been preparing for that eventuality ever since the day I interviewed for the job. That fact alone allowed me to continue on, keep working hard, and swallow my bile each time I scrubbed with Sami or shared office hours with him.

In the malignant atmosphere that my practice had become, I somehow still managed to cultivate a strong referral base and a growing reputation of excellence of which I was proud and covetous. Despite the bad air in the office, and the nearly intolerable unpleasantness in the OR whenever I worked with Sami, I pushed on. This was really just another test of endurance, but the journey had to be taken, and the trials endured. I focused on practicing in the manner which I desired, caring for patients regardless of interpersonal difficulties with my partners, and basically tried to ignore the bullshit while maintaining my position as a good, hard-working neurosurgeon.

As the years had gone on, little that went on behind the closed doors of the office was helpful to me or my goals as a spinal surgeon; more and more, the relationship with my partners appeared to be obstructive and damaging to me, my professional reputation, and to my wife and her practice. Meetings at "Seashore" went from being forums for professional and clinical debate to classic exercises in restraint, with outright threats and arguing closing many partner sessions. By 2001, Ginny had long since quit attending any meetings. As my OR schedule became more crowded, and the demands for my time accelerated, I found less reason to participate also.

In the midst of this professional chaos, Gin and I were actively trying to have a baby. We had already experienced the brief joy of a pregnancy, followed by the crushing loss of miscarriage. Once Ginny again became pregnant, our whole attitude and focus changed. Neither of us was willing to make the major life change of parenthood in the atmosphere of our miserable career circumstances at Seashore Neurosurgeons, where negative feelings and hostility were daily experiences for both of us. The trick was to find the right time, the right opportunity to leave, and to preserve the greatest thing of professional value which I owned: my reputation.

The situation was defined, attacked, and then decided finally, fittingly through Ginny's clear vision and smart sense. Eight months pregnant, Gin was having a tough time, working harder than ever and preparing a new home for a new baby. I was professionally miserable, and it was having a negative impact on pretty much everyone around me. I was coming home exhausted, frustrated, and often angry, with the cocktail of misery stirred by basically every interaction with my partners. Then, in one memorable evening, it was decided.

"I don't think I can take much more of this," I concluded, as I narrated yet another episode of Sami's antics from that day's surgeries. "I'm spent. I grit my teeth just at the thought of having to work one more day with that guy. I can't sleep, knowing that the next morning I'll be in the OR with him. I can't even hide it anymore."

Rubbing her belly, Gin smiled a bit and said, "First come over here and feel this. The baby's pretty active right now. He's kicking away."

I paused in mid-rant, as if realizing for the first time that Gin had a sizeable belly containing the gift of a child. I knelt next to her chair, breathed deeply, and stared at the visible undulations of her abdomen. I reached out, amazed again, and rubbed a bit, feeling the magic of my son's movements against my hands.

The emotions of the moment were so much in conflict that I didn't know how to react. As a result, I just kept kneeling there, numb to the thought of the work drama and seeking energy from my unborn son. "It's just so toxic anymore. I'm done, really done."

Gin was silent at first, somehow enjoying the feeling in her belly, despite the swelling of her feet. She didn't yet offer feedback, knowing that I wasn't finished stating what had been obvious for so many years. "I'm getting physically ill over this. It's been a ridiculous challenge from the beginning, and nothing makes it better except knowing that it'll be over someday. I mean, I can't keep going to work hating my life there and the people I'm working with, especially when I have some say in the matter. It's not like I was sentenced to this, but it's how I feel some days. Make that every day."

My wife let me finish without interruption, but continued to hold my hand against her belly so that I wouldn't move away. Then, in one of Gin's many memorable quotes which have defined the best parts of my life so far, she observed, "You can't keep this up. You need to either quit and start your own practice, or retire. It's not possible to stay with things the way they are."

"But I keep thinking that it's not time yet, you know, that I'm not ready for this on my own."

"Jim, you've been ready for way too long. Think of your son; think of me; think of yourself. It's killing you, and it's been really hard to watch. I was hoping that this didn't happen just as I was pushing out this baby, but you've got to do it, and do it now."

I kissed her, and told her and the baby that I loved them, and went upstairs to call my lawyer.

A month later, in easily the best day of my life so far, Aidan was born. Three weeks after that, in the best day of my professional life, I left my old practice and started Lowe Neurosurgical Associates. Both experiences have been challenging, tough at times, exhausting, and rewarding beyond any degree that I could have ever envisioned. The wonder of being a father is its own reward, and the experience of raising a child with Gin has been simply amazing. I would not dare tarnish it here by drawing a comparison to starting a nascent medical practice, but the intensity of each experience has similar roots although, of course, the emotions are different.

As Aidan grew out of that early larval stage, I enjoyed a professional rebirth of sorts in my new practice. I embraced the challenge of establishing my solo practice, joking with friends that at least now "I only had to work with one asshole." I worked longer hours, enjoying the opportunity to design my practice around my own philosophy of patient care and my own work ethic. With each change, I felt liberated and overwhelmingly satisfied that I was on the right track. The initial progress was sporadic, and it was certainly an exercise in faith while I awaited my first paycheck (some four months after I started), but the sense of accomplishment and joy with my new circumstances was clear and present. Despite working three hundred and sixty days thc first year, my exhaustion was a welcome sign of progress and success, and not a source of depression or despair. My ever-longer work days were a reflection of a growing patient list and expanding OR schedule, both of which were quickly busier beyond anything that I had previously experienced in my life at Seashore Neurosurgeons. With a sense of validation, I was enjoying the new demands of a solo experience and the rewards of having survived the painful process of maturing as a surgeon in the most stressful practice environment possible.

As the new practice grew, and my schedule continually tightened, I daydreamed more and more about getting back to the track. The feel of the challenge, which is a motivating force for me, was entirely different when I was making the new practice transition, although stress and trial were obviously part of the equation. But I knew that getting back in the seat of a race car would be the kind of "high-speed psychotherapy" that I thrive on—as well as a fine way to restore some recreational balance in my hectic work life. Quite simply, I was in need of relief, particularly the kind found in the volatile mixture of adrenaline and exhaust fumes. As I was considering my limited options for more racing, one program kept coming up among the best choices: the Skip Barber Race Series.

***

Skip Barber, a former Formula One driver, founded his eponymous race school and series back in 1975, based on his belief that race car driving was a craft that could be taught. With a focus on basic amateur instruction at the school level, Skip Barber also developed perhaps the premier amateur race series in the United States to compliment the school. One significant attraction for amateur racers in situations similar to mine was that the

Skip Barber series offered the opportunity to actually race at famous tracks around North America. As I scanned the requested literature about the series, several track names immediately popped out: Watkins Glen, Daytona, Road America, Laguna Seca. All were tracks well known to me as a spectator (though through TV viewing only—until the Russell School, I had never even been to an actual race track), and all had that special aura of history and importance in the world of motorsports. With so little time to spare, any chance to step upon hallowed ground for my rare race weekends would be a gift, an added bonus, and a strong incentive to immerse myself further in the sport.

Entering the famous "corkscrew" turn at Laguna Seca in a Skip Barber car, 2001.

In order to compete in the Skip Barber series, I first needed to complete an "advanced school" with the series' racing school. Having never run the SBRS open-wheel formula Dodge car, a two-day introduction was an ideal way to get acclimated to the equipment just before jumping into my first race weekend with the series. Better yet, I was able to schedule the advanced school days immediately prior to the race weekend, all to be done in one fast week at Laguna Seca in April of 2001. The downside was the annoyance of another cross-country trip, but that was easily trumped by the upside of getting to race at one of this country's finest road courses. I reserved my seat for the week with a minimum number of second thoughts.

I arrived Monday morning at the Skip Barber school area in the Laguna Seca paddock, helmet in hand and ready to go. I saw no reason to alter my only semblance of a routine for my first days with a new series, so I had already scouted out the location of the nearest McDonald's and had already donned my red suit and shoes. I was comforted by the similarities of the two schools early on and felt I had a good basic principles background left over from the Russell school. The two-day advanced course was challenging but straightforward, and much of the material was familiar, so my stress level was initially pretty low. The instructors were friendly, fairly laid-back (by race car driver standards), and very open with suggestions and constructive criticism. Among them were Mark Hamilton Peters, Lonnie Pechnik, Nick Nicholson, and Jim Pace—all guys with whom I would spend many racing days over the next several years (and one—Jim Pace—who would become instrumental in my pro racing career).

I was also introduced to Divina Galica, a racing legend who was one of the few females in the world who had competed at the Formula One level of motorsport. Thin and fit, Divina had a somewhat stern look and a strong handshake that completely concealed a most gentle and considerate demeanor. Then a senior vice-president at Skip Barber, Divi was in charge of the school and race events at Laguna for my first weekend. It was only at the end of the weekend that I realized that she also had final say on who among the newcomers qualified to stay and race on, and who would be sent packing for lack of ability or qualifications. With her opening talk on Friday morning, Divina welcomed us newbies for the three-day race weekend, reminding us of basic housekeeping issues—where to park, where to watch, run group schedules, etc.,—and also to enjoy the thrills of the spectacular Laguna Seca racing layout.

Constructed in 1957, Laguna Seca is a natural road course, laid out on the side of desert hills not far from Monterey, California. The Monterey bay is in full view from the top of the course, if one were to stop and look just before plunging down the world-famous Corkscrew turn. With 300 feet of elevation change, this twisting rollercoaster is the favorite of many drivers and is the highlight of many different racing series' schedules. Given the history and the layout, the opportunity to lap around Laguna Seca added a big "wow factor" in my first days with Skip Barber. Along with the wow, however, came a good deal of "pucker factor."

I suspect that the term pucker factor could be applied usefully in many different jobs and avocations, depending on the risks involved and the calculation of risk vs. reward inherent in performing certain activities. In brain surgery, the pucker factor is variable but often quite high, such as during the clipping of a brain aneurysm. During the critical part of that procedure, the moment of truth arrives with its own particular and obvious aura. The music playing during the opening of the head is turned down (but rarely off altogether), voices are lowered, and random conversations about last night's Phillies' game end without conclusion. As the surgeon manipulates the fragile balloon bulging off the artery, working with hands seemingly detached from the view through the microscope, everyone in the room realizes that a microscopic tear in the side wall of the aneurysm could lead to massive hemorrhage and death. One minor tremor at the wrong time, one momentary lapse of control as the clip's blades are released to strangle the neck of the deadly blister, and all hell breaks loose.

When an aneurysm ruptures during surgery, the intensity instantly ratchets up beyond just about any other circumstance in "routine" brain surgery. For the surgeon, the view is remarkable in its violence. A calm, meticulous, and controlled surgical bed observed at significant magnification becomes an explosion of red obscuring the entire field of view. The surgeon must act instantly, suctioning off enough blood to glimpse the architecture of the aneurysm and quickly and smoothly force a clip across the neck at the base of the actively bleeding vessel. If the clip is placed too roughly or inaccurately as the surgeon loses control of the situation, the aneurysm or even the blood vessel itself can be shredded, intensifying the bleeding and resulting in stroke or death. Take too much time to get it perfect and the brain starts to swell, damaged by the destructive bleeding and starved for vital blood flow. Lose control completely, and the damage accelerates as you struggle to stop the bleeding and swelling, almost always with devastating consequences even once the situation gets back to normal and the hemorrhage is halted.

Thankfully, the above scenario is rare, but I have experienced it enough to testify to the enormous increase in sphincter tone that accompanies such moments. The pucker factor is high and ever present during such cases, although it varies with the demands and details of the particular case, much like it does for the driver during various portions of a lap at any given racetrack. At Laguna Seca, there are at least three different sections of the course that easily qualify for that category.

The first is encountered at turn six, midway through the climb towards the peak elevation of the Laguna lap. Running hard uphill out of turn five, the driver passes under a bridge, braking lightly just before turning in for the left-handed corner. The apex of the corner is depressed, and when driven properly it seems to grab the left front wheel of the car as the grip level rises abruptly midcorner. Taking a deep breath, the driver accelerates at the apex, the rear of the car settles down, and the car powers out of the corner up the hill, tracking out beautifully on the outside curbing of Rahal straight. However, if the reluctant driver surrenders to fear and doesn't commit to power at the apex, the car will dive further left as the rear end, suffering from traction loss without power to the rear wheels, rotates away from the apex. The result is a spinning race car with the driver now struggling to avoid the walls lying just beyond the small runoff areas on either side of the road.

Once that corner is safely navigated, the next test is just over the rise. One of racing's most famous turns awaits: Laguna's turns 8 and 8A—the Corkscrew. To the casual observer, such as occurs during TV viewing, the turn is a fun-looking snaking downhill run; to the driver, it's a different animal altogether – one that photos or TV cannot begin to capture.

The Corkscrew is a blind-entry twister of an elevator drop that demands commitment to power all the way down to navigate properly. The turn in, a left-hander at the highest point on the property, is done with the car aimed at a prominent tree, as there's no other way to gauge the rest of the turn—it's simply not visible from the cockpit initially. The sensation at the first apex is that of leaping off a cliff; you can't see pavement until you're past the first apex and on your way down the chute. Position the car properly, and you clip the second apex as you wrestle the car to the right side on your way out of the turn; aim poorly and you could end up in the dirt on the right side or among the trees on the left at the exit.

There's time for a quick breath just before the last real test of the lap: turn nine, the Rainey Curve. Wayne Rainey is a famed US motorcycle racer who joins Bobby Rahal and Mario Andretti as three rare drivers who have turns named after them without it being a posthumous honor. After a few trips down the long smoothly curving lefthander, one can appreciate the advantage of grip on two wheels in negotiating this corner. Appearing relatively benign, this turn is actually where the men drive away from the boys. Not a flat out run, it requires progressive application of throttle as you struggle for more grip all the way through, while trying to set the car up on the left side at the exit in time for the next fast and right-handed turn 10.

Once that sequence is complete, the driver breathes a bit more deeply, unclenches (jaw and/or buttocks) somewhat and prepares to do it all over again in a minute or so. Not quite as scary as clipping an aneurysm, but still some big pucker factor, as they say.

***

After completing the advanced two-day Skip Barber school, I had at least become familiar with the new SBRS open-wheel single-seater and felt comfortable shifting the sequential gearbox. No longer required to "stir the stick," a driver negotiated the gears in order, pushing forward to downshift and pulling back on the stick to select the next higher gear. Heel-and-toe throttle blips were still required, but one didn't have to search for the correct slot in the H-pattern while negotiating a corner in the heat of battle. One less thing to worry about; one less advantage for the more experienced drivers of the field.

Completing the school also gave me the opportunity to learn Laguna's layout. Two days of driving with instructors nearby, and at a school pace, were sufficient to recognize the details of each turn, memorize the critical areas, and become familiar with the flow of the track. At my embryonic level of racing, it took quite a while to complete this getting-to-know-you period at any racetrack. For me, each lap over several days was a learning experience in itself as I struggled to find the proper line, gears, and brake points for each and every turn. To this day I remain amazed that experienced racers and seasoned pros can accelerate this process dramatically, often laying down fast laps that exploit the characteristics of the course perfectly after just a few laps. For those special few, somewhere in there is a genetic ability to examine the demands of the track in the context of a race car's capability and quickly approach the ideal limit of performance around each turn. For the rest of us, the process includes slow rides around a track (van-arounds—named after the laps with instructors driving Skip Barber Sprinter vans loaded with students), classroom sessions reviewing detailed track maps, and even video sessions narrated by pros describing the nuances and demands of each turn. As I prepared for my first SBRS race weekend, beginning with practice on Thursday, I was at least spared the track-learning process and freed to focus on lap times and speed.

Getting up to speed at a track is not the same thing as trying to go faster. While repetition certainly helps, not all improvements in lap time come from simple determination to increase speed. To properly understand this, the uninitiated must first realize that all drivers are pretty much going as fast as they feel they can at any given time. Other than "out" laps (leaving the pits and getting the car and tires up to adequate temperatures) and post-race "cool-down" laps, drivers usually try as hard as possible to turn the fastest laps they feel capable of. Going faster is a product of braking later, accelerating sooner, taking fast turns flat out, and searching for the limits of the mechanical and aerodynamic grip of the vehicle. In addition, different drivers have different styles and preferences in the way they take a corner—entering early and dealing with understeer on the way out perhaps, or late braking/late entry charges down to each apex, for example. However, even the slower guys out there (and I know this for sure, having spent much of my career in that category) are pushing and trying to challenge themselves and the car each and every turn. Nobody is sightseeing around a lap (although I have witnessed a few lost souls wandering a bit from time to time).

As a result, racing against another driver, and trying to overtake another car, is far more intently challenging when viewed from the cockpit of the race car. When you're approaching another car, intent on a pass, the driver ahead is essentially working just as hard as you are to keep the car on-line at the best speed possible. From the driver's seat of each car, there is a hell of a lot going on just to brake, turn, and accelerate at the right time, even without another car (or three!) in the mix. Picking the right moment to duck under another car at the turn-in, or popping out of the draft to go past off-line takes experience, planning, determination, and often a bit of trickery thrown in for good measure. Regardless of any skill discrepancy between two racers challenging each other for a corner, both are working their asses off in the cockpit just to keep pace and stay on track.

Understanding this helps explain why, when viewed from the spectator's seat, cars will often appear unable or unwilling to pass each other, even seeming somehow casually driven as they take each turn. Bumper-to-bumper, nose-to-tail racing may look orderly and choreographed from the seat in your den, but each and every turn is a loud, sweaty, and athletic battle going on inside the car.

This also helps explain why, without a lap timer (as was the case in the Skip Barber race cars) or a recurring frame of reference during my first laps, I wasn't aware exactly how much I was actually off the pace. I was working hard, trying to brake later and stay on the throttle as much as possible, but I simply had no idea where I stood in terms of lap time until I was done with the session. Only then did I get to review my all-too-obvious faults with the instructor posted at each corner and confirm my deliberate pace when the timesheets were later posted for all the world to see. Each session on Thursday and Friday was for me another exercise in fortitude, returning to the car for another go, despite the increasingly embarrassing times I was posting. I just kept trying harder and kept a good lookout in my mirrors, anticipating each overtaking car and trying to stay out of the way of the faster drivers (which was pretty much everyone).

By Friday afternoon, I had some legitimate evidence to back up my concerns. The first came in the form of an unrecognized instructor, who tracked me down a few moments after they had checkered my last practice session.

"Man, you were all over the place out there! I was behind you for, like, three or four laps. Do you know the right line here? You took a different line into every corner, like you were lost out there!"

It took me a moment to process what he was saying and figure out what had happened. I explained that I had seen a car on my tail for much of the session and that I hadn't realized it was an instructor following me. In fact, I had repeatedly moved over at each turn, trying to let the apparently faster car pass. So while I hoped he would pass and leave me alone to resume my slower practice run, he thought I was lost and erratic. His report was moments from sealing my fate and sending me home when my explanation basically saved the day—and my seat in the series.

"Well, all right, that explains a lot. I'll run out there with you next time, and we'll see what we can do to help your times."

I thanked him for his offer and silently celebrated the fact that he had at least asked me before prematurely ending my two-day-old Skip Barber career.

On the way back to the paddock tent, I ran into one of my fellow back-of-the pack drivers, a guy about my age who had come to Laguna all the way from Taiwan. He had said little to the group of new drivers in the paddock, perhaps because of a language barrier, but I had already felt a bit of a kinship after seeing his familiar lap times. Seeing that he was upset, I asked if he was OK after the last practice session.

"Not OK. Going home." With that, he turned and nearly ran off toward the driver parking area.

I looked back towards the staging area, where Divina was talking with some of the instructors, including the guy who had been shadowing me earlier. Divi looked up, saw me watching, and gestured for me as she started walking in my direction. This was cause for no small amount of alarm, given that I thought I had managed to stay successfully under the radar so far. Plus, Divina was the top dog—a no-nonsense, Formula One type, who looked pretty intimidating—and I had a policy of trying not to draw attention from those types. It had worked well for me in the Marines, and I had no intention of abandoning the technique.

I stood frozen on the spot, wondering whether I could hitch a ride with the guy from Taiwan. He certainly was moving quickly now, but I felt I could still catch him if Divi was mercifully brief in her execution.

As she reached me, she extended a hand. "Hey Jim, I'm Divina, I thought I should say hello."

"Pleased to meet you, I think. Should I try to catch up to that other guy?"

"No need. He's in a bit over his head, I'm afraid. We offered him a chance to come back for another school session, but he shouldn't be racing this weekend. Unfortunately he's headed back to Taiwan."

Lapping Laguna Seca in the Formula Dodge car, 2001

"Well, I'm pretty nervous out there also," was all I could muster.

"We've been paying attention, and you're doing just fine. The instructors say you've been driving safely, not doing anything erratic, and your times are going in the right direction. We never do know with guys who trained in other schools and other series, so we always watch more closely during practice for anyone who might need to spend more time in school before trying to race. I just wanted to let you know that we're here and available to help during your first race weekend."

I thanked her as I exhaled, realizing that I hadn't been aware up to then how close I had actually been to needing an early flight home.

***

With a renewed sense of relief, I qualified and raced in both events of the weekend without much incident. No trophies, but no crashes either. I also managed to avoid the ignominy of finishing "DFL"—Dead Fucking Last—in qualifying or in either race. For sure, I had a more, shall we say, deliberate pace than most out there, but I kept it on the blacktop and successfully avoided any conversations with mechanics about crash damage bills. I also remembered to enjoy the thrill of driving Laguna at speed and focused on racing technique—driving the right line, braking later, and passing properly when that rare opportunity occurred. Each time I exited the car I felt the adrenaline rush settle throughout my circulation, leaving that satisfied feeling behind as my heart rate returned to normal and my breathing slowed to conversational pace. Each time I dismounted my single-seater I thought about how I had just performed, when I would next get to drive, and what I might be able to do to go faster. I wasn't worried yet about finishing positions, trophies, or podium celebrations—that was clearly not on my radar, yet. But most importantly for me, I hadn't thought for a moment about work and all of the aggravation and challenges that remained such a prominent part of my other life at home.

Chapter Nine

After three seasons of running a few different events with the Skip Barber Racing Series, I was accumulating good intel on some great race tracks—Watkins Glen, Daytona, and Laguna Seca in particular. However, what became increasingly apparent was that I was making little progress towards anything resembling the front of the grid.

Averaging about two race weeks per year, I was hopelessly unable to really pick up the pace and be truly competitive when I drove. With big gaps in time between each event, I typically spent the better part of the first few days of each race weekend getting re-acclimated to the car and the feeling of the g-forces while lapping at speed. I'd get settled into the seat for the first session and try to wiggle my way into a position that at least felt familiar. Easy enough sitting in pit lane, another thing altogether at speed. It always seemed a bit of a surprise once I was up to full rpm in fifth gear: the loudness of the engine, the force of the air on my exposed face shield, the unyielding intensity of the car continuing down the straight with me along for the ride. All these sensations would become less immediately obvious as I had more sessions in the car, but until then it was always a relearning of the harsh sensory inputs and feel of the race car when driven flat out.

Further, I was typically arriving at the track exhausted from the grueling demands of my neurosurgical practice and needed some time to wind down after logging extended hours before my vacation started. An unfortunate pattern emerged in which I was front-loaded with work before I left for the track, overwhelming my schedule in the days leading up to my departure. The end result of this was too little time to work out, eat right, or generally prepare in any reasonable fashion to spend four or five straight days racing. That combination resulted in a significantly magnified challenge for my tired psyche. I wanted to drive and race hard but was simply arriving ill-equipped with any chance to compete well and spare myself disappointment when the time sheets were posted.

I listened as well as I could to instructor feedback, studied track maps, and sat in the front seats during van-arounds but still rarely ended up proud of my performance when the weekends were over. I loved the thrill of the race, the simple visceral vibe of the racetrack, and the assault on the senses that was the cockpit at speed. However, I just wasn't fast enough to be competitive. Given the amount of sparse time spent behind the wheel and my acquisition of the racing fever at a "mature" age, I frankly didn't expect much more than "just happy to be here" status. That rationalization nonetheless failed to add any sense of joy to my Sunday trips home from the track.

After returning home from a Skip Barber racing week at Daytona, Ginny caught me moping a few days later and finally called me on it. More and more, I had been ignoring the diminished enjoyment, and increasing frustration, of my sub-par performances at the track. After all, I wasn't about to pursue a career as a Formula One star, and I had some other responsibilities to tend to—a medical practice, a family, and other grown-up issues. Dealing with my selfish concerns in a race car—boo-hoo, I didn't win the race—seemed way too petty in light of the obligation of my real life. As a result, I kept this frustration to myself (or so I thought) and tried to ignore the creeping depression that went along with that tactic.

But I guess my mood, or lack of a good vibe at least, was pretty obvious. Once again I had struggled at the track, working as hard as I could have, but performing as one might expect given the minimal seat time that I had. I had again watched in wonder as other seemingly "normal" guys managed to lap the Skip Barber cars around Daytona at speeds far exceeding mine, with big deltas in our lap times always evident. And it wasn't as if I was holding anything back—quite the opposite, in fact. I tried to push harder the whole time I was out there, but it all still felt pretty foreign and unfamiliar. Unlike my indoctrination into the surgical world, where repetitive exposure in a compressed amount of time was the formula to gain familiarity and comfort, there was no such opportunity for me at the track. A few days in a row of driving, once or twice a year, just wasn't enough for me to gain a level of comfort in the cockpit. And anymore, it was getting less and less satisfying to find joy in simply being behind the wheel, regardless of where my name fell on the time sheets. Worse yet, I knew it was actually kind of risky—like the infamous doctor who flies his Bonanza "only once in a while when it's nice out." Although my racing was on the amateur level, the competition was intense and the danger real. Guys were running at high speed in open-cockpit cars, and it wasn't without risk under the best of circumstances. Add to that the fact that I wasn't always "at one" with the car, and the risk factor escalated.

Having some insight into the reality of my current racing situation, I was becoming progressively more aware that things needed to change and that the direction I'd wind up pointing likely wouldn't be a good one. After all, I did have this Neurosurgery/Act Like a Grown-up thing going on, and that was clearly a big factor interfering with my ability to brake later, or so I reasoned.

Being a self-absorbed kind of guy, I of course neglected to consider that my wife might be cognizant of my situation, or at least aware of the muted enthusiasm I was displaying upon returning from the track. I'm not exactly sure why I wouldn't have considered it (see above self-absorbed admission), but I hadn't thought to talk any of this over with the person who knew my emotions and motivations more intimately than anyone on the planet. So, in typical fashion, it was actually Ginny who broached the topic. Demonstrating her good feel for such matters, she approached me casually, almost in an offhand manner.

I was relaxing after dinner, keeping one eye on the Phillies game and the other on Aidan playing on the floor. Gin wandered into view and sat down next to me on the family room couch. I muted the TV, knowing she wasn't there to watch the ballgame. She nudged closer, but kept enough distance so as not to be too obvious. Gin certainly knew how to broach a delicate topic with me—too much hand-holding would only emphasize that something big was afoot. And that just wasn't her style anyway.

"Hey honey, I noticed you've been looking a bit down. You just went away for a couple of days of racing." She continued on without accusation. "Aren't you supposed to be rejuvenated or something like that after a week of vacation? Didn't you have a good time at the track? You haven't even mentioned it since you've been back."

I winced a bit as I began to consider just how transparent I apparently had been about it. "I'm not really depressed—more like frustrated, and kind of a bit embarrassed, I guess."

I wasn't sure how much she knew or realized, but I suspected it was more than I gave her credit for. "I really drove pretty poorly this past weekend, and I'm just not racing well enough to be competitive." I made a further admission, one that I hadn't mentioned, to anyone, up to that point. "It's still a blast driving the car, but it's pretty frustrating and disappointing to be so obviously slow out there. There's nowhere to hide it when you can't compete. I mean, it's all right out there in the open—no way to pretend you're better than the numbers show. Everybody knows it when you're slow."

"Are you stuck that way, I mean, can't you do anything to get better at it and go faster?"

I had thought quite a bit about that concept without verbalizing it to Ginny up until then. I hadn't come to any conclusion exactly, but there were a few things I knew for sure.

"I don't think I'll ever get any better than this unless I get more seat time, more time on track. Repetition and less time between races would make a big difference, I think. I don't really think I'm a lost cause, but I'm never going to get any faster or better at the rate I'm going now." Needing to hear myself pronounce it out loud, I arrived at the upshot. "Whichever way I go from here, it's not so satisfying anymore just to be driving around for the sake of being out there."

As she is apt to do, Gin put it out there in sharp focus, resulting in yet another seminal moment from the soundtrack of my life: "Well, then, you're going to have to either do a lot more racing or a lot less, because the goal is for you to be happy, instead of frustrated, embarrassed and annoyed when you get done at the track."

Gin had just then managed to resurrect and hammer home a recurrent theme in my life: if it's not right, and you're not right because of it, make it better, do it better, or get out and move forward. Be an active participant in change, if change is needed; otherwise be a spectator and embrace the passive role as a non-participant. I felt like I was eight-year-old Jimmy again, sitting on the curb, watching the big kids play, secretly wishing one of them would approach me to join in.

Despite how ill-prepared I had been to hear my wife verbalize those choices, it took only a heartbeat to choose.

"I pick more."

***

With renewed enthusiasm, I set about making plans to get more involved with an expanded Skip Barber regional series schedule. I knew a full-season schedule wouldn't be possible, given my still-exhausting work and new-family demands, but more racing was in the offing, and I planned accordingly. To conserve travel time, I decided to continue focusing on some of the tracks I knew already. As a result, the next event for me would be at Watkins Glen in upstate New York, where I previously had two separate racing weeks with the SBRS program. I expected that it would be a lot easier to take the next step when I didn't need to learn a new track layout.

Next, I contacted the Skip Barber guys at headquarters in Connecticut, inquiring about participating in their newly-established "lead-follow" program. This new program was seemingly designed just for me: running one-on-one with a private instructor, a novice driver could really up his game in the shortest amount of time possible. These sessions were conducted during the regular lapping and practice runs of the race weeks, and several guys I knew had already given the program high marks during previous weeks at other tracks. I registered for the lead-follow program immediately, and all that was left was to find an instructor who had the time to fit me in for the week. Having had little personal interaction with the coaches thus far, I relied on the recommendations of some fellow drivers and picked Gerardo Bonilla.

Gerardo was one of the well-liked and popular instructors that I had seen around the Skippy paddock at different events, usually running part of the testing program (where the cars were set up to ensure equal lap speed capability) or in the computer car. The computer car was Skip Barber's data-equipped car that generated information about each lap including braking points, acceleration curves, throttle application, g-forces, and so forth. A diminutive aspiring professional at the time, Gerardo was quick enough in the race car to set the target lap, the standard for comparison when the time came to analyze the data and make improvements for the amateur driver. Because of his easy and friendly demeanor, combined with blunt honesty about performance, Gerardo was a sought-after and busy guy at the track.

I had made arrangements with Gerardo to run lead-follow at the Glen for two full days (four sessions each) in preparation for a regional race series weekend. In yet another example of the humbling experience I encounter pretty much every day at any racetrack, Gerardo asked about my times on the 3.4 mile road course in prior events.

I mumbled a bit and then admitted a time which was actually somewhat better than the reality: "I think I did a 2:18 last time I was here."

Gerardo raised an eyebrow and grinned a bit. "Really? Was that your first time in the car or something?"

I admitted that in fact I had had at least 10 previous days in the Formula Dodge before that, but that they were spaced out over the last 24 months.

"Well, that explains it! We're going to have you going faster than that on our out-lap, just wait. You're gonna go faster this weekend than ever before. You'll see. Just do as I say."

Gerardo explained the basic idea of the lead-follow exercise. Since we didn't have radio communication, we would review the plan before pulling out of pit lane for each session. If necessary, there were a few hand signals that would work if any changes to the original plan were needed. Gerardo's routine was for me to begin the session in the lead for a few laps, so that he could observe my line and technique though each corner. Once he had seen enough, he would pull by me on the front straight, after which I was to tuck in behind him and attempt to follow him for the rest of the session. The idea was to have a moving illustration of the best way to negotiate each corner, with "permission" to push the car to the limits that Gerardo was demonstrating right in front of my car. This was particularly effective when the instructor was in front, allowing the slower car to follow and keep pace. Because the faster driver was not trying to escape the following car, it was possible to repeat the tutorial in each corner, lap after lap, and gain speed much more quickly than by routine practice lapping. Given that my primary difficulty in driving a race car was my lack of any innate ability to approach the limits of the car's capabilities, this procedure was an ideal, safe, and quick way to get me up to the next level in performance.

I pulled out in front of Gerardo, warming up with some side-to-side swerving that I hoped made me look racier than I felt. I then ran my token two lap "here's all I've got" trial with Gerardo close behind, feeling something akin to the awkwardness of trying on my first rented prom tux. Coming around the Glen's final turn 11, Gerardo raced by on my inside, and I tucked in behind him as my first real lesson began in earnest. I followed into the first turn, immediately amazed at how much speed he flowed into the first turn and down the hill into the entrance of the Glen's famous "esses." I kept at his backside as much as I could, and he constantly corrected his speed to keep me as close as possible while extending the carrot just a bit further with each turn we passed. Flying through the lap, I was less focused on the braking and line, and more intent on keeping right on Gerardo's gearbox. Lap after lap, I closed up as he pulled me along with him, each turn coming just a bit faster and each braking zone just a bit deeper.

We pulled off in tandem after the cool-down lap, and Gerardo greeted me as I dismounted the RT2000 race car.

"Pretty good laps, eh? You did OK back there, but there's a lot more where that came from. The car can go way faster than that even."

I hadn't thought about the actual times, but knew I had just been far beyond where I had ever been before that. "What do you think we were running?"

"I checked my timer a few times while we were lapping out there. I saw a couple of 2:15's and 2:16's." He said this quite casually, with almost an air of disappointment at the announcement. "We'll do better in the next session."

"Better?" I thought to myself. "Right!" Never before had I gone so fast through a turn, at least without winding up in a gravel trap; never had I run such times at the challenging Watkins Glen! At least three or four seconds had instantly evaporated from my lap times, just by following the rabbit that was Gerardo. Of course, I didn't dwell on the fact that this was more reflective of just how slow I had been going on prior expeditions, nor did I bother with the reality that I was still several seconds off the pace of the fastest drivers out there. It was all good for that moment, and I didn't wish to sully it by focusing on details that could derail my happy train of thought.

Gerardo and I ran several more lead-follow sessions over the next two days, eeking out better times with each lap, adding small doses of confidence with each run to the session's checker. Finally, it was time for the first official timed practice runs without my guide—the Friday practices just before the weekend race events being off-limits to lead-follow instructors. Just before I saddled up, Gerardo gave me a few last minute words, followed by a friendly smile to go with a pat on the helmet. "Forget that I'm not there with you. Just run the line, use the same brake points, and you'll be fine." I was skeptical, but it was no use debating him at that point, as the cars were rolling off for the beginning of the half-hour session.

Each day's sessions during a Skip Barber weekend began with the random selection of a car for the day; since all cars were tested and pronounced "equal," it usually didn't matter which race car you drew for the duration of the day's events. However, there were occasional times that one car or another fell slightly off the power grid, for reasons that were beyond my scope of knowledge. I had heard other drivers have occasion to complain about their car being slower than the others in their group; the official record always stated the complaint as "DOP"—Down On Power. Given my typical pace in previous events, I was never one to complain, as usually the problem with my lap times was anything but mechanical. In any event, making an accusation of a car being DOP was opening yourself to criticism, unless you were one of the acknowledged fast guys who could actually assess a car's power capability as separate from the driver's ability to go fast. Hence I had never had the occasion or intestinal fortitude to make a DOP claim, until that practice session at the Glen.

Again running without a timer of any kind in the cockpit, my only indication of how fast I was going in the practice session would be the progress of the other drivers and my ability to catch up and/or pass any of those close by. Since the group was well-mixed in terms of known speed and ability, it would be even harder to gauge where I stood against the other guys running in the same group. Mostly I wasn't sure who was who when out there lapping at speed. Trying to remember car numbers and drivers, let alone processing that information while trying to stay on the blacktop, was well beyond my abilities at that point. Instead, I attempted to focus on Gerardo's coaching tips and, most of all, tried to relive the sensation of grip and power through each turn that went with better lap times.

I started the session well back in the pack as we left the grid, and did a slow and deliberate warm-up, getting reacquainted with the nuances of the track, the curbing, and the transitions in the different paved surfaces which signaled changes in the grip levels. By the time I was up to speed at the beginning of lap two, I had two significantly slower cars in sight and had already been passed on the out lap by at least two other drivers. I set my sights on the cars immediately ahead, passing them both with relative ease, with open track ahead. I tried to feel the car's grip, listening for tire noise as I went through corner after corner, fixated on the track-out point at the end of each curve. In short order, I had the track immediately around me to myself, with only my own pace to keep me company as I logged miles in the Formula Dodge.

As I continued lapping, I gradually became aware of a sensation of going palpably slower, as if the car was gradually dragging a bit more weight with it as I pushed ever harder to pick up speed. With each straightaway, the view was that of an ever more stable environment; each turn slowed for me to a seemingly manageable series of adjustments and corrections, all in a vain attempt to go faster. Instead of getting quicker, I distinctly felt like the car was somehow going slower and slower. Getting progressively more frustrated, I cursed my luck to no one in particular as I drove my way to the checkered flag. I pulled into the pit lane with a few cars already parked in front of me, and the rest filing in behind me at regular intervals. I sat for a moment, regaining my wind and stewing a bit about the bad luck of getting an underperforming car, just when I wanted to demonstrate my improved pace.

Jumping out of the race car, I made a beeline for Rob Slonaker, the chief instructor in charge of the weekend. Toting a clipboard, and constantly besieged by driver and mechanic complaints alike, Rob looked up from his notes with a bit of surprise as he saw me approaching.

"What's up?" he pre-empted my introduction, expertly getting straight to the meat of the assuredly short conversation.

"My car, the blue number eleven, is definitely DOP," I blurted out, almost flinching at the embarrassment sure to come because of the source of the complaint.

"Down on power, are you sure, really?"

"Sorry, but I've never complained before. This time, I got a dog—I was crawling around out there. Definitely DOP."

Rob raised an eyebrow even higher as he was handed the run sheet for the session while we spoke. "You sure you don't want to check the times before you make the complaint?" He had a hint of a smile as he held the sheet out halfway, checking once more. "Are you sure?"

He held out the folded paper for me—one nearly identical to the ones so easily capable of inducing embarrassment on so many occasions before that. By habit, I scanned immediately to the bottom of the page—below the crease across the middle of the paper, and saw nothing. No name, no time. I looked up briefly in confusion, as Rob said, "Try the other side, big guy. Still going to complain?"

Racing with SBRS at Watkins Glen, 2003

There in black and white, for all the world (or at least the immediate world of the Skip Barber Race Series) to see, was my name hiding in plain view at the top of the list. P1. First place. No wonder I had missed it the first time.

"Really?"

"Yep. P1. Bet that's your best time, too. Still want another car?"

I had run a solid 2:14, sitting in all my glory at the sharp end of the group, having logged my fastest time and best performance ever. Even though it was only a practice session, I was inwardly stoked, surging with that feel-good buzz of personal excitement that had been conspicuously absent from my post-race debriefings.

"I think I'll keep the eleven for the rest of the weekend, if that's OK."

"Thought so." Rob smiled as he turned away to confront the next complainant in line.

Gerardo appeared over my shoulder, eyed the sheet, and chipped in, "DOP? Really?" He laughed as he pointed out the results to some of the other instructors and drivers. "The guy thinks he's down on power, after all of my hard work!"

I smiled sheepishly as I accepted a few playful shoves and fended off a wisecrack or two. Inwardly I was high and loving the feeling, finally enjoying a moment of recognition as something other than a guy who was trying hard to make up for a complete lack of ability.

Gerardo pulled me over, notes in hand.

"Want some feedback, speedy?"

I had forgotten that the ritual was still at hand, wherein the instructors critiqued our driving and technique, always pinpointing shortcomings, no matter what the finishing position and time was.

"Here's the short version: Great job, but there's more speed available, everywhere. See you next session." He smiled again and turned back to his notes as the next guy in the group stepped up to hear his feedback.

Clutching my time sheet, I jumped the pit wall, fetched my helmet, and headed off to the parking lot to grab a moment alone in my car. I had about two hours before the day's last session and wanted to preserve the good feeling as long as possible. Besides, I knew no one there well enough to share my small accomplishment, so it was just as well. A private moment of indulgence was all I permitted myself, fearing the repercussions of too much premature celebration. After all, I had won nothing yet, although I had regained a sense of enjoyment and self-respect previously lacking in the race track environment.

The rest of the weekend was somewhat anticlimactic, after the high of a personal best and P1 showing in practice. I managed to qualify for that Saturday's race in P5, which was disappointing (now I dared to be disappointed about not being in front!) but still my best ever, by a far bit. Unfortunately, during the race I spun off in the grass entering the Glen's challenging "busstop" turn, resulting in a finishing position firmly planted back in mid-pack. That meant a Sunday start (based on race one's results) around P7 or 8. From there, I never saw the front runners after the first lap and fell off the pace as I embraced some old habits (hard to give up in the heat of battle). I finished out the weekend with two top-tens, which was probably admirable given my previous ineptitude. However, I left the Glen longing for some podium hardware to confirm my newfound sense of legitimate speed, or something approaching real racing, for the first real time in my brief career. I wasn't upset or down, certainly not in any way similar to my older, slower self, but I wasn't satisfied either. That unrecognized emotion was to become much more familiar in future racing experiences (even so today), but I embraced it anew that weekend at the Glen.

10

Chapter Ten

After running a few events with Gerardo working hard on getting me up to whatever speed I might have available, I realized I was a solid, if unspectacular, mid-pack runner. Races were more of an adrenaline buzz, with closer wheel-to-wheel running providing ever increasing excitement whenever I had time for another SBRS weekend. Also, I began to notice a bit more of an established, even accepted, status within the small and close-knit Skip Barber Racing community. While I wasn't exactly the life of any party, on or off the track, I was gradually being allowed into the highly-stratified and very clique-like group of regular racers at Skippy events. Much like virtually all sports that I had been exposed to in the past, the best performers generally were the most prominent and visible members of the group. In that regards, I was way down the ladder, but at least I now had a toehold on a rung.

The most memorable step for me in this process occurred during my first trip to Daytona International Speedway for a Skip Barber event there in 2003. Still without a defined set of friends among the drivers, I generally spent time between sessions sitting alone, watching other groups run, and trying, likely without success, not to appear outwardly antisocial. When I saw guys I recognized, especially after running a tough lapping session, it was fun to talk racing and exchange pleasantries, but I wasn't exactly establishing firm ties to anyone. The typical routine was to have some fun driving, talk a bit to guys I didn't really know, assume I wasn't really a part of any group, and pick up some Whoppers at Burger King on my way back to the hotel.

All of that changed when I met Larry Revier. One of the more outgoing and easily friendly guys, Larry was also part of the of-a-certain-age Masters group within the SBRS community. I knew who he was from observation and from seeing his name near the top of the time sheets, along with a few of the other elder statesmen of the series. Having just broached the

40-year-old barrier myself, I knew I was eligible for the Masters series, but I hadn't given it any thought, as I simply didn't have the pace to run with those guys. Old or not, they were always fast and always raced hard, seeming to enjoy the social parts of the driving almost as much as running each other off into the grass for last lap passes. A real estate company owner in his late forties, Larry embodied the typical Masters runner: secure, fast, funny, and relaxed among his peers, seemingly enjoying every moment at the track. I secretly envied him, marveling at anyone having the social ease that allowed such relaxed enjoyment in a competitive environment.

In between practice sessions one morning, I was sitting on Daytona's pit wall, waiting for the other groups to finish their last laps. I was driving next, but getting geared up too soon was a job for the rookie driver only, so I continued to feign nonchalance. Larry approached, sat down beside me, and offered a hand.

"Mind if I join you? You're not wanting to be alone or anything, are you?"

I was a bit surprised, given that I was rarely approached by anyone other than mechanics who needed damage statement sheets signed.

I brushed some dirt off the cement wall next to me. "No, sorry, have a seat. I'm Jim Lowe; pleased to meet you."

"Larry Revier, thanks. Nice to meet you. OK if we talk, or are you one of those intense guys?"

Larry then proceeded to tell me about the Masters group of drivers, explaining who was who and giving me the general demographics of the core group of older but faster drivers. I was a bit confused, not wanting to admit that I was still wondering why he bothered to bring me up to speed on the topic.

"I know you're a bit new to this deal, but I thought maybe you might enjoy being part of our little Masters contingent? You seem pretty sane, although that might be a drawback in this crew. Who do you hang out with after you're done driving?"

I was at this point embarrassed enough, but for some reason, I didn't mind spilling the truth to Larry.

"I don't really know anybody here, except maybe a few of the instructors.

I'm staying at the Holiday Inn, which is pretty grungy, but I've just been going back there after I'm done here."

SBRS Masters drivers pose at Daytona, 2005

Larry ignored my whining and didn't bother with pity; he just chatted on about the track, the cars, the other drivers, and whatever other thoughts applied to my situation. We sat a few minutes until it was time for me to get in the car for my next session.

"Why don't you come join us for dinner tonight? We're heading to Gene's down Speedway Boulevard at seven; you think you might like hanging out with a few of the other old guys and me?" Larry smiled, and didn't really stop to consider the possibility that I might resist the invitation.

"Now go out there and kick some ass like a proper driver, and we'll see you at 7."

I did manage to catch up to the group later that night at Gene's, not realizing that I would be having my first of many memorable dinners there over the years. I sat next to Larry at the end of a long table of probably fifteen racers loudly talking over the best, and worst, moves of the day. I met Dick Lippert, a retired navy carrier pilot, rail-thin and fearless; Murray

Marden, a recently retired airline pilot who never drifted far from his wife Michele (she who more then held her own among the boys when it came to driving and swapping stories); Chris Wilcox, the former tire engineer and perennial series champion; financial consultant Michael Auriemma; respected psychiatrist Dr. John Greist; trader John Pew; and venture capital heavy hitter Mark Patterson. Dario Ciotti (who, I learned, owned four planes, including a seventies-era Russian fighter jet) was also there, sitting among lawyer Peter Tucker, investment banker Brent Millner, and rehab doc Ron Yarab. Each was over the age of forty, with some breaking into the sixty-plus category, and all were as comfortable behind the wheel of a race car as they were in their daily offices and boardrooms.

There was one common thread, though: they all loved to talk racing almost as much as they enjoyed the act of driving itself. Stories were nonstop, occasionally true, and often critiqued on the spot in the manner so reminiscent of my experience in football locker rooms twenty years prior. The subject was different, but the sounds, pace, and tones of the conversation were so similar that I relaxed and immersed myself in an immediate sense of comfort. No talking about esoteric surgical concepts or malpractice threats here. There was, instead, a secure refuge offering an entirely new reason to hang out and swap stories about something foreign, exciting, and worthy of tall tales and exaggeration.

I ate my steak, not daring to have wine since I was racing again in the morning, and savored the flavor of the evening. On occasion I even contributed to the conversation, but the fine art of telling racing tales is one acquired over years of driving and, more importantly, listening. I was yet again a novice, but I loved the smell and feel of the chatter over dinner that night.

A few days after the Daytona weekend, I was back doing the eighty-hour work week, putting in the long hours required by my growing solo practice in between the endless search for quality time with my son Aidan. Late one evening, after a day of surgery followed by evening rounds, I was surprised to find an email from Larry. I was copied, along with the rest of the Masters group, on some irreverent communication poking fun at one of the other driver's mishaps at the recent Daytona weekend. I followed the email string along, enjoying the occasionally witty responses and frequent forays into profanity when no other response seemed reasonable. Once again, I was witness to an easy group interaction that felt comfortable and safely removed from the routine of medical staff meetings.

"What's that you're reading?" Gin asked as she happened by while I was absorbed in my AOL screen. She stopped a moment to check out the emails, scanning down to a part where someone was seriously questioning another driver's virility.

She patted me on the shoulder. "You guys are idiots."

"I know. Isn't it great?" I smiled as she walked away.

"Don't you have a case in the morning? You better get some rest."

"I'll be up in a minute. I need to see who wins this first."

I ran a few more Skip Barber weekends that year, hanging out with the master's group of guys but not yet willing to join them on the track. I still wasn't up to their competitive speed and knew I wasn't ready to run with them until I had more seat time and instruction. I understood the intensity and style of running those guys were known for. In fact, they had their own rules within the Skip Barber system, allowing car-to-car contact and requiring each guy to be entirely responsible for his own on-track mishaps. There was more than a "just let those guys race, and we'll sort it out later" attitude towards the Masters drivers. I found that they never shied away from bumping each other leaving pit lane, or running a buddy off into the grass when a podium was at stake. In the regular SBRS run groups, a single off-track or car-to-car contact incident would result in a pit-lane inspection or getting parked altogether, depending on the significance of the offense. With the over-forty contingent, you tried to hold your own, paid for your own damage (no matter who caused it) and fought it all out later over dinner. Big boy rules, as I called them. Good to know who your friends were in this group.

I spoke with Larry several times during that year, always politely declining his invitation to run with the Masters group at each event. I was tempted by the desire to be a more accepted member of the clique, but that was tempered by the knowledge that I would need to up my game considerably in order to have a fighting chance among these crazy but fast drivers. Finally, after much coercion by Larry, I decided to make the leap at the next Skippy event at Daytona. On many levels, this seemed like a logical choice; I was familiar with the track from a technical standpoint, it wasn't the most challenging of layouts, and I now knew which hotel to stay in.

Another good reason to make my Masters series debut at Daytona was that I would be doubling up for the race weekend. Having registered for both the regular Southern Regional series and the Masters National series, I would get twice the amount of seat time each day and drive four weekend races, instead of two. For a guy in need of seat time more than oxygen, this was a critical factor when deciding when and where to take the next step. I'd also have a new instructor for the lead-follow sessions that had been so instrumental in getting me closer to the front of the regional driver's queue. Earlier that season, Gerardo had stopped doing private coaching, as he was focusing on winning a championship of his own in the upper tier of the amateur National series. As a result, I needed to find another instructor, and after some consideration, Gerardo recommended a long-time Skip Barber instructor named Jim Pace. I was reluctant at first, given that dealing with change is not the strong suit of a surgeon used to having his way and his say, but I scheduled the lead-follow sessions and made my plans to head south for another week on International Speedway Boulevard.

***

By the time I greeted Jim Pace in the garage at Daytona, I was already intimidated by what I knew about him. Gerardo had told me a bit about his racing background, and Larry and some of the other masters guys had filled in the rest. I had seen Jim at a prior event at Laguna Seca the year before and he was a daunting figure in the paddock: serious, in-charge, and all business, so it seemed. One of the senior Skippy instructors, Jim Pace was not a man I had wanted to meet, frankly, as only a significant driving transgression on my part would be cause for me to occupy his airspace.

What I hadn't known then was that I was soon to be in the presence of a guy with a significant racing pedigree: Jim had won the 24 hours of Daytona and also the 12 hours of Sebring; he had run at LeMans, and had years of winning experience in all sorts of machinery, including sports cars of seemingly every sort. I was also to find out that while he was a consummate Southern gentleman, he certainly did not suffer fools gladly.

"Hi there, I'm JP, nice to meet you, first time at Daytona?" Jim grinned just slightly as he extended his right hand. I spied the Rolex Daytona Steel Chronograph watch peeking out from the sleeve on his left hand.

"Jim Lowe, it's a pleasure. I was here last year with Skippy, but they didn't have the chicane as part of the course then, so I guess it's back to the drawing board for me." I didn't want to completely admit my relative incompetence just yet—he'd know as soon as someone broke out a stopwatch. Jesus, I thought, the guy's won in everything he's run. I'm a tired and graying neurosurgeon just trying to get a respectable lap time in the books. Just the thought of my inferiority in the company of such racing royalty was enough to make me hesitate a step as we headed together towards pit lane.

"Let's hop into the Neon for a few laps before the session starts. We'll check out the chicane, which is where all the speed comes from at this place. If you've never run it before, you'll love it, once you figure out how to get through it."

I settled into the right side seat, adjusted the seat back, and pulled the shoulder belt tight. I knew from past experience that most instructors enjoyed thrashing the SBRS-fleet Neons around when possible, taking the "Screw it, it's a rental" concept to heights never intended by the Dodge engineers. Jim didn't disappoint as he accelerated down pit lane, and my heart rate bumped up the few beats that I always felt whenever I was a passenger. He joined the track just before Daytona's infield turn three, instantly starting the narrative I would become intimately familiar with over the next several years.

JP's Mississippi drawl highlighted his otherwise unemotional description of the ideal sequence through each turn, pointing out brake points, apexes, and proper gears for each corner. "Down to the two-hundred board, maybe a little past that once you get comfortable, look down towards the apex, trail your brake until you see the curbing, then try to get back to full power, right...here." All this as he laid the Neon over onto its sidewalls, tires protesting as I hung from the overhead strap and braced myself against the passenger side door. Into each corner, Jim called out gear shifts, braking, and acceleration points in a relaxed, almost bored, fashion more suitable for reciting the daily specials at the Outback.

After completing the infield section by exiting turn six, the Neon accelerated out onto Daytona's famous 33-degree banking as JP dispensed further advice. "Once you get out here, don't forget to relax," (Relax?!)., "Wiggle your fingers and toes, check your gauges, check your mirrors, and… breathe." That last word is one I would hear hundreds of times over thousands of laps in the future, uniquely accented by Jim so that one could use it as a mantra: "Brrreeeeathhhhhe."

Jim Pace

I was transfixed on the high banking, focused on what Jim was saying as the car shook and rattled at full speed down the back straight, when I met Cayenne for the first time. Unbeknownst to me, JP had a beloved Shih Tzu who went along for the ride whenever Jim did instructional laps and track recons. I hadn't recognized that Cayenne was in his sleeping bag in the backseat of the Neon all along, apparently bored until he recognized the song of an engine at maximum rpm. At that point, he stepped onto the arm rest, and planted a wet nose unexpectedly on my elbow, scaring the living shit out of me at 120 mph. I screamed like a schoolgirl and nearly smacked my head on the roof of the car as I tried to jump out of the seat. Cayenne gave a short yelp as he rocketed into the back seat, looking almost as surprised as the passenger. Jim didn't flinch, and the car stayed on-line as he reached back, grabbed Cayenne, and launched into doggie-talk. "There's my big guy, there's my big guy," JP snuffled into Cayenne's long hair as the dog wiggled and wagged his way onto Jim's lap. "Down to the two-fifty marker, down two gears," "Who's a good boy, you are, aren't you?" "Brake about… here…look to the apex…here…" "Gimme some sugar, that's it, yes, you're a good boy," "Back to power by now, unwind the wheel to track out up the banking, up the fifth gear here, wiggle your fingers and….brrreeeathhhhhe."

My heart rate didn't return to normal until much later in lap two, after Jim had introduced me properly to Cayenne and I was able to reconcile the fact that I was tooling around Daytona at speeds far exceeding the manufacturer's intent while petting a dog and trying to remember brake points so I wouldn't get killed later that day. Just another day in a world far removed from the sterile, controlled – though sometimes intense – atmosphere of the OR.

JP also introduced me that morning to the radio—an amazing bit of technology to help the slow and the damned get up to speed. Up until then, I had never driven a race car equipped with two-way radios, a technology we now, of course, take for granted. Skip Barber cars simply weren't equipped for them, so drivers relied on the traditional flags waved by corner workers positioned at critical points on the track: yellow for caution, blue with a stripe through it for "You're about to be passed," white for last lap, black for "You've been naughty and have officially been caught." However, there was no way to advise the driver of his own technical shortcomings on a real-time basis. No way to encourage you to brake a little later, turn in earlier, or get back to power sooner. Instead, the debrief sessions with the instructor were used to recite a familiar incantation of driver shortcomings: "You've got more speed available there," "You should be flat in that corner—the car can do it," and "If you keep doing that you're eventually going to kill yourself." The problem was that once you've heard the same comments—post-event when the heart rate is back at normal levels—the effect is pretty much dulled and the value of the instruction a bit like the utility of warning a new teen driver to be careful. I needed demonstration, not rhetoric and verbal lashing. That technique had worked well for me as a new Marine, but back then I was just trying to survive boot camp, maintaining a below-the-radar status-quo until Saturday leave. On the racetrack, "status-quo" was slow and looking at the ass end of quite a lot of cars at the start of the race—something I wanted to leave behind.

Before we mounted up for the first lead-follow session, Jim taped the radio and wires into my cockpit, showing me where the talk button was positioned on the steering wheel (on the left within easy reach of my thumb without taking hands off the wheel) and how to insert my earplugs (red for right) before donning my helmet. The sensation was odd, with some of the sensory input of ambient noise removed from the equation, but the value of a voice in your head giving real-time instruction more than made up for the diminished aural feedback.

"Radio check one two three one two three," came through at top volume as I jumped a bit in the seat. "How's that volume level?" Jim reminded me not to turn it down too low, as his voice would have some competition once we were going at full song. "Copy you loud and clear. This is pretty cool."

Further instructions followed: "If you can't reply to me, if you're too busy in the cockpit, just key the mike and I'll know you heard me. You really don't need to do much talking; mostly it's for me to help you along the way. If you're having a problem, don't be afraid to interrupt me, but remember, you can only talk or listen—one or the other—I can't hear you if I'm talking at the same time. Copy that?" "Copy." "Well then, all right. Let's get going. Keep on my tail, nice and easy, and follow my line."

We set out on the warm-up lap, checking brakes and getting tires up to temp, as JP reminded me of the line through each corner. As we exited the bus stop chicane for the first time, the voice with the Mississippi drawl clicked on again: "OK, here we go. We're going to pick it up a bit. Stay with me now."

What followed that phrase was by far the fastest lap I had ever yet run in a Skip Barber car, which made it a memorable fastest lap of, well, of my life. "Come on now, get behind me and stay there." "Brake a bit later." "On the gas, full throttle now, you can do it." All said calmly in the middle of each turn, as if he was ordering lunch, all while I was getting thrashed about inside the cockpit and experiencing something closer to the limits of the grip of the car for the first time. After the first two such laps, I was amazed, excited, and, instead of being overwhelmed, straining forward at my belts, enjoying the ride thoroughly. "OK, let's pick it up a little more now. You OK back there?"

I shouted into the mike, "This is great! Awesome! I'm behind you and still with you!"

"Repeat: Are you OK back there?"

"Great! Having fun! Keep going!"

"Jim, if you're talking, I can't hear you unless you key the red button. Just confirm for me that you're OK, copy that?"

I sheepishly fumbled for the talk button with my left thumb, and found it surprisingly difficult to push, talk, and steer/shift/brake at the same time.

"OK" was all I could muster.

"Good, good," came JP's reply, "But don't slow down so much when you talk. You'll have to get used to doing a few things at the same time. For now, just get back on up here with me, and I'll do the talking. Copy?" I keyed the red button and managed another "OK" as I tried to close up on JP's gearbox. "OK then, come on now, let's get back up to speed."

We ran several laps nose-to-tail, with JP's ever-present voice rapidly becoming the focal point of each segment of the lap. Into each turn I followed him, as he talked me through key points and encouraged me to "Get back to power sooner" here, and "Get off the brakes" earlier there. I stopped worrying about losing control of the car, given that I had only the uncomplicated task of putting my wheels wherever Jim put his—basically, I was granted permission to push my car closer to its limits simply by doing what the car in front of me had already safely accomplished. In the process, I experienced a rapidly progressive acclimation to Daytona's layout and the formula Dodge's abilities in each corner—all without the drama or fear of finding limits the hard way. In other words, I was going faster than I ever had before without the risk of losing control that had always slowed my march towards the limits before.

There is a school of thought in the racing world that one needs to spin or go off course in order to truly find and define the limits of a car. Certainly, backing off a bit after overestimating the grip levels in a particular turn is effective for finding the limit, but it can be a painful or expensive lesson to learn when done that way. More cerebral drivers push limits in small bits, waiting for the tell-tale squeal of the tires and the feel of the car at the limits of adhesion, arriving there under control and somehow, in that rare genetic soup in which the super-fast pro lives, arriving there quicker than anyone else. To observe such a process live is a real treat for guys like me who understand just how difficult it is to push a car up to its limits in short order, especially in a new-car, new-track situation. I've seen drivers get in an unfamiliar race car at a track they've never driven and be up to speed three or four laps into their first session. From where I'm sitting, watching a pro beat your time in just a few laps, especially when you've put in days/weeks/months of effort to get your own time down, can be intimidating and even a little depressing. It takes a strong ego combined with a thick skin to keep trotting out there, trying lap after lap, when everyone able to read a timing and scoring sheet knows who went faster, and by how much.

There're no Rudys in racing. Unlike the movie, no one rewards heart and desire with theatrical chants of your name when you're three seconds off the pace of the fast guys. The best you can do is keep pushing, keep running hard, and make up time wherever and whenever you can. Either that or grab your helmet, throw the playbook on the coach's chair, and go home.

After two days of practice running in tandem with JP, I was officially ready for my first qualifying session of the weekend. I searched the rulebook hoping for a loophole that would allow me to qualify with JP out in front, but I was most definitely required to be out there on my own. Not only would Jim not be out on track with me, but his voice would be absent also—our radios were not permitted, as everyone else would be radio-less for the fifteen-minute session. JP did help me buckle into the car though, squatting down to offer last bits of advice before we rolled out.

"Don't focus on what anyone else is doing. Relax on the banking, trust the car to do what we've been doing all week. And get back to power sooner. I'll be watching from here." With that he patted the top of my helmet, leaving me to warm the engine and try breathing through my eyelids a la Nuke Laloosh in Bull Durham.

Qualifying was uneventful but a bit disappointing, as I unfortunately slipped into a familiar pattern of conservative driving without JP's real-time coaching in my ears. My fastest lap was a good second off what Jim and I were running routinely the day before, and I managed only an eleventh-place spot on the grid for the race later that Saturday. JP didn't come right out and tell me that I was making him look bad, but we both knew it. I sat down with him over lunch and reviewed the turns where I thought I was losing time—which was in fact pretty much all of them. I listened to Jim's Mississippi drawl as he predicted my missteps in between bites of a sandwich and playing fetch with Cayenne. "Don't worry, you're faster than that; just remember what we've been doing and trust yourself." While I didn't think he was ready to lay money on me to win, place, or show, I was reassured and more confident than I usually was before a race. I also had another thing to focus on before racing in the Regional series race: Master's qualifying was up next.

Given that this was my first Masters quali, and having already observed the apparent general nuttiness of the guys in the Masters group, I shouldn't have been surprised that the antics started before we even left pit lane. I was positioned mid-grid on the pit lane, good enough to witness a bit of bumping and brake checking on the way out of the pits. Like mischievous schoolboys spewing out into the recess yard, guys rubbed wheels and planted their noses into gearboxes as they squeezed into the funnel of the pit-out lane. Once through the gauntlet, it seemed every one of them raced deep into the first horseshoe of Daytona's infield, all wanting to get up to speed first and tackle the kink between turns three and five before stretching out through turn six and out onto the banking. I flinched a bit as several cars buzzed by me on both sides as I began my usual, conservative out lap. Once I had gotten through the slippery infield safely, I realized that I was running alone, with nobody to help with a draft. I tried to catch up with the pack, but they had pulled away in groups of three or four, working the draft to gain speed, leaving me to lope along without a partner.

Realizing that I needed to push it along on my own, I decided to focus on the one place where I knew I could make up time: the braking area for turn one. Coming down off Daytona's tri-oval banking, the Skip barber cars were light and slow enough to brake very late – all the way down at the white stripe crossing the pavement making the entrance to the turn one area. However, the sight picture of that braking area is more than a bit intimidating: keep your foot flat on the throttle right up until the tire wall and guardrail present themselves as formidable obstacles in your line of sight. Done properly, the right foot carefully and expertly applied to the brake pedal slows the car just enough to wind left around the Armco, rolling speed into the quick flat-out turn two complex. Done poorly, one's lap, if not the entire day, is ruined with a run through the grass and on into the tire wall barrier separating the runoff from turn six just on the other side.

Despite my best intentions and hopes of a higher glory, my right foot chose plan B, and pressed hard enough on the brake pedal to lock up the tires at the entry of the braking zone. Of course, once the tires are locked in position by an overzealous application of the brakes, they stop rotating, in the process losing all grip and any ability to turn the car. Instead of modulating pressure to control the brake pedal and allow the wheels to turn again, the tire wall ahead grew larger in my visor opening as I pressed even harder, hoping for some form of stopping grip to arrive quickly. I skidded on past the turn-in point and then hit the grass area on the outside of the turn, feeling the unexpected sensation of acceleration that occurs when all of the grip suddenly leaves town. I impacted the tire wall head on at about 90mph, apparently scaring the crap out of the instructor standing on the top of the tire wall—I could see him literally jump out of my peripheral vision right before the tires exploded with a wave of water raining down into my open cockpit.

Thankfully, with the exception of a bit of a sore spot on the sole of my right foot, I was unharmed. Alarmed, yes, but otherwise unharmed. It took a few beats to realize that I was seemingly intact, after which I dared to peek out over the front of the car to assess damage. As I realized that the nose was buried in the tires, the instructor, Peter Argetsinger, peeked his head comically over the tire wall as if he was expecting sniper fire.

"Are you OK?" That question again. "That was a pretty big hit!" observed Pete.

I opened my visor and replied, "Yeah, a bit embarrassed, but I think I'm OK."

"That's good. You might try slowing down for the turn next time."

I muttered into my helmet, "Thanks for the expert coaching, Captain Obvious." Then a bit louder, "Can you push me out of here, or am I stuck?"

"Back 'er on up and let's see." I engaged reverse and gunned it a bit, splashing myself with a second dose of tire water as the car pulled out of the tire wall, minus its nose cone and front wing. Pete pointed me around toward the turn two area, and reminded me, "Don't go too fast on the way back to the pits—you never know what else might fall off."

I pulled onto the track, trying to keep off line as much as possible. All sorts of nasty noises were coming from the front steering assembly, and a strangely cool breeze was blowing up through the footwell into the cockpit. I made it around to the banking and limped along on the skirt until I was able to pull off into the pits.

After I had finished debriefing with the instructors about each corner (during which I deliberately avoided Pete Argetsinger since we had already conferred about turn one), I had my first ever meeting with the mechanic responsible for the damage bill. Reluctantly I signed the sheet promising to pay for a new nose cone and wing, along with several other bits and pieces. I handed it back to the guy, who looked a little surprised.

"What's the matter? Did I screw something up?"

"No, I was just waiting for you to blame somebody else—that's what everyone else does."

"Really? Well, I did see a guy come awfully close right before I locked it up and hit the wall," I replied hopefully.

"Nice try, Lowe. With a lame excuse like that, at least I know you belong with those Masters boneheads." I stuffed the carbon copy of the bill in my pocket and turned to find several of the drivers from the Masters session waiting.

"Way to go! Nicely done! Strong effort!" and other sarcastic catcalls accompanied the golf claps and jeers from the group. Dick Lippert trotted out the typical line, just right for the occasion, "How'd that work out for you?" while Johnny Mayes kept laughing and pointing to my shoes: "I saw those red shoes sticking out of the front of your car as I passed you—nice touch!"

I endured a few other comedic insults until Larry grabbed me and pulled me away from the group. "What happened out there? First you were fine, then I saw you in the tire wall. Did you get hit?"

"Nope. Just locked them up on the way in, and that was all she wrote."

Larry was, for a moment, genuine and even gentle. "Well, a guy with a little more experience might work his way off the pedal a bit to let the tires start rolling again, you know? With braking, sometimes, a little less is more, right? You'll get the hang of it—all it takes is seat time."

I mumbled my thanks, realizing that I had just received an unexpected pearl about driving technique that I hadn't needed before then. I tucked it away for later use and remembered Larry each time I went through turn one all weekend.

The first race on Saturday afternoon was a disappointment, to say the least. After all of the practice laps, the coaching by Jim Pace, and the extra sessions provided by the Masters group entry, I went out and had a frustratingly short race. One lap into the event, I was still in the middle of a gaggle of cars despite my attempt to get forward from my P11 starting position. From there it all went wrong after rounding the blind apex of turn one. With cars on both sides of me, I accelerated towards the tight exit of the turn just in time to broadside a spinning Dodge right in my path. I managed to slow slightly right before impact, but still managed to write off another nose cone nonetheless. Several other race cars fell victim to the same scenario, with blurred impacts occurring on both sides of my skidding car. It took quite a while to get straightened out in the narrow track between the other wrecked cars, and I rejoined the race yet a few more positions down.

Despite pushing hard and trying my best to make up time and position in the next ten laps, the checker flew with me back in the all-too-familiar ass end of the running order. I recall the sensation as only a bit less frustrating than at prior events, given that the poor finish was mostly out of my control. However, the sentiment of disappointment was strongly there all the same. To make matters worse, I had just made the second race a higher mountain to climb: the finishing position on Saturday dictated one's place on the starting grid on Sunday. And twelfth place was certainly not where I had hoped to start my last run at Daytona.

Before getting that last go in race two, I had the advantage of running essentially a warm-up race first, in the form of the Masters event. I had no illusions about finishing strong in my debut in that series, but I knew that keeping pace with that contingent would sharpen my focus for the next race. Assuming, of course, that I survived the experience. And with all the bumping and banging going on, the issue of survival was still in question even in the late laps of that race. I kept my head on a swivel, but somehow got muscled aside whenever the opportunity for contesting a corner (or even the occasional straightaway) arose.

I dutifully raced hard, but clear of everyone else for most of the race, until I found myself perfectly positioned for a drafting pass behind a similarly-challenged driver on the last corner heading toward the checkered flag. I closed up on his gearbox, trying to calculate the perfect moment to break out of the draft and slingshot past on the straight. Although this maneuver looks deceptively simple from afar, much like the rest of driving well at serious speeds, it does take some practice and skills to execute perfectly. Unfortunately, those were two critical areas where I was lacking, but there's no time like the first time, right?

Foot pressed hard against the throttle pedal, I pulled out to the left as we moved through Daytona's turn four, expecting that the guy in front would push a little to the right side as we transitioned from the steep banking onto the flatter tri-oval. Good in theory, but wrong in this instance. As I started to pull alongside the leading car, the driver instead simply moved to his left, attempting to cut me off before I ran past. Since my front wheels were already even with the center of his car, there was no backing out at that point. Well, maybe there was, but I didn't consider it at that moment, given that the flag stand and waving checkers were now in sight.

I moved further left as the other car continued to ride me down towards the flat apron of the paved surface, knowing that I needed to keep my foot in it if there was to be anything resembling a happy ending to this episode. I hit the apron and squirmed a bit at the abrupt transition, and headed towards the finish line side-by-side with the other car. In a last desperate move, the driver moved a bit closer to me, forcing my left wheels onto Daytona's manicured infield grass. Flecks of dirt and grass flew off my left front tire and hit my face shield, obscuring my vision a bit. The car bucked and slid as it struggled for grip, and I struggled to keep my focus on the other car's left-side wheels and the flag stand. I pressed harder on the pedal, gripped the steering wheel to sawdust, and pulled across the line mere inches ahead of the other car. I finally took a breath as I slowed for the cool-down lap, wondering just how crazy that must have looked, given that it was a battle for fourteenth place.

Suitably warmed up, I had a short break before the final race went off. I figured that I had seen the worst of the day's traffic and aggressive driving, so I was certainly more relaxed about starting twelfth. I also knew that I was able to run faster laps than many of the guys immediately in front of me, based on my qualifying and fast-lap times. And, if worse came to worst, I knew that I could pass on the infield grass in a pinch.

Moments before the warm-up laps, I once again buckled into the open cockpit, trying to settle myself for yet another round of mach-two, hair-on-fire adrenaline rush and muscle-straining excitement. Never having been very good at the Zen-like pre-contest ritual adopted by some athletes, I just forced my eyes closed for some mental laps and good-karma thoughts.

My solitude was shattered by a loud thump as Dick Lippert wacked the side of the car and proclaimed, "We're all watching and rooting for you!" I jumped against the belts as I startled, heart rate accelerating into overdrive from the squirt of epinephrine as I looked around in surprise. Behind Dick were three or four of the other Masters guys, all enjoying a good laugh at my expense. "The boys wanted me to pass on a message: Whatever you do, don't fuck up and embarrass us." After my assurances that I lived a life in search of their approval, Dick wandered off to join the group with one last piece of advice: "Drive fast, take lots of chances."

I took the time to warm the tires, brakes, and my brain on the out-lap, swerving from side to side abruptly, putting some weight on the rubber and then alternating braking and acceleration to get the binders up to temp. Sitting back in P12, I had a great view of the front of the field as we snaked our way around turn four and towards the starter stand on the front straight. Everyone lined up two-wide, searching for the right gear and rpm to get a good launch on the start. The sound was beautiful, with engines revving up and down as drivers jockeyed for position and waited for the flag to drop. My helmet filled with the low-pitch sound of fifteen cars in first gear, resonating off Daytona's walls and seemingly right up from my feet through my chest. Heads turning left and right, we all tried to size up the location of the lead cars compared to our own, keeping one eye on the flagger and the other on the car alongside.

The sudden explosion of engine noise eliminated the need to actually see the green flag waving above as all fifteen cars accelerated simultaneously at the start. I mashed the gas pedal and tried to keep up with the upshifts while maneuvering in the mess of cars heading down towards turn one. The assault on the senses was spectacular, with the noise overwhelming the exhaust fumes generated by the pack of cars, all while I gripped the steering wheel with my left hand and shifter with my right. Feet dancing on the pedals and eyes surely bulging, I searched for a safe piece of asphalt to occupy as the cars braked heavily in unison, accordioning their way through the turn one-two complex and down into the first hairpin.

I kept to the right side on my way down into the International Horseshoe, knowing that I'd pick up a few spots over the guys stuck on the outside of the turn when we then headed up to the kink and turn five. Keeping at least three wheels on the pavement, I rode the apex curbing until the exit, keeping one eye on the cars bunched up to my left as I accelerated up through the gears.

I wasn't sure how many cars I had passed, but within moments the pack began to spread out with cars beginning to line up nose-to-tail in front of me. Trying to channel JP and taking a deep breath, I headed out of turn six up onto the banking of the oval track and was close enough to the car directly in front of me to draft by on the back straight. I had a good run through the bus stop in time to catch the next car at the exit and managed a good pass early in the oval's turn three/four section, only to be drafted by the same car on my way into turn one.

I kept on that car's gearbox until the exit of turn six, trying to fill the other guy's mirrors with a view of my nose (the car's nose, that is, not the one in my helmet, although I'm told both are visible in suitable mirrors). As I got on the power at the apex, the car in front abruptly spun out wide of the exit, allowing me to slip on by and back onto the banking. Silently celebrating, looked up in search of the next car in line. One by one, I passed several more cars—with a few passes aided by locked-up brakes, spins, or other sins of their unsuspecting drivers—but I couldn't be sure what place I was in because there was always a car in front of me each time I made my way down past start-finish for another lap.

One more car was in sight when I saw the white flag waving from the flag stand, signifying that there was one lap left in the race. I pushed as heard as possible, trying my best to brake just a little bit later and get back to power sooner, JP-style, but was simply unable to catch the guy before the lap was over. Breathless but thrilled, I steamed my way under the waving checkered flag like a kid just off the log flume ride at Disney. I hooted and whooped to myself, enjoying for the first time a cool-down lap without the usual disappointment that went with previous lackluster finishes.

First podium! Daytona, 2005

As I pulled to a stop in the pits, I could see JP, Larry, Dick and a few of the other Masters drivers waiting at the wall. They clapped as I slowed and then stopped, jumping down to pat my head and slap the sides of the car as I unbuckled.

"Nice job, Lowe! P3!," came the first announcement, straight from Larry Revier. JP chimed in like a proud teacher whose pupil just got an A (OK, B+ maybe): "Your first podium! I knew it was in there somewhere! Nice job out there."

Lippert managed, as I would come to realize is his role in this herd, to put it all in perspective: "Geez, he beats up on a bunch of slackers, but there'll be no living with him from now on!"

I beamed as Divi handed out trophies during the small podium ceremony, not caring that I occupied the lowest step nor that the cup wasn't even big enough for a proper cup of coffee. I posed for photos with the other two drivers, holding my trophy up overhead as if I had just won Monza in a Ferrari. The feeling was so unexpectedly great, the buzz so strong, that I continued to giggle a bit while collecting my gear in the paddock. I had felt good in the race car on many occasions before, but mostly out of a sense of the physical enjoyment of challenging myself with a strong effort or running a particularly good personal time. But it had been literally decades since I had the opportunity to actually celebrate an athletic accomplishment, especially one so personally desired yet unanticipated.

I carefully strapped the six-inch-high trophy into the seat next to me for the flight home, still grinning and soaking up the post-adrenaline glow of the day's events. I enjoyed the sense of satisfaction even more than I had expected and allowed myself the luxury of self-congratulation for the first time in a long while. Tomorrow there would be another surgical case, another patient to try and help, but that night was reserved for just a bit more pleasure as I replayed the race in my head

11

Chapter Eleven

After thoroughly enjoying the private thrill of my first-ever podium and racing trophy, I found it easier to settle back into the rhythm of my increasingly busy practice. Having now been working on my own for four years, I'd gotten used to the tense pace of being solely responsible for running office hours, making rounds, and taking call. I was also functioning as the chief of the Division of Neurosurgery at my hospital, which only added to the requests for my time. On a daily basis, I continued to make every effort to assist the growth of my practice and, with it, my reputation as a good surgeon. That effort, however, required a significant commitment, not just on my part but also on the part of my wife, who remained busy with our son Aidan and also with her own medical practice.

Aidan was now almost four years old and already demonstrating a diversity of activities that challenged the time and attention of both his parents and grandparents. The rate at which he was learning new concepts and developing new interests was as impressive as it was demanding of our time. Although we had help at home, mostly in the form of Gin's parents and one part-time nanny, neither Ginny nor I wished to delegate parenting unless absolutely necessary because of an unalterable conflict. As a result, we juggled our schedules whenever possible and insisted on maximizing what free time we had with Aidan. And of course, as Aidan grew, it only became more difficult when I was forced to spend time away from him. As a final stressor to a work schedule in excess of 80 hours a week, I tried to schedule race weekends with somewhat more frequency than before, remaining committed to this portion of my life.

Naturally, there were going to be some things that couldn't be easily accommodated in this increasingly busy schedule. And exercise was one of the first to drop by the wayside. Although I managed a day here and there at the gym, in general I simply had neither the time nor the incentive to spend valuable moments staying in shape. Combined with a diet that was liberal and a developing appetite for fine red wine, my weight predictably ballooned, mostly without me being directly aware of the fact. Since I basically lived in scrubs, and only occasionally put on my size 58 red Sparco race suit, my clothes offered no clue as to the extent to which I was getting deconditioned and, well, downright flabby. In reality, I simply wasn't in a physical condition that would enhance my speed and endurance at the track. Ginny was kind enough not to bring this fact to my direct attention at that point, although she was encouraging about the concept of my occasional exercising prior to my Skip Barber weekends. When a race weekend was approaching, I would make some effort to get time on my basement elliptical machine and even hit the weights a bit. Much of the demand of driving a race car was aerobic, so I would often up my meager efforts in that fashion. For her part, Ginny often joked that when she found me exercising, she suspected that either I had a girlfriend or a race weekend approaching. Fortunately for me, I was devoting my free time and emotional pursuits away from home strictly to going faster.

Over the course of the next year, I spent several race events being coached by Jim Pace, running untold lapping sessions in tandem, gradually learning race craft, and getting more familiar with the race car. In addition to JP's coaching, I essentially doubled my time in the seat of the race car by running both regional and Masters events at each race weekend. I was gradually becoming more competitive and was routinely at or near the front of the pack in regional events, and mid-pack in the Masters group. Thanks to JP's tireless efforts, I was slowly improving as a driver and able to recognize some form of progress most weekends at the track.

In September of 2005, I booked a five-day reservation for the Skip Barber event at Mid-Ohio. I arrived in Ohio to initially beautiful weather, allowing me to learn this unfamiliar racetrack under the safe tutelage of JP. However, all hell was breaking loose south of us as hurricane Katrina leveled New Orleans and parts of Mississippi, including Jim's hometown. While I was aware that there was a significant storm affecting parts of the country, and equally that my home and family were not being threatened, I was unaware of the significance of the storm to JP. In fact, he did not mention his concerns about risk to his family and damage to property back in Mississippi while he was busy indulging some other guy's racing fantasies. Instead, Jim took it in stride and kept coaching in between phone calls to check on family and friends back home. In typical JP fashion, he didn't even mention the fact that there was drama back home until later in the week, and then only after all was determined to be safe and secure in Mississippi.

As the storm moved northward, a significant amount of rain got dumped on Ohio. For two full days, the track and surrounding area were subject to soaking rains and driving winds. Several lapping sessions were canceled, and the few that were run required drivers to navigate their way around standing water and across grip-free tarmac. For much of the two days of rain, JP and I stayed undercover in the Mid-Ohio garages, talking about race technique and race craft. At one point, I finally broached the subject of racing in a different series at a more advanced level. The topic was not necessarily a new one, as I had brought up the idea to Jim previously.

At one of the prior SBRS events, while attending one of the now-typical post-race dinners with the other Masters drivers, the topic of racing in other series had been introduced. Specifically, the guys were all discussing the fact that several of the drivers had participated in the 2004 running of the Rolex 24 Hours of Daytona. Although I was aware of that famous race's existence, and I was a fan of sports car racing, I certainly was not aware that it was possible for amateurs to compete in that event or at that level of racing. I listened with growing amazement as Mark Patterson, Dario Cioti, and John Pew described their experience running a Corvette in the event, and the fact that Patterson has stepped up to the Daytona Prototype class for the 2005 race. That dinner discussion came complete with cautionary words from Dario ("I loved it, but wouldn't ever do it again") and chest-pounding from other Master's drivers who hadn't actually been there ("You'll be faster than the regular GT guys—and they can't drive in the rain like we do"), but the general look and feel had been one of assured excitement.

JP had been there for the dinner, sitting back a bit and letting the others add to the mixture of facts, myths, conjecture, and occasionally outright bullshit. Seated next to him, I directed a few questions his way but was rebuffed.

"Let's not talk about this now; there's too much going on here to get into a serious discussion over dinner. We can talk about this all day tomorrow."

"But, can we—can I—what do I have to do—is there a chance to do something like that some day?"

In a Zen-like teacher-pupil moment, JP knowingly smiled. "We'll have time to talk later, once we get some more racing done."

I don't recall having much of a serious discussion with Jim that particular weekend, but later in the days leading up to the September 2005 Skip Barber event, I reminded him that he had promised to talk about it with me. Now, sitting in the Mid-O garage and waiting out the rain, I finally had JP in something resembling a captive audience. I didn't relish the occasion of bugging him to the point of irritation, but when things were reasonably calm, I seized the moment.

"If you want me to help you, I have a few connections of teams that have GT cars that could run in Grand-Am," Jim offered. "But I really think you ought to try a few different cars first, to get an idea of what you might like and where you might feel best."

Needing one final affirmation, I risked the question that had been running through in my mind nonstop since the moment I had discovered the concept of actually racing in the 24.

"Is driving the Rolex someday still something you think I could do?" Despite the fact that I was pretty short on actual knowledge of what it would entail, I had allowed the idea to become firmly planted in my head.

"That's a reasonable goal for you, I think, but we'd have to do some serious running and get you lots of seat time before you took that on."

I ventured a compromise of sorts. "Maybe 2007, you think that would give us enough time to get me up to speed?"

JP took only a moment to answer, which encouraged me perhaps more than it should have. "I think that's a possibility. But first, let me make some calls, and find you some cars to test. Let's see if you still want to go there after driving some GT-type cars."

I agreed to go with Jim's patient approach, but much like when I decided that I wanted to be a brain surgeon while still a freshman in college, I was already tuned in to the idea of racing in the 24 Hours of Daytona. It could be done, I wanted to do it, and nothing Jim had said so far seemed like an obstacle. Equally reminiscent of my younger days, I was starting down a path towards something that I perceived as special, even elite, and worthy of the challenge. Confronting the challenge, even if I didn't really know much about it, or what exactly it would take to get there, was only a matter of beginning.

What's equally clear in my mind, even in the 20-20 vision that is hindsight, is that this was not going to be just another "bucket list" item to be crossed off. What I had learned over the years, emerging from my seat on the curb during neighborhood games, is that I wanted to be a full-on part of the action, of the activity, and not just an observer. I wanted to be on this side of the fence, not that one. The only way I had managed to conquer my fears and my reservations about failure, injury, or embarrassment was to immerse myself fully and commit to the demands of the job, sport, or avocation.

Whether it was athletics in college, going to officer's school in the Marines, tackling my medical training, or developing a spinal cord injury program at my hospital, all had been done fully and without reservation once the goal was established. Identify the endpoint, gain the necessary education or experience, and embrace the challenge that must be met. While cursory participation might be seemingly OK just to get a taste of something, I had never preferred to do it that way before. Maybe it's more curse than blessing, and possibly even a signature element of some psychiatric diagnosis, but I didn't want to do anything half-assed, ever.

I had stubbornly continued to play Division I football in college, ignoring a slew of concussions and other injuries, making the team each year despite being outgunned in the speed department but unmatched in the persistence category. I joined the Marines along with a Harvard roommate, thinking that exposure to the demands of the world's best fighting force might be a plus regardless of where life took me after that. I then left the USMC, turning down the chance for a commission to instead go to medical school, hoping that an equal commitment to neurosurgery would have equally satisfying results. Once I was on my way down that path, I managed to insert some athletic intensity during training by learning to surf and snowboard. With those pursuits, dabbling wasn't an option either: during my first year snowboarding, I competed successfully in the halfpipe (against other aging "masters"—all over the ripe old age of 25!) and eventually surfed at exotic locales such as Portugal, Mexico, the French West Indies, and El Salvador.

I had learned through all of this that opportunity presents itself in many ways, and for me the moment often occurred when least expected, and sometimes when I was least prepared. Given all of that, what came next should have been no surprise.

Before that, however, there was the small issue of actually racing that wet weekend at Mid-Ohio. Thanks to JP's tutelage, I had my first-ever pole-position qualifier during the regional race series event. I also "broke through" with a hard-fought eighth place finish in the Masters race. I was actually competitive in each event in each category—including running from last on the grid (after a qualifying spin) up to third place after two laps in the first race of the weekend. In each session, each practice, and each race, I felt more and more at home behind the wheel. With thoughts of racing at Daytona on my mind, I worried less about each turn in Ohio—and did all the better for it.

***

I hadn't heard from Jim Pace for a few weeks after the Mid-Ohio race. I had been absorbed in work, essentially running a solo private practice while tackling my Chief of Neurosurgery duties at the medical center. Between work and the fun but exhausting job of raising a three-year-old boy, my time was spoken for and all attention occupied. Additionally, I hadn't been working out or staying in shape in any real way, and I was continuing to indulge my passion for good food and even better adult beverages. This was not exactly a fine formula for preparing for a racing season, but my immediate plans at the time were more of the "just try to get through today" variety.

This was therefore the perfect time for JP to call with an opportunity.

The week Jim called, my schedule was typically hectic. I had already made it through my two long cases Monday, finishing in time to do rounds and get home that night before Aidan was asleep. Tuesday was going to be a bigger challenge, as meetings loomed on the schedule along with the usual surgeries, and then there was trauma on-call duty to add insult to injury.

Tuesday's wake-up call arrived at zero-dark-thirty, with my alarm rousing me from the usual racing dreams. The radio's intrusion was actually welcomed, as my typical racing dream wasn't one of grid girls and champagne-soaked podium glory. Rather, the dream was always an anxiety-provoked annoyance: I was near enough to a track to hear the engines but couldn't quite find the entrance to the pits. Once inside, some critical part of my race gear always seemed to be missing—a forgotten helmet, missing shoes or gloves, misplaced fire suit. This time, I was in the middle of scuffling to find my red shoelaces while my group formed up on some phantom grid somewhere when the clock radio rescued me from further aggravation.

I showered, donned scrubs, and then tip-toed past Aidan's room, pausing long enough to send a kiss the way of his still-sleeping form. Moments later I was in the truck juggling coffee and a power bar, pointed north, and headed for Atlantic City, right on schedule. I had a few trauma consults to follow up on prior to the weekly trauma service group rounds; with luck arriving just in time to weigh in on my patients' conditions and treatment plans.

I left the conference after updating the trauma docs and nursing staff on the surgical plans for the four patients that I had been consulting upon; the conference was just hitting its midpoint, but I needed to get to the other hospital in time for my 7:30 a.m. OR start. I headed West on the Atlantic City expressway, briefly enjoying taking exit 7N at felonious speeds on the way to the Mainland division of AtlantiCare Regional Medical Center. Moments later I joined my future partner Joe Zerbo in the OR locker room, where we reviewed the day's three cases: one patient getting a cervical discectomy, another undergoing a lumbar fusion, and one unplanned patient scheduled overnight for an urgent lumbar discectomy.

Our urgent case took priority in the schedule, moving up to first position in the batting order for the day. Joe and I both took a moment to meet with the patient and his family at bedside, reviewing the serious nature of the disc herniation that was damaging the nerves of the lower back. The patient himself was already well aware of the extent of the damage, and the need for an immediate operation. Because he had been leaking urine for several days, and experiencing complete incontinence since late the night before, he didn't need to be convinced about the necessity of surgery. However, both he and his wife needed to understand the risks of the procedure,

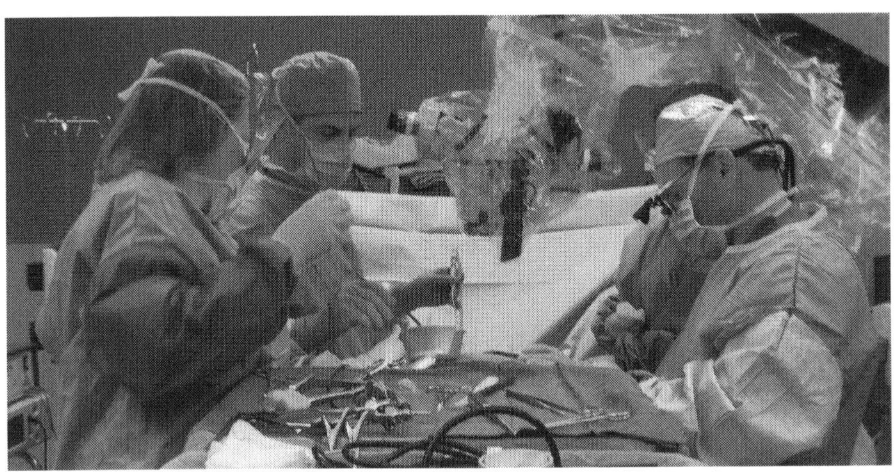

Working with the team in the OR

and also the ramifications of the problem if left untreated, before we went into the operating room.

I introduced Dr. Zerbo and myself, shaking the wife's hand and nodding at the patient at the same time. "I know you realize that George has been having a serious problem for some time now; he told you last night about the surgery, I understand?"

The missus nodded her head, throwing a sideways glance at her husband. "It's been for even longer than that. I've been telling him to get to the hospital, but he's just too stubborn. He kept insisting it was old age. He probably still wouldn't be here if I hadn't threatened him."

George was tactfully silent at this; he looked like a guy who was relishing the serenity of general anesthesia at that point, and I was going to oblige him shortly.

"Well, we'll take care of the large ruptured disc and get the pressure off the nerves. That will help a lot, but the nerves have to heal on their own after that, so don't look for instant results. It'll be a long recovery for the nerves, but this is the important first step."

After that, George received the perfunctory kiss goodbye from his wife, and Joe and I walked together into the OR suite.

Once we had George in position for the surgery, his low back was prepped with betadyne and alcohol—a combination designed to sterilize the skin prior to incision. I made the skin cut with a surgical scalpel, deepening the opening as I spread the superficial fatty tissues while Joe cauterized bleeding vessels. Joe and I both worked at stripping the muscles away from either side of the spinal bones, allowing good access and visualization of the lamina—the part of the bones lying just over the spinal canal, where the nerves were located. We proceeded to quickly remove the lamina, taking practiced bites out of George's bone with sharp, bone-eating tools called rongeurs. As the scrub nurse cleaned the bone out of the instruments, we alternated removing bits of the lamina until we had removed enough bone to expose the dura—the covering of the sac in which the nerves floated.

It was immediately obvious that George's nerves were severely compressed from a mass located in front of the sac—a mass that we knew from the pre-op MRI was most likely a massive herniated disc. Looking through the magnified operating loupes attached to our glasses, Joe and I worked to gently move the sac of nerves to one side, and then the other, exposing bit by bit the large bulk of the ruptured disc material. Once exposed, it was a relatively routine matter to pull out the disc fragments piece by piece, taking pressure off the nerves one fragment at a time. Using scraping curettes, we gently moved the fragments out of the disc space and the spinal canal itself, taking care not to stretch the nerves or place undue pressure on the dural sac. Once the disc fragments were all removed, the nerves were floating free in the spinal fluid-filled sac and, hopefully, on their way to healing from the damage caused by the huge disc herniation.

Joe broke scrub to go and speak to George's wife as I closed the wound, bringing the tissues back together with multiple layers of sutured muscle and fascia. I placed a sterile dressing over the incision site, feeling again that sense of satisfaction at a job well done, or at least done well without obvious immediate missteps. Mission accomplished for George; on the next task at hand and the next challenge to duplicate good surgical technique.

Between cases, I visited with the prior day's post-op patients and chatted with families, nurses, and case managers, trying to organize thoughts and plans for the next few days of care for each of my patients. I snacked on Graham crackers and coffee along the way, skipping lunch but not the ubiquitous junk food available in the break room back at the OR. No carrots and celery here; instead I grabbed wayward chocolate bars, pretzels, and the most prized surgical snack of all, peanut butter crackers. Before I scrubbed back in for each subsequent case, I checked by phone with the office, answering questions from my staff, and taking notes about new consult requests from the trauma docs.

I managed to get my last patient closed just in time to head over to the adjacent Bacharach Institute of Rehabilitation, taking my seat at the board meeting just a few minutes after roll call. Although my seat on the board was strictly a volunteer position, dinner was included at the monthly meetings, so I indulged in my first real meal of the day while the minutes were read. Seventy minutes later, I was finally free for the evening. I headed south down the Garden State Parkway, signing out to Joe via my hands-free mobile as I sped towards Longport and home. With any luck, Gin and Aidan would both have some energy left for a little quality time before we all collapsed into bed for the night.

Shouts of "Daddy's home!" greeted me as I opened the entry door from the garage. Aidan, who never seemed to walk anywhere, came tear-assing around the corner and literally dove into my arms. I performed a choreographed backwards fall, clutching my son to my chest as I rolled onto my back and punctuated the impact with an exaggerated "Umphhh!"

"Whoa, Bubba, did you get bigger since this morning? You're a bruiser!"

"Daddy!" I felt a wet raspberry planted on my cheek, triggering an instant memory of my own childhood, kissing my dad when he walked in the door from a long day at work. I wondered if Aidan would also remember the feel of my stubble on the smooth skin of his cheek—although my son would indeed be spared any memory of the aroma of Aqua Velva that always enveloped my dad a full generation before.

I wrestled a moment with Aidan, and looked up to see Ginny, smiling at the happy entanglement of her two boys.

"Hi honey, sorry I didn't call on the way home, I was talking shop with Dr. Joe."

"Welcome home, daddy, we both missed you a lot today."

I peeled Aidan off and got up to kiss Gin. "Hope you had a good day, sweetheart, you look beautiful, as always."

Ginny brushed off the lame compliment. "Yeah, watching Bob the Builder all day really makes me glow."

The three of us made our way upstairs to the kitchen, where Ginny's parents were stationed, Grandmom at the stove and Pop-pop at the open refrigerator. Len greeted me with a freshly made Bombay Sapphire martini, complete with three olives and a shaker of refills.

"I thought you might like this after a pretty long day," Len announced. "Were you operating all this time?

I filled my father-in-law in on the details of my day, enjoying the fact that he could easily commiserate with my hectic schedule. A pediatric neurologist still working his own busy schedule at age 75, Len was uniquely sensitive to my demanding work hours.

"They didn't beat you up too much today, I imagine?" Len was no stranger to the stresses of daily hospital politics, having earned his way to tenure in a highly competitive University hospital environment long ago.

"Nope, not today. No phone calls from upset nurses and no angry chairmen demanding my resignation." I feigned a look at my watch. "At least not yet."

"Well, go on out on the deck and enjoy a break with your drink. We've got things under control in here with Aidan."

I carefully carried the full martini glass through the sliding doors, out onto the deck overlooking the bay to my right and ocean to my left. I always enjoyed the view of the bay lapping gently against the bulwark right across the street. It was a bonus when the breeze also carried the sound of the shorebreak a block away in the other direction.

The night was cool but quiet, with none of the loud ambience associated with the peak summer crowds of only a few weeks before. I sat down on a chaise, smoothed my scrub pants out a bit, and breathed deep and slow for what seemed like the first time that day.

I was just into my second deep breath when the phone chimed and "Jim Pace" lit up on my BlackBerry caller ID.

JP started right in after the mandatory exchange of pleasantries. "I've been making a few calls, trying to see who might be in a position for us to do a test with, even if it's just a day or two driving with a couple of guys sharing a car." I would come to realize that Jim Pace was a master at getting a few guys together in race cars to practice or "test" them out (testing, as I was to find out, not only cars but the drivers themselves, on occasion), with events strung out across the country with various teams and classes of race cars. In this fashion, JP kept busy between Skip Barber Race School obligations, augmenting his income nicely and expanding his opportunities to drive in a variety of series with several different customers. JP was doing what JP did best: finding a ride for his guys and, hopefully, in the process getting some quality race time for himself as well. "I haven't been able to make anything happen with the guys I mentioned who have the Mustang, and the other team isn't running the Nissan anymore. But there is a team from California that I've run with before, and they might be a good fit."

I perked up immediately and started pacing along the deck, absently enjoying the feel of the wood on my bare feet. "Ok, I'm all ears," I said, trying to suppress the happy dance as I listened to Jim lay out the plan.

"The team's called TRG—The Racer's Group—and based near Sears Point in Sonoma. They've been a pretty big deal in sports cars for a while now. Guy named Kevin Buckler is the owner."

I recalled the team name and put together the owner's name with something in my memory bank. "Are they the ones that won the 24 in a GT car a couple of years ago?"

"Yep, that's the team. They're running Porsches in the GT class in Grand-Am right now, and I think it might be a good fit for us. Kevin's trying to put together a test next month, and he might have a seat available for you. I don't know the price or dates yet, but thought I'd run it by you first."

"Uh, well, uh…" I successfully avoided sounding halfway intelligent with my reply. "Porsches? I've never driven anything like that."

"No problem," JP replied. "Four wheels, gas on the right, brake pedal right there next to it."

"Well, I'd like to try it out, I guess, if you think this is a good way to go." I couldn't come up with anything else resembling a more reasonable response, and JP surely wasn't expecting anything different.

Not one for idle chit-chat, Jim summed it up before hanging up. "I'll get some more info and dates from Kevin, and get back to you."

I set the phone down, and looked around for someone to share the news with. Len and Mille had retreated to their downstairs bedroom for the night; Aidan and Gin were sitting on the kitchen floor, working on a puzzle. The sliding doors were open, so I merely turned around and shouted the good news through the screened opening.

"Honey, JP wants me to go drive a Porsche in California with him. Is that OK?"

I may as well have announced that I was going to swim the English Channel. "That's nice dear, now can you go and get Aidan's bath started while I clean up the kitchen?"

I half skipped up the stairs, heading for Aidan's bathroom while envisioning myself behind the wheel of a real, honest-to-goodness race car. I suppressed the urge to make engine and shifting sounds on my way up, enjoying a little fantasizing without looking too overenthusiastic. A few moments later, my son was splashing in the tub as I sat on the tile floor, still buzzed by the news.

"Daddy's gonna drive a Porsche soon. A real powerful race car. Wait till you see it!"

"Guess what, Dad? Pop-pop and I went to the playground today." Aidan punctuated his statement with a splash.

"That's pretty cool Bubba. Did you hear what I said about the race car?"

More splashing. "Then we went to the beach. Pop-pop let me watch the men fishing from the rocks."

"You know, I've never driven a Porsche before. I'll bet it's fun!"

"Pop-pop showed me how to use his laptop today. We used Google on his computer to look up fishing." Splash, splash.

I sighed, picked up the washcloth, and got back to the task at hand. "That's great, Bubba, tell daddy all about it."

It took a week or two before JP got back in touch again.

"TRG has two test dates at Sears Point coming up, but they're in November. I can make only one of them—the first one I already have scheduled elsewhere, so it would have to be the second test. Problem is, it's on the two days after Thanksgiving."

I was bummed by the news. After being so cranked up by the possibility of driving a real race car, even if only for a test, I wasn't quite prepared for disappointment. "I'll check, but I'm about 99% sure that that can't happen for me. I'm already scheduled that far out with a busy week, and Gin'll kill me if I go away for the only free time we might have together."

JP paused, as if he had anticipated this. "I told Kevin that might be a tough date. I'll call him back, and see if he has any other ideas. In the meantime, sit tight and I'll keep looking. Something's bound to come our way."

The emotional roller coaster ride continued with JP's next phone call, just a few days later. I was again sitting out on the deck, enjoying the unseasonably warm evening, watching as my son did word puzzles with his pop-pop Len. Barefoot but of course still in my scrubs, I was absently considering the long OR schedule I was facing for the next day. Racing wasn't on my mind at that moment. In fact, I hadn't been thinking much about the next racing possibility, which seemed distant at best after JP's last call. There was simply too much going on at home and work to allow myself the luxury of any racing dreaming and scheming.

So of course, Jim Pace was calling with a ride. In fact, the ride that would change my life.

Never one to beat around the bush, JP started right in with the meat of the sandwich. "Kevin Buckler called me. He has a car—a Porsche Cup car—available for us to run in the Rolex this year, if we want it. We can have the car to ourselves, or split it with some guys Kevin gets together, whatever works financially, but the ride's available if you want it."

Like Chevy Chase's character Clark Griswold in "Christmas Vacation," I couldn't have been more surprised if I had woken up with my head sewn to the carpet.

"This year's Rolex? The 24 hours?" I stammered back at JP. "Uh, that wasn't really the original plan, was it? I mean, the '06 Rolex? Like, in just three months?"

"That's what he's got available. I know it would be better to test first, like we planned, but there's nothing available until the race in January. Good news is, Grand-Am has three days of testing at Daytona right after New Year's, so that would help a lot right there."

Holy shit holy shit holy shit. It takes a lot to get my heart rate elevated, but this was doing the job. "So, we could do this, like together, and you're willing to drive with me and help me?"

"That's what we've been talking about, just sooner than we planned. But, I think we'll be able to get you ready in time, maybe even do another Skippy weekend before you go to Florida."

Jim proceeded to tell me about the cost of the event, deferring any real discussion about actual money needs until we clarified who else would be driving with us and what else we needed to get it all together.

"Go think about it some, talk to Ginny, and let's talk some more later this week once I have more details for you. But, if you want to do this, this is the best way I know to get there and do it right."

I composed myself enough to thank JP and hit "End" on the mobile. "Honey," I called out, needing to share immediately. "Honey, JP wants me to race Daytona with him!"

Gin stuck her head out through the sliding door opening. She still had her laptop bag and tote in her hands, having walked in the door from the office only moments before.

"That's nice, dear," she replied in our familiar lighthearted response appropriate for important-sounding announcements. "Can we talk about this after I put my stuff down?"

After accepting a multitude of kisses and bear hugs from Aidan, and debriefing with her parents on the boy's busy day, Gin finally pulled up a chair next to mine.

"What's this about Daytona? I thought you were just going to test for now. This is a car to drive in the 24?"

"I know, I know, not what we had planned, but JP says it's a quality ride, and I guess he spoke to the team owner who's willing to offer us the car for the race."

"Does he know you've never driven that kind of car before?"

I squirmed a bit, sounding it out on Gin before I tried it on for real. "Well, I suspect Jim didn't really tell him the full story, but JP thinks I'm ready." I added an endorsement for emphasis. "He said so himself tonight, just now."

"And who gets to pay for this little adventure—let me guess, not JP or the team owner, right?"

I hadn't thought it all the way through, but I had the makings of an early defense. "I'll try to get some sponsorship—I have a few ideas already—and we'll split the car with another driver or two, whatever it takes to make it possible."

"And what about the risk, what about that little issue, have you given that any thought?" Gin copped to her biggest concern.

I softened a bit and whistled right on by that particular graveyard. "It's only a GT car, and they're not like running a prototype. The risk is nearly non-existent, really."

Gin frowned a bit, not willing to express true misgivings right at that very moment. "Well, you'll need to talk to the insurance agent about all this, but I guess we'll talk more about that later.

I wasn't planning on her collecting on any life insurance benefits anytime in the near future, but I agreed. She had me there, and I couldn't argue it in any other direction that ended with me racing.

"OK, I'll call Bernie tomorrow, and get that straightened out, but I'm hoping it's a moot point."

"Well, for you, anyway."

"Thanks, Baby, your sincerity and tenderness are touching."

When I arrived home from work the next evening, I found a new bathroom scale laid out for me upstairs. "What's this?" I mustered, knowing full well what it was.

"I bought that for you today. You know, you can't go racing at Daytona, not in some endurance event against a bunch of pro drivers, and show up there out of shape. If you're going to do this, I figure you better get in shape and get that extra weight off."

I hugged my wife closely and kissed the top of her head. "Is that the only reason you want me to have the scale?"

"Well, it might be nice to have you around a bit longer, and I think you'd be healthier if you lost the pounds and got back in the gym. It can't hurt the racing either, right?"

"If for no other reason, I'd be embarrassed to show up there looking like an over-the-hill surgeon. Fear of embarrassment is a strong motivator, I'm guessing. We'll see, but I agree with you, and I'll try. I'll get back in the gym starting tomorrow."

Ginny laughed as she pointed out a t-shirt and shorts that she had laid out on the bed. "I'll have dinner ready right after you're done working out. Better get started, big guy. And no pasta and wine tonight."

With that, my wife squirmed out of my arms and pushed me off to get into workout mode, indicating it was time to get my act together. Of many wonderful presents that Ginny has gotten for me over time, this was surely one of the best. She had announced her support, pushed back her fears far enough to get past them, and added her own energy to my adventure.

And for that, I loved her even more, even as I sweated away in my basement gym.

Chapter Twelve

I had done what I needed to do, I thought. A thirty-plus-pound weight loss, countless hours in the gym, many more than that meeting with and talking to potential sponsors, and lots of laps running nose-to-tail with Jim Pace. The entirety of my focus, it seemed, in the last three months, had been about getting here. This moment. This place. Regardless of whether or not my preparation was adequate for the task in front of me, I at least knew that I hadn't left anything on the table. I was as ready as one might become, especially for something about which I had no personal exposure or knowledge. Like an explorer packing his kit for a place he's never been, I had guessed more than a bit and relied on hopefully sage advice to get to this point. And I knew, for sure, that the time to second-guess all of that was past.

I had arrived at Daytona for the 2006 official test days in January, Grand-Am's three-day practice session before the end of the month's Rolex 24 Hours of Daytona race.

Touching down at the Daytona airport on the runway adjacent to the track, I felt my pulse quicken as we taxied past the high stadium walls of the backstretch. From the outside, everything looked just as I remembered, having been to Daytona International Speedway a few times before for Skip Barber events. The structure was intimidating in its bulk from the outside, but I knew the real heart-quickening moment would come from viewing the track itself once inside. Like few other places in the world, Daytona's sheer scale was difficult to comprehend. For a guy used to the typical college football stadium, the scope and size of a Daytona was another world altogether. One needed to drive, not walk, from point to point inside the track; the infield would easily fit not just one, but probably a few football fields within the confines of the track surface itself. And the track—well, the track was immense. You could stand in the infield, say, in the campgrounds, and be virtually surrounded by the panorama of the high-banked asphalt turns and long stretches in between. Supersized high and wide, the place was immense and menacing, especially on first look.

Exiting the plane, I was met on the tarmac by Jim Pace and my co-driver Revere Greist. Both wore big smiles as we shook hands and exchanged greetings. JP began with his now familiar "Welcome to Daytona, Dr. Lowe," as if I was a medical conference attendee and not some guy about to don a helmet and attempt unwise things at high speed.

Despite the low-eighties temps, the hair was standing up on the back of my neck. "Hey JP, hey Revere, great to see you guys. Can't believe we're here. This is awesome!"

Revere grinned as Jim reminded me, "We're not out of the airport yet, cowboy; save some of that energy for tomorrow."

"I know, but this is great! So glad it's finally here."

"Well alright," JP drawled, "Let's get credentials and head over to the track. They should be unloading about now, so we'll meet Kevin, and say hi to the crew."

I asked Revere if he had been over there yet.

"Not yet. We were waiting on you before we went in and met everyone. I haven't seen the car yet, but I did see the TRG hauler go by when I came in. Very cool." The normally laid-back Revere added, "I can't wait to get in there and get going."

We drove over to the Grand-Am office to pick up our credentials and lanyards, joining the lines of drivers getting paperwork done and headshots taken for their hard cards. More than a few guys in line looked familiar, and JP introduced us to several guys he knew from both past racing and coaching. As I was turning to leave, Johnny O'Connell walked in, briefcase in hand and looking every bit the hired gun pro driver. I surely looked the part of the mindless fan, as I stood there, mumbling "Hello, pleased to meet you," as Jim introduced Revere and me to the multi-time Le Mans-winning factory GM driver. JP and Johnny chatted for a moment before we headed for the door.

"Good luck, fellas," offered Johnny O as he joined the line.

Sure, Johnny, it's just another race for us. On the same track as you. Probably getting in your way. Please don't hit me. "Thanks man, good to be here. See you out there." Ho hum, just another day racing against some world famous guy.

As we approached the track, JP continued with step-by-step instructions. "OK, time to get your credentials out, we'll go in the turn four tunnel, which I think is the only way in this afternoon." We flashed our hard cards to the gate security guys, who peeked and waved us through. I waved back, as if this was an everyday occurrence for me. Look like you belong, and no one will stop you, right? Surely, these guys recognized real drivers, I thought—yet I had made it past the first line of defense without any alarms going off. Not quite as exciting as The Great Escape but I felt like I had just gotten away with something all the same.

Down into the tunnel we went, painted green on the entrance side and black and white checkered on the outgoing side, emerging shortly into bright sunshine and the inner sanctum of Daytona. Feeling like a kid on the jungle ride at Disney, I watched as JP narrated the highlights of the visible track and infield sections. "Behind us is the NASCAR turn four, where there's a bump in the track from the tunnel we just came through. Straight ahead is the camping area, which will be full for race day. If you break down off the back straight, watch out for Boy Scouts as you find your way back to the garage. The paddock for Grand-Am is up to our right, but we'll have to park here for today. Later, we can probably move the car to the motor home parking spots in the driver/owner lot."

Jim continued his narration as I looked around, shocked at the magnitude of what was really only the tip of the iceberg. Having been to Daytona only for Skip Barber events, I wasn't used to anything resembling a crowded event. Running Skippy races was in fact a good way to ensure anonymity: rarely did anyone attend those events, except girlfriends and the occasional dutiful spouse, and there were no teams needed to service drivers and crew. One could probably reliably reside in the witness protection program and still safely run selected Skippy races. This scene was something completely and altogether different.

The incoming driver cars and team vans were being parked on the grass outside of the paddock gates, and a steady stream of colorfully-clad personnel were heading for the main gates. Crew guys were easily identifiable by the requisite black work pants and matching colored shirts. Drivers were more typically attired in jeans and casual shirts—as if the wearing of team shirts was passé for those who should be recognized by their famous faces alone. A few of the lucky ones rode in golf carts towards the chain linked fenced enclosure; team owners zipped by, driven by hospitality workers and assistants, seemingly oblivious to the crush to get into the entrance gates.

Behind those gates, the first immediately obvious structures were the race team haulers, neatly nosed in side-by-side, all with their back ends open and in various stages of disgorging race cars and equipment. As we approached the garages, the noise level grew, with crews shouting to each other and the gaps punctuated by the high-pitched Braaappppp of pneumatic guns in use. Revere, JP, and I walked three abreast, carrying helmet bags and backpacks towards the haulers, falling in line with a few hundred other guys similarly equipped. As Jim greeted several friends, and occasionally stopped to chat and introduce us, Revere and I just kept staring at the view ahead. Colors. Noise. Activity. Cars, golf carts, pedestrians mixing in a seemingly random fashion, everybody going everywhere all at once: watch yourself or you'll get run over – hey buddy coming thru – good time to be alert or you'll be a casualty and not a participant.

Revere and I walked together, wide-eyed at the circus literally unloading before us. "This is too cool," observed my co-driver, a bit unnecessarily. Everywhere one looked race cars were being released from haulers, gently lowered to the ground from their secure second-deck berths in the mammoth trailers, and pushed into their garages by grunting crew members. For even the most casual fans of any type of racing, the view was impressive. Cars were in various stages of undress, some up on jacks, and others with large sections of bodywork or other bits missing. It was at once wonderful and scary, like stumbling on a secret world of chaos and commotion and then plunging headlong into its center.

As we searched out the TRG garages, JP stopped frequently to introduce Revere and me to one racer after another. Drivers, engineers, crew, and team personnel alike all seemed to know Jim, and each seemed to genuinely welcome us to Daytona. While I can't now recall specific people I met, other than a few of the guys from my own team, the introductions seemed endless and the interactions overwhelming. Walk, stop, shake hands, explain in two sentences or less what I was doing there, try not to get run down by a tire carrier, and keep making my way to the end of the line. It was all a blur of motion and movement, made more intense by the adrenaline rush of commencement. After months of planning and hard work, I was finally on the ground and rushing unchecked toward my first pro event at Daytona.

The highlight of any first-day garage walk was yet to come: Approaching the last few garage stalls, I could see several blue and silver Porsche GT race cars arrayed side by side. We had finally come to the TRG encampment, where Kevin Buckler's team was arranging space for the six GT cars they were running for the event. The two Pontiac factory TRG cars occupied prime space closer to the action, but the next four garages held Porsches. Ours, number 68 (being superstitious, I was an immediate non-fan of the number, but more about that later), was third in line and already surrounded by blue-shirted mechanics and crew. As Revere, Jim, and I walked in that direction, I had to consciously restrain myself from skipping the last several feet while simultaneously considering running the other way.

With the car sitting there, being readied for action, there was no way now to change my mind and beg out. There was driving to be done, this was the machine to do it in, and all were expecting me to be one of the perpetrators behind the wheel. And this was no entry-level open wheel racer. The 400 hp, 2,800-pound GT3 Cup car was all business, with a standard six-speed transmission and a top end around 180 mph. With adjustable shocks, anti-roll bars, and ant-lock racing brakes, the Porsche was one of the better endurance racers in recent history. In the cyclical tradition of 24-hour racing, Porsches had been recently so successful that they were clearly the weapon of choice for front-of-the-pack teams. Wide shoulders, wider haunches, graceful curves, and bold striping defined the car's sleek strength and power. Standing close to the car at last, I again felt the adrenaline surge, in a familiar mixture of anticipation and dread; the thing looked mean, fast, brutish, and definitely foreign. I wasn't sure whether I would in fact ever be in charge while behind the wheel of this machine, but I knew I was shortly about to get on and attempt to ride it.

As I stared, Revere whistled softly as he circled the car, moving one hand along the bodywork and pausing occasionally to step back and look at some detail or other. JP appeared at my side and elbowed me playfully.

"What'ya think, Dr. Lowe? Pretty sweet, huh? Wait till you get some laps in her—I'll bet you forget all about driving that single-seater once you get up to speed in this thing."

I started stuttering, resurrecting an old habit that surfaced when I was overly excited or worried, or both, as was the case now. "I—ah—I'm—wow, this is—that's pretty cool—whew! I wasn't sure what to expect, but—wow."

Jim grinned at me. "Well said, Jim. I take it you're impressed."

"Yeah, a—a little, yep." I swallowed hard, failing completely in my efforts at looking calm and cool about all of this.

"Hey guys, I'm Tommy Sadler, I'm going to be the crew chief for the 68 car this month." Tommy stuck out his hand, greeting JP, Revere and me as we all stared at the car together.

Introductions were made all around, and several other crew members stopped momentarily to add to the list of names I'd have to learn over the next few days. All were welcoming, sincere, and polite enough not to ask for my driver credentials and some proof of ability. I enjoyed the feeling of the initiate again, happily being invited to play, and not yet being criticized for any lack of performance. That would surely come later, once the time sheets were out. For as much as the crew welcomed the new driver, they would know for sure if I wasn't up to snuff. These guys were pros, and they expected the drivers to bring game, or at least not to make unreasonable amounts of excess work for them. Either way, they'd soon figure it out, and I would need to come down on the "acceptable" side of the performance line or pick another dream to chase.

Finished with introductions, JP then demonstrated how to get into the car. Although this might seem obvious, there is a bit of trickery involved in inserting oneself into the race car without winding up impossibly contorted or worse. With external bodywork stretched over the internal roll cage, there is a limited opening for driver ingress and egress; the aperture is about the size of the average road car side window. With the door open, the driver has to basically sit on the horizontal bar of the roll cage, grab an overhead bar for support, and swing bent legs into the cockpit, avoiding the steering wheel and gear shift while sliding feet, then torso, down into position. Upon watching an experienced racer enter a car, one might assume that this is an easy maneuver to master. I've gotten better over the years but never perfected the art myself. However, I once witnessed a comical instance of an entry attempt gone horribly wrong—in which the driver, a somewhat rotund older chap, with supposed experience in such things, tried to get in head-first during a driver change in the middle of a race—a race!—and promptly got stuck, legs wiggling furiously out the window, Winnie-the-Pooh-like, until rescued—so I know others also find it to be a tricky maneuver.

With JP's step-by-step instructions, I seated myself in the Porsche for the first time, and did what virtually everyone does: I grabbed the steering wheel, reflexively turning it left and right, and earned a quick "Yo!" from the mechanic working on the right front wheel.

"Sorry!" I yelled, immediately dropping my hands into my lap and smiling sheepishly at Jim and Revere.

I wedged my butt down into the narrow seat, surprised at the firmness of the sides, and the softer cushion of the back. My feet sought out the pedals, and I wiggled until I actually felt like I was in something resembling a driving position. Glancing at mirrors, rear and sides, I marveled at the good visibility out of the front and side glass, along with the rear-view past the roll cage components and numerous wires hanging throughout the cockpit. Switches and buttons crowded the dash, and the steering wheel itself had several knobs and buttons, currently unlabeled, all of which added to the aircraft cockpit-like appearance of the interior.

Getting last-minute advice from JP before first laps in the Porsche at Daytona, 2006

JP leaned in the window and started the tutorial. "Here's your key buttons and switches on the dash—on the right is the master, next to that is the ignition—flip that up for 'on'—and then push the button on the left to fire her up. To shut it down, just put the ignition into the 'down' position; leave the master on until they tell you to turn it off."

I looked further down the dash as Jim continued. "Down below there's the 'low fuel' warning, which will glow red when you're getting near empty. If you see that, call it in on the radio and then hit the 'reserve' button right there next to it."

"What's the other red button down there?" I pointed to a red button, dusty and covered in plastic.

"That's pretty important. That's the fire extinguisher bottle—make sure you hit that on your way out of the car when there's a fire."

As I contemplated this tidbit of information, a mechanic stuck his head in the window. "Yeah, and if you do push it, you'll be the first driver I've ever seen do that. For some reason, you guys are always in a big hurry when the car's on fire."

I feigned a casual attitude towards the prospect of a flaming car as Jim continued on. "If you do catch fire, there's another button to push out here on the hood area—extra points if you stop to hit that one before you get away."

We laughed in the way nervous magicians do, trying on some false bravado for size. After all, if one thinks too long and hard about getting extra-crispy while driving a race car, one probably isn't cut out to be in there in the first place. And thinking a lot didn't seem to help as much as being prepared for the possibility of a quick, unplanned exit from an already tight space.

I was reflecting on how much more complicated the 'Stop, drop and roll' maneuver had just become when I heard a new voice. "Hey, what's this talk about fire? Nobody's catching on fire in one of my cars!" Kevin Buckler had arrived in his usual whirlwind style, sporting an always-on Bluetooth device in one ear, wrap-around sunglasses, and a shit-eating grin. In his late forties, the energetic and self-described "curly-haired motherfucker from California" introduced himself to Revere and me, greeting JP like an old and trusted friend. With much success already in the sports car racing world, including a surprise overall win at the 24 Hours of Daytona in 2003, Buckler was a legend in and around the paddock. Having been a successful driver, Kevin was now the owner of The Racers Group, and one of the hardest working guys in racing. Running both factory-backed pro efforts, and also a slew of customer cars for select events and series, Buckler was well-known as a 'deal guy' and someone who put asses in seats and winning efforts on the track.

This year Kevin's usual Porsche effort had been modified significantly by an agreement for TRG to run Pontiac race cars for the General Motors team. Among his eight drivers for those two cars in this year's Rolex 24 were five "factory" drivers—guys employed by GM for the sole purpose of driving their cars faster than everyone else. Because of this deal, Buckler had a mountain of work outside of the customer car Porsche efforts that the riffraff, like me, were running at the 2006 24. As a result, the apparently usually energetic TRG domo was in overdrive mode, with only a portion of the time available for the paying Porsche customers.

Despite this, it was generally agreed that manning a Porsche for the 24 Hours of Daytona was one way to optimize a driver's chance to get a win. The marque had great history at Daytona (not to mention other endurance races, like that big sister event in Le Mans), and TRG was recognized as the team to be in if one's choice was Porsche. Kevin Buckler had a rolodex that looked like a 'Who's Who' in the world of Porsche racing and the trophies to back up the big reputation. Despite the obviously strained demands on his schedule, I figured we were all likely in the right place for this event, or at least in the best place to get one's feet well wet for a first pro race.

"Great having you guys here, nice to meet you both. JP told me all about you guys. I think this is a great car and you guys are really gonna surprise some people here." Kevin never failed to exude a rapid-fire confidence, especially when it encouraged drivers willing to expand their expenditures with TRG. "Make sure you get all squared away today, because tomorrow's busy. Lots of track time. And don't forget, there's a team meeting tonight at Buca's. I'm gonna have to take this call—it's GM on the phone—see you guys later."

With that, Kevin was gone, heading on to massage the next driver and schmooze the next bigwig. I shook my head like I was trying to clear water from my ears as JP pronounced, "Well, that was Kevin in full attack mode. He's like a whirlwind—a force in the paddock." Revere, who was equally new to the pro endurance racing world, just muttered, "Wow," and resumed his inspection of the car.

Once we were all finished with settling into the seat—attempting a few adjustments to pads, belts, and steering wheel position—it was time to head out and check into the hotel. Jim deliberately took us on the long route out of the garage area, stopping by the Grand-Am trailer parked at the front of the row so that we could meet the series principles. Mark Raffauf, series managing director, was introduced, although his harried position as the main problem-solver only allowed time for an informal "Welcome, guys" interaction. Other faces appeared and vanished as I abandoned my attempts to keep up with all of the different names and job titles. As we moved on, JP reassured me, "For now, the only one you have to remember is Raffauf—he's the guy you don't want to meet with because he's the one you answer to if you screw up."

Always wanting to be keenly aware of where my low-profile efforts would be best served, I thanked Jim for the information, and silently resolved to stay off Mark's radar. Following the best advice I had been given before leaving for USMC boot camp—"Make sure your name is the last one they learn"—I vowed to avoid trouble and make sure I stayed low and out of harm's way. For sure the racing world and its inhabitants were quick to recognize those who added risk or otherwise stood out for the wrong reasons, and I was equally sure that I wanted nothing to do with that kind of recognition.

Freshly showered and shaved, I joined Jim and Revere in the lobby of the hotel, ready to head out for the TRG team dinner. As we greeted each other, I spied a number of famous faces, identifying series-regulars such as Wayne Taylor, Max Angelelli, and Hurley Haywood. All greeted Jim like a good friend, especially Wayne, who had partnered with JP for their 1996 overall win in the 24. Allowing myself to be a bit star-struck, I enjoyed brushing elbows with guys who were familiar to me only from watching and reading about races. Once again I reminded myself that we'd soon be on the same track together, and once again I silently worried that I might mess up their—not our—race.

As we were escorted into the back room of Buca di Beppo where the

TRG dinner was being held, I glimpsed more familiar racers sitting down for dinner with teammates. Everywhere, it seemed, were guys dressed in matching logoed shirts, all of whom apparently knew Jim and some of whom raised an eyebrow when introduced to his co-drivers. Entering the room reserved for Kevin's group, I spotted a few mechanics and drivers I had met earlier that afternoon; also present were several of TRG's pro drivers manning the Pontiac factory effort. Andy Lally, Kelly Collins, and Jan Magnussen stood out as guys I recognized and had already rooted for while watching various races on TV. Each now greeted Jim, Revere, and me, chatting as if we were all there for a campout or weenie roast. Formal introductions followed once Kevin made an appearance, still with phone in hand and energy level pegged.

Smiling broadly, Buckler welcomed the group to Daytona, making a point of introducing each driver and several new crew members. Kevin's ability to make each person feel a special and desired part of the proceedings was uncanny; he somehow managed to predict great things simultaneously from all of the drivers present, ignoring the unlikelihood of a six-way tie for first. Once the established pros and new and veteran amateurs were introduced, Kevin then offered up a few words of wisdom applicable to all: Keep it on the track, don't wreck yourself in the bus stop chicane, start off easy tomorrow, and more of the same. Most of the drivers just smiled. Likely none of them were entertaining thoughts of crashing anywhere soon, although I had been trying for some time not to think about that particular aspect of the coming event—with mixed results. I put on a brave face anyway, hoping I looked confident enough not to warrant any sideways glances from the regular runners.

Our route back to the hotel after dinner took us down International Speedway Boulevard and past the track. As I looked at the looming bulk of the grandstands rising in the darkness outside the passenger side window, I marveled at fact that I would be driving there in just a few hours. JP interrupted my thoughts as he pointed out, "They don't have the lights on now, but tomorrow we'll have a chance to drive with the track lit up. It'll be fun and a great way to get used to driving at night, just like in the race."

"Any tricks to that?" I asked Jim as I continued staring at the stands outside of the trioval.

"Just remember, the car doesn't know it's dark out. Relax, hit your marks, and forget about the fact that it's nighttime."

Unsure as to whether or not I might need more instruction than that the next night, I stowed away the thought and remained silent until we got back to the hotel.

With logistical specifics confirmed for the next morning, JP, Revere, and I said our good nights and dispersed to our rooms. In my room, I fussed about, trying to settle in and relax enough to actually think about sleep. Seeking comfort in routine and repetition, I packed and repacked my helmet bag and backpack, reviewing my mental checklist several times as I tried to decide what critical object to forget. I finally got horizontal and comfortable, eventually falling asleep while reading Jon Krakauer's Into Thin Air. I dreamt of climbing mountains in dark storms, wandering lost, and wondering where I had parked the car and why my friends all were walking away from me, rather than helping.

***

Shortly before 5 a.m. I sat bolt upright in bed, alert and with little of that typical "Where am I, what day is it?" waking confusion. Wondering again what it was that made me believe this was all a good idea, and questioning again Jim Pace's judgment, I headed into the bathroom to clean up. As I dressed, I fought down a sensation familiar from days long past: I was nauseated and anxious, fighting negative thoughts while recognizing excitement over the prospect of the driving just ahead. Standing at the window, I opened the bland tan curtains enough to see the shape of the track across the street emerging with the dawn. I couldn't decide whether Daytona was welcoming or threatening as its outline grew more distinct before me, and so I did what I've always done in those circumstances: I kept moving forward, grabbing my bags and heading off to breakfast, not at all certain that it was for the best.

We ate at the Hilton Garden Inn's dining room, which was noticeably crowded with racers, along with a few journalists. JP made more introductions, and I worked at perfecting an air of calm confidence. Revere, Jim, and I occupied an out of the way table, and I ate carefully as JP laid out the plan for the day.

"OK, it's a long day today, with lots of track time, and some night time running at the end. Let's relax, get comfortable in the car, and see how we feel after a few laps. I'll go first to shake off the rust and make any changes that need to be done right away. If the car is OK, we'll get you guys both in there before the end of the first session. Lots of time though, so we'll be flexible with the plan."

"Will we have time to go over the car again before we start?"

Jim was in full Sensei mode. "There will be plenty of time—remember, we've got three days here. No rushing, no panic, just put our heads down and get laps in. You're not here to impress, just to get comfortable in the car and get the feel of the track. Lots of time."

Revere and I nodded, listening to the master as he calmed our nerves.

"OK, let's saddle up and get over to the track. We'll have enough time to say hello to the crew before the drivers' meeting."

After navigating the security check at the gate and parking the car, the three of us again joined the line of drivers and crew heading towards the paddock gate. I could see that the garage area was already in full action mode, with people moving purposefully about and pit vehicles of all types playing chicken with pedestrians. Engines were firing, warming in the brisk sunshine as crews tried to get heat in the fluids and themselves. The PA system crackled, and some unintelligible test message was repeated every few seconds, interrupting the classic rock playing in the background.

As we walked closer, Revere looked at me, grinning ear to ear. "It feels just like Christmas morning."

Only slightly less anxious than before, I replied, "Yeah, well, I'm wondering whether Santa's about to kick my ass."

JP and Revere chuckled as we followed the queue through the gates.

We checked in with the guys in the garage, noting that the car was already warming up, with a mechanic working the throttle from the engine bay in the back. Tommy Sadler was hard at work, supervising two guys stringing the wheels—adjusting and checking the camber and toe of the wheels for proper set-up—and simultaneously running down his checklist.

"Hey fellas, ready to go?" JP was greeted by Tommy as he wiped his hands on a blackened rag.

"We're all good on this end. How's she doing?"

"Just getting the last bits in. I've got a few degrees of toe in her; once you warm up the tires, let me know how that works out. If you want to make a change, we can do that between sessions."

"Springs?" asked Jim.

"The usual spread—same as Kevin is running to begin with on the other Porsches. One thousand on the front and eight hundred on the rear."

"Copy that, thanks. We're going to head over to the drivers' meeting. Do you need our helmets to check the radios?"

Tommy obviously appreciated Jim's attention to detail. "Yep. Leave them with Charlie and we'll check them before the session starts."

We started to walk towards the meeting room, waving to several more drivers as they moved towards their garages. "At some point, can we sit down and go over the mechanics of the car, the settings, adjustments, and all that?" I asked Jim. "I feel like you're talking a foreign language in there."

JP again reassured me. "Not to worry, Dr. Lowe, it's just like anatomy and physiology. You'll learn the details, and as you drive the car, the different components and adjustments will make more sense. Plenty of time. But today, it's about relaxing and driving the car."

Jim sure was a big fan of being relaxed, I thought; maybe I'm thinking about this all wrong. "OK, I'm on board, but don't assume I always know what you're talking about, OK?"

"Your job today is to just relax and drive, nice and easy, just like always."

Sure, just like always. Except that there was no actual "always" for me. I had never driven a Porsche of any kind before and had never driven anything approaching these speeds. And oh yeah, there would be more than a few much faster guys out there to boot. I shook off the thought and kept pace with Revere and Jim into the meeting room.

The view on entering the drivers briefing was one that I still look forward to each January. Approximately two hundred eighty drivers, several team owners, and scores of crew chiefs and engineers were packed into Daytona's Media Center meeting room. Everywhere I looked, well-known drivers mingled with friends and fellow competitors, with virtually all disciplines of racing represented. Formula One guys, Indy car drivers, NASCAR legends, and sports car stalwarts from five different continents all jockeyed for position, filling the back of the room first, just like the cool kids in school. For most, this get-together was the first opportunity of the new season to catch up and renew contacts after what for almost all was an intolerably long offseason. I stuck close by JP and Revere as we took our seats, nudging Jim and Revere sporadically with each different sighting. I picked out Paul Tracy, Dan Wheldon, Allan McNish, Danica Patrick, Tony Stewart, Dario Franchitti, Kyle Petty, and scores of other heroes and idols as if reviewing my own living who's who list. They were all here, breathing the same stale air as one lowly and intimidated neurosurgeon rookie driver. And soon we would be sharing the same asphalt. I sat quietly, thinking that I better quickly perfect the point-by passing maneuver.

Mark Raffauf ran the meeting, eventually getting around to the usual platitudes about keeping everyone safe, looking out for the less experienced drivers (I almost raised my hand on that one), and generally being courteous on track and off. Of the few actually paying close attention, I suspected that all thought themselves excluded from the unnecessary risk-taker club; most wouldn't have been there at all if they didn't have the upmost faith in their ability to go faster than everyone else. I was painfully aware that I didn't fit into that already established club, but like the days of my Springfield childhood, I was just happy to be around the real players and this time with the opportunity to actually play.

The three of us walked back through the garage area gates and kept on out into the driver/owner lot across the alleyway where we found our RV warmed up and ready. There we changed into flame-retardant underwear and driver suits while Jim reviewed the plan and offered more advice for the day.

"Let's get out there early in the session and see what kind of shape the car's in. If I need to make any changes, I'll do that, but the goal is to get you guys in and get up to speed." I swallowed hard as Jim laid out the driver order. "Jim, you'll go after me; once you've had enough laps to work up a sweat, we'll call you in and get Revere in there." Shit. I had thought Revere would be going first. Wishful thinking perhaps, but I now needed to accelerate my mental preparation routine. Except I didn't have one of those.

I stuffed my balaclava and gloves into my helmet and headed out after JP and Revere. This wasn't some dream where I walked around outside a racetrack while trying to find my equipment, frantically realizing that they were starting without me. No, I was here, awake, at Daytona, and about to get in and drive. Really fast, with pros all around me. In full view of everyone. OK, time to man up. It's here and it's what you prepared for, right?

At the garage, Jim got ready to get into the Porsche as the mechanics warmed up the engine. I stood nearby with Revere, both of us holding our helmets, observing the routine JP used to mount up and get going. Tommy Sadler pulled up on a golf cart and offered to drive Revere and me to the pits; JP waved, and shouted through the helmet "See you in a few minutes." We both patted the car on the backside just as Jim engaged reverse and crept out of the garage; a moment later we were headed out to Daytona's pit lane and the business end of the circus.

We reached the TRG pit complex a few minutes before the session went green. With six cars running for the test, there were about forty mechanics, crew, and other personnel associated with TRG positioned along the wall. In addition, with three or four drivers per car, there was a significant volume of driver gear strewn about the tables under the pit awnings. Drivers familiar from the Buca di Beppo dinner crowded the pit area, with several already helmeted and prepared to jump in their rides. While many others wore headphones or radio earplugs, I deliberately kept mine in the pocket of my fire suit so as to get a clear first aural immersion in the sound of the session starting up. I waited along the edge of the low concrete wall, mesmerized by the sight of seventy-two race cars all lined up and ready to leave Daytona's pit lane.

As the lights at the end of pit lane turned from red to green, the immediate explosion of noise was deafening. Within seconds, all seventy-two engines had fired, followed by drivers dropping clutches and peeling out of pit lane in an attempt to get heat into their tires. One after the other, the engines protested against rev limiters on their way to full rpms while sticker tires traced black trails all the way down to the pit exit. I smiled wide until I couldn't help it anymore, and then started laughing out loud at the visceral sensation of the engine vibrations combined with the sound. Although no one could hear me over the racket, Revere looked over at me as he too failed to suppress a big grin. Although we were positioned about twenty feet apart, we did a phantom high-five before leaning back over the wall to watch the cars rolling off.

Knowing that JP would be back into the pits in a few laps, I stretched and then donned helmet and gloves in preparation for my first stint. Heart racing and mouth dry, I stood next to the pit stand, and watched the pit-in area for the sight of the 68. As Jim decelerated at the pit entry cone, I caught sight of the blue and silver Porsche, heading towards me. My ride was here.

I hopped over the wall as Jim brought the car to a halt in the pit box. As the car went up on its pneumatic jacks, JP jumped out and gestured to me as I waited alongside the left rear of the car. I took a few steps toward him and craned my neck to bring my ear closer to his helmet.

"The car feels fine. The gearbox is a little notchy, so go slow on the shifts. She moves around a bit on the banking, but just ignore that and you'll be fine. Have fun. I'll be on the radio in a minute."

The mechanic at the door stood back, holding the netting back in one hand and the door open with the other. I squeezed past him, and managed to slide into the seat just like we had practiced. I wiggled downward until I felt tight in the seat and then connected the belts, tightening each sequentially until I could barely inhale. I pressed down on the radio button and announced, "Radio check, radio check."

There was a high-pitched click as Tommy's voice came into my ears. "Radio check. Loud and clear. Go ahead and fire it up."

With my right hand I pushed the ignition toggle switch into the up position. Depressing the clutch, I reached towards the start button with my left hand. As I was about to hit the button, my forefinger stopped about two inches short of the button. I strained against the shoulder belts, but couldn't bridge the gap.

"Go ahead, let's get it started."

"Sorry, but I can't reach the starter. Give me a minute here."

Although they were too polite to laugh on the radio, I did spy several of the crew smiling as I worked the belts a little looser. Positioned better, I reached for the button and felt the beautiful vibration of the engine as I worked the throttle after it fired.

"Jim, JP here. Start out nice and easy, warm your tires and your brain, and see how you feel."

"Copy that, thanks JP, I'm on my way."

Stalling the car on first launch is a proud racing tradition, and I complied admirably with the custom. Refiring the engine, I managed to get enough revs into it to launch out of the pit box and proceeded down Daytona's pit lane for my first laps in a Porsche.

Jim's first laps in the Porsche, testing at Daytona, 2006

Arriving at the pit exit, I waited until I passed the Grand-Am official before I disengaged the pit lane speed limiter, spinning the tires a bit as I accelerated towards the pit exit. I navigated the narrow pit-out road, shifting up into second as I joined the track at the entry to the east horseshoe turn. As the car surged onto the track, I glanced into my right side mirror in time to glimpse two prototypes diving down to my right, braking late to the inside of the turn as I struggled to bend the car to the right.

I stayed wide of the apex, allowing at least two other cars to pass me on the inside, and then accelerated up towards the kink. Immediately, I had trouble getting the gearbox to cooperate, needing an extra shove to get the car into third gear. I made it through the next two turns, stirring the stick a bit in an attempt to select the proper gear. Working hard at coordinating throttle input and clutch release, I still had big trouble getting the gears to engage. I tried to ignore all that, however, as I was about to head onto the banking for the first time.

Exiting turn six, I pushed my foot flat on the floor, breathing off the gas only to shift upwards. I felt the car move up onto Daytona's banking and reminded myself that the oval section of the track would be flat out in this car. Like a climber trusting the strength of his nylon rope, I knew that I needed to have faith in the car—flat out was called for here, and there was no time like the present.

Hugging the bottom lane of the banking, I felt the smooth pull of the Porsche's flat-six engine as the view out my windscreen morphed rapidly. Accelerating around NASCAR's turn two, I gripped the steering wheel hard as the front end of the car got light and started to move. The sensation was bizarre, although I figured this was what JP had warned me about. As the speed increased, the front end of the car started to literally bounce around on the pavement. There wasn't any abrupt direction change occurring, but the intensity of the vibration and bucking of the car was simply amazing. As I transitioned down on the flatter section of the back straight, the car relaxed a bit. I eased off the throttle early and did a definitely relaxed brake into the bus stop chicane. Left, right, relax a moment, and then a quick right-left later I was back up on the banking.

The Porsche began bouncing around again as I sought out the lowest lane on the wide banked turn. I managed to find fifth and then sixth gear again, accelerating up to 165 mph as I crossed the start-finish stripe of the trioval. I tried not to think about the number on the speedo, given that the fastest I had ever been before that was about a buck-twenty in a Skip Barber car.

Looking ahead, I was alarmed at how fast the entry to turn one was approaching. In addition, several colorful shapes were visible in my mirrors as they bore down on me on the front straight. I lifted off the gas entirely too early, but given my unfamiliarity with the Porsche's brakes, I wasn't planning a hero lap just yet anyway. With amazing force, the GT3's binders engaged enough to slow me to a nearly full stop several brake markers before the actual turn-in point. I again struggled to get the transmission to cooperate, working the clutch and the stick furiously, trying to run down though the gears into the second-gear turn.

As I worked my way into the three-apex complex that was the infield's first two turns, two Daytona Prototypes bracketed me as they lost patience and passed me simultaneously. I breathed a sigh of relief as they got by and focused on the first hairpin up ahead. Slowing for the turn, I again was unable to find an easy fit as I tried to work my way down to first gear. A feeling of disbelief invaded the cockpit as I struggled with the gearshift, not willing to believe that I couldn't even execute a simple shift properly. I knew that there would be some getting used to the new gearbox after so many years of driving a sequential shifter, but this was ridiculous. Although the one-direction nature of the sequential was much easier, I hadn't thought that the old standard-H pattern would be so difficult in a racing Porsche.

I winced with each attempt to get into a new gear, but made my way through the infield one more time. But by the time I was moving out of turn six and up onto the banking again, the noise from the gearbox was awful.

"Uh, Guys, I'm having some trouble shifting out here." I didn't want to cry wolf but this was just brutal, and I was now worried that I was going to kill the thing dead.

JP clicked on. "Just go slow on the shifts, and it'll be better when it warms up some. Big blips should help."

I tried to take the advice, but by the time I was in the bus stop for the second time, I couldn't select third gear at all.

"Sorry guys, but I can't shift at all now. I think I should come in."

I could almost hear Tommy sigh over the radio. "Pit now, Pit now."

I exited the car as the mechanics engaged the pneumatic jacks and popped open the rear deck lid. "Sorry, Tommy, but I can't shift this thing. It just won't go into gear for me. I tried bigger blips, but even the upshifts are a challenge."

JP motioned for me to join him under the cover of the pit awning. "If you can't shift it, it was smart to come in. Let them take a look, and maybe you can jump back in there in a minute or two."

One of the TRG mechanics jumped into the car, fired the engine, and started to work the shifter. Horrible grinding noises emanated from the machine as I leaned helpless against a table in the pits. I couldn't believe I had broken the car in my first five minutes driving—attempting to drive—it. A new record, for sure.

A moment later, Tommy had finished conferring with the mechanics, and he made his way over to Jim, Revere, and me. "We're going back to the garage to get a better look. We can't get the gears to engage right. We'll roll it back and figure out what the problem is, but for now we're done."

JP patted me on the back, as Revere turned to collect his helmet and gloves. "Nothing to do now, we'll have to wait and see what's up. Let's head back there with the crew and check it out. Don't worry just yet."

"I don't know what went wrong. It's not like I can't work a standard shift pattern. That was crazy—I was worried a bit about shifting, but I didn't think it would be like that."

"We don't know what the deal is yet. Let's go check with the crew."

By the time we made it back to the garage, the car was already shedding pieces as the crew tore into the rear end and began the search for the problem. I wasn't sure what they would find, but I was pretty sure that the damage would have my name all over it.

As the guys worked, I stood off to one side, watching as they crawled under and around the car, trying to get different vantage points and diagnose the problem without tearing it up too much. After a few minutes of this, Tommy crawled out from under the car and motioned for JP to join him. Being the guilty party, I waited against the wall and watched as Tommy conferred with JP. I could tell the news wasn't good as I watched Tommy shaking his head and Jim grimacing while they talked. I was certain that they were reviewing my terrible technique and discussing how to break the news to me. As they talked, I wondered whether I could get some of my money back from Kevin and erase all memory of being here.

JP walked over to me, his face not betraying any misgiving just yet. "Let's go back to the RV. They're gonna be a while. We might make it out for the second session, but we're definitely done for now."

The three of us had only been in the RV for fifteen minutes or so when there was a knock on the door. JP opened it to find Kevin Buckler, clutching a sheet of paper in his hand. He motioned for Jim to come out, and JP obliged him, waving off Revere and me as he exited the RV.

A few minutes later he was back, holding the data sheet in his hands.

"Kevin wanted me to go over this with you. He's saying that you've over-revved the engine at several points, and he thinks that might have screwed up the gearbox."

"I'm finding that a little distressing since I couldn't get the thing in gear at all. How could I ruin the gearbox that way? If I over-revved it, it was because I couldn't get it into gear." I pled my case, and JP was receptive.

"I told Kevin that, and they'll take a close look at the gearbox, but he wants you to get your shifting better regardless."

I was on the defensive, but mostly because I didn't understand how it had gone so wrong. "I'm not understanding this—is he trying to blame me for the gearbox? You said yourself it wasn't right when you drove it."

Jim stayed calm, reminding me of the basic facts. "And I told Kevin that. All we know right now is the gearbox is a problem. We'll know more later. Let's not get upset yet; we don't even know what to be worried about yet."

"Well, I know I'm new to this car and all that, but that was ridiculous. There's something wrong here, and I can't believe it's all my fault." I was frustrated, more than a bit embarrassed, and disappointed—for myself, and also for Revere, who hadn't turned a wheel yet. However, I forced myself to sit and pay attention as JP proceeded to walk through the data points. Regardless of my concerns, there might be something to learn in there anyway, so I listened and tried not to scowl too much.

About thirty minutes later we could tell the first practice session was over—the background noise had stopped, and the PA music once again was audible. JP suggested we walk on over to the garage and check on the crew's progress.

"OK if I come this time?"

JP grinned. "Nobody's gonna yell at you. Let's just check it out."

As we approached the garage, I could see parts of the Porsche spread out on the floor around the stricken car. The bottom half of a mechanic was visible under the rear of the car, and several others were peering under the machine.

Tommy Sadler emerged and met us half way, wiping his smudged glasses as he motioned to us. "I've got some news, but it's not great. We think we found the problem—the clutch plate was put on backwards, and the bolts finally sheared off after a few laps."

Jim processed this as I began to realize I was off the hook, at least as far as guilt was concerned. "You mean it wasn't me that screwed it up?"

JP offered, "Well, that would explain a lot. The shifting deteriorated until it failed altogether; sounds like we've got an explanation, huh?"

Tommy admitted, "Yeah, it's a fuck-up mechanically. Nobody's fault except the guys who put it together. But for now, we've got a lot of work to do to get this fixed. It's going to be a while, and I think we should plan on missing at least the next session. We'll keep you posted, but don't expect anything real soon."

I was relieved that the problem had been found and that the problem in fact wasn't me. However, I did notice the part about missing "at least the next session." There were three more to go for the first day, with the last session beginning at 6:30 p.m. That one would be the only night session of the three-day test, so I hoped we'd get that critical practice time in before race week. If not, the end of the month would have lots of fun firsts to chalk up.

I also noticed that Buckler was nowhere to be seen at the moment. At least Tommy was on it, helping out the mechanics and organizing some sort of plan to address the problem.

Back again in the RV, I sat on the couch, relieved that that particular issue was behind me. "I'm guessing that I shouldn't hold my breath waiting for an apology from Kevin, right?"

Jim stifled a laugh. "Yeah, I wouldn't wait too long for that. Welcome to the world of pro racing, buddy. He'll probably still try to bill you for over-revving, or something like that. Don't worry, I'll talk to him and it'll be fine. What we really need to do is to be ready when they tell us it's done."

Periodically we wandered over to the garage to check on the progress of the car. With each visit, it seemed as if there were actually fewer guys working on the gearbox. At one point, there was one lonely guy seated on the garage floor, working away at the clutch with a nail file. We watched and paced, came and went, the whole time not wanting to get pushy but becoming increasingly concerned that the car would not be fixed. The next two sessions of the afternoon came and went, and it became even more obvious that the car was going nowhere fast and that the top mechanics' concerns were elsewhere for this particular moment.

At some point, I noticed JP having a conversation off to one side with Buckler. Although things didn't look too heated, it ended with Kevin stalking away, but not before visiting the garage, presumably for a talk with the lone crew guy still working. JP later told me that he thought it was time to nudge Kevin a bit, and to his credit, Buckler didn't put up a big fight. Within the hour, another fly-by of the garage area showed several more mechanics buzzing about the car. However, it was getting near dinner time, and our chance of running anytime soon still looked sketchy.

But at least Kevin was engaged and returned to the garage to give us an update. "OK, I've got my guys all over it, but it seems like we're probably done for the day. I promise you, though, we'll have it ready for tomorrow. In the meantime, we're serving dinner at the hauler, so go on over and grab a bite to eat."

Revere, Jim, and I made our way to the TRG hauler, resigned now to our fate. No running until tomorrow morning. Christmas had just been rescheduled.

I realized then that I was starving. I had eaten very little during the day, since I really don't care to drive on a full stomach. Given that we had been on full alert virtually all day, I had been very careful about my intake. Now, with the day confirmed done, I could fuel up without worry. The TRG spread was a full-on Italian meal, complete with meatballs, spicy sausage, and plenty of low-carb options for me. I ate heartily, out of hunger and also relief that the day's destruction couldn't be hung on me.

As darkness fell on the paddock area, Revere, JP, and I sat around the TRG hauler, plates balanced on our knees, talking about nothing in particular. At 6:30 p.m., we could hear the sound of the last session starting up as cars moved out onto the darkening track. The session would last until eight p.m., at least for those lucky enough to have cars under them. The three of us sat and ate, trying to ignore the fact that we weren't driving.

Moments after I had finished my second plate of meatballs, Kevin came hustling over to us. "Great news, guys! The crew guys are working hard and almost finished. They said the car will be ready for you in about thirty minutes, so get your gear and be ready to get some laps in."

The three of us exchanged glances, and headed with our plates for the trash can. JP announced, "OK, sounds like we're in business after all. Revere, I want Jim to drive this session. He's the only one who's been out there already, and I don't want your first lap to be in the dark."

Revere nodded, looking at me for confirmation. I gulped as I suddenly felt the weight of the large meal in my belly. "OK with me, I guess. Be careful what you wish for, right?"

Long before I had finished digesting dinner, I was strapped into the cockpit of the Porsche and soon on my way out of the garage area. Lights on, I navigated the alleyways back to the pit area and was flagged onto pit lane by the official at the opening in the wall. JP was again in my ear, reminding me to take it easy and warm up the tires and driver slowly. As I drove towards pit out, I took only a moment to recognize that the view out my windshield was supremely cool, with the track and pit area brightly lit and alive with activity. Refocusing on the matter at hand, I clicked off the limiter and accelerated onto the track. I immediately noted with satisfaction that the gears engaged easily, and upshifts and downshifts both were smooth and precise. Rolling onto the banking of the oval for the first time, I marveled at how little perception of darkness there was, until I approached the bus stop for the first time.

A blinking yellow arrow up on the catch fence alerted sleepy drivers, I guess, to the fact that a chicane was near; I wondered how anybody in this position could possibly not be aware of that as I proceeded into the braking zone. A bit darker than the other sections, the turns were still easily visible in my headlights as I proceeded out and back onto the oval. Smoothly accelerating up to full blast, I noticed lights in my rearview closing at an alarming rate. With little excess attention available to pay to the vibrating front end of the car at speed, I passed the start-finish line and headed into turn one's braking zone. Abruptly, a swarm of angry prototypes rushed past, outbraking me while exceeding my entry speed by easily twenty-five mph. A couple of GT cars piled on right behind them as I sawed at the wheel to not veer into the path of any of the faster cars as I turned in. The noise was deafening, even with the radio earplugs in, as cars downshifted, backfired, and went back to power all the way through the turn.

I'm sure I flinched in my seat more than once as cars went by, but after a few laps, I was able to work myself a little deeper into the braking zones and tried to lean on the car a bit at the apexes. I knew I was nowhere close to the limit of the Porsche, but at least I was facing forward in anger and shifting without drama. As I drove, the alternating dark and lighter areas of the track zipped by, punctuated by passing cars and the variable song of engines as they drew alongside, however briefly. It was a surreal experience, partly accentuated by the darkness but mostly amplified by the circumstances. Earlier in the day (was it even the same day?), I had been lamenting my ineptitude and soaking up embarrassment; moments ago, we were wrapping up a day of inactivity with a giant meal. Now I was hurtling through Florida's semi-darkness, dodging cars driven at insane speeds and wishing I could go ever faster. But inside my helmet, I was smiling a private wide grin as I passed under the waving checkered flag signaling the end of the session.

In the next two days, Revere and I got more than our share of time in the seat of the Porsche. Jim Pace ran intermittent set-up laps, working on perfecting the balance and handling of the car so that both of his rookie drivers were comfortable at speed. We perused data sheets, which contained overlaid tracings of our individual laps and JP's best lap; the visual representation of the advice Jim had been doling out was invaluable. Looking at the graphs, one could see where the faster guy was braking later, accelerating earlier, and maintaining higher mid-corner speed. Also, with each session, progress was easily visible as the gap between the two sets of data lessened, albeit slowly.

I became more settled and comfortable in the car with each session, hell, with each lap turned. The Porsche was magnificent in its power and solid feeling under braking, even if the nose did hunt around on the bumpy oval banking at speed. High speed traffic became a routine part of each lap, and I soon found the safe place on the track for my slower laps to take place. I kept it low on the banking, and learned to check all mirrors—both sides!—before turning in anywhere. Revere easily outpaced me, as I anticipated he would, but I watched as lap times went in the right direction, and my comfort level soared.

As a bonus, we finished the three-day test without putting a scratch on the car. Kevin made a point of congratulating us at the conclusion of the test, noting that we were the only one of the six TRG cars without damage. I wasn't overly impressed by this at first, but then JP pointed to a heap of car one garage over. The car, a new 996 Porsche purchased specifically for this event, was in line for lengthy repairs, and probably wouldn't see the start of the race two weeks from then. There was nothing to celebrate about that, but I was inwardly glad that there were worse stories than mine to be told about this test.

There wasn't much left to do now but wait for the end of the month. Just ahead was my first attempt at the Rolex 24 Hours of Daytona.

13

Chapter Thirteen

Around the time I was nine years old or so, my friend Billy McCole got a plastic human skeleton model for his birthday. The rather simple construct had about thirty pieces and wasn't exactly an anatomic marvel, but I was nonetheless captivated by it. This was no foreshadowing of my future occupation; rather, I recall being both fascinated by the structure and even a little spooked by the thought of the scary skeleton hanging there on its stand. Naturally, I told my mother that that skeleton model was what I truly wanted for Christmas.

Since Christmas was a good three or four months away, I had plenty of time to think about and, ultimately, obsess about the skeleton. I was pretty confident that my mom would come through and make sure I got the model, and once I had concluded that, all that was left was to fantasize about the day when I would find it under the tree. I now recall that waiting time as feeling interminably long and difficult for my obsessed young brain. I thought about the model when I woke, during the school day, and as I went to sleep at night. I imagined it hanging next to my bed, or better yet, proudly displayed between the candlesticks on the dining room table downstairs. Ultimately, I thought about it so much that the actual skeleton model was never able to measure up to the one in my imagination.

The period between the end of the Daytona test days and my departure for the race not quite three weeks later felt entirely like my wait for the skeleton. Having glimpsed a little of the scene at Daytona, I had seen enough to fuel my imagination about what awaited my return for race week. The approaching event had occupied so much of my time, for so long that it felt like an uncomfortable yet enticing obsession. I was really and truly going to drive at Daytona in the 24 Hours.

But before there was any racing to be done, I had to pay the price, physically, mentally, and emotionally.

I spent part of every day, without fail, in the gym, lifting weights and doing cardio training until I was in better shape than I had been in twenty years. After work, and before gym, I made scores of phone calls regarding sponsor deals, travel arrangements for family and friends, and final details about suit design, car graphics, and team guests. I often arrived home, beat up from a compressed work schedule, to find dozens of emails and voice mails awaiting my attention. Many hours were spent calculating and crunching the numbers to ensure that I had a realistic grip on the cost of the race, along with some reassurance about sponsor dollars that were supposedly arriving at some point. There were meetings to be had with those sponsors, including a formal introductory dinner with Harvey Rovinsky, the jewelry store owner and primary sponsor. His schedule was such that that some of the memorable meetings with his marketing team concluded well after ten p.m., leading up to my latest gym session of the month.

I juggled family time, including some reserved "fun time" with Aidan, while Ginny absorbed most of the less-glamorous parenting jobs in order to buy time for my racing obligations. I would get to play with my son a bit, reading or exploring the computer together, and then have the luxury of handing him off to Gin for bedtime chores while I went to work out. Even my partner, Joe got in on the act, absorbing some of the extra calls and weekend work, all permitting me to focus any free time on the preparation for the upcoming race. And they all contributed most by tolerating the demands I placed on their schedules and the advantage I took of their generosity and support. In the process, I discovered that what I suspected about racing at this level was true: a degree of selfishness was a prerequisite if I wanted to succeed at it while maintaining any semblance of a home life and career. I prioritized things as well as possible, relying on Ginny to redirect me when necessary, and temporarily left behind quite a few less important concerns—time wasters like TV, internet, and other mindless diversions. With non-essential activities and meetings rescheduled or cancelled altogether, my life assumed a focus unlike any I had managed since my medical training days. In fact, this was even more extreme, for back then, I had managed to fit wine, women, and song into the equation with regularity.

One driving problem that continued to worry me was eventually solved in a rather creative way. Despite the ultimate diagnosis of a mechanical fault at the test, I continued to fret about the Porsche's gearbox. Not about its layout or function, but rather about my ability to operate it successfully for the six or seven hours that I would be racing the car. I hadn't ever raced anything for any long stints that included a traditional manual H-pattern box; while not complex, it was a different world from a sequential shifter. Given that I would have a host of other concerns while racing at Daytona, including dodging prototypes and trying to maintain a respectable pace, I had some concerns that the shifting issue would come back and bite me. After all, it wasn't yet second nature for me and driving the car itself at speed was still a confusing experiment without adding in other variables. So the prospect of screwing up something elemental, such as shifting gears, was another check box on my list of fears leading up to the race week.

In an email to the Skip Barber Masters and friends group, I mentioned this fact while describing our test-day troubles with the gearbox. One of the recipients of the email, Michael Auriemma, called me almost immediately with an intriguing idea.

Mike had driven a similar Porsche race car in a Grand-Am event the year before, and was a serious Porschephile from New York. "You know," Mike began, "that gearbox you're running is the same as the one in my Porsche Turbo that I drive every day. Same setup, same feel."

Michael went on to throw his idea out there. "You know I love that Bentley GT you have. How about we trade with each other for the next few weeks; you get to run the Porsche gearbox and practice all you want, and I'll take good care of your GT."

I had to admit, it was a good call. "Standard swap rules?"

"You got it. Bring 'er back in the same condition you got her, right?"

Michael and I made arrangements, and swapped cars two days later, meeting on the Jersey turnpike to make the exchange. Mike happily drove off in my Bentley as I merged onto the roadway in the Porsche, stirring the box and enjoying the feel of the stick shift.

I drove the car exclusively for the next two weeks, commuting to and from the hospital and office, volunteering to run errands whenever possible. One week before the race, and feeling that I still needed a little time with the gearbox, I arranged an unofficial Saturday practice session on the Longport causeway near my house. Being friends with most of the local constabulary, I reminded one of Longport's finest that I would be out there taking some medium-speed runs. He gave me his "Just don't be a dumbass about it" blessing, and off I went.

I spent over two hours running up and down the one mile strip between the island and the mainland, turning off each time before making land, going down through the gears while perfecting my heel-and-toe technique. Hard on the brake with the right foot, left foot dipping the clutch at the right moment, I engaged the next lowest gear while simultaneously tipping the throttle with the right side of my foot in the classic "blip" to match the engine's revs. Over and over again I practiced, up and down the causeway, through a full tank of gas and until I thought I could do it in my sleep. Good to know considering I would soon be doing this for real in the middle of the night, with a few other challenges thrown in to make it interesting. By dusk that Saturday, I was comfortable with at least the concept of the Porsche's gearbox and no longer concerned that it would be my Achille's heel.

The last few remaining details were addressed before I left for the track on Wednesday morning. Joe already had the work schedule coordinated, managing the last two days of a busy week before departing for Daytona himself Saturday morning. I cleared my to-do list by Tuesday, double checking on the plans of a few friends who were coming to the race. With the help of Ashlei Newkirk, I confirmed the schedules of Harvey and his friends, whose happiness was critical to the financial success of the effort. Itineraries were double-checked, contact plans made, and last minute details and changes all put to rest—finally.

Before leaving for the airport, I gave Gin a big hug, reminding her that I would see her on Friday just after practice was over. She was nervous about flying, and I reassured her that it would all be OK. "Don't worry honey, once you're down there and settled into the Ramada, everything will be fine."

"Don't remind me. The things I do for you. Yeah, the Ramada. Can't wait for that. You owe me a Four Seasons weekend you know."

"Just another way to show I care. Bring your best sweatpants."

"Thanks for that image. It's not too late for me to change my mind."

I kissed her one last time. "I know all that you've done for me, for this, and I love you for it. Seriously."

Gin kissed me. "Be safe sweetheart. Call me tonight."

The last goodbye was saved for Aidan, who was of course typically busy with his own activities.

"Are you going to watch daddy race this weekend? I'll be on TV, and you can see me if you watch it."

"Are you recording it?"

"Sure bubba, why?"

Aidan looked at me in earnest, his blue eyes completely unflinching. "Because I'll probably be watching Curious George. Can we watch your race when you get home?"

Negotiating would get me nowhere with the busy schedule of my son. "It's a deal. Now give daddy a kiss before I leave for Daytona."

Aidan planted a wet one on me, and promptly turned back to his Legos. "Good luck dad."

The first afternoon of race week was unloading day, a busy time for the crews of the seventy-two cars entered for the 2006 24 Hours of Daytona. For the drivers of the TRG Porsche #68, it was time for a fun walk through the garage area and for the first view of the car all dressed in its Sunday best. Waiting as my plane touched down, Jim Pace once again collected me and my gear and off we went to the track across the street. As we approached the gates, I noticed the changes that had occurred since the test days. Bright banners and flags waved everywhere; a slew of concession trucks were parked both outside and inside the track; and campers, RVs and even a few race haulers all vied for space in the entry queues. Traffic in and around the entrance to the track was obviously busier, and several new lanes were being staffed by security guards in order to handle the increased volume moving through the gates.

For my part, I no longer bothered trying to suppress a grin as the scene unfolded in front of me. I sat shotgun as JP navigated the active infield, where quite a few people had already staked out favored camping spots and viewing stands. We made our way into the driver/owner lot, parking in front of the TRG -supplied RV. The lot was now full, and up and down the lanes, I saw million-dollar RVs parked with drivers and hospitality workers coming and going. It seemed that everywhere I looked, some recognizable driver or team owner was walking or driving by as if nothing special was happening right then. For me, it was as if I had been granted some sort of pre-event zoo tour: Come and see the racers in their natural habitat and observe how they live and work!

Once again we made the walk into the garage area, this time spotting a few friendly faces on the way in. While I in no way felt relaxed and at home, I did at least now know the way to the garage and would be able to find the men's room without a map. With over seventy additional race cars also rolled out to run the Grand-Am Cup support race on Friday, the paddock area was overflowing with people and machines. The sounds of revving engines and mechanics shouting over the din competed with the PA music and announcements, creating what amounted to a white-noise background that would last for five days. My head was on a swivel as I took in the scene, enjoying the steady stream of bright activity. The anxiety would come soon enough, but for now, it was to be a fun afternoon before the real work started tomorrow.

Revere and his dad, Dr. John Greist, met us in the garage area. I took a moment to thank Dr. Greist for his help in putting the effort together; he was gracious as always, and accepted my thanks as he described how pleased he was with the group we had for the race. Together we took a moment to thank Jim Pace, acknowledging his hard work in getting Revere and me closer to our goal. As we stood in the garage area and chatted, a good and pleasant vibe developed all around, clearly setting the tone for the weekend to come.

Our race car arrived fresh from tech, pushed back into the garage by Tommy and the new crew boss, Rogerio Reis. A quiet guy who I would later describe as "the one who looks like a lumberjack," Roger had been largely responsible for repairing our clutch and getting us back on track during the test days earlier in the month. Apparently, as some form of punishment, Kevin Buckler assigned Roger to our car for the race week. This was of course our good luck, as Roger was one of the top mechanics in sports car racing and would later win multiple Mechanic of the Year titles in the American Le Mans Series. For now though, he was stuck with us and the job of keeping the #68 up and running until Sunday.

As the car pulled into the garage stall, Kevin Buckler arrived on the scene, whirling into the space as he continued his phone conversation while greeting the six of us simultaneously. He first pointed out how great the beautiful blue Porsche looked, and as we a circled the car Buckler made a point of showing off the swooping striped livery and custom sponsor decals. However, a few critical stickers were missing, and I took a moment to remind Kevin of this. The sponsors were arriving on Thursday night, and he knew they were expecting their stickers to be on the car. Kevin assured me that it would get done properly and in time, and within minutes a TRG marketing guy was on the scene and reviewing with me what needed to be done.

Once the scene at the garage was stabilized, we made some final preparations for the coming days. After the first session was green flagged on Thursday morning, JP warned us, things would move quickly and time for addressing details would be limited. With Jim's input, we tried to square away our gear ahead of time, trying on our new TRG suits and dropping helmets off at the communications truck to double-check our radio systems. Required Grand-Am patches needed to be sewn on the suits and safety gear passed through tech. The to-do list seemed endless, but JP and Ashlei prioritized and organized until we were set and ready to go. Here Jim Pace's experience was invaluable as he knew what was coming, and what would be demanded of us, in a few short days. Like planning an ascent of Everest, the detail work needed to be done well before anyone started climbing.

With those details addressed and the car put to bed, it was time for the evening meal and a repeat trip to Gene's steakhouse. Revere, Dr. Greist, Jim, and I enjoyed a quiet meal at the famous restaurant, eating average steaks while enjoying above-average racing stories about JP's experiences at Daytona and elsewhere. Racers moved by our table, often stopping to say hello to Jim and tolerate an introduction to his rookie driving partners. More than a few guys who closely matched pictures on the wall wandered by, adding further excitement to my evening. The atmosphere was relaxed and easy, but there was a bit of a pre-game meal air about the place that I recognized from days long past. As the meal progressed, I sat back in my chair, wanting to enjoy the scene and the feel of belonging once again. We were gathered together, pre-battle, in one last relaxed setting before all hell broke loose in the morning. I savored the moment and decided that I might be in the right place after all.

Thursday's alarm was completely unnecessary as I was again easily up before the appointed hour. A Cracker Barrel breakfast was in order, and I choked down coffee and a few eggs, not wanting to load my gut before the first session's driving. Something approaching a routine emerged as we headed out to the track, made our way through the checkpoints, and unloaded into the RV. Being a creature of habit, and seeking refuge in repetition, I welcomed some semblance of the familiar as we donned race suits and assembled gear for the day.

Jim was kind enough to accompany Revere and me to the rookie driver meeting. Scheduled a half-hour before the full drivers meeting, the rookie session was a reminder to all—even Adrian Fernandez, Mexican open-wheel star and fellow Daytona newbie—of how to avoid trouble and stay out of Mark Raffauf's hot seat. Once finished, the main meeting began after the rest of the drivers shuffled in. I sat next to my partners and tried not to stare at the famous faces, certainly not wanting to be conspicuous in my gawking. I listened as Raffauf covered the usual details of such meetings—where the emergency vehicles were located, what changes had been made to the track's corners, and most importantly, how to get back to the pits if there was a mechanical problem. Mark finished with the usual rhetoric that it was unwise to try to "win practice" and admonitions against first lap heroics. As he spoke, I figured that two-hundred plus guys were nodding in agreement as they planned to set fastest laps in their first stint anyway.

The meeting concluded with a thank you from the track president, followed by a prayer and group hug. Actually there was no hug, but I felt the love anyway. I was in the midst of a few hundred type-A guys, each wanting to beat the other and all who could safely cross me off their worry list. Like being on a first-time Super Bowl team, I was firmly in the "just glad to be here" category, and that was just fine. For now.

On the way out of the meeting, we all lined up to sign several "2006 Rolex 24 Hours of Daytona" posters laid out on tables in the exit hallway. Not having anything resembling an official Jim Lowe autograph, other than the one I used to sign hospital charts and prescriptions, I tried out several different styles until I settled on one that I thought looked suitably professional. I chuckled to myself as I signed each one, thinking about how I was lowering the market value of the posters with each addition of my mark. Figuring we should continue to stay together, I signed near Jim Pace and Revere, adding the "#68" underneath just to make sure I'd be able to find it someday if I tried.

With four practice sessions available Thursday, and no clutch difficulties, there was plenty of lapping time for JP, Revere and me. With each session, I eased a bit more into a comfort zone, not impressing with my lap times but keeping safe and out of trouble for the most part. The Porsche was still a big challenge for my inexperienced hands, demanding a higher level of commitment than I had available in order to drive it at the limit. However, Jim was patient with me, reviewing data between sessions and talking me through each lap on the radio until the comfort level was there. By nightfall, both Revere and I had managed personal best laps, with Revere running about two seconds off JP's pace and me a further three seconds behind. Even in the dark, the driving was fun—and less intimidating with time. With each lap, traffic became just another part of the equation, and the busy track shrunk in scope as we focused on our own issues—braking later, rolling speed, and trying to stay clear of faster cars.

Nighttime driving during the 24 Hours of Daytona, January 2006

Once the day's last session was done, we returned to the RV for debriefing. I began by lamenting my pace, painfully aware that I was still a long way from that of my two teammates. Jim immediately countered my argument.

"Dr. Lowe, you're doing just fine out there. No mistakes, that's what this is all about. The car's still all shiny and neither of you guys put a wheel wrong today."

I wanted to avoid whining while still acknowledging that I knew where my pace needed to be. "I'm feeling better in the car, but it's tough to get down to where I need my times to be. I know I'm off the pace of you both, but I didn't think it would be three seconds."

JP made his thoughts on the matter clear. "It's not about setting fast laps here. If it were, the race would be over after qualifying. Just stay clean, and keep coming in for gas, tires, and oil. That's all you need to do. Gas, tires, and oil. Forget the rest."

"Well, that's easy to say, especially at the sharp end of things."

JP the sensei emerged and took over. "Don't let your head go there. All weekend you'll see guys ruining their races by trying to be a hero. Run well and fast, but remember—make one mistake that puts you in the garage and all the fast laps are erased."

JP reviews race technique with Jim

I chewed on that one a bit and decided to swallow my pride and return my focus to the job at hand. Much as I wanted to run faster laps, I wasn't there yet, and my job now was to hand off a good clean car to my teammates for the next stint. I was aware of this going in, but I still wanted to go just a bit faster and be just a bit more accepted in the community of race car drivers. I also wouldn't allow the fact that I had a day job excuse my driving here. There was no handicapping going on; no one would give me a mulligan just because I wasn't a true, real-life pro racer.

"Man, this is hard. I really hoped to get up to speed faster."

Jim again redirected my thoughts properly. "You're doing it all right, going about it right. Just keep taking little bites and it'll come to you. But for now, you're where you need to be." JP smiled as he offered one last thought. "In fact, you must be the fastest neurosurgeon on the property. Maybe even in the world right now."

I snorted as Revere and Dr. Greist laughed with me. "Well, thanks for that. But it's sort of like being the world's tallest architect, you know? What's the good of that?"

"The good is that you're part of a great effort, you're driving better, and you're going to do fine this weekend, if you just keep doing what you've been doing."

Properly chastised, I silently resolved to be a team player, choking back the ignominy at running too slowly once again. With renewed determination, I would get thorough the biggest race of my life by doing what JP recommended. Later, I was sure, I'd get faster. But now, my role was clear, and I would be ready.

Friday's driving time was short, with just one session in the morning and then a fifteen-minute qualifier before the Grand-Am Cup guys took to the track for their support race. We used the opportunity to sort the car one last time before JP qualified the car for Saturday's start. Since he would be running the qualifying session, our plan called for Jim to drive the Porsche for the morning practice as Revere and I watched from the pits.

I was fine with that because Ginny arrived at the track a few minutes before the session went green. I gave Gin a big hug and introduced her to Revere and some of the TRG guys. Once she was oriented, we turned back to the wall, standing side by side as the first prototypes started down the front straight at full song. As I thrilled to the visceral sensation and sound of the big V-8's thundering by at nearly two-hundred mph, I felt Gin's grip on my arm tighten. I looked down at her just in time to see tears streaming down her face.

I was surprised and confused at her response. I had literally never seen my wife cry before. "What's wrong, sweetheart?"

Gin shook her head and tucked her chin down, waiting a moment before responding. "Nothing. It's just, just, a lot scarier than I thought. I can't believe you're going to be out there."

I pulled her closer to me. "Don't worry, please. It's easier out there than it is standing in here. Really."

Gin wiped away a tear revealing her usual stoic look underneath. "I didn't expect this—for it to be like this. All I've ever seen is the Skip Barber cars, and this seems like something way beyond that. It's just that it's a bit overwhelming."

"Don't worry about all this. I'm fine, and it's really louder and scarier when you're here in the pits. Honest."

Despite my reassurances, Gin pulled me even closer. To this day she doesn't enjoy being in the pits or up close and personal with race cars at full speed. But on that first day, she hung in there. For me.

In the qualifying session, Jim ran hard, but because of a black flag caused by an errant Corvette, he only got one flying lap into the books. As a result, we were positioned seventeenth on the GT grid, roughly two miles behind the front row prototypes. Thankfully, our plans were more farsighted than that. As JP reminded us in his Southern drawl, "Pole position is just for bragging rights. In this deal, the real race doesn't even start until Sunday morning."

The rest of Friday was about fun for the drivers, with a bit of work thrown in to boot. With the crowds growing by the minute, Daytona's paddock area became the focus of attention. TRG's six race cars dominated the west end of the garages, with enough crew, drivers, friends, and fans to run a race series all by themselves. Next up for the drivers of the #68 car was driver change practice, supervised and timed by Dr. Greist. As fans crowded the garages, we practicing getting into, and then out of, the car in the fastest way possible. Manning the radio, Tommy narrated the imaginary process of entering the pit box as we rehearsed loosening our belts, unplugging the drink bottle, and preparing for the exit process once the car came to a full stop. Once the seat was clear, the next driver would be assisted with getting the belts in place and preparing to launch the car. "Radio check, radio check" was the call made when the new driver was finally ready to get moving; with each call, Dr. Greist would click off the stopwatch and announce the time. Practice ended only after all three of us demonstrated the ability to make the change in under the forty-five seconds needed to change tires and refuel the Porsche.

After working up a good sweat just exiting the stationary car, I leaned on the Porsche, drinking water and apparently appearing much like a big time race car driver. Enough so, at least, that an emboldened young kid, about seven or so, approached me with pen and book in hand. I noticed dad nudge the boy in my direction, gently encouraging the youngster to ask the sweaty guy in the fire suit for an autograph. Sensing that that particular moment wasn't the best time to burst the kid's bubble, I neglected to give full disclosure on who I was and who, in fact, I was not. Instead I knelt down and did my best "JLowe" scribble, underlining the "#68" on the blank page. The boy just stood there politely, as dad yelled his thanks from the opening to the garage.

"Would you like to go see the car up close?"

The kid's already wide eyes doubled in size. While the boy could only muster a silent nod, I heard his dad shout "Say yes, Blake, say yes."

I stood up and motioned to the boy to move closer to the Porsche. He hesitated and then looked back at his dad, awaiting the signal that it was OK to proceed. Dad responded with a smile and waved the kid on. As the boy got to the side of the car, I signaled dad to join us for some photos. Opening the door, I pointed out some of the important parts of the Porsche's interior, like where JP sat and where the fire extinguisher was.

"How'd you like to sit in the car? Would you like that?"

Wider eyes.

Dad nodded his OK as I picked up the kid and positioned him on the edge of the roll cage.

"Ok, put your feet on the seat and scoot your butt on down there. Watch your head on the way."

Blake settled into the seat and immediately grabbed the wheel, moving his hands back and forth.

Roger poked his head out from under the right front wheel. "Hey!"

Blake reflexively jumped, and offered me a guilty grin. I smiled right back. "Don't worry buddy, I did the same thing the first time I got in there."

Blake and I posed for a few photos and dad expressed his thanks several times before they moved on to continue their tour of the garages. I thanked them back and reminded dad that if they came back when JP was around, his signature would be a better one for the collection. For my part, I kept grinning and was still doing so long after Blake forgot who was driving the #68 that weekend.

Friday night was an intentionally short evening out for most drivers; we were no exception to the rule, despite the fact that our team hosted a dinner for guests and sponsors. We had reserved a room at the Chart House restaurant down near the beach, planning a nice and relaxed dinner for about thirty or so friends and a few sponsors. Ashlei Newkirk had already taken over the reins for the "meet and greet" event, ensuring that Harvey from Bernie Robbins Jewelers and the rest of the VIP guests received something closely resembling an upscale experience, all things Daytona Beach-considered. Revere, JP, and I shook a lot of hands, ensured all that we had big plans for the weekend, and called it a night early.

Since Ginny had already experienced the less-than-wonderful environment of the Ramada upon check-in that morning, the return to our room was less of a shock for her. Plus she had, as usual, a plan for dealing with the Spartan quarters and the questionable cleanliness of the bathroom, rug and bedsheets.

As I readied my gear and repacked my track bag for the fourth time, Gin busily went about her nighttime routine in the tiny bathroom. As I listened to her ready for bed, I thought about my immediate prospects for the evening. Despite my anxiety about the coming events of the weekend, I was in fact feeling somewhat amorous. I had been living a basically monastic existence for quite a while, and having a quiet and intimate moment with my wife seemed like a good way to start off the race weekend.

Finishing my final packing preparations, I jumped under the covers and waited for Ginny to join me. She emerged from the bathroom, still fully clothed and wearing wool sweat socks and shoes.

"Nice outfit, sexy."

"You haven't seen anything yet. If I could wear a snowsuit into bed, I would. This place really is skeevy."

Sensing I was losing any chance at romantic fun, I tried damage control. "I know, I know. But the sheets are fairly clean, and if you just get your feet off that rug and get in bed, it'll be better."

"Isn't there a Four Seasons around here anywhere? Never mind, I already know the answer." As Gin muttered to herself, she unpacked one last critical item. It was something I had never seen before.

I watched as visions of my night of nookie faded into the distance.

"What's that thing?"

"It's a sleep sack. I got it especially for this place, once I went on-line and saw pictures of where we were staying." Gin unzipped the silk sack, and somehow managed to hop into it and roll into bed all in one motion. "Ahh, nice and clean."

I snuggled up against her side and said, ever hopeful, "Is there room in there for two?"

Gin rolled away from me. "Not a chance. Don't even think about it. This is my sack, and I'm not touching those sheets or anything else in here."

The room was quiet for a moment as I considered my options, which were assuredly slim. I'm nothing if not persistent though, and I gave it one last-gasp effort.

"There wouldn't happen to be a hole in that sack anywhere, would there?"

I slept erratically that night, just as I expected. I was so amped by the events of the last few days—hell, the last few months—that I was grateful to eventually fall asleep at all. Just prior to doing so, I was again reviewing the path I had taken to get to that point, and the questionable wisdom of doing so. I didn't exactly recognize the coming weekend as a pivotal point in my life; in fact, if I had, there was a decent chance that I would have turned back. I was once told that some of the most important moments in one's life occur without any realization of their significance while they are happening. At least, the significance of things is easier to recognize in retrospect, I guess. But for that moment, I really wanted only to not be responsible for failure, not be a detriment to my teammates, and definitely not be a disappointment—to my father, my family, myself. I wasn't thinking fame, glory, or even positive recognition. I was imagining getting to play, and being part of a team and something very special, even if maybe I didn't belong there. Thinking these less-than inspiring thoughts, I finally drifted off, failing to reassure myself that I was in fact ready and capable.

I awoke well before dawn, again beating the alarm clock and just about every other sane driver to the wakeup as my adrenals squeezed a large bolus of adrenaline into my system. I sat bolt upright and smelled the crackle of ozone in the air. Gin slept on as I made my way in the tiny bathroom, completed my morning routine and fussed with my backpack and gear. As

I stumbled my way around the darkened room, I tried unsuccessfully to not wake my wife.

"Good morning honey, how did you sleep?"

I snickered a bit. "Fitfully." It was an old joke between us—my former partner had misused the term once, announcing his good night's sleep with "I slept fitfully—you know, I feel good, strong, and fit"—and we enjoyed using the term ever since.

A still-sleepy Ginny laughed with me. "Well, I guess you can sleep on the plane ride home tomorrow night. Are you headed out already?"

"Yep. I'm meeting Revere, his dad, and JP downstairs; Ashlei will call you later this morning and take you to the track in time for the autograph session."

I kissed Ginny goodbye after tugging at the sleep sack and exposing some lips.

"I love you baby. See you soon."

I was rewarded with a big kiss. "Relax, sweetheart. You guys will do great. And you're ready. You did everything you were supposed to, and JP has faith in you. Just keep doing what he says, and you'll do great."

The buzzing in my head increased as I opened the door and peered down into the parking lot. Jim was waiting by the rental car, talking with Revere and Dr. Greist. "Ok, time to go. I love you." I couldn't verbalize just then all that it meant to me to have Ginny there, beside me for the trip, and supporting me since day one. Besides, my wife placed little stock in sentimental words, preferring demonstration and deeds. "You know, Gin, I can't say thank you enough…"

"Yeah, yeah. Better get going. Can't be late for the bus. Love you."

I shut the door softly, and banged down the outside stairs of the Ramada, waving at the guys as I made my way toward the car. To my right, across the street, the looming bulk of Daytona was visible as it too awoke for a long weekend.

14

Chapter Fourteen

We ate at the Cracker Barrel once again, bowing to superstition and necessity at the same time. I had nothing resembling an appetite, but knew that I had better get some food down before heading over to the track. With a noon race start, my next substantial meal would probably be dinner, so breakfast was mandatory despite the simmering nausea in my gut. The sensation wasn't hard to place: I had experienced that gnawing feeling in my stomach long ago, before pretty much any looming athletic contest of my youth. What was unique was the fact that it hadn't appeared in a few decades—I don't recall ever experiencing it before tests or surgery, which basically accounted for the extent of challenges I faced over the previous twenty years. Nonetheless, I knew the drill. Eat something and ignore the churning down below. So, the four of us ate with varying degrees of enthusiasm, with the two rookie drivers looking a lot more distracted than JP did. Dr. Greist chaired an impromptu therapy session, reassuring Revere and me about our preparedness and ability, likely spotting in me the potential for a future annuity if I chose to continue racing at this level.

After making our way past the security check and then through Daytona's familiar green entrance tunnel, we parked in the driver/owner's lot next to our RV. As we climbed the steps into the RV, I could smell the coffee brewing, courtesy of Ashlei. A core member of the growing team required to survive the weekend, Ashlei was responsible for providing a steady diet of healthy food for the drivers, who would be eating at odd times and in staggered intervals. Fruit, energy bars, healthy carbs, and a variety of hydration options were spread out, lending an air of an Everest base camp mess tent to the front of the RV. Kathy Dandurand, our massage therapist, was sorting through towels and sheets, preparing to convert her area to a treatment bay once the action started in earnest. The spacious luxury RV was quickly becoming crowded with the many essentials that we would require to get through the next two days.

As the drivers staked out our territory in the back of the RV, several friends trickled in to say hi and offer best wishes. Murray and Michele Marden arrived, and settled in to chat with Ashlei and offer a hand with the to-do list. Ron Rogers, head of the video crew that we had hired to chronicle our experience, knocked on the door a few minutes after we arrived. One by one, Revere, JP, and I stepped out into the sunshine to tape a "Welcome to the Rolex 24" message as a preview to the later action on track. I took a moment to actually sit down, breathe a bit, talk with the growing group in the RV, and try to look relaxed. The distractions were actually welcome, as inside I was churning away, feeling the clock rush onwards toward noon.

We donned our new driver's suits, and I relished the feel and scent of a crisp new uniform. Once more I was a boy, thrilling to the sensation of putting on the garb that would immediately cement my association with the group—shoulder pads, cleats, camouflage gear, baseball pants—they all triggered the same reaction, and I recognized the ancient but familiar feeling right away. I just love the ceremony of putting on a uniform of any kind, and I especially enjoy the first time for each one. Kind of like unwrapping a Christmas present, it's always been a treat for me to discover the unique look and feel of each new uniform. I carefully stepped into the tri-color blue and white suit, noting the large "Bernie Robbins Jewelers Racing" embroidered on the front, along with several other patches and logos on the chest and sleeves. I mated the Velcro ends of the belt, admiring the "Jim Lowe" written in script, right there next to the small American flag. My matching new blue shoes went on last (left one first, always), and after I carefully double-tied the laces, I stood and stole a peek in the mirror. Looking back was a stranger, smiling at the reflected view of a fully-appointed driver and no doubt sizing up his doppelganger before giving approval. I wondered a bit at the image, for sure proud and satisfied with the appearance, while at the same time thinking how I looked so foreign. I had worn race suits before, at least the old red Skippy suit that I now left in the bag for emergency use, but this was different. Credentials would no longer be necessary; all I needed was to "act natural" and the uniform—the race suit—was ticket and testimony that I was a player, a soldier, a surgeon, a driver. And I now looked very much like about two-hundred or so other guys, excepting color choices, all of whom had the same free pass. I paused a moment more, said a silent thanks that I was part of something special and even looked the part, and joined my teammates gathered outside the

RV. We took a minute to check out our fire suits, commenting on how well they had come out—and how much we looked like drivers, like racers, like a team. It was time to head off to the first official team appearance, and we at least looked the part.

The impressive TRG Porsche lineup for the 2006 Rolex 24 at Daytona

JP, Revere, and I made our way through the infield over to Daytona's Victory Lane grandstands where the 9 a.m. drivers meeting was being held. I felt great, walking with my co-drivers past the garages where the cars were being readied and past the expanding crowd already lining up at the autograph session tables in the Fan Zone. Surrounding the entrance to Victory Lane was a phalanx of photographers, all jockeying for position to better shoot the approaching drivers. As the entrance narrowed to a single-file width, I delayed for just a step while following Jim and Revere. I blinked several times as numerous cameras clicked and flashed, momentarily robbing me of vision. Hesitating, I was very briefly surprised at the attention until my good vibe was promptly disrupted as a kneeling photographer politely gave me a "move out of the way, dummy" wave. I turned to my right slightly as his waving persisted, just in time to see Paul Tracy pass me by on his way into the meeting area. I shrugged, smiling at my own chutzpah, and muttered to myself as I followed after PT. "Thought they were all here for you, huh? Dumbass." Reality check number one complete, I sheepishly looked around until I spotted JP and Revere.

I joined my teammates seated in Victory Lane, enjoying several minutes people-watching. Once again, well-known drivers and famous racing faces were everywhere. As the Victory Lane bleachers filled up, I marveled at the number of my racing heroes that were sitting quite literally all around me. I must have looked somewhat comical, resisting the urge to turn my head in full circles as I spotted one star after another. In between Revere and me, JP grinned at our stargazing, waving at occasional friends and wishing luck to all who passed by. For my part, I didn't presume to wave or wish anyone luck; although I now mostly resembled the other drivers, I still had the worry in the back of my mind that someone would tap me on the shoulder and ask me to leave. And, considering the task that lay ahead, some very small part of me might have even wanted that to happen.

Revere, JP and Jim at the autograph session, Daytona, 2006

Following the meeting, we all proceeded to the tables in the Fan Zone for the pre-race autograph session. The three of us found our assigned table, equipped with a stack of our 8 x 10 inch "hero" cards which sported an image of the "Bernie Robbins Jewelers Porsche" in TRG livery. Several rows of tables had been arranged in the infield area, with ours in the middle of a long line that included many of the aforementioned stars. Fans were queuing up at the end, and a few drivers were already sitting in the hot sun. We took up our sharpies, kept sipping from water bottles, and started signing.

The large crowd was beyond anything I had ever experienced. At the 100th Harvard-Yale game, we played in front of more than 70,000 people, but this was entirely different. At the Yale Bowl, the fans were a distant backdrop, and I recall no real sense of intimacy. Here, the fans were all around us—lining up for autographs, chatting with favorite drivers, posing for pictures, and visible around every turn of the track. The feeling was one of a real connection—a shared passion. They collected signatures, objects—relics, sometimes—and lived for the thrill of the race, just as I did. And one small part of me was looking forward to a great race, much as I did when I was a fan. But there was something much different about this event.

Here, I was to be one of the players, one of the drivers who had earned the right to be on the fast side of the wall. Sitting next to my two teammates, I signed anything and everything thrust in front of me, enjoying the banter with the fans who stopped to wish us luck and success. The attention was great, for sure, and the ego stroke was gratifying, but the fun was in the confirmation: we were there to race, people were actually there to watch, and months—no years, really—of preparation were about to pay off. I wasn't sitting on the curb, waiting to be invited into someone's pick-up game. It was finally here, I was in it and part of it, and there would be no riding the bench, no too-white uniform, this time. As I looked around, at the crowd, at the grandstands, at the other drivers, I felt for once like I was participating in something rare enough and special enough to justify the time, effort, and emotion expended to get there. The race hadn't even started yet, and it was already living up to my biggest expectations.

Next up was one of the best parts of any race weekend. Except for the fact that I almost missed it. I had left the autograph tables, sweating from wearing a fire suit in the hot midday sun, and tried to follow JP as usual. As I moved through the infield fan area, I lost sight of Jim in the crowd. Worried a little, I made my way to our garage only to find it empty. There were a few mechanics straightening up the area, but no car and no drivers. They're starting without me! They're gone! With rapidly expanding anxiety, I had an immediate flashback to my familiar dream imagery of being stuck at a track, knowing the race was starting, and being critically separated from the action without a clear way in. Walking quickly now, I looked into the alleyway behind the garages, and spotted a crowd gathering at the end of the lane. I could see a few GT cars lined up there, a few hundred yards away down by the gas pumps. As I double-timed it down to the end of the line, I could hear the PA system already introducing teams and drivers. Around the corner I found the crew of the #68 waiting alongside JP, Revere, and his dad, along with Ashlei, Ginny and Murray Marden.

As I trotted up, JP called out, "You're almost late to your own party, Dr. Lowe."

The crew laughed, and Murray shook his head as I slowed up alongside the car. "Jesus, I leave you guys alone for one minute, and you try to ditch me. Man, you can't trust anyone these days."

Roger smiled that crooked smile of his, stubbed out a cigarette, and pointed at the car. "Grab a hold and give us a push, OK?"

With that we then did one of the coolest things ever: We all staked out a small piece of fender, and rolled our Porsche onto the starting grid for the

24 Hours of Daytona.

As the announcer got to our car in the lineup, I heard my name called, after Jim Pace and Revere Greist, reminding me that I was indeed expected to drive the GT Porsche. As we rolled into place on the grid, friends took pictures and fans surrounded the car and the three of us like rock stars. My partner Joe was there, along with several good friends including Kurt Eilbacher and John Mischler; Ginny smiled and circled about, along with other friends, co-workers, and sponsors. We posed for pictures, signed a few more autographs, and I even managed my first interview with the Associated Press reporter on hand for the event. The crowd seemed to grow thicker, and we continued to move in and out, grinning, shaking hands, and talking with everyone in the vicinity. We were a long way from the front where the racing royalty prototype drivers lived, but even from our distant vantage point, the crowd was swollen, loud, and right on top of us.

Like some of the best parties I've been to, the grid gathering was over just as I was getting into the ebb and flow of it. Friends came and went, the crew gathered around the car one last time, and we did one final shot of the three drivers assembled in front of the Porsche. Moments later, the Daytona security guys worked their way through the crowd in an effort to clear the grid, shooing everyone away from the cars and over the other side of the pit lane wall. This was followed by the mandatory Star Spangled Banner and the always-cool flyby of USAF jets. As I stood in the pit box area watching the planes buzz overhead, I squeezed Ginny's hand and choked back a tear. My wife was back to her stoic and in-control self; it was instead my turn to be overwhelmed.

Our pits were further up the pit wall towards the pit exit, and as a result, I could barely see the #68 at its starting position on the grid. As the PA announcer made that wonderful call—"Lady and Gentlemen, start your engines!"—I strained to see the mechanics step away from the car, signifying a successful ignition. All at once it was starting, right now, right here, and I was part of it. That familiar feeling mixed about in my gut: anxiety competing with anticipation, with anxiety currently winning on points. It's here, and you're in it. This is what you prepared for, now man up. No way to back out now, so best to go forward, and strongly so, right? In a flash I felt that sensation of being caught up in something I no longer controlled—propelled along by an unseen, non-negotiable force, unable and unwilling to alter the direction or the pace.

The noise was deafening as the cars rolled by, two-by-two, leaving the pits for the first of two paced warm-up laps. We cheered above the din as JP moved by in the blue Porsche— and then rolled on in a group of forty-two other cars, proceeding in an orderly line that would soon be shattered. The pit wall was crowded with uniformed members of the TRG contingent, along with friends and onlookers two or three rows deep, all poised to cheer on the start. As the cars came around after the pace laps, we all jockeyed for position; I leaned out as far as I dared to catch a glimpse of our car as the front of the pack approached the green flag.

As the front row of the prototype group neared the start-finish line, the engine notes changed as drivers shifted up and down in search of the best gear for the launch. Straining at the bit, one could almost imagine the pilots leaning forward against their belts as they waited for the signal to go. Standing there in the pits, I too strained forward, standing on my tip-toes and loving the vibration of the engine noise and the visceral thrill of the rush to begin the race.

I heard the race start before I actually noticed the green flag being furiously waved from the starter's stand. All at once the engine noise exploded as the drivers all went to full throttle in the run down to turn one. Thirty-six prototypes accordioned their way through the turn, miraculously managing the first section of turns without incident. Once they passed us, I refocused on the separate group of GT cars coming our way. Once again, we cheered wildly as Jim steered the Porsche down into the first turn and safely through without any problem. Less than two minutes later, the DP group was again screaming by in front of us, and the race was truly on.

As packs of race cars blew by down the front straight, I was faced with a new dilemma: What to do now? I wanted badly to watch as the early laps unfolded, but knew also that I needed to conserve energy. In my current state, pacing along the pit wall and walking around under the TRG tent, I was using up a lot of the reserve that I would later desperately need. I cheered each time I spotted the #68 moving on past the start-finish line, and anxiously awaited its return, knowing that the time for my debut was drawing near. But if I didn't get more relaxed, somehow, I'd be spent before I even got behind the wheel. Ginny recognized this quickly, pointed and then pushing me towards a folding chair parked against the back of the tent wall. I obediently abandoned my primo viewing spot and went over to sit down as Gin fetched a fresh water bottle.

Knowing that our initial strategy called for JP to run a double-stint—remaining in the seat for two pit stops, about two hours total running time—I took advantage of the extended time to hydrate as much as possible. Tommy had advised me to "drink until I was peeing every fifteen minutes," and I was doing an admirable job of following his instructions. Combined with my growing nervousness as my time to drive grew closer, I was doing the up and down, water-in, water-out deal by the time JP came in for his first fuel stop. With the first stint done and without any drama, I was on tap for the next driver change, whether it occurred after a full sixty-minute tank of gas or during an unplanned yellow flag break in the action. Between bathroom breaks, I readied my gear, checking and rechecking my radio ear plugs, balaclava, and gloves, and positioning my helmet just-so to be at the ready. Finally, I reminded Tommy to give me a ten-minute warning, if possible, so that I could start to be extra anxious even earlier.

Seated on my chair, eyes closed and ear buds taped in for good measure, I startled a bit when Tommy tapped me on the shoulder. He held up his right hand, fingers apart, and over the noise all around us mouthed "Five laps" to me. I nodded my understanding, and resisted the urge to launch right out of my seat. I donned my helmet and gloves, failing I'm sure to appear casual as I fumbled about. Roger spotted me and pointed for me to stand behind him as we waited for the car to arrive. I managed to remember to check the ground around my feet, confirming that I was clear of any hoses and wires. Lastly, I allowed myself a quick peek at the track and grandstands directly across from the pits. Nowhere near full but still holding an impressive number of fans, the sight of the colorful seats towering over the racing surface was even cooler than before, now that it seemed alive with activity.

Despite the dampening of noise from my helmet and earplugs, the buzzing in my ears intensified. Adrenaline surged through my system, and I felt like puking up breakfast right there in the pits. My overworked adrenals gave it another squeeze when Tommy looked over at me and pointed towards the pit box. As he did so, the crew assumed their ready positions, air guns and tires positioned perfectly for the coming pit stop. At once my mouth grew dry, and I swallowed hard as I looked over the wall, trying to spot the car on its way toward us.

As I stood there on tiptoes, head pounding and pulse bounding, I was temporarily shut out from the rest of the world. Since I wasn't listening to the radio at that moment, I didn't hear the call that JP had just run out of gas down by the pit entrance. In fact, I was clueless about this little drama until I saw the crew jump over the wall and start running. Looking down towards the pit entrance, I spotted the stranded blue Porsche, stuck on pit road as the mechanics sprinted to it. Despite my totally focused state, I was momentarily annoyed by this, as we had identified a problem with the reserve tank function during testing—and were reassured that it had been fixed. Apparently not. Something maybe to discuss later, but at the moment, there were bigger fish to fry.

The crew pushed the #68 down the length of pit lane, all the way to where I stood poised to make my own leap over the wall. Waiting until the door opened and Roger started pulling at JP's wires and belts, I jumped over the wall and stationed myself at the rear quarter of the Porsche. By the time I arrived at my post, Jim was most of the way out of the car. Once he had freed himself, he motioned me over, and took a moment to coach me one last time before I got in.

"Nice and easy. Warm up everything first, then go have fun. You can do this."

Wired as I was, I nodded and moved around him towards the door of the car as he patted me on the shoulder. I squirmed my way down into the form-fitting seat, grabbing for the belts even as I was still getting settled. I felt Roger's hands grab for the radio cord and drink hose velcroed to the side of my helmet as I clicked the belts into place. Raising my arms up, he snugged up the belts and gave me the thumbs up. I dutifully pushed the radio button, calling out "Radio check, radio check" and trying to sound calm.

Thomas' voice crackled into my helmet. "Loud and clear. Ready to go as soon as you are. Go go go GO!"

I dumped the clutch, accelerating out into the fast lane as I checked my mirrors, relieved to not have stalled on my first attempt. Double-checking my belts, I drove slowly onwards at the pit-lane speed limit while tightening the shoulder straps.

Thomas again came onto the radio. "Remember to reset fuel. Lots of traffic out there, remember to warm-up well. The reserve tank isn't working, so we'll call you in when it's time. Have a fun run."

I radioed my thanks as I focused ahead on the pit exit area. I tested the brakes several times, and shifted up and down once before getting to the area where I would join the track—just inside the braking area of the turn three hairpin.

Checking my right-side mirrors, I accelerated down to turn three, downshifting as I did a medium brake and turned in towards the apex. The immediate view to my front and rear seemed filled with cars: cars dove inside me on their way through the turn, with several prototypes in a fast line causing me to stay wide as I navigated the corner, while several more seemed stacked up behind. I looked up, back and all around as I exited the turn and finally got into full throttle for the first time as I headed for Daytona's infield kink. As I moved through each turn, cars passed, sometimes on both sides, as I tried to hit my marks while staying out of the way of the faster moving vehicles (which was pretty much everybody at that point).

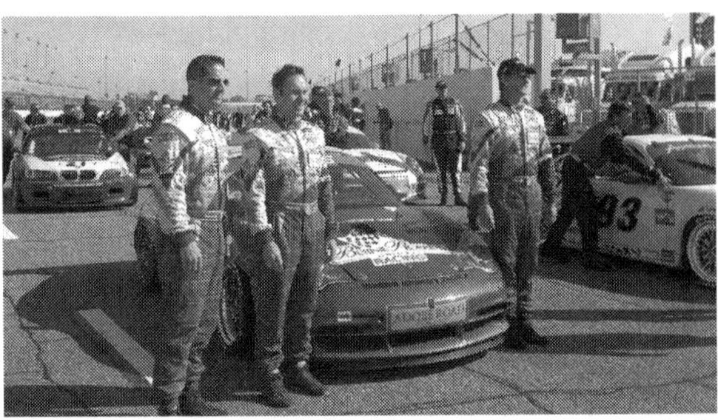

Jim, Revere and JP pause on the grid with the #68 Porsche GT3 Cup car

I made it through turn six, and sped up onto the steep banking, keeping to the low side as still more DP's blew on by to my outside on my right. As I shifted up through the gears, I became aware that for the first time in what seemed like a month, I was actually starting to relax. Intense focus was still required, but the tension of the unknown, of the unfamiliar, was receding with each turn of the wheel and each gear change. I ignored the bucking front end of the car as I raced down the back straight, easing through the bus stop for the first time and resuming my high-speed run through the tri-oval front straight. Looking up at the approaching first turn and seeing both DP- and GT-class cars entering, I strained forward a bit, actually eager to join the fight. It wasn't a fully unconscious sensation, but I was aware that I was now happy and excited to be driving the car—no longer questioning my motives or second-guessing the wisdom of the whole expedition. Like a mountaineer immersed in the

Driving through the infield at Daytona, 2006

process of taking the next step, I started thinking then only about the next turn, the next pass, the next lap.

Once I had a lap or two under my belt, I realized that there were actually a few cars on the track that were struggling more than I was to keep pace. Several times, I went into braking zones on the inside as I passed another GT car, thrilling to the feeling of going just a bit faster than someone, anyone, out there. I kept thinking about JP's mantra of "nice and easy," actually wiggling my fingers and toes while driving on the banking sections.

Although it might seem odd to the unfamiliar, the fastest parts of the lap were actually the times when I could relax a bit more. After all, the car was going in a relatively straight line, albeit at 170 mph. This created the perfect opportunity to check gauges, fidget with belts or knobs as necessary, and generally breathe a bit slower until the next turn beckoned. Though this only amounted to a few seconds here and there, there was a distinct difference to the calm of the high-speed straight and the multi-tasking chaos of each intervening turn. The mind never actually drifted, but the variations in intensity were a welcome break in the cadence of each lap.

As my stint progressed, I started to match lap times with a couple of GT cars—a Corvette, another Porsche, and a BMW all stayed around me as the group of us struggled to get by a much-slower Ferrari. As we made our way through each corner, I focused on the car immediately ahead, planning the best moment for a pass only after I identified that I was faster through a particular section. Ignoring lap times on the dash, I instead tried to get out of each turn faster, accelerate earlier, and think smartly about each passing opportunity, all while remembering to look out for the faster DP cars. I executed several good passes and managed to let a few much-faster GT cars by without any drama. There were definitely moments of "Whew, that was close," but with each lap, I felt better and better, going faster and faster. The racing for position, the planning of the passes, the jockeying with traffic, was all just so much fun. There was noise, vibration, constantly shifting g-forces—the full adrenaline onslaught—all combining to create a sensual overload that was at once delicious and thrilling. I was racing at Daytona—and enjoying the rush immensely.

At that point, I had quite honestly never felt better or more comfortable while driving a race car. So of course, feeling that good should have actually been great cause for karmic concern. My wife still has realistic doubts about my reliance upon "magical thinking," but in retrospect, I should have known. For as Robert Hunter and Jerry Garcia so expertly teamed up to observe, "When life looks like easy street, there is danger at your door." Or, in this case, straight ahead.

About forty-five minutes into the stint, I had just started a new lap as I made my way down into turn one, smoothly onto the brakes and then into the snaking section of turn two. For a change, there were no cars immediately around me, and I was looking forward to a driving for a few more turns without having to dodge prototypes or faster GT cars. I rounded the Armco section of the second part of the turn, looking up and anticipating the coming hairpin of turn three. Shifting smoothly, I went to power, flat out in the easy, s-shaped section, focusing on the next brake point a couple hundred feet ahead.

As I hit the track-out area at the exit of turn two—surely the most uneventful and least-challenging section of the Daytona lap—my rear wheels suddenly lost grip and the car snapped around in a near-instantaneous swapping of ends. Before I was fully aware that I had in fact completely lost control, I was spinning down the outside of the track surface and grass, entirely surprised by this sudden change of events. I had only a moment to understand just how significant my mistake was, and not enough time to actually panic, before the Porsche's rear end hit the wall on the outside of the turn three hairpin.

Chapter Fifteen

The Porsche smacked the wall hard, with a surprisingly loud and awful sound. The sudden booming crunch of the collision made for the perfect soundtrack of my waking nightmare. Like every wreck that I've ever been in before or since, the feeling at the moment of impact was rougher than I had expected. Had I met the wall at any other angle, it could have been much worse.

When the car completely lost grip and started spinning, I was probably going upwards of 120 mph. However, in the split second that it took me to realize that I was completely out of control, several thoughts raced at me at a million miles per hour, a combination of truly awful thoughts and images. At first, I could not believe that I had just wrecked the fucking car. Everything that we had worked for, with such dedication and diligence, was disgracefully punted out the window and completely lost because of something I had done. I just couldn't accept that it had all come down to this, in a split-second's error. And this wasn't anything that I could pretend didn't happen or hope that no one noticed. I had teammates involved who had also put their hearts and souls into the effort, and I had just screwed it all up with a stupid rookie mistake. A mistake I couldn't even wrap my arms around that very moment, sitting there in the stationary Porsche dug half deep into a tire wall.

Shell-shocked in the seat of the crumpled Porsche, I thought angrily to myself, "How the hell did I just do that?" What fundamental mistake could have possibly caused me to wreck on a relatively straight and easy part of the track? Did I lift off the throttle at a critical moment? Did I hit someone else's oil? Sand maybe? A momentary lapse of attention then? I wanted to analyze it, but no answer was immediately available. What I did know, for sure, was that I was embarrassed and immediately stricken by the extent of my failure. This was the full frontal, pants-down embarrassment of an amateur playing at a game which was well over his head at that point.

And there I was, sitting in a motionless car while a race went on past me, around me, uncaring about my distress. I was pissed off in the worst way—at myself, at my foolishness having thought that this was going to go OK, and at my stupidity for allowing myself to be responsible for the failure of an entire team through one error.

As I listened to the engine pop and crackle as it settled into an inert state, I stewed in my disbelief and epic disappointment. Shaking my head silently, I just couldn't clear the gritty taste in my mouth and the terrible knot in my gut. I was unharmed physically—in fact, not once during the course of the accident had I thought about getting hurt—but the emotion of my error was such that I knew instantly it would stay with me forever, not matter what came after.

Fortunately, the immediate matter at hand demanded that I regain some focus. There would be more time later for self-reproach and regret, but for now, I had to get some idea about the condition of the car. Was it totaled—a complete loss, forcing our retirement? I didn't smell smoke, so fire didn't seem to be an issue. How badly had I damaged the Porsche? Still strapped motionless in my seat, I realized then that I had been holding my breath, and that it was really quiet inside my helmet and inside of the car. I had tried to execute the "both feet in" maneuver suggested for the spinning driver—plant your right foot down on the brake and left on the clutch—but to no avail. I had stalled the car. The obvious next step now would be to restart the car, but first I had to confess my accident over the radio.

"Hey Tommy, do you copy, do you copy?"

Tommy came onto the radio, loud and clear. Radio worked, check.

"We copy you. How's it going?"

Although it was now apparent that the guys back in the pits weren't yet aware of my off-course excursion, I realized that I couldn't very well hide my indiscretion from my own team. Considering only briefly the concept of abandoning my vehicle and sneaking away, I instead fessed up over the radio.

"Uh, guys, I had an accident. Into the wall in three. I think it's pretty bad. I'm sorry."

Tommy ran through the mandatory questions. "Are you OK?" And then, the critical, "How's the car?"

"I'm fine, not sure about the car. Just sorting things out here."

"Can you refire it?"

"Just a minute, I'm trying." I hit the starter, praying for a good sound and ignition. The car responded, and the engine spooled up on the first try. I let out a long breath at the sound of my first request answered. The next step required no input from Tommy. I depressed the clutch, found first gear, and sucked in another breath as I gingerly tried to move forward.

The car shuddered a moment, and then extracted itself from the tires. I ran the revs up slowly, and the Porsche responded by sliding a bit as I gained traction in the grassy area outside of turn three.

"Ok, I've restarted, and I'm underway."

The car wobbled a bit and sideslipped as I accelerated slowly towards the track, finally entering the paved surface at the exit area of the turn. As soon as I gained some speed, the rear of the car put forth a hideous combination of thumping and banging, signifying a lethal injury to the unseen back end of the Porsche.

"If you can, try to drive it back to the pits and we'll take a look at it there." Tommy was hopeful, not yet understanding what I was now discovering as I attempted to drive the wounded car.

I radioed back to the pits. "I'm moving, but I think it's going to be a big problem to fix. I think we should head for the garage."

"Copy that. We'll meet you there. Be careful and stay to the inside of the track."

My distress continued as the car and I limped our way around the track, keeping low and slow while the rest of the race went on around us. The Porsche protested the whole way back, but I managed to make it back to the garage without any further incident. Roger and Tommy arrived a moment after I pulled to a stop inside our garage space; I stayed a minute longer in the seat, still buckled in as I tried to calm myself. As I sat there, disgusted about what had just happened and how quickly it had all gone so wrong, I gradually became aware of my physical distress. I sensed my rapid breathing along with a pulse pounding in my ears; as I noted that, I also realized that my internal temperature gauge was being pegged as the heat soaked into my still form.

Scrambling now to unfasten my belts and disconnect cords, I pulled at the door latch and banged my way out of the car. I fumbled with my chinstrap, pulling at the helmet and my balaclava simultaneously. My stomach lurched as I tasted bile in the back of my throat. Sure that I was going to vomit, I stumbled over to the back corner of the garage, and bent over a tool chest, shoulders heaving.

With hands on my knees and eyes closed, I took deep breaths and managed to choke back the urge to throw up what little there was in my gut. Still sweating profusely, and absolutely gutted by the events of the last few minutes, I rose up slowly and hazarded a look around.

Inches from my face was the curious visage of a young boy, who had apparently planted himself at the viewing windows of the Daytona garages as soon as he heard the car enter. His look changed nearly instantly from thrill to fright as my twisted scowl greeted him. As I stood up, he leaned away, like a kid at the zoo who wanted to distance himself just a bit more from the waking bear. Backed by his dad, he hesitated a moment, and then carefully thrust a paper and a pen through the window opening in one of the more memorable but ill-timed autograph requests ever. Not yet able to speak, and still expecting to puke any moment, I shook him off, holding up my hand to request he try again later.

By the time I had composed myself, Roger and several of the mechanics had already begun to crawl over the car. I stood off to the side, forcing myself to watch as they assessed the damaged areas of the Porsche. As I leaned against the wall, sweat puddling around my feet and my respirations slowing, several more crew members arrived to help. Just beyond the yellow line of the garage opening, several race fans had also gathered around to gape at the drama unfolding inside.

Emerging from underneath the car, Roger saw me waiting off to the side and waved me over to talk.

"This looks pretty ugly. Is JP around?"

I shook my head. "I'm not sure he even knows about this yet. He's probably still resting in the RV."

Roger looked grim. "Better go get him, and ask him to come over here. I'm not sure how bad this is, or how long it will take to figure it all out, but we should get him in on this now."

With that, Roger turned back to the car, which was forming a puddle of its own on the concrete floor.

I spun around to find Ginny standing right behind me, taking in the roughened image of her husband as she sized up the situation. She said nothing, moving a step forward to hug me, wet fire suit and all. I'm sure she was relieved to see that I was unharmed, but by then she was surely far more concerned about the distraught look on my face.

"I'm just glad you're OK."

"Thanks honey. Nothing bruised but my ego. I can't tell you how awful I feel right now."

"Can they fix it?"

I mustered up an attempt at humor. "My ego? No, that's forever scratched. Not sure about the car yet. We need to go get JP."

Gin said nothing more, and turned with me to start the walk of shame back to the RV lot.

I banged through the door of the RV, and stepped up into the center area. Ashlei was sitting on the couch, talking with Kathy Dandurand; JP was snoozing under a sheet on the massage table. Ash and Kathy looked up when I entered, quickly abbreviating their "How did it go?" when they saw the look on my face.

"What's wrong?"

JP looked up in alarm as he heard the question. "Everything OK? Is Revere in the car?"

"No, it's not good. I wrecked the car. It's back in the garage." I didn't know a good way to announce this, so it came out in one big blurt. "I hit the wall in turn three. I think it's pretty bad, but the guys are just now going over the car."

JP sat up quickly, gathering the sheet around him as he looked around for some clothes. Ashlei and Kathy started asking questions to Ginny and me all at once, but my attention was focused on my teammate. "I'm really sorry. I don't know what happened—it was going great, and then…"

"Are you OK?"

"Yeah, I'm fine. Upset, but fine physically."

"Well, let's get over to the garage and see what the deal is. Did you drive it back there, or did they tow it?"

"Drove it, but it sounded ugly." I didn't want to sugarcoat anything just then. Everyone would know soon enough anyway.

After he got hurriedly dressed, JP left the RV with me in tow. I still had my sweat-soaked suit on, oblivious to the wet odor surrounding me. I kept pace with Jim as I tried to explain what had happened out on the track; since I was unclear myself, my description probably sounded sketchy at best. My co-driver kept walking briskly, probably running through several possible scenarios in his head as we moved through the paddock. With nothing more to say about the actual crash, we both were silent as we entered the garage area.

Tommy Sadler examines the wounded Porsche

JP let out a soft whistle as the rear end of the wounded Porsche came into view. Roger appeared from around the side of the car, where he had been working under the left rear wheel well.

Neither JP nor Roger bothered with the formality of a greeting. "It took a pretty big hit to the rear; frame's probably bent, but I don't know yet just how bad the rest of the damage is until we pull the engine and gearbox."

By now, two other crew members had stopped working to join the conversation.

JP raised an eyebrow at the news of the bent frame. "Well, he drove it back, right, so the engine and gears are probably OK, I guess. The question is, can you fix it and how long will it take?"

I observed the conversation silently from my subordinate position as one unsure about the extent of the crime I had just committed. No one looked my way, but I was the guilty party, and they were now deciding my fate. Clearly, the jury of mechanics thought the death penalty was in order—and by the looks on their faces, I began to understand that no one really thought this was fixable. Or at least, worth fixing in the middle of a race.

Roger and JP talked some more, glancing occasionally at the immobile car and the mechanics standing by for further orders. I waited helplessly, wondering if I was about to have the shortest racing career on record because of my one incomprehensibly simple error. By now, Revere had joined us in the garage; he was gentlemanly enough not to ask me to rehash the crash.

Roger announced the verdict. "I don't know how long it will take, but we can get her running again if that's what you want. We'll have a better idea once the engine's out and we get to work, but I'm sure we can get it going if you want us to."

"Any reason you suspect it won't run again?"

"No, but I'm not sure how well it will handle once we work on the frame. Honestly, most of the teams I've worked for would probably retire it right now, but I'm willing to work on it if that's what you guys want."

In a moment that sealed my admiration for Jim Pace, and most likely saved my racing career, JP answered without bothering to check with his two co-drivers. "We came here to finish this race. I'd like you to work as best you can and get her back out there. I don't think we care about how long it might take; we just want to finish what we started."

"OK by me. I'll let you know how long we'll be in just a bit. Sit tight until then." Roger gave a half-smile, half-grimace, and turned back to the car. The mechanics had heard the decision, and were already back working on the car.

JP and Revere started to walk back towards the RV lot; Gin made a move to follow them, but stopped when she realized I wasn't moving yet.

"Are you coming back to the RV?"

"Not right now, thanks." I ran my hands through my still-wet hair, sprinkling Gin with little showers of sweat. "Oh shit, sorry baby, I didn't mean to do that. I wasn't thinking."

Gin shook it off. "Honey, you're still in that wet suit. Why don't you come back, get into some dry clothes, maybe rehydrate a bit?"

"You go ahead, I'll be there in a little bit. I just need to stay here for a few minutes."

My wife squeezed my hand before she turned away. "OK honey, I'll be in the RV waiting. I'll tell the guys that you'll be along soon."

I walked over to the entrance of the garage, and stepped over a couple of sets of mechanics legs as I made my way to the back of the garage space. I found an empty stretch of table, hopping up between a set of brake rotors and a tool chest. Reclining back a bit, I rested my head against the wall, closing my eyes to the sound of pneumatic tools and the crew's chatter as they worked on my wrecked car.

***

Early in my residency at Jefferson Hospital, I was on-call one night when a fresh trauma patient arrived in the ER. He was a 30-something-year-old guy who had been in a significant car crash; when I first saw him at about 3 a.m., he was unconscious and unresponsive. Mechanically ventilated through a breathing tube in his trachea, the patient had been given Pavulon, a medication that rendered him chemically paralyzed and essentially unexaminable neurologically. When faced with this familiar situation, the specialist's next step in the evaluation involved getting a CT scan of the patient's brain. Since neurologic examination was limited, treatment decisions would depend almost entirely on what was found on the scan. I followed the patient up to the radiology suite, where he underwent a head CT while I watched from the technician's booth.

As the CT-scan images unfolded on the screen before me, I saw successive slices of the patient's brain, progressing from top to bottom, revealing critical information about the state of the different compartments of the skull and their contents, one image at a time. I looked for the tell-tale bright white rim of blood pressing on the outer surface of the brain tissue which would signify a hematoma that needed emergent surgical attention. Instead, with each refreshed image, I saw only swollen white and gray matter and nothing resembling a significant bleed. With the need for an immediate operation ruled out, I left the scanner room and returned to the trauma unit to write orders about the non-surgical management of the comatose patient.

Finally finished with my tasks for the night, I collapsed into bed in the call room after 4 a.m. With less than an hour to sleep before rounds in the NICU started, I didn't even bother to change out of my dirty green scrubs. Stashing my beeper on the bedside table, I adjusted my pillow and was quickly snoring in the practiced manner of a sleep-deprived trainee with no time to spare.

Ninety minutes later, after completing rounds in the ICU, I joined the rest of the neurosurgical team for X-ray rounds in the radiology suite. A daily morning meeting attended by the chairman, other professors, and all of the residents, this was a preview of the day's scheduled cases and also a review of the previous evening's work. New trauma patients' films were routinely presented by the on-call resident, case histories discussed, and management plans formed for the coming day.

When the CT of my new patient appeared on the screen before the group, I presented the facts of the case in monotone.

"This guy came in in the middle of the night, Trauma Level I alert, unrestrained driver in an MVA. Blood alcohol over 200; two other passengers dead at the scene. He was already chemically paralyzed when I saw him, but reportedly he was unresponsive before they put him down. He just got back to the NICU an hour ago; he'll need to be checked again when the Pavulon wears off." I rattled off the required information to the team as everyone checked out the black-and-white images.

Dr. Osterholm, chairman of the department and the big boss, usually spoke up first. Expecting to hear a routine question or two and some thoughts on how to proceed with the patient's care, I was already thinking about the next set of films when his booming voice jarred me back to the matter at hand. "Did you want to take out that subdural, James?" (To this day, my mother and Dr. Osterholm are the only two people to ever call me 'James' on a regular basis.) "That's a pretty big clot, right there across both frontal lobes. Don't you want that out of there?"

The full attention of the group was now directed to the head CT. As I stared at the ghostly images, I realized that there actually was a blood clot along the front surfaces of the brain—not the usual bright white appearance but the rarer medium-gray layer of blood that blended into the gray of the adjacent brain tissue—and that it was sizeable and causing significant pressure on the patient's brain.

My chief resident, Murray, let out a humorless laugh that was his bizarre way of expressing himself under stress and in challenging situations. "Why didn't you call me about this one? That guy needs an operation!"

Dr. O grumbled his agreement. "Gotta get that clot out of there, James, it's causing a lot of pressure."

I sat there stunned, staring at the CT as if my focused gaze could make the blood clot disappear.

"I'll call the OR," Murray continued, "and we'll get him in there stat."

It was an unspoken fact that, as the junior-most resident, I wasn't going to be part of that operation. Before he left, Murray gave the marching orders for the morning's work. "You guys finish rounds, and we'll see the unit patients after I'm out of the OR."

As the group stood up in unison, the on-call attending, Dale Simpson, made his way to me and tapped me on the shoulder to get my attention. "Those are sometimes easy to miss when they look like that. But you can't afford to make that mistake again. It probably doesn't matter in this guy now, but next time, make goddamn sure that doesn't get by you."

I nodded silently, numb as the growing realization of my mistake continued to spread throughout my sleep-deprived body. As the group moved out of the room, I spent an extra moment looking at the CT on the viewbox. Even in my exhausted state, I thought I should have known enough to spot that clot reliably when called upon to do so. I couldn't understand how I had missed it, but there it was, proof of my fallibility. My failure hanging up for all to see—and a life at stake because of it.

I went about my tasks that morning, floating in the familiar foggy post-call state of the typical junior resident. I ticked item after item off my scut list, all the while keeping an eye on the clock. I knew the patient would be out of the OR eventually, and I wanted a chance to check on him once he was. I was no longer directly responsible for his care, but I definitely felt responsible for whatever condition he ended up in once he arrived back in the NICU.

An hour or so later, I peeked into the darkened intensive care room where the patient lay with head heavily bandaged and tubes protruding. I opened the door carefully, even though the comatose patient was the room's only occupant. After pulling the shades on the windows, I seated myself in a chair at the side of the hospital bed. My unknown patient was motionless and unresponsive; the only sounds came from the soft beeping of the monitors and the rush of air from the ventilator.

Turning my beeper off so that I wouldn't be interrupted, I sat in the hard chair, hands stuffed deep in the pockets of my white coat. I looked not at the supine patient but stared straight ahead, focusing on anything but that head wrapped in white gauze. I wasn't expecting any movement, any response; there would be no miracles that day—I was sure of that. Reality doesn't reward mistakes with happy endings; real-life patients don't slowly open their eyes and ask you why you're so concerned that you're sitting there at bedside in a darkened room.

I thought of my mistake, of how it was that I had missed a diagnosis and possibly altered the outcome of an already terrible situation. I had never been confronted with a personal error of that magnitude before; tripping on a few hurdles or dropping a punt just didn't compare to watching someone die with your possible assistance. In my exhausted and inexperienced state, I couldn't then consider the fact that the hematoma on that CT was something I had never seen before and wasn't ideally prepared to recognize. Learning on the job carried with it several risks, not the least of which was the likelihood that junior trainees would make mistakes. But that wasn't on my mind then—only the fact that I was the one who had erred, for whatever reason, and that failure was significant, at least to me.

Not knowing how to proceed without recognition of my fault, I said a quiet apology to the unknown patient, sat a few minutes more in silence, then stood and left the room. I silently vowed to never again fail another patient through lack of effort or preparation, and I equally hoped that there would be no more remorseful bedside vigils in my future.

Over the next few days, the trauma patient failed to make any meaningful improvement. He never regained consciousness, and was eventually pronounced brain-dead one night while I was off-call and at home. Arriving at 5:30 a.m. for rounds the next morning, I noticed the empty bed in the patient's NICU room; I didn't need any more information to understand that he had passed away while I was sleeping at home. I actually felt a guilty sense of relief—not because he had died, but because his presence had been a daily wincing reminder of my error every time I was in the unit. Although he was gone from the list of patients on the neurosurgical service, the image of that CT scan and his bandaged head stayed with me, a lingering reminder of fallibility and human limitation.

***

There is no way to appropriately compare the life-and-death circumstances encountered in medicine to the sport of car racing. I would never attempt to directly connect the act of providing healing care to a patient with a game, a sport, and the ultimately shallow drama that goes with it. As I've said many times before, nobody dies if I can't brake a bit later into turn one. However, I can attest that the sensation of wrecking a race car, of making an error that results in damage to the car, possibly ruining the race for you and your teammates, is very comparable to the feelings experienced with medical mistakes I've made. That heaviness in your gut, that gnawing sensation of failure, compounded by the visible and public aspect of the mistake, is surely physiologic as much as emotional: a regrettable stew of brain chemicals and stomach acids combines with the heavy knowledge that one's actions are not erasable in any way. With no way to un-wreck the car, only the realization that there will be opportunities for redemption in the future ultimately allows you to again seek the good feelings associated with successful performance. When I've erred in patient care, the very next patient still needs me to be focused and skillful, so there's little time and no place for dysfunctional ignominy. Like the hockey goalie who just let a weak shot through the five-hole, the surgeon who can't resume quality and dedicated work after a mistake is otherwise useless to all the rest who need his help.

So, after sitting in the garage a bit, it was only a partially conscious decision to leave the car and return to the RV. I could stay there thinking hard thoughts about my shortcomings as a race car driver, or I could go, clean up, and prepare for the possibility of another stint. I made my way through the small crowd gathered around the opening of the garage, not bothering to stop or acknowledge any of the fans straining for a look at the damaged rear end of the Porsche. A moment later, I appeared back at the RV once again. Ginny, JP, Revere, Ashlei, and Kathy were seated around the massage table, so space was at a premium. As their chatter abruptly stopped, I silently squeezed past the contingent in the front and headed for the back bedroom area. Gin got up and followed me into the back of the bus, grabbing a towel on the way.

"Let's get you out of that wet suit; Kathy's waiting to give you a massage."

I let out a sober laugh. "I hardly deserve a massage, especially after that brilliant piece of driving."

"Don't be so stubborn. A massage will do you wonders—I'll bet your muscles are already stiffening up."

I grunted my consent, wrapped the white towel around me, and headed towards the table.

I made one lame attempt at humor. "I've never had a massage before, so be gentle with me."

Kathy smiled and took me by the hand. "Just lie down on the table—we'll do your back first—and tell me if I'm hurting you. But sometimes it's best to just breathe slow and go with it so I can work on those deep muscles."

I glanced over at Gin, who nodded and reassured me. "Go ahead honey,

I'll make sure the sheet doesn't fall off if you fall asleep. Nobody wants to see your sweaty butt."

I lay face down on the table, not realizing just yet that I was exhausted—emotionally, physically, mentally—and in need of some shut-eye. It was only four in the afternoon, but I felt wiped out by the strain of the day. As Kathy worked on my back and shoulders, my mind drifted to the drama of the afternoon. I winced in pain as she dug into a particularly tender muscle, knowing that at least part of the pain was the remembrance of my wreck. I closed my eyes, and soon drifted off to the reverberating sound of the cars racing just a few yards outside of the RV. I was a world away, completely disconnected from the race, and yet only a few hundred yards from the very spot where my Porsche had hit the wall.

Ginny was still sitting at the side of the table when I awoke about forty-five minutes later. I cleared my head, and was dismayed to realize that the nightmare of my crash was still very real. Gin handed me a fresh bottle of water, which I eagerly chugged down before asking for another.

"JP said to come out to the garage when you're awake. They're still working on the car, but it sounds like it might be finished soon."

A few minutes later, after dressing again in my damp suit, I headed over to the garage. It was starting to get dark out, and the lights were already on around the track. The garage was all lit up too, and several mechanics were still moving purposefully around the car. The engine was still lying on the floor, but the rest of the car was starting to resemble a Porsche again. JP and Revere met me at the entrance, both looking a bit more upbeat than the last time I had seen them.

"Roger says they're done with the major stuff—now they just have to put the engine back in, and we'll be ready to go. I'm guessing about ninety minutes, give or take."

I didn't have to say that I was relieved to hear the news. "We'll be able to get back on track? It'll run well enough, you think?"

JP smiled. "Well, we're gonna let Revere here finally get some laps in and tell us what he thinks. Let him be the test driver this time."

I looked over to Revere. "I'm really sorry, man, I'm just so glad you'll get to run. I feel so bad…"

"No problem, not anything to do about it now. Hopefully we'll have some clean stints and finish this thing." Revere smiled, trying to pass on the good vibe that always seemed to surround him.

"I appreciate that, you don't know how much. What a relief that it's gonna be fixed. I couldn't believe…" I stammered along like that another few seconds.

JP grabbed my shoulder. "We're cool, Dr. Lowe, don't worry, we're gonna go out there, run hard, and finish just like we planned."

I smiled at that thought and turned back with my teammates to watch the crew at work.

16

Chapter Sixteen

Less than ninety minutes later, Revere was togged up and seated in the Porsche, awaiting the signal to fire the engine. JP and I stood off to the side, listening to Tommy's instructions on the radio.

"OK Revere, start 'er up, let it run for a moment to get some heat in it."

The engine boomed to life as my teammate revved the motor a few times. So far, so good.

"Alright, let's get moving. We'll push you out. Left hand down." Tommy directed my co-driver as he maneuvered out of the stall. "Once you get out to pit lane, wait for the official to wave you out. After that, take your time getting up to speed. Let me know if anything feels like a problem."

Revere acknowledged the radio, ignoring the fact that he was now officially serving as a crash test dummy. "Copy, I'm on my way."

With no further ceremony, the battle-scarred Porsche moved off through to paddock to resume our now very solitary race to the finish.

We moved to the pits, where JP and I sat and watched the race on the monitors behind the TRG pit box. Revere was running good times—1:58's and 1:59's, on par with what he had run in practice—and it seemed that the car was none the worse now that it was turning racing laps again. Tough horse, that Porsche.

As we watched, Jim described the plan for the next few hours. "We'll let Revere run a double stint, then get you back in the car after that."

I looked at him with some surprise, as my turn would normally come after his. "I want you back out there, back on the horse. You need to run some fresh clean laps, and get through a full stint to get your confidence back."

I felt a mixture of fear and relief, deciding to embrace the relief I felt at the prospect of driving again, racing again, and hopefully, redeeming myself (at least in my own eyes) with an error-free run.

About two hours later, I jumped into the driver's seat for the second time, now focused and determined to drive hard and well and, most importantly, without mistakes. Starting my stint, I pulled out of the pit exit carefully, checking my mirrors as I entered turn three. Several cars were bearing down on me, coming hard through the turn two complex on the run down into the hairpin. I stayed wide to the outside, letting the caravan pass me by, then joined the tail end of the pack as I accelerated out of the turn. I locked on to the GT car in front of me, trying to be smooth as I shifted up through the gears, lifting just a bit at the entrance to the kink, braking early for turn five as the tires came up to temp. The pack separated from me easily, but I continued to focus on the last car, using it as a rabbit as my brain came up to speed on the semi-dark track.

Down the superstretch I went, seeing red shift lights on the dash just as I went to the brakes for the bus stop chicane. The Corvette in front of me was just at the exit of the chicane, so I still had a set of taillights to chase. One check in the mirrors and I was back on the high banking, heading down the front tri-oval at an exhilarating 165 mph. The car bucked and moved on the track's bumps, but I ignored it, remembering instead to wiggle my fingers and toes as I prepared for the turn one braking zone. I wasn't gaining on the Corvette, but it wasn't getting away, either. I braked hard but without panic, relieved to find a smooth deceleration down to the first apex, easy off the brakes now, around the Armco, and back to full throttle as soon as you can stand it, through the flat-out s-shaped turn two, check your mirrors before you turn into the horseshoe, off the brake and back to power now, now, let's go, get after that guy. Kink, hairpin, turn six, back on the banking, I did it all without thinking of anything but going faster, catching that car, chasing down that guy in front of me.

And through it all, for the next forty-five minutes or so, I completely forgot to look over at the wall outside turn three, to worry about my error there that was ages ago, to seize up with fear each time through turn two. I was pushing hard, driving well, chasing other cars and giving way when called upon to do so; I was staying out of trouble, staying out of the way of the hot shoes, but still running respectable laps with good times and no scary moments. I was racing.

A short while later, I heard Tommy on the radio.

"How you doing, Jim? Everything OK?"

It took a moment before I was able to answer—I'm still pretty challenged by the occasion when I need to talk and race at full speed simultaneously—and then I managed a quick reply. "OK here. Car's good."

Tommy next words were a surprise. "You should be seeing the red fuel light any minute now. When you do, let us know, switch to the reserve, and head for the pits."

"Copy." I hadn't realized that I was anywhere near the end of my stint, so engrossed was I in the act of trying to catch up to anything nearby on the track. I felt reasonably good at that point but certainly wasn't ready to beg for a prolonged double-stretch in the car just yet.

Two laps later, with the light glowing red and the reserve now mysteriously functioning, I loosened my belts, unplugged the drink bottle, and made my way onto pit road. Shifting down through the gears, I hit the button to engage the rev limiter at the pit lane entrance, keeping my speed at the 45 mph limit. I looked up towards the TRG pit complex, excited now to do my first driver change exit in action—after all, I had missed that bit my first time out.

I spotted the waving lollipop sign pointing the way to our pit stall; I managed a smooth entrance and somehow stopped my nose on the sign, leaving the car in neutral. As I unclicked the belts, I felt the car abruptly rise up in the air on the pneumatic jacks. Someone opened the door and reached in to disconnect the radio and untangle the belts as I simultaneously began to wrestle myself out of the seat. Jumping/half-falling out of the car, I regained my balance and stumbled past JP on my way to the wall. With crewmen throwing tires this way and that, and hoses snaking around the corners of the Porsche, it was nearly impossible not to get tripped up. Half blinded by the limited view out of my helmet, I took a few steps before some faceless mechanic took pity on me and literally shoved me over the wall.

As the car pulled away in a screeching cloud of cold tire smoke, I walked a few more steps towards the back of the tented space. I realized that several people positioned around the area were clapping, congratulating the crew on a fast, mistake-free stop. Even though we were at least one hundred laps behind the class leaders, there was still enthusiasm and hard charging going on in our camp, and it was an exhilarating feeling.

Despite the buzz from my first complete stint in the race, I was starting to feel pretty worn out. It was about 11 p.m. on Saturday, I was sweat-soaked and spent from driving, and the race hadn't even hit its halfway point! I pondered this as I stripped off my wet gear back at the RV, mentioning it to Gin as I undressed.

"I can't believe we're not even into the second half of this thing yet. I'm beat, and there's a lot more to go—if we're lucky."

Feeling encouraged by the fact that we were back in running condition, and emboldened by a glass of wine or three at dinner, Gin reverted to a more comfortable sarcasm mode as she considered my comments.

"Yeah, I'd love to meet the guy who first said, 'Let's go racing for twenty-four straight hours!' right about now. I'd tell him, 'You're an idiot!'"

She thought a moment more, and then added, "And that's when everything goes well. When you wreck, it's like, 'There's goes my Valentine's Day present!'"

I couldn't help but crack a smile. Clearly she was recovering well from the emotion of my crash.

After a bite to eat and a fitful sixty-minute nap in the back of the RV, it was time again to head out for another run in the #68 car. I didn't need much prompting to clear the cobwebs, get my gear together, and stretch a bit before heading to the pits. As it was about 2:30 a.m., this was no mean feat, but it was certainly more appealing than crawling out of a call-room bed to see a trauma patient in the middle of the night.

I suited up, grabbed my helmet and gloves, and squeezed my way past the sleeping form of JP on the massage table, trying not to bang the door on my way out. Gin stayed behind in the RV, wanting to get a few more minutes of shut-eye before my next go behind the wheel. I headed out alone, into the now chilly Daytona night, enjoying the amplified soundtrack of the fifty-or-so still running engines in the background.

Helmet in hand, I made my way through the infield Fan Zone, taking a shortcut to the TRG pits. As I walked briskly through one of the gates, I found myself side-by-side with Paul Tracy, who was obviously also on his way to the pits. Actually, I was a couple of steps behind him, but I trotted a bit to catch up when I spotted him. The immediate area was deserted, so I thought this was as good an opportunity as I was going to get to do the "I'm a big fan" thing without witnesses.

I caught up beside Tracy; he didn't bother to look at me until I spoke up.

"Hey Paul, I just wanted to say hi, and…"

He looked at me with his head cocked a bit, as if he was trying to gauge whether or not I meant him any harm. He then looked down at my race suit, which I guess triggered some simultaneous relief and sleepy confusion. Why was this dude in a driver suit talking to me like a fan, in the middle of the night, in the middle of the race?

Tracy didn't break stride, nor did he say anything, so I kept stuttering on.

"…and I'm a huge fan, and it's great to be racing here with you. Just wanted to tell you…thought I'd say hello…" I trailed off, finding nothing further to say that wouldn't sound, well, weird.

I got back a grunt and maybe even a mumbled "Thanks," as he picked up the pace a bit and made a beeline for the fence gate. I figured that was my cue to fall back, as he apparently didn't want to hang out just then. I realized that I had just intruded on his "safe zone," here on the way to the pits, and didn't really expect much of a different response. But inside I felt something of a thrill—I had met one of my racing heroes, and he had said—something!—to me!

I made my way over to the TRG pits area, noting along the way several empty pit stalls, where teams had already packed up and bugged out once their cars had retired. In a way it was kind of creepy. I imagined that it must have felt similar when Navy carrier pilots found a newly empty chair in the ready room. Strewn about the back side of the fence bordering the pits was a great assortment of race team debris—car body parts, track carts, tire carriers, and the occasional crewman sleeping under a blanket.

I stepped over at least two snoring forms on my way into the brightly-lit and very much awake TRG pit tent. I went directly over to the cart, finding Tommy sitting up there, still looking at the monitors. I tapped him on the arm to get his attention.

Tommy pulled one side of the headset off his ear as he looked down at me. "Ready to go?"

"Yep, I'm here and ready."

"Did you get any rest? Eat something?"

"Yep, I'm good."

"That's good, because we need you to do a double this time. JP and Revere just doubled up; in fact, JP will probably have to do a triple stint next time."

I smiled. "He's a big showoff."

Tommy smiled back at me. "Yeah, he's an ironman. You go ahead and relax for a few. Revere will be in in about twenty minutes, but be ready just in case there's a yellow."

When Tommy gave me the ten minutes sign, I got up, geared up, and made my way towards the wall. Roger Reis was on station, leaning against the cart as he waited for the car to return. When he saw me, he motioned me over.

"Did anyone let you know—the door doesn't open anymore? We'll have to get you in through the window."

Nice. Glad I dropped those pounds for the race. "OK, no problem"

"It's a little tight, but we'll get you in there. I'll shove you in if I have to."

I nodded, trying not to imagine the prospect of getting stuck halfway into the car during the driver change.

Maybe it was the fatigue, perhaps I was just more at ease with the prospect of the task ahead of me, but this time when I got the signal to prepare for the pit stop, I was ready and focused. I was still excited, my heart rate definitely kicked up a notch, but there wasn't any sense of fear. No adrenaline-laced jitters, just a sense of the buzz of getting back out there. I was on my toes but actually relaxed; somewhere in the back of my mind, I was probably comforted by the fact that the worst that could happen, already had.

Once I had squeezed through the window—no simple task—I was back in racer mode. The radio crackled in my ears, my eyes widened to take in the bright lights and dark corners, and I felt the smooth shifter in my hand and smelled the distinct aromas of sweat, fuel, and exhaust. By the time I rejoined the race and drove down into the turn three horseshoe, I was full-on awake and hyper-processing. As heat came into the tires, I picked up speed, leaning on the car more with each turn. Fully focused, I thought only about the next braking zone, the next apex, and maybe even the next pass. There was no inner discussion of my previous failure, no consideration of wreckage or injury; there was only enough available bandwidth for me to think about what was immediately in front of the nose of my race car. And that sensation was liberating beyond belief, beyond relief.

I drove as hard as I knew how, running well off the pace of the fastest GT cars out there, but comfortable with my own personal progress. My lap times were consistent, if unspectacular. I kept eyes on my mirrors, moving off line for anything even remotely approaching from the rear. I wasn't about to add to my disrepute by getting in the way of anybody actually competing for position in the race. Blue flags waved frequently, and I obediently moved out of the way often. At one point, Tommy and I spoke about it over the radio.

Hey Jim, you OK out there? That last lap was off a bit."

Yep, I'm just keeping out of the way of traffic."

"Copy that. Just stay out of trouble."

"Yeah, well, if I'm any more polite, I'm going to win the Lady Byng trophy."

No response to that one. Guess Tommy wasn't a hockey fan.

I pitted once for refueling, staying on the same tires—I hadn't beat them up too much in the first hour. Then back out I went, quickly picking up where I left off. Lap after lap, turn after turn, I found my rhythm and pace, adjusting only when I needed to get off line and out of the way. Rarely, when the opportunity came to push just a bit harder, I tried to go deeper on the brakes or carry more speed through a corner. On occasion, I'd lock up a tire or get a little loose at the apex, but generally I left myself plenty of room at the limit. I was aware that my times were still well off those of Revere and, of course, JP, but I did manage to reset my personal best lap time more than once in that double-stint. And with each strong lap, each error-free circuit, and even with the occasional pass, I felt the sense of satisfaction and the surge of confidence that rewarded these small successes. Although I was working hard, feeling the strain of the intense workout with each corner, each lap, I was happily immersed in the buzz of the challenge.

When the time came for the next pit stop, I was ready for a break. Thrilled as I was with the powerful feeling of lapping at Daytona, I was by then worn out and quite cramped in my seat. I'd love to be macho about it and claim that I could have gone on for more, but in reality I was spent and done—and aware that there was more driving to be had later that day. So it was more than a relief when Tommy's instructions came over the radio once again.

"Pit now, pit now. Driver change and fresh tires."

"Copy that, pitting now. I'm on the back stretch."

I hit my marks coming into the pits, slowing right on down to the lollipop, ready for the dismount. Remembering that the door was stuck, I twisted around a bit in order to exit through the window. Roger reached in, pushed my head down so it would clear the opening, and then grabbed the straps on the shoulders of my fire suit. He pulled hard as I pushed through the window and then awkwardly fell down onto the pavement. I popped up immediately, hitting somebody—I think it was JP—right in the crotch with my helmet. Another set of hands reached over the wall and pulled me in the right direction as I regained my feet and cleared the wall.

Gin was there with a wet towel and water bottle in hand; I pulled my helmet off and fumbled with my gloves as I walked towards the back of the tent. Breathing rapidly, I immediately felt the temperature rise inside my suit as nausea from pure exhaustion hit me. My wife placed the wet rag around my neck as I sat down, gulping for air. Seconds later, I realized that I needed to get moving so as to not vomit right there in the pits. I jumped up, trying to spot a convenient trashcan as I turned and headed for the exit of the tent. Thankfully, there were few people around at that hour to block my path, and I moved quickly out into the cool air in the narrow alley behind the pits.

Still unsure whether I could successfully keep my last meal down, I walked away from the TRG complex, continuing my deep-breathing efforts. At one point I stopped to lean on a trash barrel, thinking I was on the verge of filling it. As I leaned down towards the opening, I glanced off to the side just long enough to spot a cameraman, red light on, recording the act for posterity. Wanting desperately to not be a perpetual "Agony of Defeat" loop on Sports Center, I swallowed hard, choked down the foul taste in my mouth, and stood back upright. Sensing a missed opportunity, camera-guy lost interest and turned away to find other B-roll elsewhere. I resumed my walking—in with the good air, out with the bad— making a loop or two of the pit area before my stomach stopped churning.

I returned to the TRG pits to collect Gin, and then walked hand-in-hand with her back to the RV. After drying off a bit, I changed into sweats, and grabbed a light jacket on my way back outside. As my exhausted wife curled up on the couch under a blanket, I headed out of the driver/owner lot just as the sun was starting to rise.

Shoulders hunched against the chilly air, I found a good observation point near the outside of the turn three horseshoe. I didn't really think much about it then, but I was standing only about fifty yards from where my car had hit the wall the day before. My focus was entirely on the cars coming through the turn, especially when car #68 came by. A few photographers stood nearby, and I was only a few feet from the flag stand, but I looked only at the track. As the darkness gradually eroded and the air lost some of its bite, I stood watch as cars screamed by. Down through the gears, the drivers braked as late as they dared, some sliding more than others as they scrambled past the apex and back up through the gears at the exit. I watched JP in growing admiration with each passing circuit made by the #68 Porsche, fascinated by his ability to bleed speed smoothly as the turn approached and then roll through the hairpin without losing momentum. I listened as he picked up the throttle early in the turn—usually right near the apex, or just past it—and marveled at his smooth acceleration down towards the kink. Fuzzy with fatigue and immersed in the noise of the race, I stood there watching, soaking up the raw feeling of amazement I felt at seeing great drivers practice their craft.

It is said that driving the sunrise stint at Daytona is a special experience for the racer; watching it unfold then, from the prospective of having just gotten out of the car, was pretty special for me, too. I held my vigil until it was completely light out, abandoning my post only after the infield area had started to awaken and people started moving about. As the area's traffic increased, with golf carts whizzing by and fans, drivers, and crew increasing their movement through the paddock, I knew my private session was over. Turning away from the racetrack, I headed back to the bus for coffee, breakfast, and some rest before my next stint.

Later that morning, while Revere was busy doing yet another prolonged and flawless run, JP and I talked about the plan for the last few hours. I sat on the couch in the bus as Jim laid out a plan: He'd get in the car for one final stint, and then hand it over to me with about forty-five minutes to go in the race. I hadn't considered until just then the possibility that we might finish the race; even less of a consideration was the thought that I'd be the one to take the checkered flag. I protested to JP, who announced his decision with tired authority.

"You're the one who put all this together, you get to drive it on home, Dr. Lowe."

"Well, that's not quite right—you and Revere worked your asses off too. I didn't do anything more than you two. And of course, I blew it yesterday, in case you forgot that little part."

JP laughed. "It's already forgotten, and now we've got a race to finish. And I spoke to Revere—he's had just about enough driving for one day, trust me, and he wants you to take the checkered. No arguing that now, big guy, we're almost there."

I couldn't muster up a super-intelligent response, so I decided to just stutter instead. "Wow, I mean, really? I didn't plan on…you didn't tell me… what about…OK, that's pretty special…"

Jim Pace cut me off. "You earned this one. Enjoy it, Doctor Lowe."

When I was back behind the wheel of the Porsche, I was pretty surprised at what the track looked like by the bright sunlight of almost-noon. As I lapped the track nearly twenty-four full hours after the race had started, I spotted the signs of the day-long fight that had gone on. Tire "marbles" were everywhere, except for one very narrow lane of blackened pavement tracking though every corner. Car-related debris was visible at several points, including the almost-intact front-end section of a long-ago-retired Daytona Prototype sitting outside the bus stop chicane. There were far fewer cars on-track also, and many of those were limping along below race pace. And in the middle of it all, two DPs and a couple of GT cars were running flat out towards the finish line, still battling for the win while everyone else struggled along just trying to make it to the end.

I enjoyed my tour of the track in the daylight, feeling absurdly calm as I raced along at top speed, keeping an eye out for wayward stragglers and fast runners alike. I checked my mirrors often, and stayed off-line at any glimpse of a faster car racing on through. With each successive lap, it seemed that other cars were slowing around me. I wasn't quite sure what was happening, until Tommy clicked onto the radio, startling me with his call.

"OK Jim, you've got about fifteen minutes to go. Kevin wants you to catch up to the other two TRG Porsches and get ready for a photo finish."

How cool is that? I grinned as I answered Tommy. "OK, but I was just about to lay down another blistering lap."

"OK champ, don't get too excited. Catch up to the 66 and 67 cars, and get alongside for the finish. And keep your eyes open for any fast guys coming by."

"Copy that, will do."

Within a lap or two, I had found the other two remaining TRG Porsches, and pulled up behind them. They were obviously struggling, going about half-speed, even out on the banking. As I stayed behind them, other cars whizzed by one after another, scaring the living shit out of me as they blew on by. The speed differential was frightening, now that I was helplessly stuck plodding along on the same track. "Please let them see me," I prayed out loud with each approaching car in my mirrors.

"Hey Tommy, could someone please ask these guys to pick up the pace a bit? They're gonna get us all killed if we keep going this slow."

"Just keep behind them, they can't go any faster right now. We'll tell you when to move alongside. Kevin really wants a shot of all three of you."

"Well, if it doesn't happen soon, he might get a shot of all three of us in a smoking pile."

Tommy's tired response was predictably laconic. "Copy."

A moment later, I saw the white flag waving from the starter stand. One lap to go.

Driving through the bus stop for the last time, I moved up alongside the other two TRG cars. As we came around the banked turn four, I looked up ahead and spotted the checkered flag waving furiously from the stand perched atop the start-finish line. As I choked back an exhausted sob, my eyes blurred with tears, we crossed the finish line three-abreast at a lazy 70 mph. I thumbed the radio button and let out a loud "Whooooo" as I drove under the waving flag. Numb, tired, elated, and disappointed seemingly all at once, I was overwhelmed at the emotion of the moment. "Thank you guys, thanks JP, thanks Revere, all of you, this is awesome!" I yelled into the radio, not caring if anyone was listening any longer. "You guys did it—we made it. Yeahhhhhh!" By then the headphones were probably off back at the pits, but I narrated my cool down lap to anyone still hanging on.

Crossing the finish line at Daytona, 2006

"We finished! Thanks guys, what an amazing feeling! This is so great! Can't say it enough! Thank you thank you."

JP came onto the radio. "I think we all copy you, Dr. Lowe." I grinned inside my helmet, still needing to negotiate the last few turns before the track exit came up.

There would be much to talk about later, after I pulled the damaged but running Porsche back into the garage—this time to cheers and grins—but the last few corners were mine to savor. As I drove, I looked around at the grandstands one final time, marveling at the scale of the racetrack and the enormity of the race I had just finished. I breathed deeply to savor the scent and feel of the car, the track, the event.

By the time I pulled the Porsche into our garage stall, there was already a bit of a crowd gathered there. Of the five TRG Porsches that started the race, the three that had finished were just arriving in the garage area. Two other immobile blue cars were off to the side, sitting alone after failing to make it to the end. One, the #69, was seriously damaged after its driver had somehow managed to flip it over in a middle-of-the-night accident that ended the car's useful racing life. However, a few feet away from those reminders of the grueling challenge that was endurance racing, celebration was commencing.

I dismounted the Porsche to claps and cheers from Revere, JP, Ginny, and other friends and crew members in the garage. There was no nausea, no dry heaves this time; I felt only the fatigued relief of a job completed as I removed my helmet and turned to greet my co-drivers. As we embraced, I thanked Revere and JP, congratulating both of them on their superb performances. Close behind was Ginny, who gave me a big hug and a kiss.

"Way to go Sweetheart, you did it! You finished! Nice job."

"Thanks honey. I love you." I looked at my exhausted wife, who had never wavered in her support all weekend—hell, from the very beginning. "Thank you for being here, with me, the whole way."

That earned me another kiss. It was turning out to be a pretty good afternoon.

Once the smoke had cleared and the cars had cooled, we took stock of our race: We had made it all the way to noon on Sunday, finishing nineteenth in class—the last running GT car. Despite our prolonged absence for repairs, we had run strong to the very end—and finished ahead of twenty-three other GT cars, along with twelve Daytona Prototypes. A later examination of the race results would reveal that Jim Pace, Revere Greist, and Jim Lowe finished in front of more than a few racing giants: Kyle Petty, Danica Patrick, Scott Pruett, Wally Dallenbach, Rusty Wallace, Allan

McNish, Scott Sharp, Sebastian Bourdais, and even Paul Tracy.

By the time the photos were done, the hugs and congratulations complete, and the trip home begun, I was able to consider what had been accomplished with less emotion to cloud my view. We had set the goal simply: To finish the race. We had successfully met that goal. I had eventually proven to myself that I was capable of competing, driving at a high level, and despite my accident, recovering focus enough to continue on well after that event greatly upped the challenge. I had been part of a team that performed well despite the odds, and the sense of accomplishment we shared was real and deserved.

I had survived—no, succeeded in—my first 24 Hours of Daytona race. For sure, I wouldn't easily forget my error and the drama that ensued and evolved over that weekend. In fact, my first race would forever serve as a benchmark, a baseline, for comparison whenever I returned to the racetrack. But on that Sunday afternoon in Daytona, I had accomplished what I had set out to do---emerging from the wreckage a successful driver, a faster racer, and a better man.

Chapter Seventeen

I started bugging Jim Pace in between driving sessions at Daytona, probably late Sunday morning. Perhaps it was the potent mixture of exhaustion and relief that we were finally running strong and clean, perhaps it was simply that I wanted to have another shot at a race, at succeeding, at competing; and perhaps it was nothing more than the fact that I didn't want to quit this one time. Regardless, at some point, before I was even finished with my first event, I broached the subject of future racing with JP.

"Dude, we need to talk about what's next."

"Well, Dr. Lowe, you're gonna get in and drive again, and we'll finish this thing, just like we talked about."

"Yeah—well, no, that's not it—not what I meant. I mean, when are we going racing again?"

JP gave it a moment's thought. "You want to do some more after all this?" Pause. "Yeah, that's something we could do, but we have to get through this first."

"I understand that, but it's good to think ahead, right? I want something more to look forward to, once I recover from this weekend. And this part, the racing bit, the circus here, I think I want more of it. If you think we can do it."

Jim didn't have to consider that concept for very long. Despite the damaged race car and his co-driver's slightly bruised confidence, he quickly threw me a bone. "No problem, we'll get to work on it once we're back home and rested. But for now, it's almost time for your next stint. Better get your head back in this game."

Even now, especially now, it's a huge deal to me that there's more racing to be done in the future. Cars can get wrecked, races lost on bad luck or poor driving, and sometimes it all goes to hell in the middle of a weekend at the track. But the simple thought that there's more to come, that I'll be back on track again, with another shot at elusive glory and success, one more chance to compete and achieve something otherwise unthinkable, that thought drove me then and still does now.

Once I had settled back in at home, and my normal work schedule had returned to something recognizable, there were still reminders of racing everywhere. It was impossible not to think about the events of that January, with the small amounts of local celebrity that had come with it. The local newspaper, The Press of Atlantic City, had given us great coverage, and my friends, colleagues, and even my patients, had all noticed. Although many confused our Daytona race with the better-known 500-miler that is run in February, it was still fun to rehash our exploits with so many interested people. I had kept a stack of hero cards from the event and finally brought a bunch to the office when several patients requested autographs. A running joke was born among my race-fan patients, when I reminded them that they had an "original" Dr. Lowe autograph on their back or neck—in the form of a surgical scar. There was talk not only of the race that had been run, but also a now-familiar question: "When are you racing again, Doc?" And with it, what was to become my stock reply: "As soon as possible."

Good to his promise, Jim Pace and I talked frequently on the phone, discussing options and ultimately developing a plan for next steps at the racetrack. Typical of "the JP approach", the plan included a first step of—you guessed it—more practice. Jim had always preached the virtues of an approach that combined a firm, reasonable plan of specific track events and more seat time—both designed to optimize chances of success for a budding racer. Instead of throwing it all against the wall and seeing what sticks, JP laid out a carefully crafted program of several test days, a Skip Barber event or two for more coachable seat time, and then several deliberately selected Grand-Am race events throughout the season. Budget also needed to be considered—for sure, there wasn't an unlimited supply of money with which to go racing—something I quickly learned about racing funding deals when a sponsor reneged on a large promised contract. But once a plan was solidified, and I received Ginny's only somewhat reluctant consent, we were off and running.

In the process of making plans for my 2006 racing season, I realized that there was a need to organize my racing activities a bit more formally, especially if I wanted to attract sponsors and stay anywhere near the professional end of the sport. Because of this, JLowe Racing was born, and a website created, along with a fan email list. The blog I had started during my first days at Daytona continued, and professional photos and videos were shared, all to promote the idea of a professional organization. The concept grew into reality very quickly, and by the time we arrived at our next Grand-Am event, we had a logo, team shirts and hats, and I was handing out cards that (very tongue-in-cheek) declared me to be the "World's Fastest Neurosurgeon." It was all a good bit of deliberate fun but also a hell of a lot more work than I originally anticipated.

While my head was filling with details about racing—sponsorships presentations, crash damage costs, options for future racing and potential teammates—I was also getting busier than ever in my medical practice. I still operated electively three days a week (and unexpectedly and frequently for emergent cases) and my duties as chief of neurosurgery at the Medical Center were demanding more and more of my free time. With each busy and often stressful day, it became more obvious to me, and probably to everyone around me, that I needed to get back on track, and soon. Recognizing a means to an end, I relied on my own instinct and some measured advice from JP, and put my head down and charged forward.

Much of our emerging 2006 plans depended on continuing a relationship with Kevin Buckler and TRG. Although I now had a JLowe Racing "operations manager" and my own hospitality and marketing people, I had nothing resembling my own race car or mechanics capable of running a professional event. For that, I continued to rely on the great resources of TRG, which included access to one of their new Porsche race cars. In early discussions with Kevin following the Rolex 24, he offered Jim Pace and me the use of the brand new racer, providing we committed to several Grand-Am events with TRG. A big upgrade from the 996 model that we had run in January, the new 997 Porsche GT3 Cup car had more power, a sequential gearbox, and a fresh, zero-hour motor. With this car, we would have equipment sufficiently updated for us to be potentially competitive with the other fast runners in the GT field. All I needed to do was to learn how to make it go fast.

The first step in the rest of my 2006 season was to run a two-day test, arranged by JP with TRG, at Virginia International Raceway. At this test, we expected to accomplish several important things. We would run our first laps in the new race car, getting familiar with its different shifting and handling characteristics, and I would learn a new track in a calm and relaxed setting. This last part was especially critical, as the deal we had with TRG included running the Grand-Am race at VIR one month later. Given the increasing demands of my schedule, we also penciled in a four-day Skip Barber practice and race event in Las Vegas, scheduled directly after the VIR test. In that way, I'd get six days of quality seat time in one week—a particularly efficient way to compress and maximize my driving time in the middle of my busy work schedule.

As we pulled into the VIR paddock area, JP gave me the overview of the track and its surrounds.

"You're gonna love this track—it's more like the old, classic tracks, with its natural terrain layout. Big elevation changes, esses, the whole deal. It'll take some laps to get it right, but once you do, it's really fun to drive."

I had noticed by now that we were deep in the woods of southern Virginia and well below the Mason-Dixon line. "Yeah, pretty neat around here. Did that security guard actually have a muzzle-loader on him?"

"Yep, you're pretty far off the reservation here, Dr. Lowe, but after a few laps, you'll thank me. Trust me, I love this place and you will, too."

As we got out of the car and headed for the TRG trailer, I took one more look at the scenery. "We're not getting in the middle of someone's reenactment of Bull Run, are we?"

JP was resolute. "Let's go see the new car. Once we're out there, you'll forget all about your Yankee upbringin."

The TRG crew had prepped the new car with an unusual twist—a race seat was installed on the right side, so that Jim Pace could do real-time teaching while I drove. Given that I was about to experience that undesirable combination of "new car/new track", I'm sure this idea was suggested by JP and strongly seconded by Kevin Buckler. Presuming that this would limit the possibilities of incurring yet more crash damage bills, I figured both Ginny and my banker would approve; I wasn't quite as sure about JP's insurance agent's consent.

Once we had been briefed on the various switches and knobs of the new car, JP and I geared up and took our respective seats—me on the left side for the inaugural voyage. Before moving out of the pits, Jim described for me the gearbox operation, which was (thankfully) quite a bit different that the standard-shifting box in the 996.

"Nice firm pulls on the stick. Pull back to upshift—keep your foot on the gas, there's no need to lift—and give a little blip while you're engaging the clutch as you push forward to shift down. Neutral is here"—he demonstrated as he pushed my hand further forward—"and you'll need to grip this lever on the shifter to engage reverse. Let's try not to experiment with that one today."

I nodded. "OK, I think I can do that. Any other last words?"

I thought I could hear JP grinning in his helmet. "Nope, let's get going. Half speed, third gear for the first lap, just like in a Skippy car."

Remembering one lesson from Daytona, I gave it some revs and dumped the clutch as we pulled out of our pit box in a cloud of blue tire smoke.

"Whoa, cowboy, no need to do that here!" Jim said immediately. "Plenty of time to warm things up out there."

I managed a mumbled "Sorry" and backed off the throttle a bit as we entered the track. Since we were one of only two cars testing that day, there was little need to spend time looking in the mirrors. Instead, I focused forward and started shifting up through the gears.

"OK, easy now, brake at the six marker this time, there's a hairpin coming up and then a double-apex left-hand sweeper that's about half speed." JP spoke the familiar language, and I understood the descriptions, at least enough to have half a clue as we entered each successive corner. "Let's get on it a bit here—apex later there—and carry some speed through these esses when you're up to it."

My first downshifts were a bit of an adventure—JP kept on me about using smaller blips—but very quickly I realized how beautifully the gearbox worked. Within a lap or two, I was taking full advantage of the no-lift upshifts, keeping my right foot planted while pulling for the next gear without engaging the clutch. Smoothly uninterrupted power flowed through the car, and the strong torque of the new Porsche felt great. Braking was another big difference; there were no anti-lock brakes, but these binders were noticeably better than the ones I had raced with in January. More confident in shifting and stopping, and hugely helped by my copilot's instant feedback, I was able to focus early on on the track itself. I drove for about thirty minutes, and was just starting to uncover the beauty that was VIR's layout, when JP tapped me on the knee.

"Pit this time, and we'll change seats."

Despite the fact that we hadn't discussed this particular part of the plan, I complied and pulled into the pits. We got out and took a quick breather before changing sides in the car.

As Jim pulled out on track, I let him know what worried me. "I'm not the world's best passenger, just so you know. I'm not a right-brain person, and not a right-seat guy either. In fact, can't stand it, if you want the truth."

Jim didn't seem to mind the potential for my discomfort. "We'll take it easy for a few laps; just give me a warning if you want to stop or you're feeling bad."

I resisted the urge to tap him on the arm before he even began, and instead cinched up my belts and hunkered down in the seat. I gave Jim the 'thumbs up' sign. "OK, but be gentle with me."

With that, JP accelerated the Porsche down to turn one and proceeded to do a three-quarter-speed lap that easily left my best full-speed efforts in the dust. Late onto the brakes, rolling speed (and allowing me to feel the lateral grip of the car properly, for once), Jim attacked the course, all the while calmly continuing his coaching.

"Down two gears here. Back to throttle right after this apex. A little breathe here, and then...back to full power ...here."

Amazed though I was by JP's demonstration of how to drive a Porsche properly, my thoughts were quickly clouded by nausea. I tried to swallow the bad taste in my mouth, but within moments knew that I was going to lose the battle if we didn't stop, and soon. I few taps on JP's arm, and he got the message. Pulling into the pits, I managed only a half-hearted "You should get paid double to sit on this side" as I breathed deeply and sucked down cool air.

"Not so fun over there, is it?" JP asked as we dismounted.

"Yeah, I'm good. No more of that for me."

"No problem. I think you got the idea now. Let's look at some data and get a drink. We'll take a break a bit, and get some more laps in after that. Plenty of time today."

Over the next four or five hours, I lapped the VIR track in the new Porsche, impressing no one with my lap times but keeping the car all nice and shiny. I loved the run up through the "esses"—S-shaped turns climbing upwards in sequence—and eventually made my peace with the "Oak Tree" corner, VIR's signature hairpin turn. By the time I noticed the fatigue in my arms and the occasional lazy mistake appearing, JP was very ready to surrender his spot in the right-hand seat and call it quits for the day.

"Nice driving, Dr. Lowe. That's some good seat time and a nice fresh car at the end of the day. Hard to beat that."

"Thanks JP. I have to admit it, I love this track, although I think it will be a long time before I feel like I've got it down."

"No problem. We've got another full day here tomorrow; more time to get your rhythm. That way, you'll be ready to get on it from the beginning when we come back here in April."

Unfortunately, Tuesday dawned cold and gray, with rain peppering the windshield of the rental Cadillac on the way to the track. By the time we were standing alongside the TRG hauler, I could feel the sting of hail on my face. Kevin, JP, and I waited it out a bit while sipping coffee, but there was no sign of any letup in the forecast. During the hour that we milled around, hoping for a break in the weather, I entertained thoughts of driving on rock-hard frozen tires and crumbling up the brand-new and as-yet unspoiled Porsche. Despite the high cost of just showing up, which wasn't to be refunded anytime soon, we elected to keep the race car under wraps, and torture the rental instead.

"Laps are laps," intoned JP, "and more time seeing the track, even if it's in that grandpop cruiser, will only help."

I was relieved at the prospect of avoiding a rainy wreck and readily agreed to running the Caddy instead.

As I was suiting up and sorting out my racing gear, my cell phone rang. I was immediately concerned when I saw my partner's number light up on the caller ID.

"Hey Joe, what's happening?"

"Hey, sorry to bother you, I thought you'd be driving by now, was just going to leave you a message."

Joe had been holding down the fort since I left, and I knew he wouldn't have called just to chat.

"Yeah, I'm sorry, there's a problem with Mr. Chancy. I'm here in the Trauma ICU, checking him out, and I think we're going to have to head back to the OR."

Mr. Chancy was a fifty-something year old guy who had fallen from a ladder at home; he had the bad luck to have fractured his thoracic spine, and the worse luck to have partially injured his spinal cord. Left with legs that were weak, but moving slightly, Mr. Chancy had needed emergent surgery to remove the bone fragments pressing on his spinal cord, followed by reconstruction with titanium rods to stabilize his spine afterwards. Joe and I had done his surgery about four days prior, and post-operatively, the guy had done fine. Great, in fact—moving better than before and recovering without incident. Up until that Tuesday morning.

Joe continued on. "The nurses called me this morning; said he stopped being able to move his legs at all. I came in to see him, and got a STAT MRI."

"Any sensation? How about rectal tone?" I quickly ran through the usual concerns with a patient in whom spinal cord function was questionable. "What's the scan show?"

"Well, there's a lot of artifact there, but I'm pretty sure there's a hematoma, and the cord looks pretty compressed." My partner was describing the rare post-op complication of a blood clot accumulating at the site of spine surgery; such a clot was often more solid than liquid, and could exert a lot of pressure on the surrounding tissues. If one of those structures happened to be the spinal cord, damage could result, often only recognized when the patient showed loss of function on later neuro checks. It was a particularly tough thing to sort out in patients that had previously had some spinal cord damage, as their levels of function often fluctuated slightly as they recovered. Joe continued on. "To my exam, he's plegic"—meaning he had complete loss of movement—"and his only chance is a trip back to the OR to explore him and evacuate any clot, if there is one."

As Joe related the situation, I felt terribly helpless—and useless. There I was, standing in the rain at a racetrack in Virginia, as one of our patients struggled and my partner was left to deal with the problem, alone.

"Shit, Joe. Should I come back? I can hop on a flight and get there in the afternoon." Even as I said it, I knew the offer was hollow—the situation was emergent, and I couldn't possibly get there in time to help.

"No, don't bother. By that time we'll be long done and out of the OR. I have Nurse Kathy here to assist, and I don't think it will take too long regardless."

"You sure?"

"Totally. Just wanted to give you a heads up. Go back and enjoy your driving. I'll call you and leave a message when we're done."

I hung up, still feeling pretty worthless. We both covered each other during absences; vacations were required for stressed out surgeons and covering one's partner had always been part of the deal. But this occasion was the first one where Joe had to manage a surgical emergency alone while I was off racing. I stood there for a moment more, and considered that here was yet more evidence of the support I had from people close to me as I indulged a passion outside of work. I was fortunate in so many ways, including some less obvious than having the seemingly simple opportunity to drive race cars.

JP interrupted my wool-gathering as he checked in. "Everything OK? You ready to drive some?"

I filled him in on what was going on at work. With a family of physicians, and nearly four years of Medical School under his belt, JP was familiar with the demands of a practicing doc. "Do you need to get home?"

I assured him that Joe had everything covered. We could go on goofing off in the Cadillac all we wanted.

"That's a good partner right there. You're lucky."

"Yep, I know it. He's the man." There was not much use in thinking it through any more than that. "Now, let's go see if this dog of a rental actually 'zigs'."

One-hundred fifty miles, and one looping spin out of the Oak Tree turn later, and I had had my fill. I had leaned on the Caddy's tires and boiled the brake fluid more than once during the day, ultimately seeing the wet track over and over again, although at a much slower pace. Regardless of which car it was, the flow and rhythm of the track was exhilarating and demanding at the same time. Get it right, and the cadence felt great; get off line and out of sorts, and the place could bite you. Although we weren't able to do any real work on setup for the 997, JP and I both knew the seat time from those two days would prove invaluable when we came back for the race weekend. That alone made it worth the price of the ticket, and there was still a lot of racing to come later in the week.

Early that afternoon, Joe called with an update on Mr. Chancy. "All good here. I found a big clot, and cleaned it out. I didn't find any active bleeding, but I made sure it was dry before I closed up."

"Any better on his neuro exam?" I was hopeful.

"Actually, he's now wiggling his toes on the right, but still nothing on the left leg. He can feel the foley, though." Sensation return in the genitals—indicative of function in the lowermost parts of the spinal cord—was usually an encouraging sign.

"Great, that's good news. How is he about all this? Is he awake yet?"

Joe reassured me further. "Yep, he's with it and understands completely what's going on. I told him we'll just have to watch him closely for now and hope he improves even more."

"Thanks Joe, that sounds good. I'm really sorry you were left with handling that on your own."

My unflappable partner—what a contrast to the guys I had worked with before!—reacted predictably. "No problem. Have fun at the track and give me a call from Vegas if you want to check in."

I hung up and, for the second time that day, said a silent prayer of thanks for the special people in my life.

18

Chapter Eighteen

Having completed the two-day test at VIR without any crash damage, and reassured by the encouraging report on Mr. Chancy, I was feeling pretty relaxed when I arrived in Las Vegas for four days of running Skip Barber cars. It was good to be back in the SBRS paddock again, shooting the shit with the rest of the SBRS Masters Group and mechanics, and generally sensing a little of that "back home again" feeling despite the foreign racetrack. There was now the added element of acceptance within the herd, given my survival—my actual finish—at the Rolex 24 just two months ago. Only one or two guys in the group of racers, plus Jim Pace, had run the 24; most were a bit in awe of the event, as I had been, and they were probably a bit mystified that I had actually been there, done that. That weekend in Vegas was my first taste in racing of being a reverse role model: quiet thoughts and occasional whispered conversations betrayed the obvious sentiment that "If Jim Lowe can do that, I know I can too." I embraced the concept much the way I did the similarly-conceived left-handed compliments of my fellow med school students, who, upon finding out that I had matched in a neurosurgery residency, remarked, "Neurosurgery!? Wow, I thought that was hard to get into. Congratulations!"

Nonetheless, I was proud to have done the big event in Daytona while waving the Skippy flag high. Jim Pace's compliments and great attitude toward our upstart success added even more legitimacy to our accomplishment among the Skip Barber coaches and drivers. Once JP had endorsed our effort, confirmed the hard luck of the race and hard fight of the crew, and publicly acknowledged my own role as an actual piece of the team, I immediately gained a foothold into the real world of racers. This bit had nothing to do with fame, fortune, or public proof of success; it was rather all about membership in a club which you can't ask to join. I don't believe that I carried myself any differently, and I most likely wasn't any faster, at least not in an open wheel Skip Barber car, but there was clearly a palpable sense of membership and inclusion that I painfully realized had been previously lacking.

With this good vibe, I approached the four-day Skip Barber Race Series Masters event at Las Vegas Motor Speedway's "Outside" track with an eye toward running more consistently and closer to the front of the pack. I wasn't gunning for points or a championship; in fact, I was hoping only to be back in the TRG Porsche again soon. The plan Jim Pace laid out for the Vegas weekend was for me to get up to speed quickly, run near the leaders, and race well each lap. Because I was stepping back into a car a good bit slower than the Porsche, but with better handling in the corners, I could really focus on improving my entry speed and car control, especially in slow and medium-speed corners. It was an ideal way to add experience and valuable seat time, especially since it would be at a fraction of the cost of running the Porsche.

Reconnecting with the Masters guys was especially fun that first day of practice. Just about the whole core contingent showed up for the weekend, I guess because of the attraction of the Vegas nightlife (not a big draw for me, especially when I had to get back in a race car the next morning). Everyone was loose and relaxed, at least outside of the car. Among the old guard, there was rarely any of the usual hard posturing around the paddock easily recognized in the younger and more aggressive junior group. Anyone still racing over the age of 40, and racing close, was pretty much exempt from the usual requirement of pre-race mind games or anything representing an honest attempt to psych-out a fellow Master. In fact, such behavior would usually lead one to be drawn and quartered by the kangaroo court, often resulting in penalties such as buying lunch or leaving the group's dinner tip. This obvious difference in attitude had nothing to do with how competitive we were; it had everything to do with how much we all wanted to enjoy the experience without seeing 50-year-old game face in the paddock. There were arguments outside of the cars, for sure, but the perspective was just so different from that of an eighteen-year-old kid trying to hustle a factory drive. We simply didn't want or need that kind of vibe. Most of the verbal jousting going on among the Masters guys was designed to lighten the situation, or to make an attempt to disable an opponent through humor. Classic confrontations were almost always recalled in admirable tones, especially if there happened to be a strong element of comic relief involved, and the best punch lines were learned and memorized quickly by newer members of the group.

Back again for the Skip Barber Vegas race weekend were Dick Lippert, Chris Wilcox, Johnny Mayes, Michael Auriemma, and several other masters-age guys, all seeming to have good thoughts about our January run at the 24. Some of them, including Dario Ciotti and Quentin Wahl, had run the race themselves and were impressed by our eventual finish, despite our early troubles.

It also was good to see Murray Marden, with whom I had spent a lot of time the month before in Daytona. Mur was a sixty-three-year-old retired airline pilot and had the same apparently relaxed approach to anything with wheels already on the ground as did Dick Lippert. However, the similarities ended there. Murray was over six-feet tall and extensively tattooed, sported a Fu Manchu-style mustache, and looked more like a Hell's Angel than the fun-loving prankster lurking just under the surface. Mur was also one of the faster guys of the group, but he was clearly going to enjoy every lap, every turn, regardless of position or result.

When I first met Mur in 2003, I was intimidated for about 20 seconds, until he called me out on my red shoes, questioned my manhood because of my choice of the road car at the time, and, upon learning what I did for a living, apologized: "Wow, I thought you guys were supposed to be smart enough not to do this shit." What followed were at least four different hilarious stories about Murray's doctor friends, all of whom seemed to have gotten blown up or arrested while in Mur's company. While I laughed with the rest of the group, I made a mental note to memorize Mur's car number in each race group we shared. Just in case.

Murray Marden

***

The so-called Outside course at Las Vegas is so named because it is not in the actual stadium or near the oval that is used by NASCAR and other circuits. Vegas' Outside course is basically a flat road course laid out in the shadows of the grandstands, in something suspiciously resembling a parking lot. In fact, the amenities there are every bit the equal to several actual abandoned parking lots I've seen. Once you drive by the almost-hidden entrance to the actual track a few times, you then proceed down a gravel road to the paddock, which is identifiable as such only by the shed standing at the pit entrance and, in this case, by the Skip Barber Racing School haulers guarding the pits.

Despite the outward appearance of the facility, the track was pretty cool: a few fast, technical sections, several passing zones, and plenty of turns just tight enough to challenge the handling limits of the Skippy cars. Basically it was a go-kart track on steroids, but it turned out to be a fun layout that was a blast to race. Although there were several sections that required focus and bravery, the backside section between turns seven and ten was the men-from-the-boys part of the track. Coming out of some twisty bits, turn seven was a flat-out left hander leading onto a medium-length straight that ran directly into a very quick chicane. When done right at racing speed, the chicane was also flat-out in a Skip Barber car, requiring big commitment to execute properly. Immediately upon exiting the chicane, there was a heavy threshold braking area leading into a 90-degree right-hander. Given the typical 100 mph-plus speed that you usually carried into the braking zone, it wasn't a particularly good passing zone, but if you didn't get the chicane right, a fast guy with guts behind you would be able to get under you for the pass entering the inside of the right-hander.

I worked hard the first two days of practice, trying to regain the feel of the open-wheel machine and relearning the shifting and braking sensation, which were so different from the heavy Porsche's. JP and I ran dozens of lead-follow laps, perfecting corner and entry speed, and especially that last chicane. I knew that the chicane was a key point for both lap time and race position; a slower driver who couldn't stay flat there had little left to defend a pass into the next turn. Ultimately, I got to the point where I was flat through the chicane, managing to clip the apex curbing and hold on without lifting my right foot until the last possible moment in the braking zone just before the right hander. Each time through, the violent banging of the car off the curbing surprised me, as did the ability of the tires to remain rooted to the asphalt despite the rapidly changing lateral g-forces.

Despite the good grip available, there was an ever-present temptation to lift off the gas, just a little bit, at the point where the car was maximally loaded and a crash seemed imminent. Of course, to do so would ensure disaster: when the car is at its limit in lateral cornering load, full commitment is required. Cracking out of the throttle, even slightly, at the wrong moment would alter the delicate balance of grip versus lateral g's, and the car would spin predictably.

With repetition comes comfort, so after two days of running flat, the chicane became less eventful, but I don't think I ever stopped holding my breath all the way through. I was mentally prepared to clench my teeth, push my foot firmly to the floor, and ride the curbs all the way to the brake zone. If the drivers behind wanted to pass me, they needed to get a better run on me somewhere else. I promised myself that the chicane would be my strong point come race time.

I qualified for the first race in sixth position, roughly mid-pack and positioned for the start one spot ahead of, and therefore right beside, Murray on the two-by-two grid. As we got prepped for the start of the race, Mur approached me with a twinkle in his eyes, a bit of gamesmanship evidently on his mind.

"Are you flat through turn seven and the chicane?"

"Pretty much, sort of. Been doing it OK with JP so far. We'll see during the race." I didn't feel obligated to answer truthfully, knowing better than to help him find a way past me.

Mur laughed out loud. "Thank God, because if you're not, I'll be so far up your ass we'll need a specialist to get me out."

He patted me on the helmet, gave me a thumbs-up, and jumped into the car behind mine. Just to remind me, he bumped my gearbox from behind on the slow exit from the pits on the warm-up lap. I gave him the one-finger salute, accelerated, and then made sure I braked ever so slightly the first time through the chicane during the out lap.

The race started in typical fashion, with that awesome acceleration of sound that happens with the drop of the green flag and fifteen engines simultaneously revving to the max. I made it clean through the first few turns, banging wheels a bit in the scramble for position on the first lap, but holding my own all the way back to the start/finish line. I then settled in for the hard running of the 30-minute sprint race, noting that I was too far back already to think about catching Dick Lippert and the front runners, and still right in front of Murray. Better get on it, son; you came here to hunt, as they say.

Mur filled my mirrors each time through turns seven and the chicane, but I stayed flat out, getting a good enough run into the 90-degree right hander each time that he simply couldn't catch up through the remainder of the lap. After five or six laps, it seemed that Murray was resigned to stay behind me for the chicane section, apparently preferring to wait until I made a mistake in one of the more obviously easy passing zones elsewhere on the track. He moved wide to the side in the braking zone of turn ten each lap, making sure I knew he was back there, hoping for an opportunity that I wasn't going to give him.

On lap seven, I got a bit sideways going into the fast left-hand turn seven, just before the chicane. In the blur of noise and vibration of the cockpit, I was able to see Mur for a moment in my right-side mirror, but I figured he had no shot at me through the chicane. I took one last glance in the mirror, saw no one, and went into the chicane flat out. I braked hard for the next turn, tried to flow good entry speed into turn ten, and got back to power early, trying to make up for my slight mistake earlier.

WHAM!!! The impact was just to the right of my cockpit, resulting in that instantaneous "Oh shit!" feeling familiar to racers and bad drivers the world over. The harsh noise of the collision easily drowned out the "Zzinngggg!" coming from the over-revved engine as the wheels broke free. However, instead of the more familiar spin that follows most impacts in these cars, I was in for a completely new experience. As Mur realized all too late that I was going hard for the apex, and that I didn't realize he was attempting a pass, he had locked up all four wheels in an attempt to avoid contact. He was terribly unsuccessful just then and slammed the nose of his car into me as I accelerated into the corner, hitting my car amidships at about a 45-degree angle—just far enough to get his left front tire in front of my right rear. When my tire met his at speed, my car was immediately catapulted skyward into a spectacular barrel roll.

From the perspective of the driver's seat, the takeoff and brief flight were really quite amazing. After the harsh noise of the impact, it was eerily quiet for a second as my visor was filled with an unexpectedly clear view of the blue sky, and it dawned on me that I was in fact airborne. How the hell did this just happen? Oh fuck, this is gonna hurt—hope it's over soon—I hope Ginny doesn't find out about—my thoughts were rudely interrupted as the brownish-green ground appeared to ambush me from the side, rotating directly into view with another loud BANG!!! as the top of the car hit the dirt inches from my helmet. This bizarre scene was repeated at least two more times as my car spun about its long axis, and I was treated to a rapidly rotating show of sky—whoa!—ground—ooof!, here it comes again—sky sequences, punctuated by heavy impacts on the roll hoop just over my head marking each full rotation. I watched in amazement as the car shed parts and fluid like a downhill skier in the midst of a wipeout. By mid-crash, I had become aware enough of my predicament to hope that I'd end up right-side-up when it was over.

Luck, gravity, and physics collided and luck came out on top as I rolled to a skidding stop right-side-up. I did a mental inventory of properly moving body parts, wiggling fingers and then toes, waiting to identify the painful areas that I was sure would be shortly announcing their presence. Strangely enough, I felt, well, nothing. Amazingly enough, I felt pretty much fine. In fact, I became immediately concerned with my position in the runoff area of turn ten and realized that I was vulnerable where I sat. In the racing world's conventional wisdom, once you come to a stop following a crash, you are by definition sitting in a spot where another errant car could follow on and hit you. As such, the first goal is usually to restart your car and move out of the impact zone to a safer area, if possible. Being at least slightly aware of this concern, I immediately tried to start up the car, hitting the starter button repeatedly.

"RURhhhhhhUrhhhhhhUrhhhhhhUrH.!" I hit the button, trying to get it fired again. As I was doing so, Stevie Debrecht, a corner instructor, arrived on the scene. He reached in and turned off the ignition switch on the control panel.

"What are you doing big guy? I don't think you're going anywhere."

He directed my attention to the front of the car, which was absent both front wheel assemblies—tire, wheel, suspension bits, everything. I tried to look in the side mirrors, but they were both gone.

"You're missing both rear wheels also, so you might as well sit tight. Are you hurt?"

I was just about to answer when Murray's head appeared next to Stevie's.

"Jesus! Are you OK?"

"I think so. What are you doing here? Shouldn't you be in your car racing?"

"Shit no, I just had to stop. I figured I had killed you, and I was gonna take your watch before anyone got to you."

"Thanks for caring, Mur. Can you help me out of here?"

"No problem. So you're really OK? I really didn't want to have to call Ginny and tell her I killed you. She'd be pissed."

Later, once I had been properly dusted off, and had a chance to survey the crumbled car coming back from turn ten on the wrecker, I debriefed with the rest of the Masters crew. As we gathered around and gawked at the totaled car, Mur was actively retelling the story, pantomiming my car rolling overhead, all the while narrating the crash blow-by-blow.

"His eyes were THIS BIG," holding thumbs and forefingers three inches apart, "as he flew over top of me!"

Dick Lippert chimed in with the classic deadpan line, "I'm a pilot, and I'm pretty sure that anything that flies that far ought to have a stewardess on it."

I reminded any and all who would listen that What Happens in Vegas, Stays in Vegas, but I was equally sure that this would all come back to bite me when the inevitable happened, and Gin found out about my unscheduled flight. Until then though, I had an immortal contribution to make to future sessions of "bench racing," the time-honored tradition of swapping "my car crashed worse than yours" stories, not to mention having a leg up on Mur for, well, forever.

***

I flew home from Vegas with one top-five finish in the second race and a fragment of brake rotor (which was pretty much all that was left of my car on Saturday) in my carry-on. I had had a strongly competitive weekend, performing relatively well in the same series where I had been clearly outclassed just two seasons prior. In my homecoming of sorts, I enjoyed the great feel of being back at the track with like-minded friends, all of whom shared my need for high-speed psychotherapy. And in the process, I acquired another great story to tell—to anyone other than my wife, that is. Having already stretched Ginny's tolerance for risk farther than I dared, I didn't feel any need to give her the gory details of my airborne experience. No harm, no foul, right? And no need to add unnecessary worry where none was needed.

Two days later, I made rounds at the City Division of AtlantiCare Regional Medical Center, site of the Trauma center and temporary home of Mr. Chancy. I made my way through the maze of the ICU, and entered Mr. Chancy's room to find him sitting up in bed.

"Hey doc, how's it going?"

I smiled, relieved already. "Good to see you upright. Dr. Zerbo told me about what went on while I was gone."

Our patient pushed his breakfast tray aside to make room for a demonstration. "Yep Doc, pretty scary. But I'm doing good now." With that, the patient lifted his right leg off the bed. "Check this out. I can move the toes on my left leg now, too."

"That's great; a real good sign of recovery. I'm encouraged by your improvement already, compared to what Dr. Zerbo described to me."

"Yeah doc, damnedest thing, that blood clot. But the therapists tell me I'll be walking again, and I'm a fighter. I'm gonna get right again, thanks to you guys."

I wasn't totally in agreement with that last "Thanks to you guys" part, given the surgical complication that was at the very least a serious setback for the man, but I joined him in optimism. "Well, keep up the good work. We'll keep checking on you."

I exited the room, smiling as I considered yet again how fortunate I was to have the chance to care for patients like Mr. Chancy, and to have my partner treat them, and me, so well.

19

Chapter Nineteen

When I returned to Virginia International raceway for the Grand-Am event in April 2006, the scene I encountered was decidedly different from our private test days just one month before. Even on the move-in day, a full four days before the race itself, the paddock was abuzz with activity. After parking on the hill outside of the half-paved paddock lot, JP and I joined the other drivers and crew members heading toward the area where the Grand-Am contingent was located. As we walked down the narrow road, carrying our backpacks and helmet bags, I could see into the crowed lot, with colorful team trailers, merchandising carts, and the usual assortment of pit vehicles and race cars scattered about. Straight ahead, the pro race teams had lined up haulers side-by-side, with awnings spread out to the side to create outdoor garage space for the mechanics. Further towards the track itself, other Grand-Am teams—mostly from the elite prototype ranks—occupied the trackside garages. To the left of the large paddock, support series encampments and equipment-related trucks and other vehicles were spread out, all the way up to the false grid area. Having last seen the paddock quietly unoccupied, the view at once was as intimidating as it was impressive.

On our way to the Racer's Group encampment, Jim and I ran into several drivers that we had last seen at Daytona. Most were still unfamiliar with me, and JP was kind enough to introduce me to several guys I knew only from TV and my rubbernecking at the last drivers' meeting. I was inwardly surprised that so many drivers were so friendly Many expressed congratulations on the fact that we were still running in Grand-Am races after the 24. It was obvious that my co-driver was well-liked and well-respected. For me, there seemed to be instant credibility in the fact that Jim Pace was still running with his unknown amateur teammate—although there were a few eyebrows raised when we encountered some of the other drivers and crew. After all, JP was a seasoned and decorated pro—with major race wins, a Le Mans start, and an impeccable reputation in every paddock he stepped into. That it was a big deal to still be entering races with JP—especially since I had done nothing to wow anyone thus far—wasn't lost on me. For now, I received the benefit of the doubt, but eventually I was going to have to pull my weight and earn my rights to the ride. That would only come with seat time and—you guessed it—hard work. I wanted to be a racer, not just an occasional field-filler in a backmarker rental car. And the weekend's Grand-Am sprint race at VIR was just the next step in what I hoped would be a long journey.

Kevin once again welcomed us into the TRG paddock area, enthusiastic in his greeting as always.

"Hey guys, welcome to VIR. Did you see your car yet? It looks great—you're gonna love what we did to it—we got the Bernie Robbins logos on it and even have the new JLowe Racing stickers for it."

I handed Kevin one of my newly printed business cards. "Check this out. Something a bit different."

Kevin looked down at the card and laughed when he got to the tag line. "World's Fastest Neurosurgeon, huh? That's beautiful!"

"Yeah—I'm aware no one around here gives a shit about fast doctors—but we thought we'd have some fun with it. Plus, nobody's challenged me on it yet."

Kevin was off in a flash. "Great to have you both back. Gotta go see how the Pontiac boys are doing. Don't forget about dinner tonight."

I looked over to the far side of the makeshift garage and spotted Mike Johnson, who was tasked with the job of crew chief for our car. Mike was going over a checklist taped to the windshield of our Porsche, which was admittedly looking sharp and fast in its new livery. JP and I made our way over, greeting mechanics on the way, and saying a quick hello to Andy Lally, who was driving one of the TRG Pontiacs. I stepped carefully over and around various hoses, tires, and other equipment, trying not to make any of the mechanics' already busy day any busier. Besides, I was well acquainted to the ritual of being a new member of any group in a foreign environment, having stepped into many different OR's for the first time during med school and residency. One thing I knew for sure from those experiences: you don't want to piss off the people actually running the place—mechanics or nurses alike.

While JP and I chatted with Mike, a few of the other TRG drivers made their way over and said hello. The Pontiac factory drivers, Kelly Collins and Paul Edwards, took a minute and checked in with us. While Paul was quiet and intense, the bespectacled Collins oozed California cool, his laid-back approach giving me instant flashbacks to my surfing days. He walked right over to JP, extending his hand for a brah-shake as he joined us.

"Dude, sooo cool that you guys are here. Are you going to run more this season?"

JP gave him the lowdown. "We've got a few more planned for Jim here…" Jim turned to me. "Dr. Lowe, say hello to Kelly Collins—he's driving one of the TRG Pontiacs."

I shook Kelly's hand, somewhat in awe of this guy also. A driver who made his living as a factory-paid hired gun, with winning credentials to back up his obvious relaxed demeanor.

Kelly grabbed my hand as he turned sideways towards JP. "Just do whatever this guy says. He's a legend. He'll definitely keep you locked on and wired tight."

After introducing Paul, the four of us chatted a few more minutes about the cars, the upcoming weekend, about anything racing. The feeling was locker room all over again—I was in the inner sanctum, talking story with drivers in their own private, off-limits area, just another guy about to go racing once again. Standing there, all casual-like, I probably even looked like just another driver to any unsuspecting and less-knowledgeable observer. But I knew better and knew equally that the next few days would likely prove the difference.

Thursday and Friday were official Grand-Am practice days, with all of the Daytona Prototype and GT teams sharing track time, in between sessions for the support series. Grand-Am's circus traveled with various other amateur and semi-pro series scheduled around the main event, and track time was at a premium. Practice sessions were scattered among the Skip Barber and second-tier Grand-Am Cup series practices, so seat time was short and needed to be effectively used to get the car setup adjusted for the race. With relatively few opportunities for me to take practice runs after

JP made changes to shocks, springs, and wing settings, it was obvious how valuable our testing time in March had been. At least I had a jump on things, having some idea about the track layout and the potential of the Porsche, instead of feeling it out from scratch as a VIR rookie. Nonetheless, despite having a nice dry track, the lap times came to me slowly, and the data sessions afterwards were nothing short of embarrassing. Whatever large ego I've been accused of having in the past was swallowed whole as I compared my plodding efforts to JP's tracings.

"You're way late to power here…"—JP stabbed a finger at the data sheet—"…and you're getting killed up through the esses. You have to trust the car more. It can do it—you're almost twenty miles an hour slower than me up through there."

I defended myself feebly, realizing that there was no place to hide in those tracings. "I'm working up to it, but that's still pretty hairy going through there." It wasn't necessary to convince my partner that I still wasn't comfortable with the new car's performance.

"You'll feel better if you feed in more power. The car loves it. If you're tentative, the car will feel unsettled, and you'll feel too much on edge. Give it some more gas and you'll see."

There was just so much to absorb, so many points of data, so many things to consider as I tried to pick up pace. Lap after lap, I was absorbed in my brake points and track-outs, and trying to roll speed through the climbing esses and get back to power at each apex. Immersed as I was, I thought of little else for those two days—even when I was done for the day and away from the track. But Saturday's qualifying session loomed—my first in Grand-Am—and I desperately wanted more practice time. Just like a resident participating in his first operation, there was an expectation of extensive training and some sort of helpful practice first, right? Except here, in the often bizarre world of 180 mph race cars and deadly mistakes, I felt wholly inadequate and unprepared. But this was the big league, with big-boy rules; I swallowed my concerns and pushed hard to settle dark thoughts into the back parts of my mind. As my high-school football coach was fond of saying, "If you can't play with the big dogs, stay on the porch."

***

Saturday morning's first look outside proved the weatherman right for a change—gray skies blanketed the southwestern part of Virginia, promising that rain couldn't be far off. As JP and I made the trip to the track, he continued his coaching, walking me through the necessary adjustments for wet running.

"We'll get the car set up nice and soft, with more wing for better downforce. The engine is hanging over the rear wheels, so that'll help for grip. Since all the practice sessions were dry, and you've never run this car in the wet yet, start out nice and easy. Stay off the painted surfaces, but you might find some grip near the apex."

I pointed out that I had always hated running the Skip barber open-wheel cars in the rain. "I always felt right on the edge of disaster in those single-seater races. The grip seemed to be just awful, and I was always off pace."

"Don't forget, you've done quite a bit more driving since your last time in the rain in a Skippy car, and this will be completely different—heavier, which is good, but a lot more power too. Gentle on the throttle, brake a little early."

"You mean drive just like I normally do?"

JP laughed with me. "Well, come to think of it, Dr. Lowe, you'll be just fine if you do that."

I was much more relaxed than I had a right to be for the morning practice session, considering the rain bucketing down periodically over the twisting VIR road course. This unusual change in my demeanor arose directly as a result of a change in the Grand-Am qualifying procedure, newly announced just for this race. Normally, the qualifying session was a frantic fifteen minute deal, with the qualifying driver required to also start the race. Conventional wisdom called for the slower driver (we were all quite sure who that was) to start, hang in there near the leaders as best he could, and then hand off to the faster guy to make up places to the finish. Given that, I would have been expected to do a few firsts that weekend: drive the Porsche in the rain, qualify, and then make my first Grand-Am start.

Instead, the Grand-Am powers-that-be decided to try something different and declared that qualifying would be a thirty-minute race, with the finishing order determining Sunday's starting position. In addition, the qualifying driver would now be prohibited from starting the race, so we could use the much more experienced driver for the wet quali race, and I would do the start (from an even better position on the grid). Buoyed by the knowledge that I was off the hook for qualifying, I was greatly relieved when I took the wheel for a few laps in the morning practice: I had one less "first" to worry about.

My relaxed attitude contributed greatly to a fun and fast practice session in the rain. I drove the first forty minutes of the practice, enjoying, for a change, the enhanced sensation of grip in the Porsche despite the wet conditions. Rather than hanging on for dear life, as it usually felt in the open-wheel cars, the heavy rear-engine Porsche felt firm, planted, and much more predictable and controllable. I did manage a few slides on the slippery track, but everything seemed to happen in a linear fashion—no sudden swapping of ends, no big surprises as I went to the brakes. At one point, on a good run up through the esses, I came up quickly behind Paul Edwards, who was obviously struggling with the Pontiac. He slipped sideways as I crested the last right-hander of the sequence, just as I was ready to back off and fall in behind him for the left-handed downhill blast that followed. Instead he checked up to the left, and I was forced over, off-line, to the right. Normally, that path would have been a disaster, with the car all loaded up—with all of the weight on the wrong side of the car for the next turn—and way off the apex. Instead, I found grip there and, rather than sliding off into the grass, found my nose perfectly pointed toward the track out, with room to spare. I flew on past Paul easily, as he continued to search for useful grip in his front-engine Pontiac GTO.R. So I did manage a "first" that morning after all—passing another driver in anger, in difficult conditions. No time to celebrate, though, as I was still trying to survive a lap with lots of other opportunities to screw up surely awaiting.

I made good time through the Oak Tree turn and thanks to the grip level, got to power early, heading onto VIR's long back straight. In dry conditions, the speed at the end of the straight was about 160 mph for the GT car; in the wet, with full wing, it was quite a bit slower. Despite that, it was still an attention-getter all the way down the straight, which had a delicious dip in the middle, right before an abrupt rise, and then a downhill section into the braking area. I tiptoed upwards, turned to the right, and then rolled down through the "Hog Pen," the rollercoaster section before the last, high-speed, high-g downhill right-hander onto the front straight. With a four-wheel slide on exit, I managed to roll enough speed that I had a bit of a head of steam for the long run down to turn one.

As I went by start-finish, Mike Johnson cracked onto the radio.

"Nice lap, Jim, best one so far."

"Best one today?"

Mike's answer surprised me. "Nope. Best one of the week so far. You just went faster than you went yesterday."

I pondered this for a moment before answering. "I guess that's not because I was so lightning fast just now."

JP clicked on. "Don't worry about that right now, Dr. Lowe. Just keep doing what you're doing, and don't try to break any records."

I pulled into the pit box a few laps later, swapping places with JP so that he got a few laps to see the conditions before the qualifying race. As I watched his times renew on the timing and scoring screen, I marveled at his ability to progressively pick up pace despite the steady rain. And while he was doing so, he continued to talk with Mike on the radio, making suggestions for setup changes, describing different sections of track and the varying conditions, and occasionally calling out the bad behavior of another driver. If you didn't know any better, JP sounded as if he were out for just another Saturday drive, chatting away while he made his way through light traffic. I of course was aware of the chasm between our abilities, but never was it more evident than when I was watching and listening at the same time.

When the qualifying race started, I was positioned on the TRG pit cart for a good view, radios tuned in to the #66 car's frequency. Watching the two columns of cars arrive on the front straight, I was absolutely thrilled—excited about watching a good scrap in the rain and even more excited that I wasn't out there in the middle of it.

As the green flag was called over the radio for the start, the lead group of GT cars exploded in a cloud of wet mist. Left sightless, with all of the cars simply disappearing in the cloud, I waited to hear of progress from JP.

A few minutes later, I heard Jim's voice over the radio. "Pretty wet out here; my visibility's lousy. All fogged up."

"Copy that," replied the helpless Mike Johnson. "Are your vents all turned up towards the windshield?"

"Yep, everything's pointed the right way. I'm just gonna live with it until I can't see anymore."

A moment later, the #66 blew on by down the front straight, running in fifth place after JP had made up more than seven places on the first lap. As the rain intensified, I watched, mouth no doubt hanging open, as JP stayed out near the leaders lap after lap. At one point, he called in that he couldn't see at all; with nothing to offer, Mike just wished him luck, reminding him that he was already halfway done.

"I'm going to have to do something about this. I can't see at all," JP advised. There was silence for a moment, and then, "There, that's better."

We were all curious; Mike asked for us. "What're you up to out there, JP?"

"No problem, I had to undo my belts so I could lean forward and clear the windshield."

Mike looked over at me and raised an eyebrow. I responded with a "What did you expect?" shrug of the shoulders. Just another day in JP-land.

As the rain got even heavier, Jim called in about standing water at several sections of the track. Shortly after that, he let us know that he had just slid off in turn eleven. "Nothing damaged, just couldn't see or feel anything. I'm underway again."

With that misstep, JP fell back to twelfth place, where he ultimately finished. In conditions that would have had me begging for mercy, he had done yeoman's work to get me closer to the front of the pack for the next day's start. Now it was up to me not to screw it all up when my turn came.

Sometime before we left the VIR paddock for the day, I ran into Divina Galica, who was roaming the area during a break from her Skip Barber series duties. We took a moment to catch up, and I reminded her that we had met shortly after my first not-so-quick laps with the Skip Barber series back at Laguna Seca. I figured she wouldn't remember the details, but felt it necessary to mention my first meeting with her.

"Thanks for not sending me home all those years ago."

"Divi was confused at first. "You're going to have to help me out—should I remember something here, or maybe apologize?"

I laughed. "No, nothing like that. You just encouraged me at a moment when I was expecting to be kicked out of racing forever, and now, here I am."

"Well, look how far you've come. I guess I'm glad I didn't ask you to leave back then."

"Me too, for sure. Thanks again Divi."

We shook hands. "You've made us proud, Jim. Good luck to you and JP tomorrow."

The next morning, I waited for JP to arrive for the third-world continental breakfast being served for the downtrodden at the Danville Marriott. As I sipped gray-black coffee, Kelly Collins strolled up and grabbed a seat next to me.

"Dude, I think we're starting right next to each other."

I looked over the rim of my cup, surprised at the news. "Really? How badly did you guys mess up the quali race?"

"No worries dude, we're gonna do fine. Just follow me right down into turn one. Stay right on my tail."

"Dude, in case you haven't noticed, I can't follow you, but thanks for offering."

Kelly smiled and slapped me on the knee as he got up. "You've got JP. He's the secret weapon. You guys will kill it. See you out there."

A few hours later, I was strapped into the cockpit of the Porsche, sitting on the pre-race grid next to Kelly's GTO.R. Trying desperately not to think about my first pro race start, my mind wandered a bit. I was aware of this, and in fact encouraged it to do so. Every time I thought about the race start, I got queasy anyway, so happy thoughts were in order. I started with the fact that the day had dawned without rain, and the track was in fact dry as a bone. The positive vibes from that realization led me then to consider a few different scenarios from my prior, non-racing life.

I considered for a moment that, on any given typical April Sunday, I'd likely be still sipping coffee and tuning into the Phillies' game right about then. If I hadn't been called in to do some emergency surgery, I always loved the luxury of a quiet Sunday. Putter around the house some, watch the Phillies, maybe even sneak in the forbidden nap. Instead, I felt the compression of my helmet's padding around my head and listened absently to the mechanics talk on the radio. I wiggled my fingers inside my driving gloves, looked out of the visor, and squirmed a bit to get the belts settled just right around my shoulders.

Despite my best efforts, I couldn't help but consider my current predicament with concern. OK hotshot, you ran one endurance race so far, and nobody cared much about your pace then. And we all know how that turned out. This is a sprint race—and you're surrounded by some very serious guys who don't give a damn if you were the smartest kid at Our Lady of Perpetual Help or the fastest guy at your hospital. They're just waiting to kick your ass any minute now. You really need to be balls-out from the start. I'm not sure I'm ready for this, but it's a little late to be lacking confidence just now, huh? Oh shit, What was I thinking?

The thoughts flashing through my head were interrupted by the faint sound of the National Anthem drifting over the radio, punctuated by the whoooosh of the flyover. I craned my neck a bit to try and spot the planes, thinking simultaneously, "This is just too cool." All at once, I stopped questioning myself, stopped doubting the wisdom of spending my Sunday in harm's way, and instead pictured the drive, the fight, the strain of pushing myself once more. It was OK, right there, even if I failed; I was part of it again, belonged there, and wanted to be nowhere else that very moment.

After firing up the Porsche's 3.6 litre flat six, I waited for my signal to move out on the pace lap. Two by two the GT cars crawled forward, until it was my turn. I waited a moment for Kelly to get underway, and followed him on down the front straight. I was too far back to see the pace car, but I really didn't need to anyway—all I needed to focus on was the rear end of the blue Pontiac directly in front of me.

Mike clicked on the radio, startling me a bit. "OK, warm those tires, get some heat in there, keep pace with the car right in front of you. Two pace laps—we'll go green second time by. I'll call it for you."

I looked up to see Kelly weaving back and forth, warming his slicks as we headed into turns two and three. He was really leaning on it—so much so that I marveled at how he managed to not spin the car. I made a few perfunctory back-and-forth gestures with my car, sure that if I pushed it as far at Kelly did, I'd wind up facing backwards or committing some equally senseless mistake on the pace lap. I abandoned that in favor of braking/accelerating rapidly, generating heat that way, and staying off the dirty far edges of the track.

On the second go-round, we obediently slowed down through the last turn just as Mike called out, "Pace car's off, get ready…get ready…remember, don't pull out or pass until the call."

I closed up next to Kelly and behind the BMW directly in front of me. Second gear, mid-range revs, I was wide-eyed and listening for Mike. I couldn't see the flagger, but I wasn't at all concerned—my whole world was inches off my front bumper.

"GreenGreenGreen!!!" Mike announced in my ears. At once, the noise enveloped me, as all twenty engines redlined simultaneously. I stomped down on the throttle, pulling back for the first upshift as the tach needle sprang into the red zone. Unfortunately, the BMW directly ahead hesitated just enough that I had to crack out of the throttle to avoid running into him. I backed off, and then attempted to accelerate as five GT cars streamed on by me down into the first turn. Kelly—that S.O.B!—didn't bother to wait for me, and he was long gone by the time I made it through the right-hander and headed towards turn two.

Just like that, there was a gap between me and the next closest car. I gulped at the evidence of my crappy start, and tried to get back on it as the next sequence of turns approached. Bit by bit, I could see some progress—as I went into the esses for the first time, I made up ground, and through the Oak Tree turn I managed to catch up to the BMW once again. Working hard, biting down on the drink tubing and gripping the steering wheel to sawdust, I locked onto the back of the BMW and drove.

Right on the tail of the BMW past start/finish, I thought for a moment that I might be able to pass in the braking zone of turn one. Instead, I was too early and too light on the brakes, and managed to lock them up just enough to slide off the track at the outside of the turn. I made one slow revolution before I stopped, with my rear end ever so slightly in touch with the tire wall. Flustered but relieved that there seemed to be no big impact, I restarted the car, and rejoined the race, now in P19.

I did my best to hustle the car back up to speed, but it was definitely tough. I had to focus a bit harder, and reassure myself that the only way to get back in it was at full pace, forgetting my lazy error. I bore down, clenched my jaw a bit harder, and tried to push just a bit more.

Midway through that lap, I found myself surrounded by prototypes. The DP's had started well ahead of us, and with my slow pace and early off, they had caught me and the poor bastard behind me, rather easily. I tried not to flinch as, one after the other, and often in pairs, the faster prototypes zoomed on by, ignorant of my plight. I kept to the racing line, tried not to make any unpredictable moves, and eventually headed on down into turn one for what I hoped would be my first successful attempt at speed. I went to the brakes a bit early, relieved at the great bite and urgent deceleration of the car. At I trailed the brakes into the corner and pointed down towards the apex, I took a quick scan of my rearview mirror. I saw a flash of a purple Daytona Prototype right behind me on my right side. Despite the fact that I had the line and the corner, I decided not to chance it and gave the faster car plenty of room to pass me on the inside.

With a harsh Bang!! the Crown Royal Special Reserve car hit me broadside, punting me one full car width to the left as I tried to turn down towards the apex. I backed out of the throttle and tried to hold my new trajectory as the prototype rubbed alongside of me for a moment—sort of like when Sammy Marcozzi used to rub his hand in my face before he got off me after a fight—before launching off the apex and disappearing down towards turn two.

"Effing Eddie Cheever just ran into me in turn one!" I called over the radio. Mom! He hit me! I realized I sounded all too petulant, but couldn't resist anyway. I was also aware that we had some guests likely listening in on the radio, so I added, "That wasn't so special or very reserved."

Mike checked up on me. "Are you alright?"

"Yeah, I'm fine, the car seems OK; just wondering why he used me as a turn-in point."

Mike was diplomatic, sort-of. "Well, he's Eddie Cheever, and, well, you're…umm…not."

I responded a few turns later, when I had a moment to breathe. "Well yeah, but I can't wait for him to come back around again a few laps from now. No moving over next time."

JP felt then that it was time to chime in. "Ok, Dr. Lowe, time to focus, and get back to driving your race. Come on now."

I raced onwards, maybe a bit harder now that I was suitably mad—not at Eddie, that was just more evidence of my problem—but mad at the fact that I was driving like a dumbass. Getting passed on the start, screwing up turn one, getting caught up in a DP dust-up. All things that I should have known better to avoid. The adrenaline combined with the flush of anger worked well: I picked up pace, pushing hard to make up ground to the next set of taillights in front of me. I spotted the BMW once again, and realized soon that I was in fact getting closer. As I came up behind the GT car, two Prototypes passed by me, just at the entrance to the Oak Tree turn. I latched onto the second DP's tail, and managed a sneaky pass of the BMW as it moved aside for the faster cars. Following the last DP through the turn on-line, I was able to get onto power earlier and drag-race the GT car on down the long straight. As I pulled away easily, the sensation was exhilarating. Noise, torque, fumes, fun—and so much more race to run. I smiled, wiggled a bit in the seat like a horse taking the bit, and raced on.

For the next several laps I managed to keep the Porsche on the black stuff, setting personal bests that were, of course, a long way off from the front-runner's times. I celebrated two additional passes, of two different Corvettes, both gratifying rewards for the hard work of first catching, and then cleanly overtaking the struggling GT's. I was having big fun now. I actually drove as if I wanted to get into and through the next corner even faster. I didn't question the wisdom of being there anymore, although the occasional passing of an aggressive DP definitely made me question the sanity of the whole concept.

Coming down through turn seventeen once again, I looked up through the corner to spot a crumbled-up Daytona Prototype positioned sideways across the track-out area. After an initial burst of panic, thinking that I was going to collect the immobile car, I hit the brakes, and managed to whoa-up my Porsche. It's not quite as easy as it sounds—I was fully loaded up, leaning hard on the left side of my car and trying to roll speed at a fast part of the track when the damaged car came into view. The accident must have just happened, as there weren't even any yellow flags waving yet. My car squirmed a bit as I slowed down and then made my way through the debris field generated by the substantial wreck. I gave silent thanks for having avoided adding my own sheet metal and bank account to the carnage. I certainly needed to keep the car shiny, especially when wrecks were avoidable with a little luck.

Having somehow remained in one piece thus far, I called the yellow flag in on the radio, to which Mike replied, "Yeah, we can see it on the TV. Nice job avoiding that. Pull up to the car in front of you. No passing under the yellow."

I caught up to the orange DP in front of me, piloted by Oz Negri. He was co-driving with Mark Patterson, another of the Skip Barber guys who had evolved (or devolved, as the case may be) into a Grand-Am regular and podium finisher. I felt strangely comforted just to be behind a guy I knew, and someone I figured at least wouldn't try to kill me on a restart.

The yellow flag period dragged on for quite a while, during which I realized that I was in fact bored with weaving back and forth at three-tenths speed. After a few laps of that, I figured it was a good time to check back in with the crew.

"Man, this yellow is lasting longer than my first marriage!"

I could hear Mike laughing when he decided to weigh in on the radio with some encouragement.

"Nice consistent laps, Jim. 3:35. 3:34, 3:35. Way to go."

It only took me a few seconds to get it—the typical fast laps under race conditions being under two minutes.

"Thanks for the support, bud. What's on TV? Should I wave?"

"Nope, but I'll keep you posted. For now, stay out, and we'll keep running this tank out. Repeat, stay out."

"Copy that, staying out. You guys are no fun."

When we finally went green again, I spit myself out of the Prototype sandwich I was in, pulling off line to let the fast runners get by. I managed to avoid Christian Fittipaldi, Cheever's co-driver in the Crown Royal car, who apparently hadn't paid attention to Eddie's pre-race driving instructions. Once I was clear, I picked up the chase behind the next GT cars ahead of me. I passed the first unwitting Corvette—might have been the guy I passed the last time, I wasn't sure—and then another GT car before heading on down the long back straight once again.

I wouldn't see it until days later, when I watched the Speed TV replay out of morbid curiosity, but a few laps later, I blew on by a waving red and yellow-striped flag—signifying "slippery" conditions on the back straight ahead. I ran over the rise at full speed and straight down toward the heavy threshold braking zone of turn fourteen. Lining up on the outside of the turn in area, I hit the brakes firmly, right at my marker, anticipating the quick uphill braking area followed by a right-left sequence called "The Rollercoaster." Unfortunately, I didn't notice then that a DP with a blown engine had just finished oiling down the line in that area, only seconds before I arrived.

The instant I touched the brakes, my right rear wheel slid off the track onto the grassy edge, sending me into an immediate high-speed spin. In the blink of an eye, I was rotating rapidly, foot hard on the brake pedal, spinning up the track towards the aforementioned roller coaster ride. I was disappointed, to say the least, realizing immediately that I was in the midst of a very big off. However, instead of panicking or thinking black thoughts about my mortality, a new problem confronted me.

"Shit, this is on TV, and it's gonna be big enough to make the highlights. Ginny will be watching at home. Hope this ends OK."

In that familiar eternity that is a spinning race car, I thought only about what my wife would be thinking when she saw me crash. After all, she had never actually seen such an event in slow motion, hi-def carbon fiber shards and all; this would undoubtedly be really ugly. She didn't ever like to see other guys crash on TV; I was pretty sure she would just hate this one.

And then a funny thing happened: my car made a few more revolutions, slid up over the top of the hill and across to the grass on the other side of the track, and…stopped. I couldn't believe it. From 155 mph to 0 in a blink, with only my racing heart and some wild skid marks as evidence of my spin.

I blinked several times, thinking it somehow odd that I was intact and the car hadn't made any nasty crashing noises. I looked up to see the corner worker waving the yellow furiously and pointing the way for me to re-enter the racing surface. Once I had the car restarted, I took a series of deep breaths, and radioed in to Mike what had happened.

"Hey guys, I just had a big spin, but didn't hit anything. I'm getting underway, but not sure what shape the car's in. I don't think anything's broke."

Mike replied immediately. "We didn't see anything back here, but Grand-Am just called it on the radio. Get going if you can, and let us know how it is."

I pulled onto the track after checking to make sure the path was clear. I slowly got back up to speed, taking a few extra quick turns side-to-side to make sure the suspension and tires were OK. I immediately felt a deep vibration coming from the tires.

"Big vibration in the front tires. Must be flat-spotted."

Mike gave me instructions. "Come on by down the front straight, and we'll look and listen."

By the time I was halfway down the straightaway, my teeth were chattering from the staccato vibration of the squared-off tires. Mike immediately confirmed this on the radio.

"You're chattering away there. You're going to have to come in now; can't risk a blow-out. Let's pit now for a driver change and four tires with fuel."

With that, my first starting-driver experience in a professional race—about fifty minutes that felt like three days—was over. I unplugged my cords and drink hose, loosened my belts, and dutifully returned to the pits to hand the car over to JP.

Jim Pace took over after I pitted from 16th place, which I thought wasn't too bad, considering the wild and varied adventures I had just experienced. As I cooled off in the shade of the TRG pit tent, JP ran the Porsche the way it was meant to be run—hard and aggressively. In five laps, my partner had wrung the neck of the GT car all the way up to P12. I watched the dual-display timing and scoring, alternating with the Speed TV feed, as JP made up ground and attempted to restore our honor.

Unfortunately, the Speed TV crew came out of a commercial just in time to pick up the ending of a crash, zooming in on the back end of a suspiciously familiar blue Porsche protruding from the tire wall in the run-off area at the end of the esses. As I watched, JP emerged from the stationary car, displaying a disgusted look on his face. I sat there stunned, wondering what had just happened, while the crew scrambled all about me getting ready for the car to get towed back to the garage area.

As we collected things in preparation to meet the wrecker at the garages, the TV returned from the yellow-flag commercial break. I looked up in time to see the blue #66 car emerge from the tires and get underway once again. A few shouts later, the crew had returned to the box and checked up with JP on the radio.

"I just hate it when I damage a race car," Jim's Mississippi drawl was evident on the radio. "I just hit him from the back corner, it was my mistake. Sorry guys."

"We all saw the end of it, but didn't see the hit," Mike advised.

"I'm moving now. She doesn't seem to have anything wrong that I can't race with."

With that, JP returned to the race with solid, if unspectacular laps, finishing up in P17 after about forty minutes of quiet running. Once the checker was out, the Porsche returned to the pits, looking for all the world like a battle cruiser returning to port one torpedo hit shy of a sinking.

JP emerged from the car, looking a bit beat up himself. We did the hug thing, exchanging regrets for having made the day all too long for each other. I reminded my co-driver that it was a great day nonetheless, given that I had made my first start, survived a baptism under fire, and in the end, we finished well better than DFL.

My ride home was in a stylish Gulfstream jet—not actually for me but arranged by us for the day's use of three potential sponsors. My marketing guy had recently introduced me to our first allegedly legitimate contacts for potential investment in our racing efforts. Unfortunately, in the process he also introduced me to the harsh reality of such interactions. We had hired the jet for the day to give high-ranking C-level types from KPMG, Marriott, and The American Cancer Society a chance to see us up close and in action. All three brought guests, all paid for by me, who traveled from Philadelphia to get wined and dined around the VIR paddock. After a fine outing, all six of them talked excitedly about their experience as we rode home in style. Each pledged to make every effort to "make something happen", and to work with us to put a real sponsor relationship together. After a rough couple of days in the Grand-Am school of hard knocks (literally), I was thrilled that we seemed to have something viable to work on with our guests as the new JLowe Racing team emerged.

In the days and then weeks that followed, not one of them would return our calls and email requests for follow-up or further discussion. They didn't return the logoed golf shirts, either.

Chapter Twenty

"OOOh, oooh, Mr. Lowe! Mr. Lowe!!" Braving the scariest moment yet of my entire racing career, I fought to remain calm in front of forty not-so-calm classmates of Aidan. I had just asked the boys to guess what my HANS device helped prevent; I had thought they might be interested in the oddly-shaped contraption that I wore while racing. Several hands shot up, and a few of the boys struggled to stay properly seated. "Mr. Lowe! Ohh, Missterrrr LOWE!!"

Seated on a tiny chair alongside my son, who was proudly perched in the seat of honor, I was just beginning my first attempt at being an official guest parent career/role model for Aidan's kindergarten class. Earlier in the year, when I had originally volunteered, I had thought that the discussions would be crafted around my career as a physician and surgeon. However, Aidan had made it clear a few weeks before my scheduled appearance that he had something else in mind.

"Hey dad, you know how you're going to come to my class for career day in May?" I could tell by Aidan's approach that he had more in mind than just confirming that I was going to show up.

"Yep, Bubba, I'm looking forward to it."

"Well, you know how you do two things—being a doctor and racing?"

I cocked one eyebrow as I looked up from reading my paper. "Yeah..?"

My son had obviously thought this through, and the rehearsed words came out carefully. He obviously didn't want to offend me with his thoughts.

"Well, I've been thinking about it, and I think maybe the kids would like to hear about the race car driving the most." He said this as more of a question than a request.

"So, not so much the doctor part, huh?"

Aidan seemed relieved that I didn't sound upset. "Yeah, well, that part's OK, a little, I guess, but the racing stuff is probably a little more exciting."

"Yep, you're probably right about that. Anything in particular you want me to show them or talk about?"

This, too, had evidently been considered already.

"Could you maybe bring some of your fireproof underwear?"

So, there I sat on the hot seat as kids expertly dodged my Q&A session efforts.

Holding up the black HANS device, I decided to go on the offensive. "Brandon? Do you have any idea what this is for?" I directed attention over to one boy who was jabbing his hand urgently skyward.

"Mr. Lowe, have you ever been in a crash?" Brandon was literally hopping in his seat.

"Well, yes I have, but first let's talk a bit about safety…"

The boys collectively smiled and whispered excitedly when I first admitted to being in a real, live, wreck. Few were focused on the HANS at that point.

"Ohhh, Mr. Lowe!"

I gave it another try. "Alright…" I pointed towards Trip. "Do you know what a helmet does?"

Trip shot out of his seat. "Mr. Lowe, have you ever crashed…" he gestured with his hands slapping together... "like this?!"

I tried once more to brush it aside and return to my planned topic. "Well, yes I have…"—big grins from all of the boys, and a few partially muffled cheers thrown in— "but let's talk just a little about safety, OK?"

"Ooo, Aidan's dad, Aidan's dad!!" More little hands shot up eagerly.

I pointed to another classmate. "OK, Max, how about you? Do you know why I wear a helmet?"

Max stood, shifting his weight from one foot to the other. He had a comically serious look on his face, and now we both had the attention of the other boys. "Mr. Lowe, have you ever crashed..." once again, with hand gestures "...UPSIDE DOWN like this??" Max's eyes were wide as he turned both hands palms-up, animating a twisting, inverted impact.

Aidan's classmates bounced excitedly in their seats. Clearly I was overmatched and outwitted. Leaning forward, I said in a conspiratorial tone, "OK. First you have to promise me that you won't tell Mrs. Lowe."

The room fell silent, and forty heads nodded in anxious affirmation. The boys inched forward in the seats, and I waited a tick until answering.

"Yes, I sure have!"

"Woohoo!!" The boys erupted in joyous whoops and yelps, and beside me Aidan beamed a Cheshire cat grin that matched his newly elevated status among the kindergarten elite. At that point, I could have only made them happier if I had burst into flames right then and there.

As the commotion died down, I felt Aidan tugging at my elbow. I looked down to see him holding out my Nomex shirt and longjohns.

It was clearly time to give up on accomplishing anything remotely educational. "Who wants to see my fireproof underwear?"

"Yeaaaayyyy!!"

Later that afternoon, when I arrived in the car line for pickup at Aidan's school, I could see my son standing with some of his classmates. I pulled up in time to see several of the boys pointing in my direction and talking excitedly with Aidan. My son broke away from the little gathering and headed to the car. A few of the boys waved hello, and one yelled out "Cool car!" as Aidan jumped into the Porsche's front seat. I chuckled to myself as I realized that Aidan was sitting up just a bit taller than could have been accounted for by the booster seat alone.

"Hey dad, thanks for speaking to my class today."

I smiled wider. "No problem, bubba. How did I do? Do you think they liked it?"

My son nodded, anxious to put my mind at ease. "Oh yeah. Everybody liked it. Even Mrs. Higgins said she liked your talk."

I rarely got so much out of my son during our rides home from school, so I thought I'd carefully take advantage of his unusually loquacious mood. "What part did they like the best?"

"You mean besides the underwear?"

Laughing, I reminded myself of the simple pleasures of a kindergarten kid. "Yeah, other than seeing my fireproof underwear."

"Well, I think they all really liked the part about you crashing."

"OK, well then, I guess something good comes out of wrecking a race car after all."

Aidan fell silent, and I figured that I had gotten the maximum out of my usually reticent son. Several minutes passed before he spoke up again.

"Hey dad, do you think I could go to one of your races sometime? I mean, not ride in the car, you know what I mean, just go and watch maybe?"

This was clearly a day of bigger and bigger grins, at least for me.

"Sure thing Bubba, I think we could do that. Not my next race—it's already too late to do that—but I'll speak with mommy and we'll figure something out soon, OK?"

Aidan was clearly satisfied with my answer. "OK. Can I shift again, please?"

He grabbed the stick shift with his left hand. I reminded him of our routine. "OK, just wait until I say 'Go' and then pull it down, alright?"

Both content, we drove on home. "Go" was the only word spoken after that.

***

In late May, I headed off to the Finger Lakes region of New York for my next scheduled Grand-Am race. As per the carefully crafted plans of Jim Pace, we had entered the #66 TRG Porsche in the "Six Hours of the Glen," the endurance classic run annually at Watkins Glen International. I was excited about going back to the Glen, having raced there several times in Skip Barber events over the past few years. On the downside, the race was to take place on our wedding anniversary, so Ginny and I would be celebrating at the track, blurring the focus on the "us" as I worried only about going faster. I had been watching the calendar for this one for some time, eagerly awaiting the trek up the PA turnpike and Rt. 81.

While venues such as Long Beach have glamour and tracks like Indianapolis and Daytona have drama, few places on the American motor racing circuit have the palpable sense of history found at Watkins Glen. Names like Jim Clark, Graham Hill, Briggs Cunningham, Jackie Stewart, and Stirling Moss hang in the air, which drips with the aura of great and fast men racing, and occasionally dying, on this classic twisting road course. For a student of the history of motor racing like me, the small town of Watkins Glen and the phenomenal track just up the hill occupy a priority position.

Watkins Glen first hosted a motor race, organized by Cameron Argetsinger, in 1948. Undeniably brave men raced on a 6.6 mile circuit laid out on the town's streets, in the European fashion popular for the sport at that time. Even braver spectators watched from too-close positions around the streets, and the death of a young boy in 1952 prompted relocation of the course further outside the town center for the 1953 race. The first permanent, purpose-built, track was constructed in 1956, moving the racing off the public roads for good. Since then, an addition ("the Boot") was added in 1977, and a bus-stop-style chicane in 1992. But, in one form or other, the track which I was to drive was hallowed ground, covered with the footprints of giants.

Knowing that I was enamored with the history of the place, my co-driver had a bit of a treat planned for me on our first day at the Glen. Once JP and I checked in with the crew, eyeballed the Porsche, and said hello to Kevin Buckler, we headed out of the paddock towards our hotel and an early dinner. However, instead of heading directly back to home base in Corning, JP made a surprise detour in the middle of town. Pulling into the parking lot of a non-descript municipal-looking structure, JP announced proudly, "I think you're going to enjoy this visit, Dr. Lowe."

Standing at the front door was Michael Argetsinger, the brother of Peter, and son of the guy who started the tradition of racing at the Glen. JP introduced me to Michael, who welcomed us to the International Motor Racing Research Center, a treasure trove of all things racing. With extensive documents, photos, books, and memorabilia, along with video and movies, the Center was a collection of so many touchable items related to the history of my sport that my heart raced as I toured the two-story museum. Michael's mom, Mrs. Jean Argetsinger, served as a tour guide, pointing out special objects here and there, and unfailingly describing the history and significance of each artifact as I walked along with the group, dumbstruck.

I related to Michael and Mrs. Argetsinger how my son and I were fortunate enough to own a signed program from the 1961 Formula One race—The "US Grand Prix"—containing signatures of Jimmy Clark, Innes Ireland, and Stirling Moss; I described the three-minute home video my friend had given me along with the program, showing a rare behind-the-scenes glimpse of his experience as a young fan on race day back in 1961. Both Michael and his mom expressed interest in my small but meaningful collection of Watkins Glen memorabilia, and I promised to check and see if it was OK with Aidan to lend the items to the Research Center. As we walked further and talked more, Michael was kind enough to show us his newly-published book on Walt Hansgen, a sports car racing legend from the 1950s and '60s. Before we left the Center, I was doubly pleased to receive an autographed copy of Michael's book, with the following inscription:

"For Aidan, a race enthusiast! Your dad's a great driver. I hope you enjoy this story."

It was signed, "Michael Argetsinger, Watkins Glen, 2006."

I thanked the Argetsingers for my very special tour of the Center and clutched the book proudly as Jim Pace and I headed back to the hotel. The inscription on the title page of the book was special, no doubt, and I of course realized that Michael had been all too generous with his description of my driving ability. But my young son wouldn't have to be confronted with that rough truth for quite some time anyway, so I let it pass just then and enjoyed the small treasure.

I quietly continued considering my diminutive place in the racing cosmos, especially here where you could live and breathe the history of great men, when JP interrupted my woolgathering.

"Well, Dr. Lowe, what'd you think about all that?"

There was little to say that could properly express the overwhelming thoughts I had about the Center and my brief trip there. So I said little, for once.

"Wow."

On the first practice day, Watkins Glen lived up to another aspect of its reputation: rain greeted the drivers standing bunched around the Grand-Am trailer for the pre-practice meeting. As I alternated views between the dark sky and Mark Raffauf's podium where he detailed the running order and various race housekeeping items, my mind wandered to the challenge of running on a wet track at the Glen. I had done so before, actually on many occasions, and basically had hated the experience each time. Racing an open-wheel single seater in the rain was tough enough anywhere; at WGI, with its blind turns and elevation changes, it was damn near impossible for anyone with any reasonably cognizant sense of their own mortality. Much like the rollercoaster that was VIR, Watkins Glen was a true natural-terrain road course, without any artificial alterations or man-made segments. And it had one added feature that threatened all who drove there: menacing blue Armco guardrails outlined most of the track, seemingly placed with malice aforethought at the areas where one might most likely crash. Trying not to think too much about these little details until I absolutely had to, I swallowed hard and put on a face of false bravado in front of the other drivers. Standing in small groups, I laughed and smiled as we exchanged idle chatter before splitting up to go to our respective race haulers. As we headed towards our car and the wet driving experience that awaited me beyond that, I brought up the whole driving in the rain deal to JP.

"God, you know I love this track, but I think I hate driving it in the rain."

JP tried to be reassuring. "You've got a lot of laps here, which means a lot of laps in the rain, right? And you did just fine at VIR. You'll do fine here—just focus on smooth, easy power down, and slow hands." Jim said this calmly, as if he was describing a chess move.

"Oh yeah? Easy power down, huh? It sounds a little too much like me trying to convince you how easy spine surgery is."

JP, given his medical school and family background, was no stranger to the concepts and challenges of surgery. "If I had a vote, I'd bet surgery was quite a bit tougher than driving a car."

I felt obligated to counter his argument. "No way. I've done enough of both to sleep a lot better the night before a big operation."

At this point, JP sensed a need to get me back on the right path as we neared the time to drive. "Look," he said, stopping and turning to me, "you've driven in the rain, you've driven in all sorts of conditions. You're here now because one, you can do this, two you're good at it, and C, because you love it. So shake it off, and let's go have some fun, OK?"

I blinked twice as I tried to decide whether he was being supportive, or just plain tired of hearing me whine. I decided it was a little of both.

"OK, I'm in. I'll be better when I'm strapped into the car and not standing around thinking all the time."

"Copy that. Let's go get the car warmed up and rolled out."

Unfortunately, the weather failed to cooperate, and the rainy mess plagued our practice sessions from the start. JP took the Porsche out for the first part of the first session, making changes every few laps or so—a little more wing here, a little bit softer on the springs, full soft on the roll bars—all in an attempt to set the car up so that I would be more confident in the wet. I watched from a seat on the pit cart, bundled up in a parka, bullshitting with Murray Marden as he too waited to drive. Mur had gotten a seat in one of the other TRG Porsches and was making his Grand-Am debut that weekend. Maybe he was just good at hiding any anxiety, or maybe it was just his pilot's training that helped him here, but he looked and sounded a whole lot more relaxed that I did. However, neither one of us had been on track at the Glen in a Porsche yet, let alone in the rain, so we didn't bother comparing notes about anything other than our completely-irrelevant Skip Barber experience.

Mike Johnson finally pointed over in my direction, and I shed my jacket, donned my helmet, and waited obediently for the GT3 Cup car to return to the pits. As Jim Pace jumped out, and I stepped toward the open driver's side door, he grabbed my arm and motioned for me to listen.

"It's pretty slippery out there, but the car is set up real nice right now. There's a stream running across the laces at the track out; make sure your hands are straight when you go over it. Remember, nice and easy, little inputs."

I nodded, eyes probably a little wider than usual, and moved around him to get into the car.

Once underway, I moved down pit lane towards the exit, which was a rather sharp downhill right-hand turn—just the first of the track's many challenges. On my way, I wiggled the steering wheel as I tried to get a feel of what kind of grip the grooved rain tires offered. Satisfied that I wasn't on roller skates, I took a deep breath, checked my mirrors, and moved out onto the racing surface down towards turn two.

Watkins' turn two, at the beginning of the famed S-shaped uphill section, the "esses," is a banked right hander that the driver enters downhill and exits uphill; the car compresses fully when at race pace, and most cars can do the full sequence flat—no braking, no lifting off the throttle—all the way through. Done properly, the car is all loaded up, pulling maximum g's at the apex of the turn, with the driver holding firmly on the steering wheel to keep the car pointed up towards the right side of the track at the exit. As the car starts to move uphill, still at full throttle, the driver must unwind his hands and begin the turn to the left for the next apex. There's an upshift to be made in the middle of the transition over to the left, and the hands are pretty busy at this point. Subtle moves are necessary, as turning too abruptly not only unsettles the car but also sets up the nose of the car for a deadly "early" entry to the last part of the esses. The final apex is done blind, and if the car arrives there before the apex—"early"—the driver will be headed directly for the blue guardrails lining the track out area as he crests the hill.

In a properly set-up car, especially one with good downforce, the esses become a relatively simple matter of "grip it and rip it"—full power, all the way through, with the driver already focused on the long straightaway to follow. But in the wet, or in a car not quite up to the task, the sequence of turns can be a real adventure. I moved through turn two and on up the hill carefully my first time through, trying to get some heat into the cold wet tires and simultaneously stealing a glance at the track surface to try and spot any developing dry sections. The Porsche felt solid and stable, but I was nowhere near the full-throttle that would be expected of me come race day.

Pleased that I had survived the first few turns, I accelerated up to fifth gear, not quite making it all the way to sixth as I did a relatively slow run down the back straight to the bus stop chicane. Down two gears, a quick right/left/right sequence later, and I was on my way towards the "Boot." Taken together from an overhead view, the next few turns are shaped like a boot, beginning with the downhill (why did everything at the Glen seem to be impossibly downhill?) off-camber left-hander, which was always slippery, even when dry. The run-off area here was one of the few places where there was a tire wall—and for good reason. It's quite easy to lock one's brakes when heading into the "laces," and a driver who is not back on the throttle early as the car turns downhill robs the rear end of traction. The result is a predictable spin-off into the tire wall, usually marked by paired black skid marks all the way in.

I stayed wide, on the "wet line"—out where the cars usually didn't run in the dry and where there was much less slippery wet rubber laid down—and looked out for the water streaming across the track that JP had mentioned. I crossed the little river with hands straight as instructed, feeling the car shiver a little as first the front, then the rear tires, hydroplaned on through. I managed to get back on the throttle a bit after the exit, still pointed downhill towards the "toe."

The toe of the boot was a sharp, banked right-handed hairpin, with a fun, full-power track-out section that led to a blind uphill run and then down again (of course!) to turn eight, the "heel." With little banking, the heel was a challenging right-hand turn that dares the driver to brake just a bit later each time through. Carry too much speed here, however, and there's a rather large sand trap awaiting you—where many a racer has sat, miserably watching the other cars go by while waiting to get towed out.

I made it on through the Boot, and approached the most slippery turn at the Glen—turn nine, also called "NASCAR nine" because it's where the short course—run by the stock cars—joins the Boot section. The entry is tricky, as the car is coming out of a deep dip between eight and nine, and the road flattens out immediately at entry as you crest the hill and turn left. As the driver moves onto the flat, wide surface of the turn, trying to bend the car towards the apex, the nose of the car gets very light, and it's quite easy to slide all the way around the turn. In this rain-slick section of track, I deliberately entered at the outside edge of the paved surface and again kept on the outermost part of the turn—doing a "rimshot", driving out where the grip tends to be better, away from the now-slippery typical path cutting across the turn to the apex—and filed another piece of good intel away for later use when I found good grip there also. It was no surprise as the car shimmied and slid on re-entering the usual path at the turn's exit, but my wide line had allowed me to straighten up the steering wheel earlier so that I wasn't trying to turn and gain traction at the same time on the wet surface. I was able to give it some decent throttle on the short chute that led to turn ten, a typically fast (and often flat in the dry) left-hander that was now pretty scary with the track watered down. Once again, the wide rain-line saved me, and good grip was to be had along the outside path, just like they taught me in racing school.

I held tight as I negotiated the Glen's last turn, eleven, a banked 90-degree right-hander that required commitment and an early application of power in order to give the driver a good jump on the long front straight. It was a little hairy in the rain, and there was little room to try anything resembling a wide line here, so I tried to point the car early through the apex, let it slide a bit until the tires hooked up near the exit, and made my way onto the front straight still unscathed.

I'm not sure, but I think my first truly deep breath came only once I was set up for the downward right-handed turn one. This turn was pretty fast and technical in dry conditions and in previous years had been downright frightful in the rain: there was an expansive sand trap running along the outside of the turn, and even a slight error anywhere from entry onwards would heavily penalize the errant driver with a trip over the curbing and a long subsequent beaching. However, in 2005, the year before my first Grand-Am run there, the runoff area had been fully paved, allowing anyone overcooking the turn to simply run wide over the outside curbing, often rejoining with little penalty once the driver gathered his wits about him. This was especially comforting to me as I made my way through there in a semi-relaxed fashion and prepared to once again confront the darkly wet esses.

As I wiggled the rear end of the car down into a deliberately wide apex in turn two, the yellow caution light on the dash started blinking, almost simultaneous with the waving black flag of the corner worker. Flashing back to my early Skip Barber days, I immediately assumed that I had committed some dire transgression, wondering just what I had done to deserve censure so soon in the session. My mind was quickly eased with the next radio call, however.

“Black flag all, black flag all.”

“Hey Mike,” I answered only once I was on the straight part of the backstretch. “I thought that was for me. What gives? Somebody wrecked somewhere?”

Mike seemed puzzled that I didn’t know why the session was being flagged. “Did you happen to notice the fog? We can’t see beans up here on the front straight.”

I realized that I had been pretty focused on the ten yards immediately beyond my front bumper—classic rookie driving—and hadn’t realized that visibility was nearly zilch in thickening fog.

“OK, I, um, see that now. I’m on my way through the Toe and coming back now.”

“Copy that, be careful, and don’t run over anybody. Lots of slow movers out there right now.”

I reassured the crew back on the wall. “Not to worry, I think I’m one of them.”

Thus after one glorious half-speed wet lap, I had officially started my professional experience at Watkins Glen. All would be well and good if only the weather would cooperate so I could get dry laps in for practice—and hopefully then during the race.

The next and now only real practice day dawned cloudy but dry, and I was encouraged enough to volunteer for first laps in the #66 Porsche. I was thinking that it would be great to get a nice solid dry run in, and by the time I was buckled into the seat, I was feeling pretty good about myself. That all went to hell a few moments later when my first lap times started showing on the dash. Too timid through just about every turn, I drove the car as if it were still wet out—not trusting the grip in the corners, late to power, hesitant everywhere. I had no idea where exactly my times needed to be to be competitive, but I knew I was off pace. A lot.

A few laps later, Mike called me. "Everything feel all right Jim?"

"I'm not sure, but I think the car's fine. I just can't get it going right." I was frustrated but didn't want to sound too whiny over the radio. Blame the car for something like this and everybody will soon know the truth anyway, once they get a look and find nothing mechanical amiss.

"Is the car OK?"

"Yeah, the only problem is the soft part between the steering wheel and the seat."

I could hear Mike chuckle. "Copy that. Let's get JP in the car for some laps."

I dutifully returned the car to the TRG pits, and swapped seats with Jim Pace. Not bothering to listen on the radio, I slumped down in my seat on the pit cart and watched as JP reeled off several fast laps in a row. Fifteen minutes later, Mike looked over at me as he listened on the radio. Holding the blue headset off one ear, he let me in on the conversation.

"JP says the car is fine. He wants you to get back in and drive some more. You up for that?"

I nodded, and Mike repeated the news to JP. "OK, he's coming in next time by. Get ready. There's about a half-hour left in the session, so plenty of time to get some solid laps in."

I was geared up and waiting by the pit wall when JP brought the Porsche to a stop in our pit box. Jim twisted himself out of the car and motioned to me to stop and talk for a moment.

"The car's fine. The problem is here." He punctuated the word by firmly planting his foot on top of my right racing boot. "You need to put that—he was still standing on my foot—down more." As he spoke he grabbed both of my shoulders. "More power is what you need. There's a whole lot more car under you than you've been using, and you have to trust that in order to make it work. More gas, less brake."

I stayed silent as Jim let me have it. "The car is set up perfectly for you to go faster. Just get on the throttle, and do it like I taught you. Now get in there."

Embarrassed, I set my jaw as I drove the car down to the pit exit, trying to shake the bad air from my brain. I knew JP was right, especially about the source of the problem—me. Running bullshit slow laps at the Glen wasn't going to cut it, and it was now or never for me to decide if I wanted to do this right. Otherwise, there were plenty of good seats in the stands still available.

I pushed the car harder up through the esses, feeling the car lean over hard, but staying glued to the track all the way up the hill. I used a lot of curbing at each apex of the bus stop, rolling momentum better for once. At the next critical downhill turns—the laces, the toe, and turn eight—I went to power sooner and harder, surprised at how much better the car felt under power. Drivers talk about the feel of a car under load, but it's something that can't be taught—you just have to experience it in order to understand. And here, on this intimidating, undulating track in the middle of New York, I finally felt it. And it felt marvelous, with the rear end delivering great gobs of grip as I fed it throttle earlier and earlier. No sliding, no slipping, just a constant feel of speed delivered as the car worked just the way it was designed. Want to go faster? OK, push on the gas. Downhill, uphill, off-camber? It doesn't matter, just push on the gas and feel the grip and the torque deliver as promised.

My first lap was a full eight seconds faster than what I had done earlier in the session; over the next few laps, I took several seconds off each successive lap. In the back of my mind, I was aware that much of the improvement was a simple reflection of just how poorly I was driving earlier, but I didn't care anymore. I was back on pace, driving the way JP had taught me and thoroughly enjoying the experience. At one point, I was even held up by another Porsche driver struggling through the toe, though I was sympathetic only for a moment.

When the checkered flags waved signifying the end of the session, I was both surprised and disappointed. The feel of managing the Porsche at speed had finally clicked—thanks to the tough love from JP and some intestinal fortitude on my part. I didn't want to stop at that point, knowing that there was much more progress to be had. I just needed more time in the seat, but Grand-Am and the event organizers hadn't considered Jim Lowe's plight closely enough when planning the schedule.

I did a cool-down lap—probably closely resembling my earlier laps of the day—and made my way into the garage area. As the mechanics waved me into the parking spot under the blue tent, I could see JP standing off to the side, grinning. I tugged off my helmet after emerging from the car.

"Nice job, Dr. Lowe."

"Yeah, that's a little more like it, I guess."

JP was still smiling at his pupil. "I knew you could do it, once it clicked in there." He pointed at my sweaty head.

"Yep, that felt good. I'm ready for tomorrow, I think. As long as it doesn't rain, that is."

When we returned to the RV late that afternoon, we were met by Ginny, Ashlei, and my parents. Somehow, for the second time, my mother had been convinced to come see me race at Watkins Glen. The first had been a bit of a trial for her, so I was somewhat surprised to see her there as promised. Despite her brave greeting, I could tell by the look on her face that she hadn't forgotten the weekend when she and my dad had come to watch me drive in a Skip Barber race.

Jim and mom Bette at Watkins Glen, 2004

About two years before the '06 Grand-Am race, I had managed to convince my mom to come up to the Glen, where she and my dad could watch me race in person (a first for my mom; dad had already been to a few Skippy events). Afterwards they would visit with my sister and her family in Buffalo. I figured it would be a win-win but hadn't anticipated just how anxious my mother would be when the action on the track started. After all, she had always been the strong one when I was a kid, taking me to the ER with various broken bones and sprained joints or carting me off to the doctor with assorted bleeding appendages. My mother had constantly exhorted me to "be careful," surely realizing by the end of my first decade that my definition of "careful" didn't mesh with hers. Given that discrepancy, Bette Lowe took up the issue with God, praying in church daily, but never actually forbidding me from playing any sport. However, in the matter of the sport of car racing—the one she surely knew as potentially deadly—she had had no say. Perhaps that fact was the source of greatly intensified concern, but, if so, I hadn't really considered it before inviting my mom to watch me race.

When the races began on that Skip Barber weekend, I wasn't scheduled in the first group to run, so I joined my parents in the grandstands overlooking turn one. I encouraged my mom and dad to sit high up in the stands, where the view would be better and the noise from the cars slightly less intense. In this way, I figured the view of fifteen cars barreling into the first turn would be less threatening, and perhaps more enjoyable for my mom when viewed from afar. I thought it would be even better that I was sitting safely right next to her as the race began. What I hadn't anticipated was the possibility of other people around my mom screwing up my master plan.

Sitting one row in front of Bette and Bob was a young mother (probably around my age) whose eighteen-year-old son was running in group one. This petite woman chatted calmly with my parents as the warm-up laps began, proudly talking about her son's success thus far in the series and how nice it was that she had been able to watch him race several times before. Like a seasoned veteran, she reassured my mom several times—"You're going to love the racing," and "Don't worry, they're not going that fast." Having listened to several similarly-misdirected statements over the years, my mom was appropriately unconvinced but otherwise politely silent.

As the race started, the woman excitedly cheered her son on, clapping and jumping up and down each time he drove on by down the front straight. My mother watched dutifully, looking neither upset nor nervous, undoubtedly calmed by the fact that her son wasn't racing just yet. This state of relaxed calm lasted exactly three laps, until two different cars (neither driven by the aforementioned mother's son) tried to go deep into turn one simultaneously. I had watched this develop over the first two laps and, having seen similar such incidents before, had some idea of what was going to happen next.

As the two drivers went into the braking zone of turn one, nose-to-tail, the lead car braked just a fraction of a second earlier than the following driver. In a flash, the second car climbed up over the rear wing of the lead car, flying over the top of the rollbar (damn, another set of skidmarks to brush out of a helmet), and balancing on top of the other car for a brief moment before both cars spun harmlessly off into the kitty litter outside the turn. As this unfolded, young mom stood bolt upright and started screaming as if the offending cars had just parked on top of her baby.

"Oh My God Oh My God Oh My God!!"

I was sympathetic at first, as the crash did admittedly look quite ugly, though I knew it appeared much worse than it actually was for the drivers. Young mom, however, evidently remained concerned, and continued escalating the screaming.

"OHMYGODOHMYGODOHMYGOD!!!" This was now being screamed in a full stream of unpunctuated verbiage. And as it continued, my mother's eyes grew wider and wider while I watched her shoulders tense and the color drain out of her face.

The earsplitting screams continued on inexplicably, as both drivers were by now out of their respective cars and chatting amicably while standing in the gravel trap next to the wounded race cars.

"OhMyGodOhMyGodOhMyGod! OH. MY. GOD." It seemed that she was losing some steam, and by now people were starting to stare in our direction as the hysterical woman showed amazing endurance. I put one arm around my mom's shoulders, pointing out the fact that both drivers were now walking across the track and on their way back to the pit area.

"It's OK mom, really. See? They're both walking away, everything's fine."

"Oh. My. God." Young mom was still at it, a little quieter now, as she started walking down towards the grandstand exit. Her son was safely circulating around behind the pace car, now much closer to P1 as a result of the two cars having crashed out. I figured she ought to be happy, but she obviously hadn't yet begun to see it my way. My dad stayed seated alongside my mom, who remained silent and stoic as she managed her distress privately. Finally, Bob weighed in with a question.

"What the hell was she screaming so much for?"

My mother finally looked up at me. "Oh, Jimmy," was all she could manage.

To her credit, Bette stayed up in the grandstands and watched my (much more uneventful) races later that day. But it was clearly above and beyond the call of duty when she returned to the Glen two years later to watch my Grand-Am race.

***

Jim and Ginny with Bette and Bob at Watkins Glen, 2006

Since it was our wedding anniversary, I hosted the team along with my parents and my wife, of course, at the fine dining establishment that is Chili's. Gin was once again a trooper, putting up with the suspicious food and even more questionable rendition of "Happy Anniversary" by the waitstaff and a few of the TRG mechanics. She endured this not-so-elegant version of a celebration, partly because of the lack of any better option on a race weekend, and in part because of our agreed-upon "matching gifts program." In that fashion, we both knew that I owed her one when my wife indulged my inner child/racer at the expense of her special occasions. In reality, it was a fine way to celebrate a special event—surrounded by friends singing badly and relishing the thought of better mental health through racing. My improved psyche was a good addition to our union, so Gin was surely also happy with that concept. That and some fine jewelry and we'd be square.

Proving again that the race gods were completely indifferent to the fate of Jim Lowe, I awoke Saturday morning to a rather significant rainstorm. I slogged through the mud in the paddock bundled in a lined rain slicker and followed JP to the TRG hauler in time for the early morning practice. Race time was 2 pm, so there was time for one more go at the setup of the Porsche that morning before we went live and in color that afternoon. I didn't say much—I wasn't the talkative type on race mornings anyway—as I glumly considered the prospect of racing in the rain once again.

Jim Pace, Mike Johnson, Kevin Buckler, and I huddled in the front office of the race hauler, balancing hot coffee cups as we reviewed set-up sheets and talked forecasts and strategy. It wasn't yet clear whether or not the wet stuff would be with us for the duration of the race; the radar showed sporadic gaps in between nasty green blobs overlying most of western and central New York. Ultimately, JP made the call, suggesting that he get the car set up best for wet running, using the one short practice session to get the car sorted for the race. Given the damage the weather had done to the schedule, the usual Grand-Am qualifying session had been cancelled the day before in lieu of more practice time. So we were gridded based on points, putting us safely back in P18 for the start. Since there was no actual qualifying driver, the rules allowed that we could have either driver start the race. Better yet, since there were only two drivers in the #66 TRG Porsche, our best strategy now called for the faster driver—no doubting who that was—to start first and then also run it to the finish in the last stint. Hence the wisdom of setting up the car for JP to optimize the start. And, since I had run well in the dry conditions of the day before, it would only be a bonus if the rain held off. If it didn't, well then I'd just have to take my first laps in the rain under race conditions. Once more unto the breach and all that.

As race time neared, the rain actually tapered off, and parts of the track appeared on the monitors to be visibly drying. Since there was a made-for-TV big-screen monitor just opposite our pits, we were able to watch the track video feed from where we sat. I noticed improvement in the track surface as the cameras followed the safety vehicles making their way around to their positions well before race time. Bits of lighter gray were appearing in between the darkened pavement, especially around the more exposed sections of pavement, where wind helped dry the asphalt and concrete. I figured I was getting a break and thought that maybe my pilgrimage to the Motor Racing Research Center had paid off in some unanticipated way. "Positive thinking, big guy, happy thoughts, it'll be dry, just you wait."

And basically dry it was, for the start at least. I was enjoying the fact that there were no raindrops spoiling my view from the perch up high in the TRG pit cart as I snuggled deep in my thick parka. With both hands stuffed in my pockets and head tucked in against the chill air, I watched as JP took the green flag and began working hard right away. In the half-dry track conditions, Jim was inspired behind the wheel of the Porsche, pushing hard from the start and making passes from the first turn onwards. Where other drivers were too timid, Jim was aggressively pushing the Porsche, making up places quite literally left and right. There were several yellow-flag caution periods, and each one offered JP an opportunity to close up behind the car directly in front, and shortly afterwards make the next pass. I watched as JP's name climbed up the timing and scoring screen displayed proudly on the TRG monitor right next to the weather radar. As his name crept higher, I noticed that the green blob that was the next rainstorm had moved closer and closer to us. A few sprinkles started to fall as JP made one final pass on a Pontiac going up the esses, this time in full glory for all to see on the giant TV screen trackside. Forty five minutes into the six hour race, I looked again at the big screen and there was JP's picture in living color, sitting alone atop the GT standings on Speed TV. Even though I had just watched it happen, I was still pretty shocked. We were in first place.

Better yet, Jim kept up the pace even after cycling through the first two pit stops. With each stop, he kept running back up to the front, never dropping lower than fourth place over the next two hours as he wrung out every bit of performance from the Porsche. I huddled next to Ginny, my parents watched from the stands, and all was right with the world as JP drove a masterful race.

Then it began to rain in earnest. On cue, as if the weather gods told the racing gods to 'mind your own business, his ass is ours,' it started pouring just as Mike gave me the ten-minute warning. I silently cursed Graham Hill and Jimmy Clark for their apparent inattention as I shrugged off the parka and geared up for my first run.

A glimmer of hope appeared in the form of a full-course yellow, which occurred just in time for our planned pit stop. At least I would be able to get into the car without it being a full-on mad scramble. I'd also get to see the wet track under one-quarter speed a few times around before going green. Maybe Graham and Jimmy were tuned in after all. We were currently P4, and not quite halfway through the race. All I had to do is not fuck it all up from here. Survive for an hour or two, and get JP back in there for a good finish. No problem.

I pulled out of our pits, tightened my belts, and headed for the downhill pit out as I keyed the radio.

"OK Mike, any last words of advice?"

There was a long pause before Mike answered. "I just took a poll here in the pits. We all want you to go as fast as you can without wrecking."

I would have appreciated the humor in that much more, had I not been searching for the windshield wiper switch while making sure the lights were on, and trying not to crash in my first thirty seconds in the car. Although it was not quite five o'clock, the clouds and rain made it pretty dark as I strained to make out the tail end of the pack of cars. I tried to hustle the car up through the esses but felt the tires slipping and sliding as they slowly (oh, so slowly) came up to temperature. As I leveled out on the back straight, I saw the flashing lights of the pace car up ahead, with just a handful of cars lined up behind it. Not my usual view from the cheap seats.

As rain pounded the windscreen, I joined up with the pack of cars, and settled in for several slow laps around the eleven turns of the Glen. Through the foggy dark mist, I could make out the blurry lights of most of the cars in front of me; one Pontiac and two Porsches occupied the GT positions directly ahead. Behind me, I could see a set of headlights swerving back and forth as the driver tried to keep his tires warm.

"Who's that behind me?" I called in to the pits.

Mike gave me the news. "That's Andy Pilgrim in the other TRG Pontiac."

I contemplated this as we continued to circulate about under the prolonged yellow. Andy was another of the superstar Pontiac factory drivers; he was a multi-time driver champion, two-time Daytona 24 winner, Sebring 12-hours winner, and universally acknowledged super fast guy. And now, he was right behind me. In the rain. At the Glen. Holy shit, Batman.

"Is there any way I could point him by me under yellow?"

"Don't worry, you're faster than him in the rain. At least that's what JP said to tell you."

"Thanks guys, nice to know you have my back."

After several more quiet yellow laps (at least this time, Mike didn't compliment my consistent pace), I got the call again from the pits.

"OK Jim, Grand-Am says we'll be going green next time by. Make sure you take a good look at the track on this last yellow lap and be ready for my call."

I gripped the wheel just a bit tighter and tried to swerve a bit to get more heat into the tires. There was some grip at the outside of several of the turns, and I tried liberal brief applications of throttle to see what I might get away with on the next laps. As we came up out of the Toe for the last time under yellow, the pack slowed to a crawl, and I saw the pace car's flashing lights go dark. I waited for the call from Mike as we approached turn eleven.

"OK Jim, wait for it…GreenGreenGreen!"

I resisted the urge to punch the throttle, knowing that I would simply lose all traction if I overdid it now. Instead, I squeezed onto the gas, happy to feel the rear wheels settle as the car accelerated around the last turn and onto the front straight.

Spray was everywhere, giving the impression of driving headlong into a cloud as I pulled gears and accelerated directly into the wet air hanging over the long straight. I could see well enough to spot the brake markers and hit the brake pedal well before my usual "300" sign, knowing that there would be an adventure with slowing the car, especially the first time through. The Porsche slowed nicely, however, and I kept to the outside of turn one as I tried to stay near the taillights of the car in front of me. I expected to see Andy come flying by at any moment, so I took a quick peek in my mirrors before I redirected all of my attention to the upcoming esses.

I actually made up ground on the GT car in front of me as I approached the entry to the esses, feeling the spray invade the cockpit as the cars once again closed up ranks on the way up the hill. I moved my head side to side, straining for a better view out of the opaque windshield.

On down the back straight we went, with the visibility varying with following distance and speed. Once we slowed for the chicane, the view out the front was clearer, and I was able to actually look at the track for signs of a better line. On through the carousel and down into the laces, the car strained at the bit, but I wouldn't add more power, not just yet. First, I had to make it through the Laces.

I stayed wide, found grip despite a lurid slide at the entrance to the left-handed turn, and found myself side-by-side with the GT car that had been in front of me moments ago. I tried to apply progressive throttle, just like JP taught me, and won the race down into the hairpin. I again moved to the wide side and easily kept ahead as we exited the Toe. The car wiggled and squirmed with each gear change, but I stayed pointed forward and kept making up ground.

I was racing once again. No dark thoughts, no weight of embarrassment, no grimacing at the thought of failure, just the thrill of the drive, the rush of excitement with each turn, each lap. Yeah, it was dark and wet, and I had no actual idea if my lap times were competitive or not, but I didn't care just then. I was racing. Try to catch the guy ahead, try not to get caught. Wet or dry, clear conditions or Victory at Sea, this was racing and I was totally immersed.

I raced on, loving the Porsche's great grip on the slick surface. The GT car that I had passed into the Toe finally got by me a few laps later, when I overdid it just a bit and slid wide through NASCAR nine. I managed to get back on his tail and stay there for a few more laps, enjoying the dice with the other driver as I tried to find a way past him at several different points. In what seemed like only a moment later, I heard Kevin Buckler's voice on the radio.

"Great job out there, Jim. Still in P4. Keep up the good work."

"Where's Andy Pilgrim? Anybody know what happened to him?"

Kevin was quick to answer. "Don't look now, but he's right behind you."

I allowed myself a brief smile, and then went back to driving. Don't screw it all up now.

A blink later, and Mike was back in my ears. "OK, pit this lap, pit this lap."

I was definitely disappointed and at least a tiny bit relieved to get the call. The rain was still heavy, and I knew that, fun or not, my luck would likely run out at some point.

"Copy that, pitting now."

JP took over with less than two hours to go. The skies remained dark, but the rain slowed to a drizzle and then stopped altogether. I bundled up and resumed my place in the pits, Ginny at my side, as JP drove the #66 car on into the evening. In the last hour, the running order had settled itself so that we were running in sixth place, well ahead of the next GT car and not in hunting distance of the P5 car.

With a half hour to go, JP called in to the pits. "I don't think I have anything for the guys in front of me. How far ahead of the next car are we?"

Mike confirmed that our finishing position was likely safe as we ran. JP then offered, "Why don't we put Jim in the car to finish it up?"

Mike pointed over to me as I simultaneously started pulling off the headphones and looked for my helmet. I gave Gin a kiss, trying to appear valiant as I donned my gear and headed over to the pit wall. I hadn't expected to drive again, but there were only about thirty minutes left, and the track was nearly dry, so I figured there was little risk in getting back into the Porsche at that point. We were two full laps ahead of P7, so the pressure was off and I could cruise around, ticking off laps and enjoying the smell of the campers' barbecues.

I reentered the Porsche, pulled away with confidence, and rejoined the race in almost complete darkness. The track was indeed mostly dry, although there were some devilishly tricky wet sections left to keep you on your toes. I made several circuits around the Glen, generally trying to keep pace without risking a wreck. I also kept out of the way of the prototypes whenever they happened by, wanting to avoid the ignominy of screwing up someone else's race while I was busy bringing it home.

Mike gave me the "Ten minutes left", and then later the "Two laps left" call over the radio as I made my way out of the Boot and back towards the start of my last lap. As I rounded turn eleven, Mike sent out a warning call: "Prototype race leaders are going to catch you on the front straight. Heads up."

Suitably warned, I kept my eyes in the mirrors as I moved on down the front straight, foot flat on the throttle the whole way. I watched as the flock of three DPs contending for the win caught up to me about halfway down the straight. I stayed far left and made myself as narrow as possible as Jorg Bergmeister, Alex Gurney and Ryan Briscoe roared on past me at nearly 180 mph. Once they were by me, I breathed a short-lived sigh of relief, until I looked up just in time to see my 300 brake marker go whizzing by while I was still at full throttle.

Way past the point of making the turn, I hit the brakes hard, slowing only marginally as I flew on by the usual turn-in point for the first turn. I continued trying to slow the car as I ran off the outside of the entry area, straight onto the newly-paved asphalt of the now-dark runoff area. As the car finally slowed to a manageable speed, the outside tire wall came into view. I squeezed the wheel tightly and willed the car to turn as I tried not to lock up the steering and the tires all at once.

With great relief, the car turned right, tracing an arc just inside the tire wall as I got the nose turned back towards the track. I rejoined the racing surface at the track-out area, and calmly resumed my run towards the esses for the last time. Considering that I would have been beached permanently in the kitty litter just one year before, I counted my blessings and correctly figured that the worst was now safely behind me. I also took a moment to consider that maybe, just maybe, Jimmy Clark and Graham Hill were still paying attention.

I figured a radio call was in order, now that I was home-free. "Wow, that was interesting."

Mike came back with, "What was that?"

"Didn't you guys see that?"

Mike explained the confusion. "It's pretty hard to see back here. Everything OK?"

I didn't feel the need to fess up to this one. "Yep, all's well. Just seeing if you guys are paying attention."

"Copy that. We weren't."

I brought the Porsche around to take the checker, which was barely visible in the gloom of the evening. It still felt great, especially when Kevin sent his congratulations over the radio.

"Great job you guys! P6, P6! Nice run, nice drive, both of you."

"Thanks Kevin, thanks guys, fun run today. Thanks for everything."

JP chimed in. "Nice driving, Dr. Lowe. Ginny's happy, your mom and dad are happy, good day at the track, I figure."

"Thanks partner. Pretty good job yourself. See you in a few minutes."

I navigated my way back to the TRG camp in the paddock, pulling in under the brightly lit tented area to applause from Ginny, JP, my parents, and assorted other friends and family members.

Once I had finally shed my helmet and gloves, I hugged my wife and then made my way over to where my parents stood. My mom still had that look of resigned concern on her face, but it clearly softened as she saw the happiness in my features. I shook my dad's hand and then gave my mom a big hug.

"That wasn't so bad, was it?"

I could tell my seventy-seven-year-old mom was shaking a bit as we embraced. "No, not so bad, but isn't that enough now? Can't you stop now?"

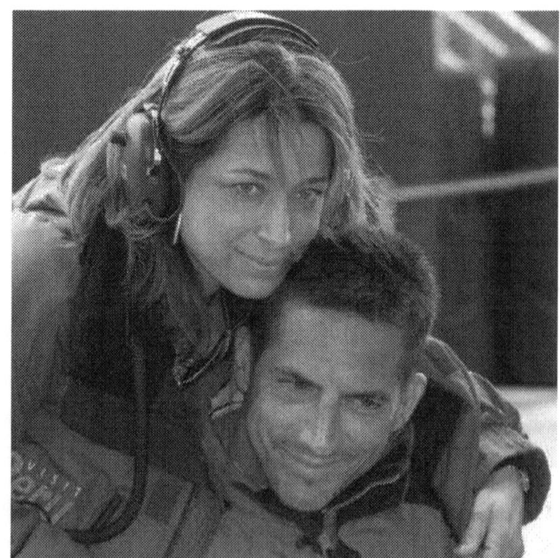

Jim and Ginny watch the monitors as JP runs the Porsche out front at the Six Hours of Watkins Glen, 2006

I felt like I was sixteen again, begging the doctor to let me play as soon as possible after some injury or other. "Stop now? We're just getting going! Why would I want to stop this feeling? I know you're worried, but this is no big deal. Really. Come on over here, relax, and enjoy it with the rest of the team. We'll talk about this another time—maybe."

Resigned to her pleas falling on my deaf ears, my mom just shook her head. "Oh, James, won't you ever listen to me?"

I smiled at her without answering and then turned away as someone tugged on my arm, diverting my attention elsewhere in the hectic post-race scene.

Chapter Twenty-One

The Grand-Am circuit had a full month that June 2006, beginning with the six-hour Watkins Glen Race and continuing with two more races in a one-month span: the Mid Ohio Sports Car Course Race on June 24 and the Brumos Porsche 250 at Daytona in early July. However busy the Grand-Am circuit drivers were, I respectfully submit that at this time I was quite a bit busier. In a rare circumstance for me, I was scheduled to drive my second race in less than a month, having committed to race again with Jim Pace in the TRG #66 Porsche at the Brumos race in Daytona. In between the Glen and Daytona, I had a predictably stressful time trying to cram roughly five weeks of neurosurgical work into a three week period. This was amplified by the ramp-up of the trauma season at the Jersey Shore, which officially commenced with Memorial Day and got progressively more active as the weather got nicer and the crowds got bigger.

As the local population swelled with tourists, the number of "trauma alerts"—calls for emergent care—increased exponentially. Traffic volume around Atlantic City increased dramatically, and with it, car accident victims visited our ER with steady regularity. On top of that, visitors managed to do infuriatingly dumb things as if they were somehow immune because they were "on vacation": diving into shallow pools, strolling mindlessly across busy streets, and partying at the casinos and then driving home drunk being some of the more common bad decisions resulting in chance meetings with the trauma team. And when their luck really ran dry, they found themselves—if they were conscious—looking up at a neurosurgeon who was describing the ten-hour operation they needed to repair the damage. It wasn't always life-or-death, but it was often a matter of more basic human function: Doc, will I ever walk again? Will my fingers ever work again? Will I be strong enough to hold my son again?

I answered the calls when it was my turn, and in between the emergent cases, fit pieces of my elective practice together like a jigsaw puzzle. Two days a week of scheduled office hours and three days of elective (if you can call surgery to relieve excruciating pain elective) surgery. Spackled around that schedule were the mundane tasks of running a small business—I had nine employees, a large overhead, and a rapidly expanding office to steer through daily challenges. And through all that, I leaned heavily on Ginny, who did much of the administrative work, and Joe, who shouldered more than his share of the medical grunt work. I pedaled as fast as I could, but there were times when I felt overwhelmed by the demands coming at me from all directions.

Jim Pace had warned me, but I initially felt that I had it all under control. I was juggling three jobs—team owner, physician, and driver—and somewhere in there needed to carve out time to be husband and father. I was in serious danger of replacing what scant free time I had with the demands of my new passion for racing at a seriously advanced level.

There was work to be done on the new website and meetings to be had in what seemed already to be a never-ending quest for sponsorship. Ideas were constantly presented by my team marketing staffer, who regularly debriefed with me during my commute home. Many ideas were somewhat admittedly farfetched, although several seemed to have potential. Given the position of sports car racing within a demographic that was somewhat different than NASCAR's, we initially attempted sponsorship with "luxury brand" types of companies. This included jewelry companies, Porsche dealerships, watch companies, and private jet companies. Despite all of our efforts, however, and despite countless hours spent scheming, planning, creating presentations, and occasional face to face meetings, little in the way of any true progress was made. Notable failures ranged from the now-familiar but always insulting lack of any response whatsoever to phone call and meeting requests and presentations, to outright breeches of contracts and, in one notable case, a check bouncing from the marketing director of a to-remain-nameless private jet company.

With all of the accumulating stresses, I was experiencing strain that was over the top for me, even in comparison to all of my various prior challenges. I typically approach episodes of increased demand in a headstrong fashion: confront whatever it is face-on, and work through the problem—like soldiers in an ambush—not away from it. But this period was like a non-stop test on my ability to keep up. I was getting hit from multiple sources, from multiple directions, and really felt like a guy juggling chainsaws. Catch 'em all, or else. And don't ever admit that you're struggling. When I was a surgical intern, it was a common aphorism that asking for help was a sign of weakness. So I bore down, pushed on, and continued the only way I knew how.

While I may have thought I was managing reasonably well, apparently there were signs of cracks in the foundation. Sleep-deprived, testy, and generally stressed, I was actually a pretty difficult guy to be around most of the time. Thankfully, I had a wife who was really the ultimate partner—when I needed it most, she was the clear-headed navigator who steered us through the roughest of spots. When I was in need of help, even if I wasn't able to acknowledge it or even verbalize the problem, she sensed that need and responded thoughtfully. This time was no different. Knowing me as she does, Gin didn't expect that I'd make any effort at a new approach, so she took matters into her own hands.

The antidote arrived in the form of a well-executed plan that would rival some itineraries suitable for summit day on Everest. With little assistance from me, Ginny had crafted a schedule that combined my next race event in Daytona with a family-focused excursion to Disney World. She examined the various race dates, and had come up with a program that called for the Lowe family to travel to Orlando for four days in Disney World, and then drive up to Daytona for the one-day event that was the Brumos Porsche 250 race. Gin's brilliant design allowed for a renewed family effort that demanded of me relaxation, vacation, and fascination with the joy of a five-year old confronted with Mickey Mouse for the first time. Admittedly, on my own I likely wouldn't have considered a trip to Disney World, grossly underestimating the value of four days in Orlando with my family and especially Aidan. However, when faced with the alternative of long days in the OR and office, and predictably several sleepless nights operating on unfortunately fractured spines, I readily agreed to the expanded trip schedule. Plus, the bonus was that I would be able to fulfill Aidan's request to finally come and watch a race in person.

While in Orlando, thoughts of race tracks and race cars were no longer front and center, as I instead experienced unanticipated enjoyment in revisiting some of the features of the park that I had last seen at age twelve. And for a change, I had left behind a relatively stable neurosurgical practice, without dumping any leftover work or other disasters in my partner's lap. Additionally, I had little opportunity to think about the business aspects of my growing racing devotion, as the immediate future called only for me to perform better behind the wheel. Issues of financing the rest of the racing season and any future racing could certainly wait until after I had completed my second professional event at Daytona.

This is not to say that I didn't occasionally think about racing while at Disney. There were times that I silently wished that the monorail driver would brake later and go back to power sooner, and at least once or twice I found myself predictably unimpressed with several of the roller coaster rides. While the high G-forces remained enjoyable, I was often uncomfortable owing to any lack of control over the machines themselves. I knew in fact that I would be much more at ease in just a few short days when I steered a different type of E-ticket ride around Daytona's high banked racing surface.

In our four days at Disney, I did manage to focus quite a bit on race preparation physically. While the 95+ degree temperatures were undoubtedly unpleasant for most of the tourists, and anybody wearing a fuzzy animal outfit, for me the brutal weather was a godsend. I was able to acclimate to the high temps over a week-long period, upping my cardio and strength workouts by happily carrying the fifty-pound Aidan around on my shoulders for most of each day. I bonded ever more with my boy while he enjoyed the best seat and best view of the park. We hit all of the main events, thrilled to the fireworks, and soaked up the G-rated fun over four days of otherworldly distraction. We enjoyed the rides, swam together, ate ice cream, and did whatever we wanted—together. It was more than a distraction—it was the reality of the best part of life, happening right in front of me.

But, behind it all, I didn't really let the racing go. Nor could I easily avoid occasional thoughts of some of the more challenging cases of my neurosurgical practice. In fact, it proved to be difficult to put all of the thoughts and images of both medicine and racing away. What can I say? I'm an A-type through and through, and even a place like Disney has limits to what it can accomplish, psychotherapy-wise. But focusing on family and having genuine off-time turned out to be hugely therapeutic. The goal wasn't to be entertained by the rides, it was to re-bond with Aidan and Gin and wash away the hardness of the previous weeks. And the result of this family vacation, combined with the sauna-like workout conditions, was that I arrived at Daytona relaxed, rested, and in shape for the fast-paced one-day event to follow.

***

Once we settled into our hotel room, we made our way west on Speedway Boulevard so that Gin and Aidan could join the team for pre-race dinner at Buca di Beppo. It was great fun to proudly introduce Aidan to JP and Ashlei, and to several other racers we bumped into on our way into dinner. Though somewhat shy, Aidan was his usual polite and perceptive self. He seemed to enjoy meeting people whom his father obviously thought were important, even if he was doing it mostly because it pleased his dad. For their part, the other racers were great, stopping to say hello and being unfailingly engaging and welcoming to both Aidan and Ginny. This all contributed greatly to my sense of belonging, adding to the comfort of returning to familiar surroundings at a familiar track and seeing some familiar and friendly faces. For a change, I was able to include my family in the "other" world that mattered so much to me.

Mur and Jim chat during a break in the action in the pits at Daytona

Similarly, the morning routine was quite comforting, beginning with a mandatory breakfast at the Cracker Barrel prior to heading over to the track. This time was slightly different since I could spend a few minutes with my wife and my son at the hotel room before leaving for the track. The feeling of familiarity was further reinforced by the typical circus atmosphere awaiting us when we pulled through Daytona's checkered-flag colored entry tunnel.

The Grand-Am Brumos 250 event was a one-day race, unlike any that I had previously been involved in, owing to the fact that it was sharing time on the schedule with the weekend NASCAR event. The Grand-Am cars were allotted a one-day period to practice, qualify, and then race into the night, after which we were unceremoniously kicked out of the paddock in preparation for the stock car boys beginning their race weekend the next day. Because the NASCAR boys were in town, the crowds were notably larger and somewhat more colorful. The campground area ringed the entry road to the paddock, allowing for some enjoyable viewing when we arrived at the track. In a slightly different show than occurred with the sports car racing at Daytona in January, the NASCAR encampment included a significantly higher percentage of campers of all shapes and sizes, many equipped with overhead observation decks and inflatable pools alongside. Most flew flags supporting their favorite drivers; I searched in vain for a JLowe Racing banner, but figured we could fix that situation with a free giveaway later. Despite the fact that it was not quite eight in the morning, there were quite a few bare-chested NASCAR fans already on their second Budweiser, sitting on rooftop observations decks anticipating the stock car practice sessions in the middle of the day.

As we slowly made our way through the crowds, I remarked to Jim Pace, "I know they're not here to watch us, but it is kinda cool to run in front of a crowd this size."

To which JP replied, "Well Dr. Lowe, racin's racin' and you'd be surprised at how many of these folks are gonna be taking time from their beer drinkin' to check out our race tonight."

I smiled at the mental image and followed my partner into the paddock as we sought out the #66 TRG Porsche.

A short two hours later, I was strapped into the cockpit of the Porsche GT racer, awaiting the signal to start the first practice session. After I got settled into the seat in pit lane, I then received the signal to roll out and join the starting lineup at the pit exit area. However, the start of our practice session was then delayed because of some technical difficulty that the Daytona flag stands were having in communicating with each other. Their troubleshooting turned into a thirty-minute delay before we were able to go green and begin our first practice session.

While I waited in the sauna-cockpit of the Porsche, I realized that the exterior temperature of nearly 100 degrees was likely a chilly environment compared to what I was currently enjoying inside the car. Wearing fireproof underwear, a three-layer fire suit, and a helmet over a balaclava, I was a poster boy for heatstroke. Despite wearing a cool suit, which circulated ice water through a tubing system embedded in my undershirt, my temperature was creeping skyward with each passing moment. As I sat inside the Porsche, I realized that I was in fact quite relaxed, if not actually sleepy. I closed my eyes and thought about the practice session to begin, until it dawned on me that I was in fact about to fall asleep sitting right there in the starting lineup.

At that point I became concerned when I considered that I might be actually starting to pass out from the heat rather than simply falling asleep. I struggled a bit to stay awake and realized that I needed to jump-start my brain. I decided one of the best ways to do so was to find something to do, someone to talk to. Falling back on tried-and-true techniques that had always worked for me in the OR, I started telling jokes on the radio to the crew. As I keyed the mic and launched into a bawdy "good news bad news" doctor joke, Kevin Buckler cracked onto the radio.

"Hey Jim, love the jokes, but just be aware that the Pontiac factory people are here and probably listening in on the radio."

I considered this for a moment before I answered. "Well then, I'll make sure I speak slower and use little words."

"Nice." Mike Johnson had joined in the conversation. I could hear giggling over the open circuit. Bunch of schoolgirls back there in the pits, apparently.

A few minutes later, Jim Pace came on the radio to warn me that the session was in fact finally going to begin. "Hey now, time to get focused. They just gave the five minutes before the green signal. Goal here is for you to start out fast, get on pace, and run nice clean laps to get your brain and the car up to speed."

"Copy that, thanks JP, I'm here and ready."

I took a deep breath, closed the visor, and retested the cool suit once more prior to firing up the Porsche and rolling forward to the starting line. A moment later I was twisting through the pit lane exit, joining the track at Turn 3. Several turns later I was spit out onto the banking, once again enjoying the familiar feel and sight of driving at Daytona.

I enjoyed the return to the rhythm of Daytona's banked oval section followed by the six turns through the infield. I felt a comfortable familiarity with the car and the track, although I was certainly not anywhere near the top of the timesheet in comparison to all of the other GT cars. Nonetheless, the feeling at this point in my return to Daytona was completely different from that I experienced in January.

Looking in the side and rear view mirrors was a second nature event as I made my way through the infield and out onto the low side of the banking. There was no longer any element of fear or even significant concern in the management of the traffic. I simply focused on doing my best to progress through each section of the track at a maximum lap speed while not impeding the progress of faster GT cars and the Prototypes.

A few minutes later, Mike Johnson called me over the radio. It was time to jump out for a quick breather while JP did setup work on the car.

"How's the car handling? Your lap times are consistent, and already looking stronger and more steady than January."

I answered Mike back as I pulled onto pit lane and headed his direction. "The car feels good and stable. Not doing anything scary."

"Copy that. We are going to get JP in now and work on some setup so we can get it ready before qualifying."

Once I handed off to Jim Pace, he quickly got up to proper Porsche speed, of course eclipsed my times, and made several stops during which small changes were made to improve the handling of the car. Although I certainly had no specific complaints in the setup of the car, it was clear when I listened to Jim's radio communications that there were several aspects of the car's performance that he felt needed attention. With each stop, tweaks were made to shock settings and wing adjustments performed until Jim felt that the car was optimized. At that point, he reentered the pits so that I could get in for the last few laps to try the new setup.

Once I got back out on track, the changes that JP and Mike made became immediately evident in the improved performance of the car. The car turned in better, and I was able to get back to power sooner with each turn, so that without much effort my lap times showed improvement immediately. Two or three laps later, as I was enjoying one of my best laps ever in a GT car at Daytona, the practice session was checkered, and I proceeded obediently into the pits.

"Nice job, Dr. Lowe," Mike Johnson called out. "How'd you like the new setup?"

"Yeah, the car feels great. There's no drama in the changes, but clearly the car feels faster. I'm guessing my lap times look better?"

"Yep," Mike answered, "you're right on pace from last year, even allowing for the hot track conditions. Everyone else seems to be down a second or two a lap."

I smiled as I came to a stop at the TRG pit box. No drama, no crashes, no embarrassing moments (so far). Just the way I had hoped and certainly a nice way to start a busy day. Certainly, it was a good frame of mind to be in prior to beginning my first-ever qualifying session in a Grand-Am car.

The good and the bad news about qualifying sessions for Grand-Am is essentially the same fact: the session only lasts fifteen minutes. If you're a mid- to back-of-the-pack runner, as I am, it's mercifully quick, and there is little time to think about anything other than trying to get in a decent, mistake-free lap. If you're a contender for the pole, you have precious little time to get the tires warmed up and the car up to speed, and make that run to the front. Either way (and it's probably no different for the fastest guys), the experience of qualifying goes by in a blink. It was definitely that way for me in my first qualifying session at Daytona. I went out in the middle of the pack, stayed in the middle of the pack, and ran what I hoped were consistent laps that would not earn me any jeers when I returned to the pit box. The radio remained silent during the entire qualifying session, as I made my own private attempts to brake just a little bit later and get back to power just a little bit sooner. Certainly, I was not about to try a "ten-tenths" lap, given that there would be no time to repair a damaged race car before the evening race if I screwed it up now. Instead, I drove hard but overall cautiously, with the goal of coming back in one piece and avoiding the dreaded DFL designation once again. Ultimately, I was successful on both fronts, being gridded in thirteenth place out of eighteen starters in the GT class and returning with a shiny undamaged Porsche.

In between qualifying and the 8 o'clock race start, there was plenty of time to walk around the Grand-Am paddock with Aidan, giving him a tour of the various team haulers and race cars sitting within easy reach of a five-year old. I introduced Aidan to several drivers, including Hurley Haywood and David Donahue; Aidan was again polite but probably not quite as excited as his dad to have a moment chatting with those guys. I enjoyed holding his hand, savoring the one-on-one moment that seemed so private despite the circus going on around us. After a lap or two of the paddock, we rejoined the TRG team members under the blue canopy, regrouping before the next scheduled part of the event.

After our paddock tour, the next stop was a Grand-Am driver autograph session, set up with tables staked out in the infield fan area. This was another enjoyable moment for myself and my son, as Aidan sat in my lap while JP and I signed "TRG #66 Porsche" hero cards for a long line of mostly NASCAR fans. Once again, I suspect Aidan was a little confused as to what the big deal was with regards to all of the people lining up for autographed posters, but he happily went along with the program, enjoying the attention from the stream of fans, and no doubt creating just a little bit of extra good will for our underdog team.

After a very light dinner, it was time to get down to work. JP and I suited up in the RV, grabbed our gear, and then walked over to the paddock together. A moment later, standing alongside the Porsche race car, JP shared a few tidbits of advice with me before I got strapped in to the cockpit.

"Now this is just like a start of any other race you've been in. Stay close to the bumper of the guy in front of you and try not to let him gap you before the flag drops. Remember, this isn't an endurance race. Everybody's gonna be on this from the beginning, so you're gonna need to have your tires warmed up and your head warmed up before you go green. Once you go green, find a lane going into the first couple of turns, and stick on the bumper of the guy ahead of you."

I nodded silently, probably with wider eyes than usual, betraying my increasing nervousness. "Oh yeah, and don't forget to have fun." JP grinned that wide grin of his, slapped me on the shoulder, and opened the door to the car for me.

I looked at the open car door and the empty seat, and wondered whether or not I could execute some last minute negotiation to get JP to start the car for me. I mean, what business did I have starting a sprint race, for God's sakes, in a professional racing series, with a bunch of famous fast guys, all of whom had already written me off in their pre-race planning? JP nudged me, interrupting my woolgathering.

"She's not gonna drive herself, Dr. Lowe."

I dutifully nodded, and swung my right leg up and over the roll cage bar, sliding into the seat in what I hoped looked like a practiced manner. JP reached in and helped me arrange the five-point harness, as I fiddled with the belts, and wiggled my way down into the proper seating position. Once I slid the seat forward and tested the position of the steering wheel with my arms and the position of the pedals with my feet, I gave JP the thumbs up sign. Jim thumped the roof of the Porsche with his hand as he yelled "Good luck!" Before I could object, he had turned and walked away, leaving me to my thoughts in the silent Porsche.

My isolation lasted only a moment before Mike Johnson came on the radio. "Hey Jim, it's Mike, do you copy? Do you copy?"

"Copy you Mike. Loud and clear."

"Great. I'm over in the pit box already. In a minute they're gonna line you up in the paddock, and you're gonna roll out onto the grid. Once you're all lined up, you're gonna roll through pit lane without stopping and take two warm-up laps prior to getting the green. Do you copy?"

"Copy that Mike, two warm up laps."

"And don't forget, there is no passing until you pass the start/finish line. No passing on the start. Copy?"

"Copy. I got that. No passing on the start. I'm allowed to pass later though, right?"

Mike came back quickly on that one. "Hopefully you'll do quite a bit of passing, buddy."

The radio fell silent, and I was left to my increasingly rapid and scattered thoughts as I awaited the signal to roll on out. I could feel my temperature rise and my heart rate slowly accelerate. Since the Porsche's engine was not yet running, I could actually hear the throb of my pulse in my ears. With a little effort, I switched my brain over to mentally reviewing each turn of the track. Eyes closed and mind occupied elsewhere, I was startled by a thump on the side of the car. I strained against the Hans device as I rotated my head to the left, enjoying the view as both Aidan's and Ginny's face filled the window opening.

Aidan had on oversized red aviation headphones for ear protection, a suitable black JLowe Racing cap, and his white golf shirt that was covered with autographs of both his dad and the much more famous Jim Pace. Ginny stooped down alongside Aidan, as both my wife and my son smiled broadly.

"Good luck, Daddy!" they called in unison.

I forced a smile and gave them a little wave. A muffled "thanks guys" was about all I could muster, however, as I already had my game face on and was in full "I'm a little too freaked out right now to talk" mode.

Ginny grabbed Aidan and gently directed him away from the car, as both of them waved and again wished me luck. My second half-hearted wave was then interrupted by the roar of the Porsche directly in front of me firing up its engine.

Time to get on with it.

Once I had made my way down through pit lane and out onto the track, dutifully remaining behind the Porsche and the Corvette directly to my front, I started to experience an ease of the tension, along with a palpable sense of heightened awareness. My senses were bombarded, as the visual imagery outside of the cockpit combined with the aural and tactile experience within it. I swerved my Porsche left and right in an attempt to warm up the tires, alternating accelerating and braking for the same reason, as the cars ahead of and behind me did the same. The view spread out in front of me was that of a slow motion wavering line of multicolored race cars, further visually enhanced by the contrast of the bright lights of the track against the darkening night sky. Stretched out in front of me were thirty-nine cars, counting the front-running Daytona Prototypes and the twelve GT cars ahead of me. We snaked around the Daytona infield; once we were through the bus stop chicane, we then lined up in a two-by-two fashion and prepared for the start. I obediently moved to the left side and lined up behind the Corvette of Vic Rice. The pace car was too far to the front of the lineup for me to actually see its lights go out as it rounded Turn 4 and headed for the pit lane. However, Mike was in my ears at that point, reminding me to close up against the Corvette and shift down into low gear for the start.

"Wait for my call, wait for my call…"

My grip on the wheel tightened, my eyes widened, and I tried to watch the tachometer in order to make sure my revs weren't too high for the drop of the green flag. As I was coming through Turn 4, I realized that the Corvette had gained a little bit of a gap on me, and I attempted to close up the gap. Just as I reached the bumper of the Corvette, Mike the call on the radio.

"Green! Green! Green!"

I couldn't see the flagger waving the green flag, but quite honestly Mike's call was unnecessary. Once the race went green, the sudden increase in noise around me was like a detonation. Simultaneously, each driver went to full throttle, with rapid upshifts proceeding as soon as drivers could grab gears on their way to full speed. Unfortunately, because I had tried to accelerate up to the Corvette right before the green flag, I had to check up in order to keep from wrecking both of us before we even got to the start/finish line. As a result, I backed out of the throttle and lost a significant amount of momentum. Trying to recover by getting back on the gas as aggressively as possible, I was already well behind the eight-ball by Turn 1. As I braked for the first turn, four different GT cars came zipping by me on both sides, taking up valuable positions while I was trying to get my act together. Once I followed them through the Turn 1 apex, I got on the gas and was able to stay right on the gear box of the first car in front of me. I suffered a bit of target fixation but maintained some focus that allowed me to stay inches from the rear bumper of the next GT car. Pushing hard, I frantically followed that car around the Turn 3 hairpin, through the kink, and through Turns 5 and 6 and out onto the banking.

I was no longer considering my qualifications, or lack thereof, when it came to racing in a professional race at Daytona. There was only the car in front of me and the need to make up places. I drove with a determination that was its own reward for all of the hard work, both physical and mental, that had gotten me to this point. The only real thought process now included the need to recognize my brake point for the bus stop chicane coming up in just a few seconds and the gear shift sequence through that turn and the rest of the lap.

I proceeded to follow the car in front of me until I could spot the places in the infield where he was clearly braking just a bit earlier and maybe going back to power a little bit later than me. I finally set up a good pass on the exit of Turn 6 and was able to perform a classic overtaking move on the banking. I repeated this at least two more times, generally avoiding the infield hairpins when it came to passing attempts, given that they were typically occupied by much faster Prototypes or other GT cars. I made a total of three passes on the banking and was thoroughly enjoying my lapping once the race finally settled down to a comfortable lap pace for me and the GT cars around me.

Approximately twenty minutes into the race I was making my way through the infield when the radio clicked on and I heard Kevin Buckler's familiar voice.

"Hey Jim, I got somebody here who wants to talk to you if this is an OK time."

I took a few seconds to answer as I downshifted and braked hard for the first hairpin. "Now's as good a time as any, sure." I didn't bother trying to guess who was going to talk to me at that point, but I was definitely surprised by the small voice that I heard after a long pause over dead air.

"Hey Daddy, it's Aidan, are you there?"

I laughed and smiled so hard at the same time that I almost drove past the braking zone of Turn 5.

"Hey Bubba, is that you?" Downshift, downshift, back to power, on my way to Turn 6.

"Hey Daddy, I just saw you go by!" Brake, downshift, downshift, turn towards the apex.

"That's pretty cool, Bubba. Are you having fun at your first race?" Upshift, upshift, eyes up, out onto the banking.

"Yes Daddy, we're up on the grandstands. Can you see us?" Upshift, upshift, wiggle fingers and toes, check the gauges, here it comes, get ready for the bus stop.

"Well, I'm a little busy right now Bubba, but I'll definitely see you when I get out of the car." Brake hard, downshift two gears, turn into the bus stop.

"OK Daddy, see you later! Have a great race!" Apex, turn, apex, apex, turn, apex, back to power and back up onto the steep banking.

With that the radio was again silent, and I was left with the relative quiet in my ears and a face-splitting grin as the chaos of the racing all around me continued full blast.

I made it through the rest of my planned stint, neither gaining nor losing many places at that point. As cars began to cycle through pit stops, and various drivers in faster GT cars came around and lapped me, the race order became quite jumbled. I was no longer aware of exactly where I stood in the standings, nor was it an immediate concern. I drove as hard as I could and with as much daring as I could muster, while still being mindful of the need to keep the car in one piece. When the call came on the radio to "Pit now, Pit now", I was exceptionally disappointed and relieved all at once. I had done my job, made up a few places from my original starting gaffe, and had kept the car shiny side up.

I pitted from twelfth or thirteenth place, lower than I had hoped, but overall pretty respectable considering the events of my first-ever professional race start. Jim and I executed a reasonable driver change during a well-crafted TRG pit stop, and our race was now in the hands of our pro.

As I got mostly undressed in the pits, removing my helmet and stripping halfway out of my soaked race suit and cool shirt, Ginny and Aidan arrived in the pits. Aidan had a rather large grin on his face, and his mother looked to be half pleased and half relieved. I gave a sweaty hug to Aidan, although Ginny declined anything up close and personal in my current overheated and wet-dog state. We excitedly discussed the race thus far, and I confirmed again with Aidan that he had enjoyed not only watching the race but talking on the radio as I drove. As we chatted, Kevin Buckler wandered over, and I had the opportunity to thank him for arranging the radio call with Aidan.

"I thought you'd like that, bud," Kevin remarked. "I wasn't sure if things were going well enough for a long conversation, but you both seemed to have enjoyed that a lot."

"Yeah Kevin, that was pretty special. Thanks for setting that one up. That's another great racing memory right there."

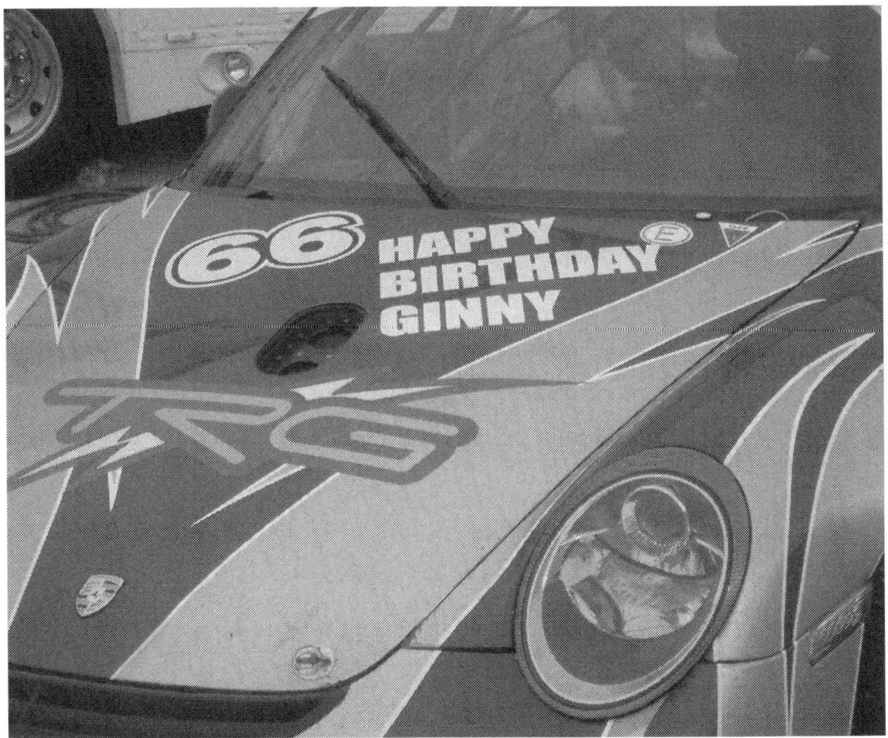

Ginny's "birthday car" at the Brumos Daytona race, 2006

Jim Pace proceeded to drive a typically masterful stint, hunting down each car in front of him over the course of the next hour and a half. His fast lap in the Porsche was just one second off the fast GT lap of the race. Jim managed to pick up two places overall, and in the end he brought the car in for a solid and respectable tenth place.

Once JP arrived back in the TRG pits, we began the now familiar post-race celebration. We exchanged sweaty hugs, and shook hands, patted backs, and exchanged high fives with various crew members and TRG personnel. I took a moment to remark to Jim that tenth place was a bit of a disappointment, considering our recent successes and goals for this race; JP immediately redirected my enthusiasm to the fact that we had just accomplished our second top ten finish in a professional race. A later review of the results sheet would reveal that we came in, in fact, in front of quite a few accomplished racers, including Nick Jonsson, Andy Wallace, Terry Borcheller, Kelly Collins, and Sylvain Tremblay.

Aidan and Ginny disappeared back to the motor home while JP and I did the post-race debrief with Kevin Buckler and Mike Johnson. We reviewed the setup and handling of the car and talked a bit about how the different characteristics of the Porsche would potentially help us when we returned once again to Daytona in the winter. I also spent some time recording a post-race wrap up segment with our faithful video crew, and spent a few more minutes supplying quotes for the TRG press release. This time, there was no reason for remorse, recrimination, or self-flagellation. No tears or harsh thoughts, only the challenge of coming up with an original cliché instead of "I just hope I helped the team" sort of stuff. Afterward, helmets in hand, JP and I walked side by side back to the motor home. We talked only about the enjoyment of a good run, soaking in the good vibe that would probably carry us right through to our next event.

When I arrived back at the RV, Aidan was fast asleep on one of the couches. He still had his oversized headphones on and was clutching his blue teddy bear in one hand and the radio in the other. As Ashlei served a late dinner, Ginny, JP, and I, along with a few scattered visitors, enjoyed a rehash of the night's events. We chattered excitedly as Aidan slept right on through our impromptu party. Not long after that, I slung my still sleeping son over my shoulder and carried him out to the car. We caught a late flight out of Daytona, and arrived back home in the dead of night. Aidan slept through the whole affair, while Ginny also caught a moment of sleep or two in-flight. For my part, I remained awake and vigilant as I reviewed the events of a great week with my family and friends in Florida.

Chapter Twenty-Two

As my racing schedule accelerated in a fairly dramatic fashion, with several races scattered over the summer and other planned events such as testing (the racers' word for practicing), my work schedule became exceptionally pressured. With my now-mature surgical practice, the demand for both busy office hours and surgeries was fairly significant—and thankfully so. However, between work and racing, there was little time for simple relaxation, with the exception of formally planned events such as the trip to Disney World—and even that was tied into a race event. The upshot of all of this was that the majority of my available free time was in fact spoken for long in advance, and I rarely had the luxury of off days. This concept bled over into my birthday, which fell in the middle of the summer, but nonetheless required me to have a normal working surgical schedule on that day. However, the unusual events of this particular summer day would result in a longstanding policy to never again perform surgery on my birthday.

Bernie Mathers became my patient in a consultation after his family practice physician referred him to me for evaluation. Bernie was a seventy-something-year-old who had been suffering from progressively worsening clumsiness of his hands, pain in his neck, and numbness in his arms. Over the past six months his gait had deteriorated to the point where he was no longer able to ambulate even short distances; in fact when he came to me he was essentially wheelchair-bound.

A rather obese aging gentleman, Bernie was absolutely pleasant from the moment we met. He was accompanied by his wife, Helen, and it was clear that they were one of those rare longstanding couples-for-life. In fact, the briefest of interactions with Bernie and Helen led one to believe that they were both gentle God-fearing folk who were destined to be together 'til death do they part. Of course, at our first meeting I had no inkling that I would play any role in the fulfillment of that last concept.

Once I had examined Bernie and reviewed his imaging studies, I pointed out the findings of great concern. As he and Helen sat in my office examining room, I stood in front of a light box, where his MRI studies were hung.

"If you look up at this picture, right where I have the red marks, you'll be able to see just what I'm talking about." I used a wax pencil, circling areas of concern on Bernie's neck images, especially the parts where the bone and discs in his neck were squeezing and damaging his spinal cord. "Right here is what the normal area looks like, where there is plenty of room for the spinal cord. But if you look down here,"…I pointed the tip of the red pencil a little lower... "There is a significant amount of bone and disc material that is pressing right up against your spinal cord and basically crushing it." Both Bernie and Helen paid very close attention as I continued my little teaching session.

"If you look at the spinal cord itself,"—that's this gray stripe down the middle—you'll see that there is a white area inside it. That's the kind of thing we see when the spinal cord is already showing significant damage." Bernie and Helen nodded in unison, as I suspected they had done for the last sixty years or so. "If this problem is left untreated, it will continue to further damage your spinal cord, and things can only get worse. You already lost most of the ability to walk because of this; eventually you'll lose the use of your hands and arms altogether."

At this point, Bernie remained silent but Helen spoke up. "Doctor, what's the worst thing that can happen if we leave this be? I'm very concerned because Bernie isn't the healthiest guy, obviously."

"Well, you're probably aware that the spinal cord controls not only the movement and sensations of the arms and legs, and bowel and bladder function, but that level of the spinal cord also controls breathing. If something isn't done, eventually the damage could be severe enough that breathing could be interrupted." At this point Bernie spoke up. "Doc, I think I'm following you here, but I want to be clear about this. If that kind of problem occurs then I don't survive, right?"

I looked Bernie directly in the eye and tried to simultaneously engage Helen. "I've had a lot of experience in these kinds of problems," I said, "and it's quite obvious to me that this is a severe enough case that it's in fact a possibility if we don't get on this thing and fix it."

With that, Bernie and Helen reflexively grabbed each other's hands. Bernie made the pronouncement but it was clearly unnecessary. "While I'm sure Helen agrees, I can speak up here: at this point, Doc whatever you have to do to fix it, let's hear it."

I spent the better part of an hour that day explaining to Bernie and Helen the anatomy of the neck and what needed to be done. The operation would be a rather significant one, and in fact was two operations in one. It required me to make an incision on the front of Bernie's neck, doing a dissection long enough to expose the bones and discs of his neck from essentially just underneath the jawline all the way down to the collar bone. Once everything had been properly exposed, I explained how I would drill away the bones and remove the discs in between them, all the way back towards where the spinal cord was. Using a microscope and a high speed drill (I brag to my mechanics that I have cooler tools than they do), pieces of bone and disc would be removed in a careful fashion, including those that were pressing up against the spinal cord and nerves. At each area enough bone and disc material would be removed until I could actually see the spinal cord float back up into a normal position, and assume a relaxed, uncompressed state, as I watched. Once that was done, a long metallic mesh cylinder would be placed in the gap that I had created, after first filling it with bone harvested from a separate incision in Bernie's pelvis. On top of this a long titanium structural plate would be fastened, screwing into the last visible healthy bone above and the first visible one below, spanning the entire construct and adding instant strength. Once that part of the surgery was done, there would still be much more work to do. While still asleep, Bernie would be flipped over, face down, and a second operation performed on the back of his neck. An incision would be made to expose all of the back side of the bones of the spine extending from just below the base of the skull down to the region of the shoulders. Once those bones were exposed, I would use the high speed drill again, benefiting from its 76,000 rpm technology, to make a cut in the bone in a strategic fashion that would allow me to remove the bone from the back side of the spinal cord without damaging the delicate spinal cord tissue underneath. Once that decompression was completed, screws and rods would be placed on either side in a paired fashion, further adding strength and fixation from top to bottom. The job was finished when little morsels of bone were implanted in the outer edges of the joints that were remaining, with the ultimate goal that they would grow into a nice, solid, healthy union—a "fusion."

As I described that surgery to the Mathers, I outlined the procedure details in as clear a way as possible, knowing that they very much needed to understand the severity of the problem and the significance of the solution. They also needed to know that the operation was anticipated to take somewhere between eight to ten hours and that there were many risks associated with surgery of this sort. Although the risks were typically well controlled, I informed them, I did note that several complications were known to occur.

"We don't anticipate problems, but we're always prepared to handle bad things that can happen during and after surgery. That includes bleeding, infection, damage to the nerves or spinal cord, and other problems such as blood clots in the legs, which can break off and go to your lungs and result in death."

Several times during those aspects of the discussion, both Bernie and Helen reassured me in a typical fashion. "Doc, we're listening to you, but we don't really see any way around this." Bernie finally concluded, "If I want to have any chance of living the rest of my years in a functional fashion, I need to do this, right? Whatever you say to do, we're gonna do it. We're in your hands."

As chance and circumstances would have it, Bernie's surgery was scheduled to be performed on my birthday. Shortly before seven a.m. the nurse anesthetist and the circulating nurse from the OR wheeled Bernie into the operating room on a stretcher. With their assistance, he was able to scooch himself off of his stretcher onto the operating table, lying down on his back on top of a warming blanket and gel padding for comfort. As he lay there, no doubt staring into the bright overhead lights and wondering just what the immediate future held, Bernie requested of the nurses around him that he have a moment to talk with me. Amidst the controlled bustle of a team preparing for surgery, I was busy reviewing Bernie's chart and MRI images in my usual routine prior to operating. When I heard Bernie's request, I looked up from the chart, closed the plastic book, and walked over to the side of the operating table. As I arrived at the side of the table, Bernie grabbed my hands in his right arm and said "Doctor, if it's OK with you I'd like to pray with you."

When he made his request, the OR room quieted perceptibly. Although there were several people continuing to go about their tasks, clearly people had heard Bernie's request, and respectfully quieted themselves as they worked. I stood next to Bernie, my hands enveloped in his, and honored his request. I am not a visibly religious person, and my faith remains a typically private matter, but I was more than willing to participate in anything that Bernie felt was important to him. I looked around the room and became aware that all eyes were on both Bernie and me. I was aware of the gentle beep of the monitor and the ambient noise of a busy operating suite, but I was equally aware that virtually everyone in the room had now stopped to participate in this particular prayer.

"Dear Lord," Bernie began, "please guide the hands of this surgeon in his work today. Bless him with your wisdom and lend your healing powers

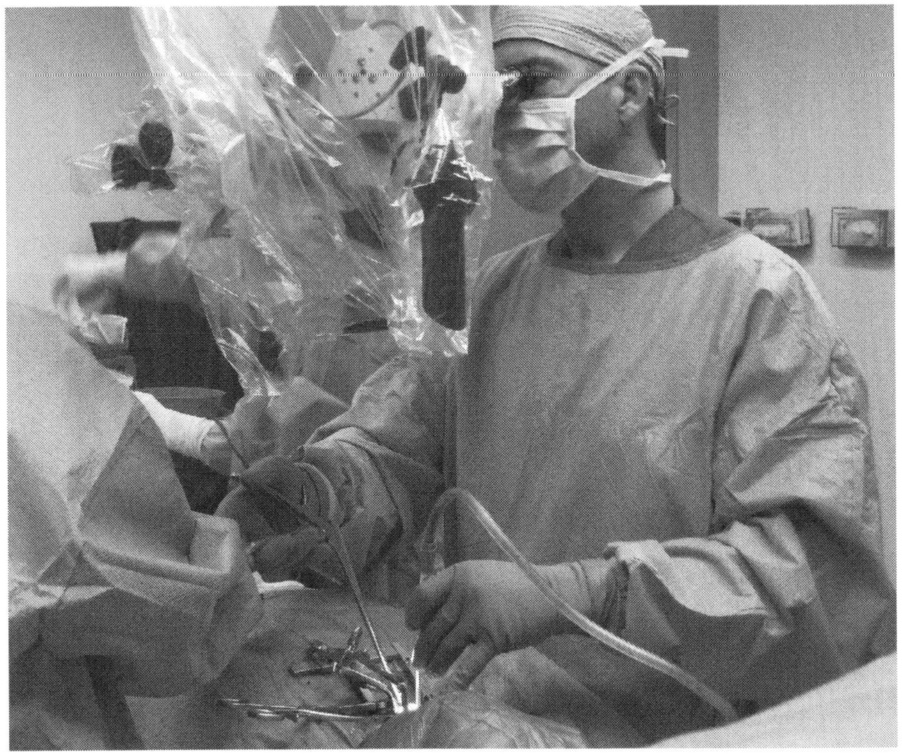

Jim working under the operating microscope

to him today as you work through him to treat my body. Guide him and his team on a clear path of healing, and help him, and me, Your faithful servant, accept the consequences of today's healing treatments. And bless everyone in this room who is taking the time to exercise the skill to help me. Bless them and their faith in You as they do their best to help me through this physical ailment. I remain, Lord, in Your hands through Dr. Lowe and his team and gladly accept this healing burden. All praise be to You, my Lord. Amen."

I stood there silently as Bernie continued to hold onto my hands. His grip was tight, but clearly no longer robust or refined. He pulled me somewhat closer to him, so that I could hear him whisper. "Hey Doc, I hope all this is OK with you. Hope my prayer didn't bother you." I stood back erect over Bernie and replied, in a normal voice, "Bernie, it's my pleasure to take care of you as best I can. Any help I can get from upstairs is fine with me."

"Well Doc, that's a good thing, because I'm hoping for a good day for all of us today. After all, it's my birthday."

I was surprised at this as I hadn't noticed the date of birth on Bernie's registration information.

"Wow what a coincidence, it's my birthday too, how 'bout that! I don't think I have ever operated on someone I've shared a birthday with, let alone on our birthdays."

Before Bernie could answer, the anesthetist's head bobbed up from behind the drapes. "It's your birthdays? That's weird, it's my birthday today too."

At that point, there were several exclamations of surprise from the others in the room, as we all thought through the unlikely nature of this coincidence.

"Wow," I observed quietly, "this is starting to freak me out a little bit!"

Bernie looked at me and gave me a half smile. "Well Doc, it's just another good sign, huh?"

With that, the anesthesiologist gave Bernie some medication for relaxation through his IV prior to inserting the breathing tube and putting him all the way under.

Bernie's surgery turned out to be an uneventful affair. It was certainly a prolonged operation, and I worked steadily onward, with the assistance of my nurse and the OR staff, from approximately seven-thirty in the morning continuously until nearly five o'clock in the afternoon. Bernie's surgery proceeded as planned, appropriately routine, with one notable exception.

At various points during the course of these operations, x-rays are taken of the patient's neck so that we can determine that the various screws and plates and cages are inserted in a proper fashion. Midway through the procedure, while I was busily working on Bernie's spine, the x-ray technician arrived in the operating room, opening the door to the suite with a dramatic bang.

"Everybody be nice to me today, it's my birthday!" he loudly announced. With that, there were several audible gasps from the various nurses and technicians in the operating room. For my part, I stopped working and simply looked up at him, remaining silent at first. While I'm quite a superstitious guy, I have no actual tangible belief in anything supernatural. But this definitely got my attention. "Say that again, please?"

The x-ray tech looked around him, wondering what it was that he had said that had so captured everyone's attention. "All I said was, 'it's my birthday', that's OK isn't it?"

I looked back down at Bernie's spinal cord pulsating just past my fingertips. I shook my head silently as I went back to work. I muttered quietly to myself, "You guys are really freaking me out today."

The remainder of Bernie's surgery proceeded uneventfully with no further birthday, anniversary, or bar mitzvah announcements made. After completing the surgery, I accompanied Bernie to the recovery room, where he slowly awoke from the long procedure.

As he came to, Bernie's eyes tracked left and then right (his neck was rigid in a collar) until he made eye contact with me. He then smiled a somewhat crooked smile, and said "Hey Doc, how'd it go?"

I informed Bernie that everything had gone exceptionally well and reassured myself by checking the fact that he could wiggle his fingers and toes and give me a good squeeze with his hands. "Looks like everything is working great, Bernie," I reassured him. "The nurses are gonna give you something for the pain, and I'd like you to just relax and wake up nice and slow. I'm gonna go give Mrs. the good news."

Bernie made sure to remind me. "I knew God would take good care of me in your hands, Doc. Thank you for everything."

I was somewhat uncomfortable with the continued praise, and did my best to deflect it. "The whole team did a great job for you today Bernie, and I'm really glad to see that you're doing so well. Now you get some rest while I go talk to your wife."

I stopped in the surgical waiting room area on my way out of the hospital, spending a few minutes with Helen to describe Bernie's condition and to reassure her that all was going exactly as planned. I reminded her that we were going to keep him in the intensive care unit overnight for observation reasons, noting that otherwise Bernie was doing quite well despite his advanced age and his other medical problems. After assuring her that I would be in to see him first thing in the morning on my way to the office, I said my goodbyes and headed out of the hospital.

That evening, my wife treated me to a special birthday dinner at my favorite sushi restaurant, Sagami. After a long day in the OR, a private birthday dinner was the perfect way to celebrate another good year. Overall, I thought, my birthday, despite being a working affair, was turning out to be quite a remarkable day.

On my way home from the restaurant, my beeper went off, with a digital request from one of the ICU nurses that I contact her regarding my patient, Bernie Mathers. I dutifully picked up my cell phone as Ginny drove, expecting to get a routine checkup report from the intensive care nurse. Instead, I received undeniably shocking news.

"Your patient, Mr. Mathers, in Room 12, just coded."

I pulled the phone away from my ear and stared at the offending object as if it had somehow magically delivered me the terrible news.

"Can you please say that again? Did you say that Bernie just coded?"

The nurse started to explain. "Yes Doctor, the code team's in there now, but they're having a hard time resuscitating him—it's not going very well—I thought you'd want to know."

Before hanging up, I informed the nurse that I was nearly 45 minutes away from the hospital, but that I would be there as soon as possible. I turned to look at Ginny, who could already tell that the call was bad news. "Bernie Mathers just coded in the ICU. He'll probably be dead before I get there. I can't believe it."

Ginny reached out for my hand and we headed together to the hospital.

When I arrived in the ICU, there was no need for the nurse to fill me in on the current condition of Bernie. His room was semi-dark, and he was its only inhabitant. The code team, having finished its work unsuccessfully, had long since departed. Two or three ICU nurses were sitting in a small circle at the nurses' station several feet outside of the closed door to Bernie's room. When I saw this scene, familiar to me in so many ways over so many years, I knew without needing further confirmation that my patient had died. In unison, the nurses looked up and, once they recognized me, decided collectively not to impede my progress into Bernie's room. I opened the door to the room quietly and took note of the silent monitors over the bed. A breathing tube had been inserted in Bernie's throat, but it was no longer connected to a ventilator.

I approached my patient's bedside and took his right hand in mine. It was cold and lifeless, so unlike the firm grasp that I had last received when checking him just a few hours before in the recovery room. I bowed my head and said a quick prayer, not bothering to question the whole "power of prayer" thing given the bizarre circumstances of the day.

As I exited Bernie's room I closed the door quietly behind me. The nurse looked up, and I acknowledged her and her colleagues with a nod. "Has anyone spoken to Mrs. Mathers?"

The nurse responded, "Yes, we called her as soon as we had a moment. She's actually just arrived and is in the waiting room waiting to speak with you."

"Thanks," I said halfheartedly. "Before I go in there though, can you please fill me in a little bit on what happened here?"

"Well it was the strangest thing," the nurse began to explain. "Bernie called me about an hour after his wife left and told me that he wasn't feeling so good. I went in there to check on him and everything seemed OK at first. But while I was doing his vitals, he repeated 'I don't feel so good,' and then he flatlined and coded."

"That's it?" I asked admittedly unnecessarily. "Nothing? No warning? No sign on the monitor that there was any problem?"

"Nothing, Doctor. He went from having a normal rate and rhythm to a complete code blue."

I shook my head once again and tried to clear my thoughts as I headed out of the ICU to the adjoining waiting room. Helen sat there, oversized purse on her lap, looking small and quite alone. As I entered the room, she looked up in a questioning fashion, recognized me, and stood with arms outstretched. I headed immediately towards her in a similar fashion.

"Oh Helen, I'm so sorry about this. I know they did everything possible."

"Doctor, it's such a shock. I still don't understand what happened!"

I did my best to explain what little ideas I had formulated at that point. "Well, when we see this kind of sudden event, we often assume that it's a blood clot that went to the lungs. What we call a pulmonary embolism. I'm so sorry that this happened. I feel so terribly."

With that, Helen told me the final shocking postscript to my day. "You know Doctor, Bernie told me tonight that he was going to die."

I stood there, stunned and silent.

"Yes, he did. In fact, he told me several times before I left. I was getting up to leave when visiting hours were over, and I said to Bernie 'I'll see you tomorrow sweetheart' and gave him a big kiss. His response was simply 'No you won't, I'm going to die tonight.'"

By this time, I think my mouth was hanging open a bit, as I stood there holding her hands in mine. She was dry eyed and lucid as she related the story to me.

"I told Bernie, 'Don't be ridiculous Bernie, I'll see you in the morning, I love you'. But he wouldn't hear any of it. He just kept saying 'No, you're not gonna see me again, I'm gonna die tonight.' I didn't believe him of course, and finally told him, 'Bernie you're being ridiculous. I've gotta go now. See you tomorrow. Bye.'" She paused for a minute as she looked up at me. "And that's the last I saw of Bernie, until the nurses called me with this." As she said "this" she pulled her hands from mine and gestured towards the ICU door.

I was too shocked to say anything meaningful at that point, so I recall just repeating "I'm sorry, I'm so sorry." When there was nothing further to say, Helen concluded our visit by asking me, "Can I see him now?"

After escorting Helen back into the ICU room, I left both Helen and her husband in the compassionate hands of the ICU nursing staff. There was nothing further for me to offer at that point, and I felt useless, unnecessary. As I exited the ICU and headed for the elevators, I checked my watch. It was just a few minutes after midnight. It was no longer my birthday.

In the many years that have passed since Bernie's operation, I have had the occasional patient request to pray with him or her prior to their surgery. I have never denied any of those requests, but I have to admit that on each occasion the hairs on the back of my neck stand up just a little bit. And since the time of Bernie's surgery, I have never again operated willingly on my birthday.

Chapter Twenty-Three

The last bits and pieces of Jim Pace's original plan for my first professional racing season were to be run out by the end of the 2006 summer. This included two days of testing with TRG at the newly constructed Miller Motorsports Park in Tooele, Utah. Practice time at the track would be excellent prep for the scheduled Grand-Am finale race at the same facility on Labor Day weekend. Along with the usual herd of TRG Porsches, JP and I were scheduled to run the blue #66 Porsche at the inaugural nine-hour endurance event. The opportunity to spend two days of unlimited practice time at the new track prior to the official race weekend, learning its twenty-four turns, was therefore a golden opportunity.

So I dutifully made my way out to Utah in midsummer, disappointed somewhat by the fact that there was no snowboarding to be had in Salt Lake City at that time of year. Quite different from my prior trips to Utah for winter adventures, the summer scene outside of Utah was notable only for the fact that it was, well, not very notable. There was essentially one main road heading from Salt Lake City out to the area of the racetrack, dotted with the apparently mandatory low-mid-range hotel chains within easy driving distance. We ate our first, second, and probably last dinners at an Applebee's, where I swear we were served by the same waitress that had taken care of us at Daytona, Virginia, and Watkins Glen. The meals there were hardly memorable, with the possible exception of the hilarity that ensued when one of the group's otherwise clueless TRG drivers managed to ask the waitress what the name was of "that big lake out there?"

The two days of testing at the new track continued the developing theme of "Nothing to see here, return to your homes." The track's twenty-four turns were almost entirely flat, lacking in any features whatsoever. A brand new layout, Miller's runoff areas were all sand, with no grass and nothing to set apart one turn from another. In a notable difference from most racetracks, the turns weren't numbered but had cute little sign posts inside each apex declaring different names ("Diablo," "Faster," and "Maybe you'll make it"). As clever as this might have appeared to the track's designers, it was definitely unappreciated by the engineers during our debriefing session when we all finally realized that no one knew which turns we were talking about.

Nonetheless, the two days of the testing did allow us to generate at least a degree of a sight memory for the track and its many turns. The testing also gave us a sense that we would have a head start when we returned for the race event at the end of the summer. The bonus was that I didn't put any new dents in the Porsche, a fact which contributed to the Lowe household budget in a nicely positive fashion.

I made it through the summer working side by side with my partner Joe, managing the unfortunately frequent requests for our surgical services for spinal trauma patients. With the increased population at the resort area surrounding Atlantic City, the summer OR schedule was, as always, hot and heavy. By the time I departed for the Labor Day weekend race in Tooele, I was once again worn out and badly in need of a racing fix.

Being back at the track with the entire Grand-Am contingent in its full glory was quite a different experience from our rather quiet testing experience earlier that summer. This time the featureless landscape was completely obscured by the many multicolored haulers and trailers that accompany the Grand-Am army. And this time, in an increasingly comfortable fashion, Jim Pace and I seamlessly blended into the racing landscape, just one of many different entries for that weekend's event. While none of the other drivers were fretting the entry of the #66 TRG Porsche, at least I was starting to feel like one of the necessary clowns at this particular circus.

At the first drivers meeting, I settled into a seat in the middle of the classroom, right behind Jim Pace and right next to Boris Said and Max Papis. While I'm sure there was some important information being imparted to the drivers by Mark Raffauf, I actually heard very little of it. Like being planted in the middle of the cool kids at a high school assembly, all I could hear was the playful banter of Boris and Buddy Rice, both attempting to do their best Max Papis impersonations. I slouched down in my chair so as to avoid being included in the inevitable reprimands that were forthcoming. Smiling to myself, I considered the fact that the circumstances had clearly changed, but the venue was just so familiar: same nondescript room, same folding chairs, same authoritative voice somewhere towards the front of the room. Whether it was an Indian Guides meeting, Little League baseball draft, high school football pre-game meeting, or Marine Corps boot camp lecture, the scene felt the same. I looked around, soaked up the atmosphere, and savored it.

The several practice sessions before the race were thankfully also uneventful. Two particular moments, however, stand out in my memory. The first was when I had finally strapped into the Porsche for the first time in seven long weeks, preparing to go out for my first practice session. As always, JP was standing not far from the car as I prepared to depart pit lane. Seconds before I peeled out of the pit box, JP bent down into the window on the passenger's side of the car and thumped the roof to get my attention. As I looked at him, he gestured toward my seatbelt and was obviously trying to tell me something. I wasn't able to understand him with the noise of the engine and the muffled hearing inside my helmet. At that very moment, the crew chief gave me the twirling finger sign and several mechanics starting pushing me out of the pit. I engaged first, laid down a nice stream of rubber, and headed down the pit lane, all the time wondering what JP was trying to tell me.

As I entered onto the racetrack at pit exit, I made my way down towards to Turn 1, at approximately 50% speed the first time around. Before I got there, however, JP's voice crackled in my ears.

"I was just trying to tell you that if you're on fire…"

I broke into the conversation at that point. "I'm what? On fire!?"

"I was just trying to tell you that if you're on fire, you're lap belt buckle is backwards."

"On fire? Jesus, I thought you were trying to tell me I was on fire!"

JP then brought up a good point. "If you thought you were on fire how come you kept driving?"

"I was trying to do that Michael Schumacher thing where I put out the fire by going fast."

With the mic open, I could hear the mechanics laughing. JP's fatherly voice didn't quit though. "Well Dr. Lowe, I was just trying to let you know that if you need to get out of the car quickly your buckle's backwards. But in the future, I recommend that if you think you might be on fire, it's probably best not to start a lap."

"Copy that JP. I'm gonna do my best to remember that particular tidbit."

The second most memorable aspect of that weekend was my first session driving the car in truly dark conditions. Since Sunday's race was going to be a nine-hour event, the finishing driver would be bringing the car home in darkness. Therefore, one of the practice sessions scheduled by Grand-Am was an evening session in the dark. And, unlike Daytona, this track was truly dark: no lights, very few reflectors, and essentially no features. Where the track in Florida had infield and grandstand lights that essentially eliminated the guesswork through virtually all of its turns, the track in Utah was simply dark. Damn dark.

I went out for the night session, dependent only on my headlights for illumination of the critical points of each turn. Unfortunately I soon discovered that the headlights pointed forward, whereas the critical parts of the turn, such as the apex and track-out point, were, naturally, to one side or the other. This created a surreal sensation of driving down the front straightaway at over 150 mph, braking at the usual marker, and not being able to see into the actual corner including the apex and the expected track-out point. The old Skip Barber technique of "eyes up" didn't do much here when you couldn't see anything if you actually bothered looking up through the turn.

I quickly learned to depend on the instinct of turning down into the dark corner regardless of the limited visibility, understanding that the corner was essentially in the same place it was in the daytime. Mastering this concept certainly took many laps and much reinforcement, and I managed to cover the car in dust from the run-off areas at multiple spots before I got the hang of it. By the end of the nighttime session, however, I at least felt that I was not likely to kill myself independent of some other untoward event, and that the car still behaved as desired. Like JP had always said, "The car doesn't know it's dark out."

As for the race itself, I certainly enjoyed the Grand-Am finale event at Miller Motor Sports Park. I felt that surviving the nine-hour event was a decent accomplishment, and definitely worth some story time in the distant future when I was called upon to tell racing tall tales. Jim Pace qualified our car tenth out of fourteen GT entries, approximately .5 seconds off the next closest runner in P9, and he was at least 1.5 seconds faster than our fastest run up to that point. Come race time, our team was bolstered further by the addition of Barry Waddell, a friend and fellow racer of JP's who had significant road course experience as a strategist and a driver. Having both JP and Barry with me for this weekend was a special deal and was a huge contribution to my continuing challenged progress during that event. Like secret weapons, the two of them were constantly in my ears with advice and recommendations, both in the car and out of it.

At the beginning of the race, JP did a double stint, which turned out to be quite a bit longer than our typical racing stints. Because of the altitude, we found that a full tank of gas lasted almost 90 minutes. Thus, a double stint in Utah was the equivalent of three sessions in the car under our usual normal sea-level conditions. Despite the extended driving time, JP did amazingly consistent laps within one second of each other during his three very hot hours in the Porsche. Teammate RJ Valentine, who joined us for this weekend, took over and ran steady laps for an additional tank of gas. Right on schedule, RJ brought the car back to the pits in eighth place, still all nice and shiny just like the engineers asked.

I then took over the driving duties of the Porsche, rejoining the race in twelfth position after the crew changed tires and refueled. I survived several "warm up" laps trying to get my brain up to speed on the now very slippery and greasy track. In short order, I started to feel comfortable in the car—that is mentally comfortable, but not physically. I quickly discovered that the cool suit was not working and did my best to drink more than typical in order to avoid becoming totally dehydrated. I did manage to make the ninety-minute stint without any incident (inside the car or out) and managed to give the car back to JP in tenth place.

Once I was out of the car, I initially experienced fairly significant sweating and carefully and aggressively rehydrated in order to avoid cramping or worse. I spent some time in the hauler relaxing and even enjoyed a truncated but effective massage by Kathy Dandurand. Afterwards, I changed into dry Nomex underwear, donned my damp race suit, and headed out to the pit wall, assuming that I would be watching JP finish the race. Just when I had settled into the role of happy spectator, Barry Waddell informed me that I would in fact be finishing up the nighttime run. Surprised as I was, I had to admit it made some sense considering that I had the nighttime laps in practice. Had I paid more attention, I might have guessed back then what JP and BW had in store for me. On the other hand, I now had little time to worry about racing in the dark.

I strapped into the Porsche and launched out of the pits, heading down the front straight directly into the setting sun. As I made my way down into Turn 1, I adjusted the tilt of my face shield, prepared with racer's tape across the bottom to act as a sun blocker. Barry came onto the radio in a reassuring voice and said, "Ninety minutes to go, just take it easy and bring her home."

Thirty minutes later the course was in full darkness. Thankfully the Grand-Am organizers had persuaded the track to install more reflectors at the corners, so I was 4% less scared than I was during my first nighttime practice laps earlier in the weekend. With so many cars on the track, and the top Prototype drivers still battling head to tail for the win, it was nerve wracking at best to negotiate the turns in total darkness. The off-line area of the track was now covered with incredible amounts of rubber scraps ("marbles"), and anytime you went off-line the hot tires picked up a massive amount of rubber. With the extra rubber bits stuck to the tires, it felt like driving with a flat tire. That persisted for several turns until the bits then flew off in the next fast section. When that first happened, I thought that the car was disintegrating as the rubber chunks loudly impacted the body work around the tires. Alarmed at first, I gradually learned to ignore both the odd sensation and the loud sounds coming from the tires intermittently.

Every so often another group of prototypes would blow by me (how can they possibly be seeing what I can't?), reminding me that I was in the middle of a race. I did my best to up the intensity, still trying to brake deeper and roll speed through the turns. Nonetheless, the sensation remained a typically solitary one as I drove on in the dark, a race going on all around me.

Barry finally broke the silence with a "last lap" radio call, and I took the checkered flag in P9—another top-10 finish!—with the paint on the car still intact. I did a slow-down run, radioing in my thanks to Jim Pace, Barry Waddell, and the whole TRG crew, finally enjoying a lap, in Utah, in the darkness.

As I circled the dark four-and-a-half-mile track at half speed, I took a moment to consider that I was in fact on my last racing lap of the season. I knew that plans for future racing couldn't be far off, but my continuing partnership with Jim Pace hadn't been finalized. However, even at that point I was quite sure that it wouldn't be long before we would firm up the blueprint for the 2007 season—and beyond. I had jumped in with both feet, was in up to my neck, and was happily refusing all rescue efforts.

***

After that, a significant amount of hard work and perseverance eventually paid off, and plans for our '07 Grand-Am season came nicely together. Kevin Buckler played a big part, offering up the TRG name as affirmation to Stuttgart that I was an appropriate buyer for a brand-new 2007 Porsche GT3 Cup car—JLowe Racing's first ever race car. Together with the help of Kevin, JP and I crafted a plan to run the new red-on-white race car under the JLowe Racing banner with the help of TRG's mighty crew. But before that could become reality, there was more practice, more driving, and more testing to be done. If I wanted to have anything resembling a legitimate chance at a competitive run in the '07 Rolex 24 at Daytona, I needed to up my game. Seriously.

When it comes right down to it, it wasn't that hard to recall that I was in fact a neurosurgeon who had been squirming in front of his timesheets for the last few years, typically cringing when I saw my times posted in comparison to the fast guys. For a competitive guy, albeit one who had not been swaddled in Nomex nor glued to the seat of a go-kart since age five, it was often a bitter pill to swallow to see that I was so far off the pace of the fast guys. But frankly, in my new environment amongst the professional racers of Grand-Am, nobody but me really gave a shit. I had had a partial rookie season in the professional series, and beyond that guys named Wolfe and Hans were still getting paid handsome sums of money to kick my butt at the racetrack on a regular basis. I was humbled, to say the least, and more than a bit frustrated by the impossibility of besting the hotshoes. More than once, I fantasized about getting a chance to even the score through fair competition on my turf in the operating room. Pop some scrubs on a few of these guys, show them how to wash their hands, and see if they're not a little wide-eyed at the prospect of cutting open a dying patient. And televise the event—all while an announcer critiques their performance.

About that time in my nascent career, it crossed my mind that I had a few choices. On one hand, I could be satisfied by a few top ten finishes, resulting in a great buzz that produced an instant smile every time I thought about them. I in fact actually considered this route, considering for a second or two the possibility of an early retirement at what anyone would have expected would surely be the top of my particular game. Happily, however, I more strongly considered the other option as too compelling: I could try to go faster, do better, and achieve a greater degree of success whenever I ran.

Going faster, for all of us not born into the lucky sperm club, certainly takes more than simple determination. In racing, it takes time—seat time, combined with good coaching. Fortunately the old-fashioned approach was a repeated concept in just about every sport that I ever played. And that was the direction that I took, comforted by the familiar sense of applying hard work and determination. After all, that concept had seemingly taken me quite far when it came to brain and spine surgery, so why not apply it to racing? With this in mind, my off season plans, in between my tight neurosurgical schedule, involved driving as much as humanly possible. This started off with running with TRG in the #66 Porsche GT3 in the Porsche Club Racing event at Daytona and later included the Grand-Am official off-season test at Daytona. Those two events would certainly satisfy the desire for more seat time, more laps, and more repetition of all things racing, and they would be at the place that I would confront once again come January.

The first event, held in October 2006, was Porsche Club Racing's first-ever weekend event at Daytona. For that event, Kevin Buckler arranged for Murray Marden to join me in the #66 car, in what for both of us was to be our first exposure to the PCA event style. Part of that style included surprisingly strict entrance requirements, including a rather challenging application for my club racing license. On that application, I listed my 2006 Grand-Am results at the 24 Hours at Daytona, along with professional racing results at VIR, 6 Hours at the Glen, Brumos Porsche 250, and the 9 Hour Miller race. However, during the long telephone interview that was a prerequisite to the final licensing for the Porsche Club racing group, I was asked for actual proof of my results. Somewhat flummoxed, I finally offered up the possibility of presenting copies of receipts for the damage repairs to the Porsche that I had raced all year. Thankfully this wasn't necessary and my application was, apparently somewhat reluctantly, approved.

On the evening when I arrived in Daytona, Murray and I immediately headed for the Daytona Infield briefing room for a three-hour (yes, three hour) drivers meeting for rookies and those not yet properly brainwashed by the PCA's "no touching" rules. Seeking safety in numbers, Murray and I sat shoulder to shoulder in the room crowded with over 200 drivers, comforted somewhat by the presence of Andy Lally. In his role as one of the TRG coaches for the weekend, Andy attended the rookie meeting in a good-natured fashion, quietly sitting through the mundane details of the long meeting with only a few snickers here and there. Despite the fact that Murray's and my experience paled in the comparison to Andy's, the three of us became collectively worried when the meeting's moderator asked for a show of hands of everybody who had driven at Daytona before and ours were the only hands held aloft.

I must admit that there are several parts of the long meeting where I did not particularly pay close attention, although I did keep my ears tuned for seemingly important information. One point that was hammered home repeatedly was the fact that "Porsche Club Racing rules were different." In fact, the moderator emphasized, over and over again, Porsche Club Racing flags might actually be different from those used in other racing series and that at all times, "our rules must be followed, no matter what you might've been used to in the past." Particular emphasis was placed on the fact that the green and checkered flags for each session would be displayed from the starter's stand at the start/finish line, and nowhere else on the track. I tuned in long enough to absorb this rule, and did my best to remember it amongst the smattering of other seemingly minor details that were discussed, ad nauseum, during the meeting.

Sure enough, once I had the chance to get back on the track the next day, I had an enjoyable time running our '06 spec TRG #66 Porsche GT3 cup car. I admittedly had a somewhat anxious first session, given the wide variety of speeds, techniques, and lines exhibited by the other racers on the track. At one point, I found myself braking shortly after the start/finish line on my way into Turn 1. When that happened, Kevin Buckler clicked onto the radio.

"Hey Jim, what's happening out there?"

Jim and TRG's Kevin Buckler chat in the pits at Laguna Seca

"Nothing much, just trying to keep myself in one piece out here with all of the madness."

Kevin explained why he was calling in, "Well I just saw you hit the brakes not too far after the start/finish. Is there something wrong?"

I didn't realize I needed to explain myself but I wanted to make sure it was clear. "Nope, nothing wrong here on my end, there's just no way I'm going to go deep in the brake zone behind one of these guys who're still figuring out which way the track goes!"

"Copy that Jim," Kevin came back, "just try and keep that car shiny and don't get into any trouble out there."

I drove on through the first practice session, until I saw a checkered flag waving at Turn 6 in the infield. Smiling to myself as I recalled the admonition of the moderator of the previous evening's instructional session, I promptly ignored that particular flag. After all, it wasn't waving from the starter's stand, so … I completed my run through the oval, chuckling to myself as the cars in front of me obediently split off down through the pit entry lane to finish their session. At full throttle and 180 mph I blew through the front tri-oval, past the waving checkered flag at start/finish. Once past start/finish, I dutifully slowed down to 50 percent throttle, taking my time completing a cool down lap through the infield, passing several flaggers furiously waving at me at various points at Turn 3, Turn 5, and Turn 6. I waved back, taking the time to make sure I gave everybody a big thumbs up on my way by.

On my way off the hot track down through the pit entry, I passed the deceleration cones, and prepared to turn left into the paddock. However, before I could do so, one of the Porsche Club officials quite literally threw himself in front of my car waving frantically and screaming at me as if I had just ran over his grandmother. I brought the car to a stop as he finally collected himself and ran screaming to my driver's side window.

"Just what the hell do you think you're doing??"

I paused a moment, turned, and looked at him calmly. "I'm sorry, but you're going to have to stop screaming if you want to talk to me."

He was unreceptive to my request and continued screaming at literally the top of his lungs. "Just what the hell do you think that was all about? You got a checkered flag, and you blew the checker, and ignored everybody flagging you to come in!!"

Once again I paused for effect. It was quite a turn for me to be the calm one in any spirited conversation, so I relished the role. Slowly, I lifted my face shield and stared at him once more.

"No, No, No," I slowly shook my head for effect, "You guys aren't changing the rules on me. I went to your meeting, and you said that the flag was gonna be waved only at the start/finish. Nobody gave me a flag at the start/finish until my last lap. I therefore ignored the checkered flag in Turn 6, just like I was told!"

"I—I—I don't care what you were told in that meeting—you were told—there was a flag at Turn 6—and you, you just ignored it!" At this point, there was spittle flying out of his mouth and I thought it prudent to put my face shield back down.

"Look buddy, I don't know what your role here is but I went to the meeting that you guys told me I had to go to, and I actually listened to what you told me. And I was told specifically not to pay any attention to any flags that weren't at the start/finish stand. So if you want to give me a hard time about that, go right ahead."

Surprisingly, the official at this point became only more aggravated.

"You know, we really have a problem with you new guys around here and if you're not gonna follow the rules we can't have you running with us! You're a danger to everyone out here!"

At that point, I frankly had had enough. "Hey buddy, I've got more laps around here than you or anybody else on the property at the moment. And frankly, if you want me to follow your rules, I'll follow your rules, and if you're gonna change the rules you better let me know ahead of time!" At that, I engaged the car in gear and started to pull away while the guy was still busily trying to see if I would come around to his way of thinking.

Shortly thereafter, I had the delightful opportunity, with Kevin buckler in attendance, to discuss the issue a little bit further with the Porsche Club Racing officials. Ultimately, we all collectively decided that we would call it a draw. I was permitted to race on, but advised to pay attention to all flags (regardless of what the prior instructions had in fact been). So sue me if I'm a literal guy and occasionally even stay awake in meetings.

The good news about that weekend was that I got three solid days of running, sharing the Porsche with Murray Marden, which turned out to be a thoroughly enjoyable experience. Murray and I took turns running hot laps in and around the occasional struggling Porsche Club racing drivers. Clearly, we had bought a bit of a cannon to a knife fight, but it felt good nonetheless to pass cars at will and easily lap well out of range of virtually all of the other cars. Despite our slight disadvantage of running on Hoosier Tires (with all of the other fast runners sporting Michelins), Murray and I managed to dominate the ninety-minute Sunday enduro-race, and I managed to run times several seconds better than my prior laps at either Grand-Am Daytona race. The weekend ended with more good vibes and more invaluable seat time in a Porsche at Daytona. An added bonus was the absence of any further ideological exchanges with the Porsche Club racing Feldgendarmerie.

Following a few uneventful weeks at work, thankfully survived by both me and all of my patients, I returned to Daytona for the official off season Grand-Am test. This time, Murray and I had the benefit of Jim Pace's coaching, relying heavily on his expertise to find the ideal setup for our

Porsche. While Murray and I again shared one car, the test was made even more enjoyable by the presence of Murray's future co-drivers for the '07 Rolex 24, Dr. Mike Gomez, Brent Milner, and John Peterson. Murray's co-drivers were quite familiar to me from our shared Skip Barber days, and it certainly felt like a bit of a reunion when we first got together to exchange notes prior to the first day's running. However, I did notice that the newbies were sporting a bit of the wide-eyed look that was now so familiar to me, having shaved with a guy who looked just like that on every race day of the past year.

Once we had dispensed with the pleasantries, it was all business, and both Murray and I got to work quickly, running laps that once again represented improvement from our prior driving. There was a decidedly comfortable feel to the seat of the car, for a change, and with each session, I ran more consistent laps, in a more and more relaxed fashion. And despite the fact that the safety net of Jim Pace on the radio was ever present, I felt completely different in the car, enjoying the new found confidence.

On the last day of the test, conditions were ideal. There were clouds early but no rain. I ran initially on old tires, noticing that the dash was showing consistent times regardless of traffic. As I drove, I was actually able to appreciate the change in the handling of the car with tire wear and with the changing track conditions. I focused on managing the traffic, including trying to set up the imminent passes of Daytona Prototypes at the proper points so that my own laps wouldn't be ruined. With JP in my ear, I laid down a personal best lap which actually felt slower and more in control than many of my earlier laps. Once my personal best was established, I quickly backed that up with several laps within a tenth of a second, just to make sure that it wasn't a fluke. Once the session was concluded, JP and I retired to the RV to review data downloaded from the Porsche's brain. The data engineer had printed out overlapping tracings of Jim Pace's best laps and mine; despite my personal best times, I remained awed by the fact that JP was still several seconds ahead of me. I was humbled by Jim's awesome performance, and recognized it for what it was: a testimonial to a great education and both how far I had come and how far I had yet to go.

I departed Daytona for the last time in 2006 with a sense of accomplishment and satisfaction, knowing that I had come a long way from the dramatic first laps in January. I also had the satisfaction of knowing that I would be back shortly, this time in a brand new 2007 Porsche race car. A plan had been set in motion and was continuing to move in the right direction. When I came back to Florida in January, we would have a contingent of professional racers ready to make a legitimate and competitive run at my second Rolex 24 Hours of Daytona.

***

It didn't take me long after I returned from Daytona to settle back into my usual work routine. Pre-dawn departures for work, long days in the OR and the office, and late arrivals for a delayed dinner with Ginny and Aidan were the norm. Late one particular evening, I arrived home as Ginny was busy getting Aidan ready for bed and preparing for his school day the next morning. As usual, when Ginny spotted me coming through the door, she inquired about how my day had gone.

"Hi honey, Welcome home, how was your day? How did things go in the OR?"

I filled her in with a brief sketch of my day, assuring her that all of my patients were doing fine after surgery. However, I was aware from the subtle inflection in her voice that there was something more to be said.

"You sound a little concerned—is there something wrong?"

At that point Ginny reminded me of her day at Aidan's school. "You probably forgot, I spent the afternoon as the guest celebrity reader for Aidan's class."

I didn't know what exactly was coming, but I was pretty sure it wasn't going to be good.

"You know, when you talk to the kids you learn some very interesting things."

Uh-Oh.

Ginny finally filled me in on what had happened. "When were you going to tell me that you had a crash where you flipped upside down in a race car?"

Those little stinkers. "Uh, I'm not sure what you're talking about?" I made the lame effort, but was sure it was futile.

"I believe you know exactly what I'm talking about. I arrived at Aidan's class to do the reading, and the first words out of their mouths were 'Did you know Mr. Lowe crashed upside down?'"

Damn. "But those guys promised they weren't gonna tell anybody."

"Well, you should have known better than to trust a bunch of six-year-olds. They couldn't wait till they told me all about it."

Defeated, I headed off towards the pantry to pour myself a glass of wine. Shaking my head, I muttered to myself, "Damn, I thought we had a deal."

24

Chapter Twenty-Four

"Life is what happens to you while you're busy making other plans," John Lennon theorized in his song "Beautiful Boy (Darling Boy)." Indeed, this could have been the theme of my life while I was making preparations for another go at the Rolex 24 at Daytona in 2007. While I was in the midst of daily meetings and phone calls crafting plans for the upcoming January race, the rest of my life was settling down nicely, seemingly almost without any assistance or input from me. With each tightly scheduled day, now filled from wake-up to lights-out with activity—professional, family, and racing—life was indeed happening.

In retrospect, the non-racing aspects of my life had never been more simultaneously settled and unsettled. However, the unsettled aspects were representative of growth and positive change, unlike some of the prior acrimonious events in my old practice and in my emerging days as a new physician. Dr. Zerbo had formally joined my practice, and we now had an official partnership to go with our association that had grown over the years while working closely together. I previously remarked quite frequently that "Joe was more of a partner to me (when he was in his prior practice) than my original partners had ever been." Now, with our new arrangement, we worked together officially daily, saw patients together in the office, and solved practice problems, both clinical and business-wise, together. I enjoyed the partnership, especially in contrast to what I had experienced in past iterations, and for the first time I felt a true sense of satisfaction in that specific part of my professional life.

During that same period the practice continued exponential growth, both in good will and patient demands. Joe and I continued and even upped our efforts at giving frequent lectures, going to meetings, and maintaining a good level of general visibility regarding our particular area of expertise in spinal surgery. I found that my duties as Chief of neurosurgery at the hospital carried more responsibilities than previously demanded –

some pleasant, others not so much. In addition, Ginny had settled into her role in our practice, both in the clinical aspects of her work as a spinal cord injury spasticity specialist and also as an oversight administrator. In this fashion, I found professional comfort, satisfaction, and success working with both my wife and my partner to grow and maintain our core business. Although the daily running of a neurosurgical practice did not approximate the thrills and spills of driving a race car, clearly there were challenges to be met, and immediate focus, attention, and determination were required in order to keep us at the sharp end of things. As we planned the future of the practice, there was scant time to realize that the current state of the practice was in fact quite successful and satisfying.

With all the demands on my time, there was certainly a risk that I might neglect my most important career of all: that of being a father. Recognizing this, and with the thoughtful input from my wife, we created "Daddy night." Understanding that there was a need for not just quality time but a quantity of time to spend with my son, I made plans to reserve Monday night time with my son no matter what the schedule demands were. Once again, I leaned on my partner for assistance with this; Monday nights became Joe's time on-call while I was able to essentially shut down the beeper and phone and dedicate all my attention to my son. I would pick him up at school, and he was aware that the rest of the evening was already reserved for time together, just the two of us. Whether we simply went out to dinner, went to an arcade, or attended fly-tying classes together, the time was ours and ours alone. For sure, there were certainly other moments that we spent together, and in those times on other days I considered that something of a bonus. But I found myself looking forward to Monday's "Daddy night" with each day of the week. I am not sure who enjoyed those periods more—Aidan or me—but to this day we have continued the tradition that reminds me always of my privileges and priorities with my son.

Increasingly, the business of medicine and the business of racing were being mixed in my small piece of the world. For our 2007 Rolex 24 effort, I had come up with the idea of combining my visibility as a neurosurgeon with my love of the racetrack. A program was developed wherein we invited physicians to come to Daytona so that they could experience the race weekend from the insider's point of view, while attending educational programs, seminars, and lectures from experts in the world of spine surgery. As we worked on developing this program, it became evident that there was a significant demand for not only other physicians but also for an expanding circle of friends, families, and even patients to come enjoy the unique atmosphere of Daytona with us. The guest list grew exponentially and at one point we realized that we had over 150 guests planned for the end of January. As the guest list grew, so did the need for detail, planning, and attention to every possible aspect of the weekend so that we delivered on our promise for a great event. And, of course, none of this had anything to do with me actually focusing on getter faster.

The 2007 event would also be the debut of the JLowe Racing Team's first formal effort that was officially combined with the support of TRG, but with the logo and branding of the JLowe Team being first and foremost. Our new 2007 Porsche GT3 Cup car was scheduled to be delivered just in time to be prepped for the January testing days; in the meantime, we spent endless hours reviewing plans for car livery, color schemes, and the appearance of drivers' suits, banners, and signage. I became a bit of an expert in graphic design, marketing, economics, and sales, all on the fly while I also was busy spending time functioning as a neurosurgeon. I leaned heavily on the expertise of friends and family, relied increasingly on Joe to pick up the slack in the practice while I was busy, and spent daily time on the phone with Jim Pace discussing specifics of planning for January. All in all it was a demanding, busy, and intense time; and for sure, life continued to happen while I was in the middle of making these other plans.

***

Life was also happening for my patients, including those who required my unscheduled services, sometimes in an emergent fashion. One such case was that of Joey DeVoto, a young roofer who had the misfortune of working on New Year's Eve.

Perhaps Joey was distracted by thoughts of the upcoming midnight celebration after he got off work for the day, and perhaps he was simply the victim of incredibly bad luck. However, while working on a flat roof, Joey picked up a large sheet of plywood on his own, planning to toss it off the side of the roof. With massively ill timing, a huge gust of wind occurred just as Joey picked up the plywood, blowing him and the plywood over the edge, down to the hard ground two stories below.

Joey was taken by ambulance to the emergency room, strapped flat on a spine board for his own safety so that he wouldn't inadvertently move and cause more damage to his injured spine. The emergency room physicians and the trauma docs did their routine initial examination and called me shortly after Joey's admission that afternoon.

The trauma doctor presented the case to me on the telephone, giving me enough basic details so that I knew I had a true emergency on my hands.

"I've got a 25-year-old here who got blown off a building," the trauma doctor began. "He's complaining of numbness from the waist down and reporting that he can't move very well. To my examination, he only has small bits of movement in his legs, and he has no sensation in his perineum." The doc was describing to me neurologic damage that happens with a classic injury to the tip of the spinal cord, which not only causes weakness and numbness in the legs but numbness in the "saddle region," affecting critical parts of bowel, bladder, sexual function and sensation.

"What do you see on the films?"

The trauma doc continued his narrative. "CT scan shows significant burst fracture at T12, with deformity, and lots of bone fragments in the spinal canal. The patient is on his way to MRI, but I figured this was a good time to call you, guessing that you would probably want to operate on this one."

The basic details were certainly enough to get my attention, and I knew that I would now be spending my New Year's Eve in the operating room. "I'm on my way. I'll meet him in the MRI scanner, but we better let the OR know that we're gonna need to do a case." With that, I hung up, headed for the car, and started dialing my partner to let him know we had a case to do.

Within the hour, I was meeting with Joey and his family, reviewing the results of the CT scan showing the significant fracture as well as the MRI showing the damage where the bone fragments had crushed the tip of the spinal cord and the nerves around it. I explained to the patient and his family that the injury was "incomplete"—there was actually some small amount of neurologic function still remaining—and told them that in these cases it was thought that emergent surgical treatment could be of great benefit. I described the procedure that would combine several different incisions on Joey's trunk to gain access to the damaged bones, to remove the fragments away from the spinal cord, and to stabilize the spine with hooks and rods. Although there wasn't time for the typical prolonged, detailed, and extensive surgical discussion we normally did with elective cases in the office, I sketched a few basics on the white sheet of the stretcher and did my best to draw out for the patient and his family what the incisions would look like. Concluding my discussion, questions were asked and answered, and I cleared the path for the anesthesiologist to get to work to get the patient into the operating room.

Joey's surgery started somewhere around six or seven o'clock that evening and began with an approach to the patient's fractured bone through the side of his trunk. The trauma surgeon made an incision in a curved fashion at the bottom of the rib cage on the left side and, through that incision, cut down attachments of the patient's diaphragm and then moved the critical abdominal organs out of the way to gain access to the bone at the mid-spine region. Critical tissues were cleared away and bone exposed, at which time it became quite clear that there was severe damage to the structure of the vertebral body. I looked over the shoulder of the trauma surgeon as he completed his exposure and recognized a significant amount of tissue disruption.

"Geez, it looks like a grenade went off in there. There's so much damage at that level you don't even need an x-ray to make sure we're at the right area."

"I took an x-ray anyway and identified the discs above and below the broken bones so I knew how far to dissect." The surgeon, Pete Thompson, was one of the more experienced guys with performing these exposures, and I had the utmost confidence in his ability to perform a dissection that allowed me to easily see the fractured bone, and the normal bones above and below it.

I looked over the table at Joe and nodded. "We're gonna go scrub, we'll see you in 10 minutes. Hold that pose."

Joe and I scrubbed in and got to work. Using a high speed drill, fragments of bone were progressively drilled away at the site of the fractured bone, with the goal to remove all of the crumbled portions of bone in a piecemeal fashion. Initially this was quite simple, drilling away bony fragments that were not critically placed. However, with further bony removal, we got closer and closer to the spinal canal, right where the spinal cord lived. Under magnified vision, I was able to identify several very large pieces of bone that had actually been pushed into the spinal canal and were crushing Joey's spinal cord. In a meticulous fashion, I poked and prodded each piece of bone, removed several portions of ligament that were involved, and eventually took all of the pressure off the spinal cord. Bit by bit bleeding areas were controlled as we worked, with Joe suctioning away blood while I gently removed the offending fragments. After we completed this portion of the operation, we could see the soft tissues including the dura—the thick covering over the spinal cord—and the nerves at the fracture level; it was clear that they were now free of any compression. Whether or not they would recover function was an issue for another day, but at least at this point there was no further pressure being applied.

Removing all of the fractured bits of bone had, of course, left a large gaping hole in the structure of the spine with critical supporting bone now missing. In essence, if the patient now was able to sit up, he would quite literally break in half, as there was nothing to support his spine now that the bone had been removed. This therefore necessitated a reconstructive fusion—placing a structural cage where the bone used to be, along with some bony elements to allow eventual ingrowth and stability. I selected a cylindrical mesh titanium cage, packed it with bone morsels taken from Joey's pelvis, and placed it in the gap where the original fractured bone had been. The unique property of this cage was its ability to be expanded by turning a ratchet inside, allowing us to achieve the perfect size and fit of the device in the bone. After this was in place successfully, a plate was affixed across the gap, with screws and bolts securing the ends of the plate to the normal healthy bone above and below the fracture site. Despite the severity of the patient's injury and the gravity of the clinical situation, I must admit that this little bit of carpentry was quite interesting and entertaining. It was truly a tinker-toy approach to rebuilding a patient's spine, and I enjoyed solving the mechanical problem in addition to the prospect of greatly helping the patient's neurologic condition.

That incision was then closed by Dr. Thompson, after which Joe and I needed to perform the second half of the procedure. It was now approximately one o'clock in the morning, and we still had several hours of work to do. With the patient still asleep, we flipped Joey over onto his belly on a special padded frame, and prepared his back for more surgery. The skin was sterilized with a mixture of Betadine soap and alcohol, and sterile drapes were placed to outline the surgical site. A long incision was made over the mid-center region of Joey's back and through that incision Joe and I worked to expose the bones at the fracture site and also the healthy bones above and below the damaged area.

More evidence of disruption and significant fracture was found when we performed this exposure. At the same level of the fractured bone we had encountered in the front of the spine, the portions of bone in the back of the spine were also fractured severely. Fragments of bone were actually pushing into the spinal cord from the back side, and there was leakage of clear spinal fluid from traumatic tears in the dura. Once again working in a meticulous fashion, the fragments of bone were removed from the spinal cord, and the openings in the dura were repaired with a miniscule water-proof stitch. After that work was done, it was clear that the spinal cord was now under no further pressure from the front or the back sides. All that was left was to complete the stabilization procedure.

Fashioning hooks around the back side of the bones of the spine (the lamina), a claw purchase was obtained to secure rods crossing the fractured area. Rods were secured into the hooks on the patient's lamina and bent into a proper position so that the patient might ultimately assume a relatively normal anatomic alignment when he healed. Once the rods were secured, we took an x-ray of the patient's spine to determine that all of the nuts, bolts, cages, screws, and rods had been placed properly and remained in a good position.

I took a moment before closing to check the x-ray, letting out a long slow whistle as I examined the picture of the rather complicated carpentry in front of me. "Wow, that's a pretty extensive amount of work in there. Looks great though, if I don't say so myself!"

The circulating nurse wasn't about to let that comment pass without her own sarcastic observation. "Yes Doctor, you're wonderful, now please could you get back to work and close the patient. It's the middle of the night."

I got back to work, closing the patient's long incision and taping sterile dressings in place.

We returned Joey to the recovery room sometime after four a.m. He was still heavily anesthetized, and I was unable to do any form of examination to confirm whether or not he had any improvement in the neurologic function in his legs. Thankfully, he was otherwise stable, so there was no need for me to remain on watch at that point. I proceeded to the waiting room, where I gave the news to Joey's parents.

"Well, everything went just as planned. There was a severe amount of bony damage, and the fracture fragments were causing a significant amount of pressure on the spinal cord. But just like we planned, all of that is gone now. There is no more pressure, and we were able to stabilize everything with the hooks, rods, and cages."

"Doctor, how did the spinal cord look?" Joey's father was of course very concerned and asked the question that I've heard so many times before.

"Well the only thing I can tell you about the spinal cord at this point is that there was certainly evidence of damage and a lot of pressure there. However, the best measure of whether or not Joey's spinal cord is going to recover is actually going to be his examination over the next couple of days. The nurses, the trauma doctors, and Dr. Zerbo and I will do repeated examinations to determine whether or not there is some return of good function. Given that we got to him so quickly, and that there was some function preserved before surgery, I'm hopeful that we'll have a good return of function eventually. How much return, however, I simply can't tell at this time."

At this point, Mom chipped in, giving voice to her biggest fear. "Doctor, will he walk again?"

As optimistic as I might have been for a good recovery, I had to be careful here. I didn't want to give Joey's parents unfounded hope, and clearly there was no completely predictable recovery to be had, at least from the perspective of a surgery that was now only one hour old. "There's just no way to tell for sure, but I am expecting that there'll be some degree of neurologic recovery. How much recovery we can't predict accurately now; the next few days will really tell us what we need to know about that. I'm hopeful, but I don't have any way of knowing for sure until we see how Joey does over the next 72 hours."

The parents nodded and accepted this information with limited optimism combined with exhaustion.

"I'll be back in the morning"—I corrected myself—"I mean this afternoon, and I'll check Joey to see how he's doing. If you're here then we can talk about what his status is at that point." Joey's parents assured me that they would be there for the remainder of the day.

"Well, make sure you both get some rest. Joey is too asleep now to appreciate that you're here; it might be best if you take the opportunity yourselves to get some sleep, so that you are in better shape when he wakes up."

Dad spoke up. "We're gonna be right here in case he needs us, but thank you for your thoughtfulness. We'll see you when you get back."

I drove home on New Year's Day with the rising sun in my eyes. It had been a long night, but I was still buzzing with a combination of fatigue, caffeine, and dwindling adrenaline. I fantasized about taking a nap when I got home, but knew at this point that that was about the worst thing I could consider doing. There was more work to be done that afternoon: we were still on call for the hospital for any further trauma patients, and I had last minute preparations to do for my trip to Daytona the next day.

Arriving home to a quiet house, I poured myself a fresh cup of coffee, and started packing my things for Daytona. I made a few trips in and out of the bedroom, managing to somehow avoid waking Ginny while I collected my necessary clothing. My new JLowe Racing branded travel bag was still in the living room from when it had been delivered the other day; I sat on the couch in front of the bag as I carefully organized my helmet, fire suit, Nomex underwear, and various other articles that needed to go south with me. Once I had everything suitably organized (and counted twice), I figured it was safe to take a moment to relax on the couch. I reclined on a couple of pillows, clicked on the TV with the volume low, and took a deep breath for seemingly the first time in twenty-four hours.

I was startled and disoriented when Ginny gently nudged me awake several hours later. Looking around, it took me a minute to figure out where I was and get oriented to the time, place, and events of last night. "I figured you better not sleep all the way through the night, but you looked so nice and relaxed sleeping there," my wife said.

"No, no, thanks," I mumbled sleepily, "I have to go back to the hospital anyway. What time is it?"

"It's just a little after three in the afternoon. I figured you might need some more rest."

I shook the cobwebs out of my brain, sat up, and started heading towards the bedroom. "I'm just gonna clean up, get a shower, and head to the hospital." As I headed up the stairs past Ginny, she grabbed me for a quick peck on the cheek. "Oh by the way, Happy New Year!"

I yawned. "Yeah, nice start to '07. I hope this isn't a bad omen."

I made my way to the hospital and found Joey in his Trauma ICU room, surrounded by family. He was off the ventilator and slightly sedated but otherwise awake. I said hello to the various family members and then politely asked them to give us a moment so that I could examine Joey privately.

I went over Joey's neurologic examination carefully, doing my best to check the strength in his legs. I also performed a rectal examination, trying to get a sense of whether or not he had any sensation in that area and any voluntary muscular function. Unfortunately, he still had a significant problem with sensation in that area and couldn't even feel my tugging on the Foley catheter in his bladder. There was some encouraging findings however, as he seemed to be moving his legs in a somewhat stronger fashion than before.

I called the family members back into the room and gave them a quick update on his condition. "There are some signs of improvement especially in his strength, but there are also still some critical problems where we were worried before. He still has a significant problem with sensation in his saddle area; this might be something that takes quite a long time to improve, if it's going to. However, it's certainly never bad news to see some neurologic improvement like we're seeing here. And it's very early of course."

I stuck around to answer a few questions and to reassure the family that we would continue our examinations of Joey. I also alerted them that Dr. Zerbo would be doing the next several visits, as I was going to be away for a few days. I said my goodbyes and left the several family members and friends at Joey's bedside.

On my way home, I made one last phone call to Jim Pace, wishing him a Happy New Year, and confirming my arrival time at Daytona Beach the next morning. I then signed out to Joe, completing the transfer of all the necessary call duties and any future emergencies to my partner in anticipation of leaving town in the morning. With all those boxes checked, I was finally able to shut the surgical part of my brain down and focus entirely on the next racing task at hand: the official test days for the 2007 Rolex 24 Hours of Daytona.

***

Engineer Sebastien Constans

I had long ago learned, sometime during medical school or internship, a surprising thing about staying up all night on call: the worst day was actually the second day after an all-nighter, with adrenaline and necessity usually allowing me to perform reasonably well in the hours immediately after spending a night without sleep. However, when I finally did get some sleep the next night, waking the following morning was usually an arduous task. After a long stretch working without sleep, usually fueled by caffeine, ill-advised sugar boluses from the vending machine, and a combination of anxiety and exhaustion, a single night's sleep was not enough for adequate recovery. I had grown used to the concept that I would have more of a sensation of fatigue upon waking up the next morning, even more so than on the immediate post-call days. It was in this condition that I arrived at Daytona the next morning, just over twenty-four hours after last walking out of the operating room.

In the fuzziness that surrounded me in my fatigued state, emotional thoughts and sensory inputs were perceived as if surrounded by a thin veil of fog. I was able to appreciate what was going on, I was genuinely engaged and involved, but I was somehow just a tick of the watch removed from much that was occurring around me. This sensation was heightened further by the déjà vu that was meeting Jim Pace once again on the tarmac at Daytona's airport.

"You look like you been rode hard and put up wet," JP welcomed me

Ralf Kelleners

with his Mississippi drawl.

"Thanks, I was hoping I would at least look like the hammered shit I feel like after a couple days on call."

"Well Dr. Lowe, if walking through the paddock this afternoon doesn't wake you up, I'm sure driving around the banking tomorrow morning will certainly get your attention!"

I reassured Jim Pace that I only needed a little bit of time to make a full recovery. "A little bit of lunch, a cup of coffee, and maybe a nap before I drive, and I'll be on it," I promised. "Don't worry—what is it you always say—'It's not my first rodeo.'"

"Copy that, Dr. Lowe." JP smiled, grabbed my helmet bag, and steered me over to his rental car.

As we made the quick drive over to the paddock, JP ran down his first impressions after meeting some of our new crew members. He noted that he had already checked in with our new engineer Sebastien Constans, simply stating "I hope he's as good an engineer as he is tall." I didn't quite understand JP's statement until meeting Sebastien a few hours later and realizing that he was at least six feet eight, maybe more if he ever actually stretched himself out of his perpetual slouch. Jim reassured me that I was going to have a good time meeting Thomas Blam, our new strategist, and he noted also that Roger Reis would be joining us once again as crew chief. The only remaining two members of the team not yet present were Johannes van Overbeek and Ralf Kelleners, the two pro drivers to fill out the lineup. Oh, and one other new member of the team: our brand new 2007 997 Porsche GT3 Cup car. My 2007 Porsche Cup Car. The joys, and occasional sorrows, of race car ownership were now officially upon me.

As we wandered through the paddock and the fuzziness receded from around the edges of my vision, I felt the quickening in my heart rate as

I saw the familiar sights and sounds of crews at work. I enjoyed walking with JP as cars were unloaded from haulers and rolled down to tech as the general chaos of the day began. I strolled around recognizing many familiar faces, having brief moments to chat with a few of the friendlier drivers who knew me from the past year in the paddock. Although I no longer had any lingering fear of being barred from entry to this particular game, I was certainly aware of submerged concern about my own performance lurking just under the surface of my enthusiasm.

As JP and I walked through the paddock, I could see down to the end garages that a decent crowd was already in place around the TRG section. With four other cars entered, in addition to my #64 car, the group of crewman, engineers, and assorted team personnel from the TRG group was truly impressive in size. Somewhere underneath a few layers of that crowd lurked my new car.

JP and I made our way to the new car, still in its delivery white colors, with an ersatz #64 painted on the nose and sides. Standing next to it was Kevin Buckler, along with the aforementioned very tall engineer, and Roger Reis. As I arrived, they looked up in unison and smiled while Kevin spread his hands out as if to present the car to me in a royal fashion.

"Dr. Lowe, your stallion awaits!" I stopped in my tracks a few steps from the car, and took my time to get an overall image of the beautiful new vehicle stamped on my brain.

"Wow, if she's as fast as she looks, this is gonna be a pretty good month."

"She's even faster than she looks, Dr. Lowe," JP corrected me with an elbow to the ribs.

"And just wait 'til you guys get some time behind the wheel. You and JP are gonna love this little buggy," Kevin assured us, "and the other two hotshoes, Johannes and Ralf, are gonna kick ass in this thing also. I think the only thing the rest of the TRG team cars have to worry about is #64 right here."

As usual, Kevin was his effusive self, emanating good vibes, deserved or not. He then proceeded to introduce me to Sebastien Constans and patted me on the shoulder as he was off to other duties and concerns of the huge effort he was running.

I chatted a bit with our crew chief, thanking him for once again drawing the short straw and being saddled with both the slowest and the fastest neurosurgeon in the paddock. Roger just squinted his eyes in his usual twinkle, smiled ever so slightly while shrugging his shoulders, and opined, "I'm thinking we're gonna have a pretty good month."

I spent some time walking around the Porsche, quite literally kicking the tires, and inspecting the various body work pieces that were added by Porsche to improve the aerodynamic characteristics of the car. Finally, after first getting a thumbs-up from Roger, I pulled my wallet and keys out of my pocket, handed them off to JP, and assumed my position behind the wheel in the tight driver's seat.

Virtually every race car that I had been in up until that point represented a challenge for me to achieve anything resembling a comfortable position. Usually, there is a great deal of fiddling—adjusting the seat rake, angle, and position, and quite often adding or subtracting padding in order to get my apparently atypical form to fit into a standard seat. However, for some reason, in this car, in that seat, I felt immediately comfortable and at home. The shoulders were exactly as wide as I needed them, and the angle of the seat, with a small cushion preset in the small of my back, fit perfectly. I wiggled my butt a little bit, found the pedals with my feet, and of course did what we all do, sawed the wheel back and forth in a moment of juvenile enthusiasm.

"You look pretty good behind the wheel there, JLowe," remarked Jim Pace.

Thomas stuck his head in the opposite window. "Well at least you're comfortable, so we won't have too much fiddling to do tomorrow when we get down to business."

"What kind of sizes are Johannes and Ralf?" I asked.

Thomas had worked extensively with Johannes on the American Le Mans series Porsche team where Johannes was a principal driver. "Johannes has a very thin torso and long legs. But he can probably fit in just about any situation, just like I'm sure Mr. Pace here can."

JP confirmed the obvious. "You just get yourself settled in and the three of us will work around you, Dr. Lowe. Nothing for you to fret about at this point."

I reluctantly dismounted from the car, and stepped away as the mechanics attached the pneumatic hose and raised the car up on its air jacks. In moments, wheels were removed and suspension checks and other various nuts and bolts were tightened under the watchful eye of Roger. JP tugged at my arm and motioned me out into the garage entrance area.

Johannes van Overbeek

"Let's walk a little bit, say hello to a few people, drop our helmets off to get the radios checked, and get out of here. We've got a lot of work to do in the morning, and we don't want to waste all our energy on the pregame show."

"I'm following you JP, you lead and I'm right behind you."

JP restated his objective for this particular event: "From here on out it's a lot of hard work and it's all business, Dr. Lowe. We're gonna have to be on our game if we want to be at the sharp end of things at the end of the month."

With that we headed off to the trailer, making our way through the paddock with time to say a few quick hellos. After checking out the RV situation in the Driver/Owner lot area, and dropping off my helmet bag and a few other pieces of clothing for the next three days, JP and I settled onto the couches in the front area of the RV to take a deep breath and relax. We talked a little shop, such as discussing plans for the race weekend, including the fact that we would have Kathy Dandurand, the World's Greatest Massage Therapist, back to help our effort. We had also planned to rent a second RV to use as a "quiet" space for the weekend. JP reminded me that the team RV became a bit of a busy place once the green flag dropped, with drivers and friends and family trudging in and out for the next twenty-four hours. With a second RV, we would have a designated place for drivers to sleep and/or rest while getting a massage; it would also mean that those who needed to eat or get ready to drive could do so with lights on and no restrictions on their sometimes noisy activity.

We continued to discuss a few of the seemingly unimportant odds and ends of the coming month; JP had taught me from his vast experience that sometimes those little odds and ends made a difference in the long run. It was also best to address them at calm moments, rather than trying to address seemingly minor details in the heat of battle with more pressing issues at hand.

We had nearly completed that bit of housekeeping when there was a knock on the door, and both Ralf Kelleners and Johannes van Overbeek stepped into the RV. We all said hellos, shaking hands as we made introductions. Johannes was tall and thin, not quite lanky, with dark hair; he was seriously lacking the crow's feet and early gray hair that were both prominent features on both JP and me. Ralf, on the other hand, was the shortest of the four of us, but he also was slight and built like a prototypical race car driver. He had beach blonde hair in a punk style, complimenting his sharply angular features. Both guys seemed entirely pleasant, and I breathed a slight sigh of relief guessing that there would be an easy chemistry between the four drivers for the rest of the month. I was mostly right about this, although Ralf and JP would clash on occasion especially when it came to car setup and expectations. Overall, however, the initial impression and ongoing concept of the month was one of a good core group of fast guys to complement, and perhaps overcome, any of my shortcomings.

While we were busy getting acquainted in the RV, Thomas, Roger, and Sebastien stopped in, and we spread out for our first official JLowe Racing team meeting—Sebastien with his laptop and Roger and Thomas with notebooks and pencils. Thomas led the meeting, setting out a driver order strategy for the coming three days of testing time. Considering that we needed to shake down a brand new car that had never turned a wheel before, Jim Pace was elected to run the inaugural laps in the Porsche. This would be followed by me, getting in a few laps to see the track in the new car, after which the real work of testing would begin. Johannes, Ralf, Jim, and I would then rotate in order, making changes as necessary in order to establish a baseline setup for the car for the endurance event to come later in the month. Although three days of testing seemed like a lot of time, we all knew from various amounts of experience that the third day would come all too quickly, and we had to have our act together well before then.

We performed the various rituals of the night before testing, including dinner at Buca di Beppo with old team members and new ones together; this time we also took a few minutes to meet with some of the new guys from Kevin Buckler's TRG cars, including friends Murray Marden, Michael Gomez, and Brent Milner from my Skip Barber days. The temptation was to spend time over a glass of wine yucking it up over days past and races run, but the looming schedule ahead of us and the necessity to take our program in a competitive direction negated any late night reunion time. Instead I made myself retire from the festivities early, hitting the rack in a timely fashion to expect a reasonable night of sleep. Unlike last year's pre-event jitters, this time I fell asleep in a relaxed fashion thinking happy thoughts about the three ringers I had driving with me for the rest of the month.

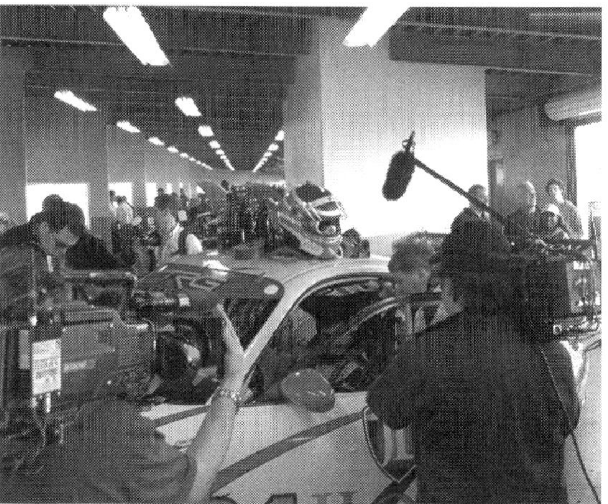

TV time in the Daytona garages, 2007

Immediately upon beginning Thursday morning testing, it was obvious that the car was fast right off the truck. JP ran a couple shake-down laps, and then I jumped behind the wheel of my new car to get a good view of the track from behind the wheel of a better and faster car than I had ever driven. After a few brief laps for me to clear my head, I handed off the car to Johannes. He proceeded to take all of about 10 seconds to get up to speed in the car, making a few comments over the radio while he knocked off second after second from his lap time. We ended the short first session quite happy with the feel of a car that was quick from the start, knowing that cars that are slow off the truck often never get to a point of being competitive regardless of engineering changes.

The giddy sensation of fast times evaporated quickly in the second timed Grand-Am session later that morning. As I stood in the pits watching the cars go by approximately every two minutes, I noticed several laps into the session that the white #64 car had disappeared from sight. A few minutes later, the car reappeared—suspended on the end of a tow hook behind the wrecker. Johannes appeared shortly afterwards at my elbow, apologizing profusely for having lost control of the car. A later analysis of the telemetry data from the car showed that the throttle had hung up on Johannes just long enough to send the car sliding into the tire wall at Turn 5. However, the sight of my brand new race car, which I had spent all of three laps in, coming back on the wrecker was certainly my first experience in the distinct "downs" of car ownership. I swallowed hard and took it all in stride,

The team rolls onto the grid at Daytona, 2007

remarking to anybody that commented, that this was certainly nothing to get too agitated about. "Yeah, it's not like anybody is dying around here at the moment," I stated. "In fact, that's sort of what race cars do, isn't it?" There was certainly an element of false bravado to my statements, knowing that that little accident had probably just cost me about $30,000. However, the critical issues were that Johannes was unhurt and the car was definitely fixable. After that, I had to put it all out of mind and look forward to getting back in the car when it was straightened back out.

While the car was being repaired for the rest of the afternoon, the non-mechanical members of the team retired to the RV to spend time talking about strategy and generally getting to know each other. We discussed concepts of car setup and discovered several differences in philosophy between Jim, Sebastien, and Ralf that would ultimately lead to some acrimony. For my part, the afternoon was a crash course (literally) in engineering and aerodynamics. My head was spinning with information about the not-so-basic principles of managing suspension, wing, brake, and ride height settings to improve the handling characteristics of the race car in different circumstances. Our particular team's challenge in terms of setup was to manage to make the car capable for a wide range of driver skill (to say the least). In addition to simply making the car fast on the straight away sections of the banking and on the slow winding sections of the infield, the car had to be as drivable for the amateur neurosurgeon as it was for the expert Porsche racers. After something less than a heated discussion, JP, Johannes, and Ralf finally settled with Sebastien on a baseline setup with which to begin the rest of the testing sessions. Thereafter we ran the last session Friday and the morning session Saturday in a controlled and thankfully uneventful fashion. The times came down for all the drivers, including me; for their part, Jim, Ralf, and Johannes ran times at approximately 1:53 to 1:54. As we watched the Grand-Am monitors, it was quite clear that the car was competitive and near the front of the pack in the GT times. After the three hotshoes had become comfortable with the setup and the handling of the car, there was only one more variable to address: Jim Lowe's lap times.

The last session Saturday afternoon was reserved for the weakest link in our driver lineup; for my part I was quite pleased to get the majority of the time behind the wheel, augmented by coaching in my ear from JP and coaching on the sidelines from Ralf and Johannes. I set out originally to minimize embarrassment in the face of my three incredibly talented driving partners, knowing that the rest of the team was busting their butts in order to make us all look better. For their part, Johannes, Jim, and Thomas suggested that my previous best time of 1:57 would be "just fine", but I was aware that they were perhaps being overly polite to the car owner and the guy who signed their checks. For my part, up until that point I had felt comfortable, perhaps too comfortable, in the car. I suspected that there was more out there for me, especially if I could get some clean traffic-free laps. And here was my opportunity.

Late that afternoon, mounted comfortably in my new car, I pulled out onto the track to begin the last session of the three-day test. I could relax and work on getting up to time gradually, knowing that the session was mine and there was nothing more to be done other than work on my own particular personal level of comfort and speed in the car. With that in mind, I took a warm-up lap, enjoying the sound and feel of the powerful car underneath me.

Within the first few laps, my radio failed, stealing with it my usual security blanket of Jim Pace coaching in my ear. I tried keying the radio several times, calling out in a hopeful fashion "JLowe to pits, JLowe to pits, do you copy, do you copy?" but heard nothing but static in my ears. While this was happening, I noticed that the lap timer in the dash continued to show 0:00, so I was without any real-time feedback of my actual lap times either. Deprived of all sensation other than what was immediately in front of me on the track, I put my head down, tried to keep my eyes up, and got to work. I remembered JP's usual advice, trying to "brake later, get back to power sooner" and simply focused on running hard. Ignoring the faster Prototypes moving around me, except when I needed to guard the apex of a turn in order to protect my own lap time, I pushed harder each time around. Managing both faster traffic and slower traffic, I repeated lap after lap, eyes up and jaw clenched, trying to remember to wiggle my fingers and toes on the straightaways. There was no drama, no scary moments, and no looming barriers approaching my field of view from odd directions. I kept it securely on the blacktop, hit my marks as deeply as possible when braking, and focused only on the next turn.

Before I knew it, the yellow light was flashing in the car and the checkered flag was waving from the front stretch starter stand. I took the checker, returned to the pits, and immediately saw by the big grin on JP's face that I had made some progress. I got out of the car and was greeted by JP, Johannes, and Thomas who announced that I had turned a 1:56.6. This was my best time by over a second from previous sessions, and it eclipsed somewhat the personal goal I had privately set for myself prior to the weekend's test. To cap off my sense of accomplishment, Kevin Buckler wandered by and paused briefly to give me the racer's best compliment—the international sign language for "big cojones." There were smiles all around at this point as I unbuckled my gear and then joined the other drivers on the way back to the RV.

I was a driver, pulling something resembling my own weight, and perhaps even better than what might have been expected by my accomplished professional partners. I had accomplished goal one for the month: I was part of something special and competitive and, so far, not simply an anchor weighing down the team. I wasn't going to set anybody on fire by the way I drove, but I was certainly going to be able to play my part when the time came. And it would come in just over two weeks.

***

I hustled through the next two weeks at work, fitting as many surgeries and as much time in the office as possible in order to make up for the lost time at the beginning and the end of the month. As always, my partner Joe was an ironman, picking up more than his fair share of the work, while my focus remained divided. While I spent days in the OR or seeing patients in the office, my ride home and time after arriving was devoted to racing. I spent hours on the phone discussing all of the necessary planning details of not only running a twenty-four hour endurance race, designing a sponsor scheme for the car, and working on the business aspects of the deal, but also preparing for the 150+ guests we had planned for the weekend. Once I got home, I ate dinner followed by an immediate trip down to my basement gym where I exercised for an hour or two, working on my aerobic fitness in a last ditch effort to prepare for the rigors of the end of the month. Simultaneously, the time seemed to fly and crawl. I spent nights dreaming of my white race car with red stripes, fantasizing about winning a Rolex watch, and joining the ranks of the elite. In my more lucid moments, I thought only about redeeming myself after last year's ignominious first try at the 24 Hours of Daytona. I secretly hoped that we had assembled the right group of drivers and crew in order to make a good go of things, but in reality I hoped only for a respectable showing and some degree of personal satisfaction with a performance that was surely going to be an improvement on the prior year's.

On Wednesday, January 24, I made my way dutifully to Daytona. I tried hard not to put on a game face just yet and instead surely bounced a bit on the edge of my airplane seat as we circled over the giant track on Speedway Boulevard before landing on the airstrip right next to the back stretch. Once again, JP was there to meet me, and off we went to meet the crew in the paddock and walk around spying on all the other GT teams. While I was not particularly worried about Santa kicking my ass this year, I did have a sense of anticipation mixed with anxiety. I felt comfortable and somewhat at home in the paddock, but I still tingled at the thought of putting on a uniform and rolling out on the track amongst all of these professional and accomplished drivers.

We met up with Johannes and Ralf at the #64 JLowe Racing Porsche, which was looking beautiful in its newly outfitted red and white livery. After brief hellos, we took a walk through the garage area together. I inwardly chuckled at my newly found status as a driver on a respectably competitive team. I had no misconceptions that I had suddenly developed blazing speed, but clearly the other drivers knew JP, Johannes, and Ralf well enough to respect their abilities and their potential for a good finish in the race. I remarked to more than one inquiring friend that I felt like the geeky kid in high school who had suddenly acquired three body-builder buddies. Nobody was going to mess with me now, and the days of atomic wedgies in the gym locker room were apparently over for little Jim Lowe, at least for that weekend.

We had two days of practice available, if we needed it; Thursday was the long day of the two on the schedule and included mandatory night practice for all of the participating teams. During the day, we all ran good, fast, and effective laps in the #64 Porsche, with Johannes and Ralf setting times repeatedly near the top of the timesheet and JP doing his usual yeoman's work in a steady fashion. For my part, I ran several laps faster than my personal best of the test earlier in the month, but nobody seemed to notice. All eyes were focused on Saturday.

Midday on Thursday, a fifteen-minute qualifying session was scheduled for the GT field. Early that morning, the four drivers met with strategist Thomas and engineer Sebastien, to go over the plans for qualifying and the racing day lineup. By Grand-Am rules, the driver who qualified the car was also required to start the car on Saturday at the 1:30 p.m. green flag. Typically, given that driver order was not a huge part of strategy in the 24 hour race, the fastest driver would qualify and start the car. By the previous test days' times, it was clear that Johannes was currently topping our personal timesheets in the car, although JP and Ralf were certainly right behind him. When the discussion turned to who would do the qualifying, Thomas and Sebastien first suggested that Johannes get the call. However JP spoke up somewhat abruptly, saying, "I would be honored if I could be the one to qualify and start Jim Lowe's car for this race." I was initially surprised by this, not giving it much thought up until that point, but recognized

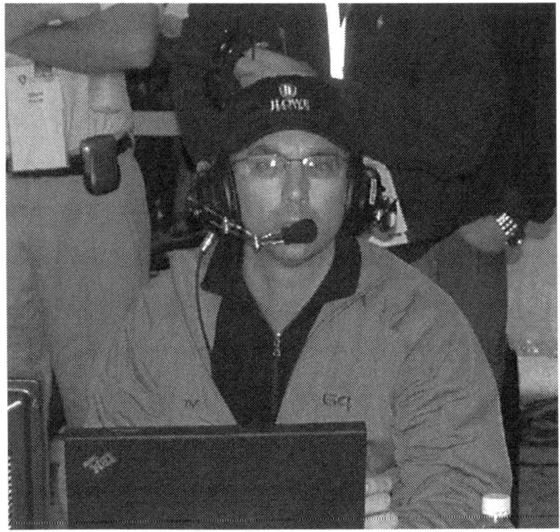

Thomas Blam

the compliment from JP combined with his rather forceful recommendation for strategy. Clearly, JP rightfully felt that this effort was mine, made possible only by his guidance and efforts; he didn't want to leave the opening stint up to chance with the pro drivers and potentially compromise my effort early on. He needn't have worried; Johannes readily agreed to this arrangement, and Sebastien and Thomas had no reservations. Ralf, for his part, remained silent, realizing that he had little say in the matter regardless of his feelings about who should be running the first laps.

That little bit of strategizing out of the way, we spent the rest of the meeting talking about a reasonable lineup for race day, which included Johannes following Jim, then Ralf, and then me. We debated the wisdom of this arrangement, thinking that occasionally teams did better by inserting the less experienced driver earlier so that he got clear laps in daylight conditions. However, this was measured against the risk of there being more cars on the track at a faster pace earlier in the race. Once I reassured them that I felt equally comfortable in the car in daylight and setting sun conditions, it was determined to run me fourth and keep me in the rotation for as long as it seemed reasonable. Although it was unlikely in the circumstances, given my duel role as driver and owner, nobody suggested that I take a seat and watch from the curb.

Jim Pace qualified the car admirably, in a fifteen-minute session including over forty cars in the GT class on the track simultaneously. Jim complained several times that he could not get one single open run through the bus stop or down through Turn 1; I could hear his frustration over the radio as he repeatedly worked at improving his position on the grid. He made his way steadily forward but ran afoul of traffic on his last flying lap, resulting in seventeenth place on the grid for Saturday's start. I knew JP wanted a better position for the start, but we all acknowledged that this was the one race where it was not a huge concern. In fact, our qualifying place was high enough that we did not have to go through a second qualifying session on Friday. The bonus of this was that the crew could spend its time working on final race prep of the car, and the drivers could devote all their time to driver change practice and other non-track activities.

Instead of running unnecessary setup laps for Friday's second qualifying session, we decided to forego that exercise in favor of one simple short installation session, scrubbing tires and bedding a set of brakes to be used late in the race on Sunday morning. Thereafter we handed over the #64 car to the crew to do the necessary work for Saturday's race. Instead of scrapping together parts to repair a damaged car, they did last minute finishing touches and were able to get away from the track early. This was a huge bonus given the fact that they would likely arrive early Saturday morning and spend the next thirty or so hours awake and working hard. For our part, the drivers repeatedly practiced driver changes, until we easily had the time down to less than that required to fill the tank with fuel. That mundane but necessary task behind us, we had the rest of Friday afternoon to basically goof off and find some version of personal relaxation.

For the rest of the afternoon, I welcomed a fairly steady stream of friends and guests as they arrived at the paddock and made their way on behind-the-scene tours through the garage and pit lane area. One highlight, or maybe low-light, was bumping into a camera crew from the Jimmy Kimmel Show. The focus of this particular bit was two wash-outs from the first round of Fox TV's American Idol; these poor guys were dressed in ill-fitting race suits and were being subjected to all sorts of semi-humiliating activities in and around my race car. For my part, I gamely mugged for the cameras and tried not to say anything too particularly stupid in response to their obviously scripted questions. I signed a release, hoping my parents wouldn't stumble upon a later telecast that included their brain surgeon son acting like a bit of a clown. Actually, it was a moment of relaxing fun and a nice way to divert my growing anxiety in anticipation of the completely different clowning around I would be doing the next day.

By Friday night, rather than having easy relaxation, the intensity only seemed to grow, and the vibe, not just in and around the paddock area, but in the town of Daytona Beach itself, seemed to expand. By early evening most of our 150 guests had checked into the hotel, and I spent some, but not all, of my time greeting them and shaking hands. In addition, Ginny had finally made her way from the airport to the hotel, along with several other members of her family. I attended the team dinner, where I found myself the less-than-desired focus of attention and greeted everybody with unscripted remarks.

During my dinner speech, I managed to somehow introduce the key members of the team without too many mispronunciations. I talked about our goals, thanked our sponsors, and reassured everybody present that we were up to the task of getting the car up to the front end of things. A little luck, I assured everybody, and we would be in it to win it. I thought it at least sounded convincing, regardless of my lingering subsurface concerns.

Once dinner was finished, Ginny and my two brothers-in-law, Paul and David Graziani, retired to the hotel restaurant bar with a few other friends. I stopped by momentarily and said my goodnights, entrusting Ginny into the care of her brothers. For my part, I knew that if I did not disengage myself then, I was only going to pay the price when the morning came and it was time to get serious about racing. It was time to get my game face on and get down to the serious business of endurance racing, which certainly included getting some rest the night before.

Chapter Twenty-Five

I bent over and vomited for a second time into the toilet, trying to do so quietly so as not to wake my sleeping wife. I had forced down a nasty concoction of coffee and warm water, brewed by the hotel's malfunctioning single-serve coffee maker that had been collecting dust on the counter top. Desperate for some caffeine, I had made the regrettable decision to drink the ersatz coffee and ten minutes later was paying the price.

I washed my face, rinsed out my mouth, and stared into the mirror at a somewhat bleary eyed guy staring back. In just a few short hours I would don a Nomex race suit, and begin a twenty-four hour adventure racing at Daytona. I was as physically prepared as possible, having devoted months—no, over a year—to getting into the best condition of my life. I had toiled and studied under the watchful eye of Jim Pace and was a veteran of six Grand-Am events up until this point. I was as prepared as any forty-two-year-old brain surgeon possibly could be to go run a professional race—and I was pretty much scared shitless.

Exactly one year prior, I had entered the first Rolex 24 of my new career and had promptly thrown our race right into the dumpster when I wrecked the car in my first ever stint at Daytona. Although we recovered and finished the race, the memory of my mistake had stayed with me somewhere buried, though not too deeply, in my memory. Certainly, it was something I couldn't help but think about each time I strapped myself back into a race car. And today, I was sure, would be no different.

No, actually today was quite different. After spending all the time practicing, getting more comfortable in the race car, and getting more acclimated to the level of competition, the 2007 Rolex 24 at Daytona would be completely different for me and hopefully for my teammates. Instead of running a "happy to be there car" with amateur drivers, we had spent a lot of time putting together a concerted, serious effort. While I had no grand plans of winning the race, I did entertain fantasy thoughts of maybe a Top Ten finish, maybe even higher than that if we got lucky. But most of all, I thought about being competitive. Respected. Or at least taken seriously by other teams and other drivers. In essence, I hoped to be officially joining their club today, driving in a car for a team that was recognized as a real part of the race. In order to do so, I was painfully aware that I had to make sure that my own performance was up to snuff.

Considering all of the above, I promptly hunched over and wretched a third time into the toilet, hoping that that would be the end of that particular bit of nastiness.

I met Jim Pace in the lobby, and off we went to a breakfast at IHOP. The other members of the team were on a slightly different breakfast schedule, so this time it was just JP and me. We chose the IHOP after I refused another breakfast at the Cracker Barrel, noting that I keep wrecking cars when we eat there. For his part, JP could remember two podium finishes after having breakfast at IHOP, so the choice was clear.

JP and I ate rather quietly, chatting about the previous two days' testing, JP offering the usual counsel with regards to approaches to driving the 24.

Jim at Daytona, 2007

"Gas, tires, oil. That's all you need to be worrying about, and that's all we should be doing if we're going to have any chance at doing well in this race."

I had heard this bit of wisdom from JP before, but it was always good to hear it again. I was well aware of the concept of keeping the car in one piece and needing only "routine" service.

"We're gonna keep the car out of the garage and work on our own particular pace. Ralf and Johannes are gonna be working on putting in fast laps, but your job is to be consistent. Start out strong, but don't be trying to set any records. It's a long race, and you just gotta go with it!"

I nodded back at JP. "Right, no hero moves. No passing in the bus stop. I remember. I promise." With that little bit of wisdom digested, along with bacon and eggs, we headed off for the track to meet the rest of the team and prepare for the two days ahead.

JP and I checked into the RV, just a few minutes ahead of Johannes and then Ralf. Everybody at this point was wearing JLowe Racing golf shirts, which looked quite nice with the new red and black logo over the standard issue white shirt. Even Ralf, who was turning out to be the nonconformist, was decked out in the JLowe shirt. While none of us were perhaps bright-eyed and bushy-tailed, everybody looked suitably well rested, although I expect I was the only one puking into a toilet just a few hours prior. Shortly after the drivers arrived, Roger Reis joined us along with Sebastien Constans; Roger carried a notebook and Sebastien a laptop, both containing their particular items that needed to be covered in our little pre-race debrief. Ashlei had arrived early enough to have hot coffee (the good kind) brewing and breakfast snacks for the other two drivers who had their own particular routines to follow.

We spent the next half hour going over several pre-race details, including where we had to be when (drivers meeting, autograph session, and car rollout); Sebastien also discussed the driver order plans for the race. Jim Pace, who had qualified the car, would start, with a single stint being run in order to cycle all the drivers through early in the race. Johannes would go next followed by Ralf, and then it would be my turn. Once we had all had a chance to get warmed up, we'd then run the pros in double-stints, allowing for more rest for each driver between sessions in the car. I wasn't the least bit offended to see that I would be expected to drive only single stints—minimizing the impact if I was running too far off the race pace.

Roger reviewed a few housekeeping items for the car, including the pit entry procedure (loosen belts, unplug water bottle, and make sure the pit lane speed limiter is engaged at the right time). He also reminded us where the reserve fuel tank button was and to keep an eye out for the glowing red light that signified it was time to hit the reserve.

"We think we have the reserve button all functioning normal at this point. When that red light lights up, you have at least one lap to get in. Hit the reserve and call the pits to let us know you're coming. If you're anywhere on the track before the bus stop, you should call the pits and plan on pitting

Jim, JP and Johannes pose with the TRG JLowe Racing Porsche, Daytona, 2007

immediately. From that point you may not have enough fuel in the reserve to get around twice." JP chimed in. "I lost the podium here once when my teammate ran out of the gas on the last lap. It isn't fun, and there's really no excuse for it."

I thought about this and expressed a concern as to whether or not I would be able to judge, in the heat of the battle, whether I could make an extra lap or not. Johannes made it easier than that.

"Just call the pits, and do whatever they say. You're better off not having to think too much, especially when you're just trying to stay in one piece."

I mostly observed through the rest of the meeting, passively absorbing bits and pieces of driver and engineer wisdom, also observing the approach taken by the engineer, the crew chief, and the drivers, when solving little problems that might come up. There was an easy willingness to work together, but everybody had his own perspective. For me, my perspective was that of the student who in reality had little further to contribute. Just keep the car off the guardrail.

Shortly before 9:45, the seven of us made our way over to the pre-race drivers meeting in Victory Lane. I felt a little less self-conscious than last year and actually braved a few waves and handshakes to some of the drivers I had seen more than once in the past year. While I wasn't going to be running for class president, clearly I felt a little more comfortable, seeing some familiar faces and, as before, enjoying spotting several unfamiliar but famous faces. Names like Jeff Gordon, Juan Pablo Montoya, Jimmy Johnson, Helio Castroneves, and Sam Hornish popped up as drivers straggled in. Once things settled down, Richard Petty, the Grand Marshall for the weekend, welcomed the almost 300 hundred drivers and team members, who collectively represented one of the more amazing and unique assemblies of racing talent found in one space at any point during the entire year. As I did the year before, I spent much of the meeting rubber necking, spotting famous faces and enjoying the fact that I was sitting in the middle of such an esteemed group. I was also sitting shoulder to shoulder with some great drivers with whom I would be sharing a car in just a few hours. It was a "pinch me" moment, the first of many I would have that weekend.

Once the drivers meeting was over, we made our way to the mandatory driver autograph session. By this point, I was fully into game day mode and relishing the feelings that came with it. After all, I was a forty-two-year-old neurosurgeon, and the concept of grown adult men experiencing that sensation was completely foreign. Unless you're one of those rare gracefully aging professional athletes, the average forty-something male is long past the time where game day preparation was a reality. Real life intruded—issues of raising children, making a living, and behaving like a grown up

Jim and crew escort the car to the starting grid, Daytona, 2007

took precedence—and none of us were expected to be competing at a high level in anything other than the occasional golf club championship. And here I was, team shirt proudly displayed, joining a few hundred other guys who were all about to go at recklessly dangerous speeds in an attempt to simply drive just a little bit further than the other guy over the next 24 hours. And a lot was at stake: decent prize money, lifelong recognition as an accomplished driver, and entry into a very small and exclusive club. And the winner also took home a brand new Rolex watch. And not just any watch: although you could buy the nearly identical version, only a select few drivers in the world sported Rolex Daytona official cosmographs, engraved on the back with "Winner, 24 Hours of Daytona." In fact, I had purchased one such watch, the unengraved kind, which I wore fifty-one weeks of the year. The other week, at the end of January, I refused to wear it out of principle.

I thoroughly enjoyed the autograph session, with what appeared to be a sizable increase in attendance this year. Part of that increase might have simply been the crowd connected to JLowe Racing and the #64 TRG Porsche. We had a sizable number of guests, along with several repeat visitors; several members of my family, a couple of my employees, and more than a few friends made their way by our table to say hello and grab a hero card. I chuckled to myself as I used a Sharpie to sign my name on the cards, thinking that I would have to remember the following week not to add "64" under my signature on medical charts.

Following the drivers meeting, we had a few other necessary housekeeping items to complete before race time. A quick lunch of tomatoes and cheese was followed by the official TRG paddock photo. Four drivers from the #64 car rolled out in our brand new silver, blue, and white suits, sporting the "JLowe Racing" logo prominently along with the well-recognized TRG logo. Four other Porsches were parked next to the #64 car, and 20 blue-suited drivers and approximately 100 TRG staffers showed up for the photo opportunity. It was evident that Kevin Buckler's operation was quite a large scale and successful model and certainly much more intimidating and impressive than the seven people I had assembled in order to run our race that particular weekend. But I stood next to the car along with the other drivers and tried to appear as professional-looking as possible while inside I thrilled to the sensation of being a part—even a small part—of such a big deal.

The sensation continued to build, as we proceeded then to do one of my favorite non-driving moments of the weekend. The drivers and crew surrounded the #64 car and pushed the car out onto the grid, posing briefly for the official 2007 Rolex 24 picture. Once we pushed the car into position among the other GT cars, we had approximately twenty to thirty minutes before race start to relax—sort of. At that point, the grid was flooded with fans, and I spent most of the time saying hello to our guests, getting introduced to new faces, and posing for photos with various combinations of drivers and other crew members. I scanned the crowd repeatedly and realized there was no sign of my wife. In all the hubbub of the morning, I hadn't had a chance to speak with her, wanting not to interrupt a hopefully relaxing morning prior to what would surely be a very busy weekend for her also.

I noticed that there were large numbers of fans walking through the infield grass and out onto the banking of the tri-oval; as I watched them attempt to climb up the steep bank surface, I realized that despite all of the laps that I had run at Daytona thus far, I had never actually set foot on its surface. I then considered that this was probably a good thing, given that most drivers' only opportunity to walk on the track would be immediately after disengaging themselves from a wrecked car.

As I mulled all this over, horns sounded, and Daytona security guards started the task of clearing the track for the race start. Peopled seemed to scatter left and right, and I did my best to make my way towards the TRG pit area. On the way, I ran into quite a few of my fellow drivers taking similar routes to their pits; we generally exchanged half-hearted well wishes, since it would take too much time to say something like "I hope you run great and I hope I beat you!"

Arriving at the TRG tent, I made my way over toward the wall, trying to grab an ideal post from which to view the start of the race. The area was quite crowded with all the aforementioned JLowe guests, multiplied four-fold by the presence of the other TRG guests. For my part, I staked out a spot right in front of our pit cart, where I could have a good view of the track at the start/finish and also an easy view of the monitors running the official Grand-Am timing and scoring. As I settled into my position, and the grid continued to clear, I exchanged hellos with a few additional guests. Kevin Buckler made it a point of coming by for one last handshake and a sincere "good luck to you guys." For my part, I spent the last few minutes before the start enjoying the national anthem and the subsequent choreographed fly-over, all while trying to drink continuously in order to stay hydrated in the hot suit.

A moment before the "Gentlemen, start your engines" was called out over the Daytona sound system, I felt an arm around my waist. I jumped just a little bit, and looked down to see Ginny sneak in to the small space left beside me. I smiled at the perfectly timed gift of my wife arriving just at the moment when the cars were rolling off the grid for the race. A hug and kiss later she reassured me that she was in good shape for the race, despite having celebrated heartily with her brother and a few of our friends late into the night.

Ginny securely at my elbow, I clapped, hooted, and hollered as the first cars came around to take the green flag. Alex Gurney, in the Gainsco Daytona Prototype rolled by, guarded closely by Max Angelelli in the SunTrust machine. As I cheered alongside everybody else, I felt the vibration of the accelerating machines deep in my chest. When the GT pack swarmed by, led by the Synergy Racing Porsche driven by Patrick Huisman, I looked over and checked on Ginny. At least this time she wasn't crying. The #81 Synergy Porsche made its way down to the first turn, chased by the Tafel Racing Porsche of Wolf Henzler; 40 other GT cars made their way down into Turn 1 without any cars getting banged up prior to completing turn one of the first lap.

I felt Ginny's arm tighten around my waist as the stream of cars went by, with the white and red-striped #64 car making it down into the breaking point of the turn without any drama. I watched anxiously over the next two minutes, waiting for the cars to reappear. Shortly thereafter, Jim Pace came flying by in fifteenth place after one lap, to the cheers of our assembled guests. I started jumping up and down a little bit, cheering as Jim went by, until Thomas Blam tapped me on the shoulder.

Suitably warned, I ceased my jumping and clapping and obediently allowed Ginny to steer me to a chair in the pits where I could see most of the action while off my feet.

I settled in to watch the first exciting laps of the race, during which the cars would be running closer than any point up until the last hour or so on Sunday. Despite the repeated admonitions of Mark Raffauf in the drivers meeting, lots of drivers were still making questionable decisions in the first few minutes of the twenty-four hour race. This led to some close racing, and it also ultimately led to one of the more unfortunate yet exciting moments of drama early in the race.

Pit stop, 24 hours of Daytona, 2007

Good friend Michael Auriemma (he who loaned me his Porsche to practice my shifting before my first Rolex 24) was driving the #42 Team Sahlen Porsche GT3 at the start of the race. This was Michael's first Rolex 24 event, although he did have experience driving previous Grand-Am events, and was known by those of us in the Skip Barber ranks to be an accomplished and careful driver. Unfortunately, Michael's good name was besmirched in an instant, when, while rounding NASCAR Turn 4 on the oval, the bonnet clasps of his hood suddenly broke loose. Unfortunately for Michael, this resulted in the lights being turned out without warning, as the hood flew up and completely blocked his windscreen view. Quite predictably, Michael slowed and made a heroic effort to try and maintain his initial line of travel. However, in the instant of transitioning from a clear track to completely blind driving, Michael's car suffered a very understandable wiggle. More unfortunately, this occurred just as Alex Gurney, whose prototype was still leading the race seven laps in, was on his way by Michael. Most unfortunately, Gurney's Daytona Prototype was sideswiped by Michael's car, in full view of 50,000 spectators overlooking the front straight. Gurney's injured car was able to continue down the track, pitting three or four minutes later for repairs; Michael for his part made YouTube history as he carefully guided the Porsche, completely blindly, off the track across the infield grass and to his pit stall, solely on the directions of his engineer. Later, post-race write-ups would criticize Michael for driving a "wayward Porsche" and causing the accident with Gurney; all of us who were watching, including

I suspect every driver not actually wearing a Gainsco suit, felt sympathetic for the plight of the rookie driver in that situation.

The rest of Jim Pace's first stint behind the wheel was uneventful, as he steadily climbed northward in the standings. The call came for a driver change just over one hour into the race, and Johannes switched placed with JP without incident.

As Johannes pulled away, amidst the cheers and clapping of the JLowe fans in the TRG pit, Jim Pace pulled off his helmet and found me in the back of the tent.

"There's a lot of questionable driving going on out there," warned JP. "When you get out there, you gotta pay attention and expect the unexpected. I could have wrecked two or three times if I wasn't on my toes. You especially have to watch out for those knuckleheads in the red Ferrari."

I listened intently as JP described a few issues with the car handling, none of which sounded scary. JP then seemed to realize that I was standing there in the pits, and reminded me of the need to rest up a bit and try and relax before I got out there.

"You should be off your feet, Dr. Lowe. Try not to use up all your energy before you even get in the car. It's a long race."

JP, Jim and Ralf debrief during the race, Daytona, 2007

With that, JP was off to the RV for a massage and some nutrition, while I resumed my spot, sitting in the back of the tent. I respected the need to try and relax a little bit, but there is no way I would miss the initial excitement of getting to watch, up close and personal, a terrific race.

Johannes had a great run in the next hour, gradually and consistently moving the #64 car up further in the field. The radio stayed mainly silent, with the exception of the occasional call from Johannes to report details of the handling of the car. I listened carefully and was pleased to hear that most of Johannes' comments about the car handling were positive. He did report, on occasion, about questionable driving of other GT cars (and occasional Prototypes also); more than once a warning about the red Ferrari came over the radio.

Ralf was up next and appeared five to ten minutes before the appointed time, geared up and ready to go. The crew executed another flawless pit stop, exchanging Ralf for Johannes. As Ralf pulled away, I realized that that was in essence the signal for me to start getting my act together.

The tent was still crowded with bodies moving about, some of them purposefully, so I moved over into a corner of the tent, where I managed to stake out a little bit of room to begin stretching. With my back to the action, I went through my pre-driving stretching routine, carefully working from the ground up, paying special attention to my problem areas (Achilles and hips). Ginny appeared nearby and waited expectantly alongside my gear, one eye on the monitors, to determine when I might be needed. At that point, I was really not paying attention to anything other than listening for a call for the unexpected yellow flag. I simply needed to check my watch and wait for the nearly one-hour stint to be over and for the call to action.

As that time got closer, the periphery of my vision got fuzzier and fuzzier, and I managed to block out all of the extraneous activity around me. I had but one focus at that point—getting into the car without delay and without misstep—and all of my efforts were geared towards that and only that. I assumed a place next to my gear and waited for the sign from Thomas Blam. Seemingly seconds later, Thomas turned from his perch on the pit box and gave me the ten-finger 10-minute sign. I geared up in a deliberate fashion, making sure not to dislodge any of the various wires and connections hanging from my helmet. With a little help from Ginny, moments later I was outfitted with helmet, HANS device, and gloves, suit properly zipped and earplugs plugged in. I then assumed a position on the side of the pit box, approximately two feet from the knee-high concrete wall separating the pit lane from the pit itself. I stood as still as possible, alternating between closing my eyes and breathing deeply, and focused on a distant part of the stands. As I went through this routine, I could feel my heart rate slow and a sense of relaxation and confidence arrive. I had spent a year preparing for this moment— waiting for the opportunity at redemption, the opportunity for success, the opportunity to compete once again. And my time arrived momentarily, at the 45 mph pit lane speed limit.

Ralf pulled into the pit box expertly hitting the marks, leaving enough room on the left side of the car for the mechanics to change tires. The door was opened, Ralf's lines were unclipped, and he exited the car just as I was moving from the back of the car towards the driver's seat. I slipped in right behind Ralf, just like we had practiced; I fell into the seat, reached for my buckles, and managed to get everything connected quickly. I cinched the seat forward so that the buckles were tight and confirmed that this time I actually was able to reach all the knobs and buttons along with the steering wheel and shifter.

"Radio check, radio check," I called. I remembered to release the red button this time.

"We got you loud and clear Jim. Remember, start out nice and easy, get the tires warmed up, and keep your eye out for traffic. Ralf says it's still pretty busy out there."

Before I could get out a "copy that," a second call came in my ears. "GO, GO, GO, GO, GO!!!"

I looked up to see Roger furiously spinning his finger encouraging me to get moving. I dropped the clutch as I simultaneously hit the gas, laying a nice long set of black streaks out of the pit box onto pit lane. I remembered to keep the pit lane speed limiter engaged until I passed the green cones at the end of pit out. This slow exit speed gave me several seconds to look around, check my mirrors, and get my eyes oriented to the track and the cars around me. Seconds later I crossed the acceleration line at pit out, disengaged the pit lane limiter, and sped up into second gear. I shifted up once and back down once, in order to negotiate the tight pit exit left-hander (where I had seen, and would see, many a driver crumple up the nose of their cars in the slippery conditions). As I accelerated out of the pit exit down to Turn 3, I was thinking only about what might be coming in my right-side mirror. I kept wide on the entry and carefully accelerated, trying not to spin out on the first corner of my first lap.

Several corners later, I was back out onto the banking at Daytona, thrilled to be back up to speed, and simultaneously hypervigilant about the cars around me. I kept to the low side of the banked surface, in a steady line of GT cars, and made sure to leave plenty of room for the Daytona Prototypes passing on the high side at their much faster speed. Making my way down to the bus stop, I braked early just in case the brakes were not yet up to full temp. I easily made my way through the four-turn complex and headed back out for my first trip past start/finish on the front straight. The engine was pulling beautifully and the sensation of speed and power and thrust from the rear end of the car was awesome. The noise was pretty substantial too, including the intensified sounds that occurred whenever a car was nearby.

I plowed on through Turn 1 uneventfully and proceeded dutifully through the six infield turns and back out onto the banking. I started to get myself into a rhythm, remembering Jim Pace's advice: each time I went down to the bus stop, Turn one, and the various points in the infield, I tried to brake just a little bit later, without getting beyond myself.

I soon found that there were several GT cars scattered around the track that were well off the pace. I managed to negotiate clean passes most of the time, usually attempting to do so on the straightaway sections of the track. This was relatively easy to do as long as I was able to get a good run out of the exit of the prior turn. With the superior horsepower of the Porsche, and the great jumps that I was getting out of the apex from the prior turn, I found it possible to pass several GT cars (and even a struggling Daytona Prototype) early on the straightaway sections. I kept myself off the radio, not wanting any additional distractions, as the field of view in front of me was offering plenty to keep me occupied.

What seemed like only moments later Thomas came on the radio.

"Hey Jim, what's happening out there?"

I hit the red button on the steering wheel. "Everything's going fine. No worries. A little busy right now."

I could hear several of the crew chuckle on the radio as Thomas replied.

"Well just keep on going then. Your lap times are coming down progressively in case you haven't noticed. You're down to pretty consistent 1:57s, and we think you just set a personal best lap time a few laps back."

#64 on the banking, Daytona, 2007

I wasn't feeling particularly chatty but I couldn't resist. "Well I'm just gonna have to keep trying to get better than that, right?" The answer came immediately from several sources that all sounded alarmed. "No, no, no, no!—you're doing just fine! No need to push it!"

"Copy that." With that the radio fell silent and I got back to the business of driving.

A short time later, just as I was lining up a Corvette for an infield pass under braking for Turn 6, I got another call from Thomas. "Hey Jim are you seeing the red light yet?"

I looked down, and sheepishly realized that the red fuel light was in fact lit up. "Uh, yeah, there's a red light on. Sorry I didn't call it in."

"Pit now, pit now, pit now." Thomas also remembered to calmly remind me, "and don't forget to hit the reserve button when she stumbles."

Just as I was accelerating to pass the Corvette I felt the Porsche's 3.6L engine stutter as the last bits of gas in the primary tank drained dry. Since I was in the middle of a corner, I perhaps wasn't paying close enough attention and nearly hit the fire bottle button, conveniently located right next to the reserve tank button. Thankfully, the fire bottle button was covered in plastic, and I could feel the flat surface on my fingers just well enough to realize I was heading for disaster. I glanced down quickly, reoriented myself, and managed to engage the reserve tank button without filling the cockpit with fire extinguisher foam.

A few seconds later I was braking for the pit lane entrance, trying to get down to the required 45 mph speed limit at the entry cone. From there on I hit the pit limiter button, taking my time loosening belts and disconnecting the hoses on my way into the pit box. I managed to hit the crew's marks perfectly, and before I knew it, the door was opened, the net was yanked down, and I was being pulled rather forcefully out of the car. I got my footing and jumped out of the way over the wall, just in time for Jim Pace to sneak by me. As he did, he gave me a pat on the shoulder and then hopped into the still-running Porsche.

A sweaty moment, minutes after getting out of the car

I hadn't had any sensation of fatigue or physical discomfort at all during my driving stint; however as I pulled my helmet off, that familiar flush and rise of heat once again took over. As I stumbled past a couple of patrons applauding for the crew as they finished their pit stop, Ginny was standing ready with a cold drink, a wet washcloth, and a chair. I plopped down into the chair, and covered the steam rising from my head with a wet washcloth. Leaning back, I felt an incredible sense of pleasant fatigue, combined with that drained feeling of a great work out completed. A huge sense of satisfaction came over me, as both Thomas and Roger made their way back to my chair. Both were smiling broadly, as Thomas informed me that I actually made up a few spots during my run. "Nice job Jim, all nice and shiny and in good shape for JP's second stint. Just like the doctor ordered."

At that point, I was flushed enough to simply offer up a smile and a shrug, in between gulps of water being fed to me by my ever watchful wife.

"Now's a good time to go get some rest. Make sure you get a massage and be back here in about three hours to do it all over again. Just like you did just now."

With that, Roger and Thomas returned to the pit box, exchanging seats with Sebastien, who made his way to me. Sebastien knelt down by the chair, laptop balanced on his knees (which were nearly at eye level considering his six foot eight frame), and reviewed the car handling issues with me. We discussed whether or not the car was loose in the corner, whether or not there was any under-steer, and what I thought about tire degradation. I told him what I could about the car and noted in summary that I overall felt the car was very drivable, especially for my particular style (that is, slower and more conservative than the pros). Sebastien made a few notes in French on his laptop and returned to his station on the pit box to confer with Thomas.

My duties immediately post-stint were quickly over and I was free to return to the RV for some R&R. With Ginny carrying my helmet, and a fresh wet rag draped around my neck, I made my way down the lane behind the tented pit boxes and through the fan zone toward the driver/owner lot. On the way, I spotted several other drivers in various stages of finishing, or preparing for, their own stints. There was time for brief hellos to one or two of the Skip Barber alumni, including Mark Patterson whose Daytona Prototype was running near the front end of the field at that point.

Ginny dropped me off at the motor home and made her way with Ashlei back to the hotel so she could actually get some rest. She was, of course, relieved that I was intact and unharmed and even more relieved that there was no psychological drama to confront such as occurred just one year prior. I kissed Gin goodbye, and she promised to be back in time for my next stint.

After a snack and a nearly hour-long massage, I drifted off face down on the massage table, relaxed and comfortable, and without any distress to consider. I was looking forward only to my next stint and another go behind the wheel of a Porsche.

After something resembling a nap, I reassembled my still somewhat soggy uniform and gathered my gear together prior to leaving for the pits. Walking over to the "lights on" RV where I would pick up a golf cart for my trip to the pits, I again made note of the constant droning noise in the background. I remembered the sensation from 2006, when at times, especially in the middle of the night, it felt as if it wouldn't ever go away. I had entered the middle stretches of a very long race, during which the usual measurements of time no longer seemed to function well. Instead, time was measured by whether or not I had time to eat, sleep, and/or relax just a few more minutes before heading for the pits. Then, once in the car, time accelerated in some warp-speed fashion, as my entire world focus transitioned to the area contained in the car's windshield.

I noted that there was a bit of a chill in the air now and could tell, even with the darkening skies, that clouds had rolled in. They had forecast the likelihood of rain at some point during the night, but none had shown up yet, thankfully. I checked in at the pits and settled down in my assigned seat, waiting for the call. While I sat there, I checked monitors, which included not only the Grand-Am timing and scoring feed but also the Speed Channel TV feed. There, I saw repeated highlights of the race thus far, including the usual "thrills and spills" segments. These now included the #22 Porsche driven by Mark Bassing spinning off into the Turn 1 tire wall; it was able to restart and proceed, but the wreck actually looked pretty substantial from the vantage point of a TV cameraman. Other various offending drivers were shown in their full glory, as car after car seemed to make hard to understand mistakes, typically ruining the team's races in the process. In the meantime, I noticed the #64 car climbing steadily up on the timing charts, now planted at approximately eighth place in the GT class.

Thomas roused me from my thousand yard stare by coming into my field of vision and tapping me on the shoulder. "Ten minutes to go; Ralf will be in in just a few laps."

"Sounds good. I'm ready. Is he saying anything about the car?"

Thomas shook his head and smiled. "He's been quiet the whole time and just ran the fastest GT lap of the race. I'm guessing everything's doing just fine." With that Thomas smiled, patted me on the shoulder, and returned to the pit stand.

I gathered my gear, got everything in place, and double checked my helmet connections to make sure the radio was attached and the drink hose positioned properly. I assumed the "next driver in" position on the wall and watched as Ralf came steaming into the pits. I was amazed at the condition of the car at this point, noting that my beautiful Porsche, previously a pristine white and red, was now speckled with black pieces of rubber and other grit, along with exhibiting a pockmarked nose. I could spot a dent here, a crack in the body work there, and overall, the thing was starting to

The #64 TRG JLowe Racing Porsche, nighttime at Daytona 2007

look a bit worn out.

As I jumped into the seat, I immediately noted that the temperature within the car was now quite high in comparison to the ambient air outside; the seat itself was also starting to feel suspiciously wet. I fumbled for the belts, clicked in, and waited patiently as Roger made the appropriate connections and slammed the door shut. I called out the radio check, and got the signal to go from the front tire man. Accelerating out onto pit lane, I was back in the race.

Whereas only moments before I was still exhibiting those fuzzy-around-the-edges sensations from my recent nap, now I was fully amped, alert, and on edge. Prototypes and GT cars whizzed by me on my inside as I rejoined the race. Nobody stopped to acknowledge the fact that I was once again part of the ongoing contest. With the jarring sensation of getting "switched on" so abruptly after being relatively sedated moments before, it was overwhelmingly obvious that the race had been going forward, with blatant indifference to my participation. Whether I joined in or not, it was going to continue right on up to its conclusion Sunday afternoon. If I wanted to be any part of the great history of 24 Hours of Daytona, I needed to get back on my horse, and quickly. I put my right foot down, looked up through the turn, and tried to breathe the throttle as little as possible right before entering the kink.

I drove lap after lap in a steady fashion, searching out the bright white colored headlights in my rearview mirror, signifying an approaching Prototype; I was less concerned about the yellow tinted headlights of the GT cars, although there were several of those that seemed to be gaining slightly on me. I focused on my line, my brake points, and watched my lap times on the dash settle into a fairly consistent repeating rhythm. I drove on, occasionally executing passes on wayward Porsches and other GT cars, until I fell in line in a group that was clearly being held up by a red Ferrari. Groaning inwardly, I knew that this was going to be somewhat problematic as I watched the two or three GT drivers in front of me struggle to get around the Italian car. Whereas the Prototype racers had little trouble negotiating this straggler, because of their significant speed differential and ability to get out of the corners quicker, the GT cars one by one had to exercise great care in trying to get around this obviously inexperienced driver. While most drivers of any level of experience in the professional ranks knew to drive a typical "line" around Daytona, this driver did not seem to recognize any reasonable standard of where to put his car on the track in any given turn. As such, he was the most threatening type of driver in the eyes of my fellow participants: one who acted in an unpredictable fashion.

When it came my turn behind the red Ferrari, I certainly did my best to at least guess where he was going to go next. As we made our way, nose to tail, through the various turns of the infield, it was quite obvious that attempting to pass this driver under braking was a rather foolish thought, given his propensity to "slam the door" and move down towards the apex in an unexpected fashion. Whereas the typically experienced driver would know he was being passed as soon as a car appeared alongside, and just as typically intelligently give way to that faster driver, this driver seemed to have no knowledge of that concept. Time after time I stuck my nose to the left or to the right to make sure he knew I was there; each time, he responded by either moving directly in front of me or making no acknowledgement of my presence as he drifted from side to side himself.

I called in to Thomas on the radio to complain. "There's a crazy guy out here in a red Ferrari. Somebody ought to be calling Grand-Am to get this guy out of here. He's a danger."

Thomas clicked in a second later. "Yeah, we've been hearing complaints about him all night. Just remember you're currently running in P7 and he's in P25."

"Yeah well, I'm getting a little frustrated back here."

Thomas consoled me. "Just back off and get a run on him through the banking. Just watch out for Prototypes behind you when you pull out."

I heeded Thomas' advice, and the next time through Turn 6 before we got out onto the banking, I saw my opportunity. The Ferrari was well wide of the apex and drifting wide on the turn exit; I lagged back just a little bit and then went to power early. I snuck down on the inside of the Ferrari, ready to make my way onto the lowest lane of Daytona's steep banking. Just as I did, the Ferrari turned down, almost as if he wanted to make one last ditch effort at keeping me behind him. Just as I pushed hard down on the throttle, I felt the Ferrari bang its nose off my right rear bumper. At impact, my sturdy Porsche shuddered a tiny bit, a stallion annoyed by the rider's spurs. Although the thud was loud, I suspected that the impact was relatively minor, feeling nothing unusual in the grip and sensation of the car as I accelerated up onto the banking. I went up through the gears, leaving the Ferrari headlights growing smaller in my rearview mirror and finally stretched my legs. The car felt fine, with no scary noises coming from the rear end. I accelerated onto the back straight at something approaching 160 mph, and shortly thereafter braked hard for the bus stop without any unusual response from my Porsche. I flew on through the bus stop and back out onto the steep Daytona banking, relieved to have escaped the Ferrari clash apparently unscathed.

Once I was sure the car was unhurt, I called Thomas to alert him that I had been involved in a little bit of argy-bargy. I asked him to take a look at the car as I came down the front straight and make sure that nothing unusual was happening. He gave me the all clear as I went by the pit box area, and I once again started a new lap.

I completed the rest of my second stint without any further drama and, thankfully, never stumbled across the red Ferrari again. I dropped the car off dutifully back at the pit box, hitting the extended "TRG 64" marker with the nose of the car, and leaving enough space on the left side of the car so that the tire changers could work between the wall and the car itself. I hopped out after all my various wires and hoses were disconnected, making way for JP once again.

Stumbling over the wall, I was surprised to find that the pits were still crowded with fans, mechanics, and other team members, despite the fact that it was nearly midnight. The lights were on under the tent, the monitors were showing the Speed Channel feed and the Grand-Am timing and scoring run down, and the appearance of everybody was anything but subdued. I checked out the back flap of the tent and saw golf carts going both ways down Daytona's narrow pit road behind the pit boxes, taking drivers to and from their appointed rounds in between driving stints and transporting fresh sets of tires; various journalists and photographers were running about while appearing purposeful. After the controlled environment of the cockpit, the view immediately in and around the pit area was one of semi-organized chaos.

I got rid of my helmet and balaclava, slapped a wet towel around the back of my neck, and reached down into the ice chest for a fresh bottle of water. I was still breathing relatively heavily, but I had no discomfort, no nausea, and only a refreshing sense of having had a good hard work out. I stuffed my wet driving gloves inside my helmet, grabbed it by the strap, and made my way down pit lane heading towards the RV park. Before I left the pits, however, I did stop and check the Grand-Am timing and scoring board. We were in P7 and only one lap off the lead lap from the GT front runner. I shook my head and smiled, and then waved to both Roger and Thomas before I left the pits.

Back in the RV, Ashlei had laid out a great late-night snack of tomatoes and mozzarella with fresh basil. I shucked out of my wet suit, hung it on a hanger in the back of the RV, and sat in my Nomex underwear while I ate dinner and drank a second bottle of water. There were fewer bodies moving about the RV at this point, but there was still a fair amount of activity. Fortunately we had the foresight to have a second RV so I would be able to get a massage and some rest, now that we were well into the depth of the nighttime running.

After eating, I slipped into a clean sweatshirt and sweatpants and made my way over to the "quiet" RV. The air was crisp and somewhat chilly, and I had that sharp cold sensation around my still damp hair that contrasted with my warm, well-fed core. As I walked between the two RVs, I paused for a moment, acknowledging again the constant and incessant repeated sounds of the race still going on somewhere beyond the fence line. Cars came into the hairpin on full throttle, and I could hear the different engine notes as the drivers lifted off the throttle and decelerated as they went down through the gears for the turn. You could tell the moment when the car was at its minimal speed, and you could tell which drivers were actually coasting a little bit and which were quick to get back on the throttle. As the cars accelerated again, the noise reached a crescendo as they moved on toward the full throttle kink. Over and over again, sometimes with different engine sounds overlapping other ones, the cars moved through in a constant symphony of varied notes of both descending and ascending volume. Like good jazz, to the untrained ear it was a confusing cacophony of seemingly unrelated noise; to a driver, the individual sounds all meant something and could be related to specific parts of the racing experience. I smiled as I listened for just a moment more, and then made my way over to the darkened RV.

Kathy Dandurand was already set up and waiting for me. Hopping onto the massage table, I enjoyed forty-five minutes of Kathy's expert hands finding every knotted and sore muscle and working out every kink as I tried my best to relax. The TV at the front end of the RV was visible, although the volume was down so as not to disturb anyone. I watched as the Speed Channel feed continued off-air, noting various thrills and spills as they continued through the session. I variably watched and dozed a little bit, as Kathy finished her task. Once she was done I made my way to the darkened bedroom in the back of the RV and flopped down onto the bed. Ginny had long since returned to the hotel to get some actual sleep, so I had the bed to myself. Sprawled out comfortably in the dark, I took note of the unrelenting noise of the race outside of the RV one last time before I fell asleep.

I woke up with a start, initially disoriented, and then fully realizing that something was completely wrong. In the darkened back room of the RV, I had no understanding of what time it was, but I was aware of one fact: it was quiet. Completely quiet. The sounds of the race were gone—completely absent, as if I had woken up in some sort of sensory deprivation chamber. Looking around somewhat frantically as I sat up, my first thought was "son of a bitch! Those guys finished the race without me." I couldn't believe that they would let me just continue sleeping through the rest of the race, and go on without me. The thought that immediately followed that one was "well, who could blame them? They had a shot at winning this thing as long as I kept sleeping."

Within the next few seconds however, my head cleared enough to realize that it was still dark out. I opened the door to the RV and found Kathy

Dandurand and Ashlei sitting in the front chatting quietly. Ashlei greeted me first.

"Well hello Sleeping Beauty. Are you ready for your next stint?"

I was scheduled to get up somewhere around two a.m. to make my way to the pits for my next driving session.

"I think I'm ready, but what the hell is going on out there? It's way too quiet for a race to be going on."

Ashlei and Kathy laughed.

"There was a red flag just about an hour ago. Apparently a GT driver hit the guardrail and it had to be repaired and they parked everybody. They're still waiting to restart this thing."

"Huh. What should I do? Do they want me over at the pits?"

"JP stopped in just a little while ago and said that Thomas wants you there sometime shortly after they restart the race. You'll be next after Johannes is done."

I stepped into my flip flops and made my way out into the cool, incredibly quiet night. There was a surreal absence of noise; unlike being in the woods where one could hear crickets and various nocturnal animals moving around, this was spooky calm and seemingly void of all sound. Finally, in the distance a golf cart started up, and it felt like the seal was broken. Once again I could hear a few sounds coming from the paddock and was comforted that I hadn't stepped into some form of alternate universe.

After dressing back in my racing togs, I grabbed a golf cart and made my way back to pit lane. I presented myself to Thomas, who was still amazingly awake and vigilant on the pit box despite the fact that he drank no caffeinated beverages whatsoever. As I approached, Thomas held up one hand in my direction, fingers spread wide apart. I stopped dead in my tracks, recognizing the "Halt!" sign, and simultaneously wondering where exactly I had transgressed to get the wave-off. I raised a questioning eyebrow in Thomas' direction, at which point he fortunately recognized my confusion.

"No, I didn't mean stay away, I meant we're in P5—Johannes is in fifth place—and running strong, even with the rain earlier."

I hadn't even noticed the wet surface as I walked into the tent; much of the pit lane was already drying, but clearly there were signs of a pretty good downpour earlier.

"He must have had a good run in the wet, huh?

"Yeah, considering the wiper stopped working right after it started coming down really hard, it was pretty miraculous. He had one brief off in the grass when he couldn't see but was able to continue, right on pace. Guy's amazing, really."

I nodded in agreement, silently thankful again that the racing gods had seen fit to keep the wet stuff from happening during my time in the car. Another good omen, I thought.

Up to speed with Thomas' situation report, awake, and suitably impressed with the need to get my act together in a strong fashion for my next turn in the Porsche, I assumed the ready position in a chair against the back wall and waited for the call to action.

Chapter Twenty-Six

The call came somewhere between three and four o'clock in the morning, when Thomas made his now-familiar trip down from atop the pit box and headed in my direction. Halfway there, he gestured toward me demonstrating putting on an imaginary helmet and gloves. With that he detoured left and out of the pit box, presumably heading for the men's room. I found myself surprised that my superhuman race strategist actually did need to occasionally answer the call of nature.

Donning helmet and gloves, I made sure that my radio connection was taped firmly to the helmet and checked all the attachments of the Hans device compulsively. Roger wandered back at that point and leaned close to my helmet with a few last minute words of wisdom.

"I just talked to Johannes. He says the car feels great, but the throttle has been sticking occasionally, so watch out for that. If it happens, try downshifting but be aware that it's been a little bit of an issue in the last couple of hours. Also, Johannes says that the track is getting a little bit slippery in the bus stop, so keep heads up out there."

I nodded my understanding, not bothering to ask any more questions. Roger was a no-nonsense guy, and didn't need to be bothered with questions about foolish things that neurosurgeons worry about in the middle of the night. Before turning away, Roger paused a moment as he listened into his headset, and then tapped me on the side of the helmet. "One lap, and he'll be in. Be ready."

On cue, my throat tightened and my heart rate picked up, and I once again felt the harshness of anticipation somewhere deep in the pit of my stomach. We were running strong, we were running near the front, and this was no time for mistakes. It was time to again get up off the sidelines and into the thick of it. And I was completely aware that nobody really cared whether the guy behind the wheel was an anxious spine surgeon or seasoned veteran racer. Nope—here I was in the middle of The Real Deal. And my job was to run hard until Thomas called me in and, above all else, bring the car back in one piece.

Speaking of one piece, I was quite amazed when Johannes finally pulled up in the Porsche. It was really starting to look like a pile of shit. Half of the front splitter was broken off and the nose was sandblasted, even more so than the last time I had seen her. The beautiful pearl white paintjob was starting to look downright tawdry, and when I got in the car, well frankly, she really was starting to smell a bit too.

I managed to get myself strapped in for what I realized would be my last stint at Daytona. There was no way I would let it be a regrettable one—not now, when my teammates needed me to step up. Pushing evil thoughts of wrecking out of my mind, I refocused on the task at hand and settled in behind the wheel. All of my senses came up to full function, full alert, and full power. I became hyper-aware of my surroundings as I accelerated on down pit lane, passed the last Grand-Am marshal, and disengaged the pit lane speed limiter button. The Porsche surged under my over-excited right foot and skidded sideways a little as I headed down the narrowing pit lane. I avoided adding more damage to the nose of the Porsche when I remembered to slow for the sharp left-hander in the middle of the pit lane exit road, and tiptoed my way safely around the still-damp surface and back out onto the track. Once on track, I was amazed by the distortion of the lights—from overhead and from the cars themselves—that created a surreal landscape. It was like landing on some oddly lit planet, and nobody had bothered to tell these guys that it was still dark in the real world. Prototypes whizzed by as my vision accommodated to the new view, and two different GT cars managed to overtake me while I waited for my tires to warm up. I slotted in behind the GT cars coming out of Turn three, moved aside once at Turn 5 for another fast-moving DP and, just like that, was back in the race.

I drove on for the next forty minutes, managing to keep pace with almost every GT car out there, suffering only one or two further passes by GT cars. By now, I was basically ignoring the Prototypes circling about in the midst of their own race. I saw no red Ferrari, or any other dangerous looking characters, and kept looking as far forward as I could, while keeping to myself. Like Bobby Jones worrying only about beating par, and not his opponents, I focused only on the next turn, the next straightaway, the next braking point. I wasn't interested in passing or being passed, nor did I particularly care. My job was to bring this thing back to the pits in one piece so that the fast guys could take over and do what they were brought here to do. And I managed to do that.

When I saw the two GT cars crumpled into the tire wall outside of the bus stop, I knew the call from Thomas was coming. I had already backed out of the throttle when the radio clicked in my ears.

"Full course yellow. Pit now, pit now."

"Copy that, pitting now."

I had a few seconds of relaxation just then, realizing that this would be my last up-close look at Daytona's high-banked turns. No matter where I was racing, I had always tried to savor my last lap, and this was no different. As I regrettably slowed for the pits and did the loosen-the-belts sequence, I took in the view of the mighty track before me. Big, bright, awesome. Despite the sleep-deprivation and stress, there was only excitement and the electric taste of adrenaline in my mouth. I breathed deeply and tried to hold onto the image as I made my way down pit lane for the last time.

I came to a stop with the nose of the Porsche centered right on the dangling #64 sign. Hopping out, with only a moderate amount of assistance from Roger, I slapped JP on the rump as he jumped into the car. I then half-rolled, half-jumped over the wall, and was surprised when I looked up to see that our tent was nearly full with spectators. Despite the fact that it was not yet dawn, the crowd in the TRG tent area had grown appreciably.

Shucking out of my helmet, gloves, and the top half of my race suit, I toweled off as I gave a quick rundown of the car handling issues to Thomas and Roger and gave a short quote to the TRG press agent. Ginny was nearby, as were several of my friends from work, and even my partner, Joe. I didn't bother to think how odd it was for them to be standing there in the middle of the night in the post-rain Florida chill, but there they were anyway. As focused as I was on the race at hand, and as concerned as I was with my ability to continue performing, I didn't really make note of the fact that friends, family, and co-workers were right there with me. I was peripherally aware of them but wasn't fully cognizant of their support or their presence individually. But for sure, to this day when I look at pictures from that time, I remain pleasantly surprised at the number of recognizable faces that are surrounding me in each and every image.

Once I performed the perfunctory walk about the back lane of the paddock, allowing my heart rate and respiratory rate to return to something resembling normal, I had cooled down enough to return to the tent. The skies were definitely starting to lighten up, and I could sense that we were truly coming down the home stretch. Not wanting to miss another minute of the race, I decided to forego a trip back to the RV, and instead ate breakfast in the TRG pit area while watching my teammates drive. I crawled up onto the box next to Thomas and clutched a steaming mug of coffee as I watched the pros go to work.

While I was watching, our video crew came by to grab another sound bite and quick update of our position in the race. Bending down from the pit box, I answered the camera man's questions about our position. I smiled a bit, noting that we were now running in P5 and feeling pretty strong about ourselves. As I spoke, I felt a nudge in my ribs from Thomas, interrupting my soliloquy. Thomas whispered in my ear, and my smile grew even broader. I amended my update on the fly, probably with a look of disbelief on my face, as I informed the unseen audience, "apparently, we're now in P4 and really running strong." I couldn't believe the good luck of our continued march to the front, but even at that late point in the race, I expected nothing beyond what we had already achieved. My wildest dreams had pretty much always stopped there—I hadn't dared consider the possibility of an even better finish.

As the sun came up, and we were finally running once again in full daylight, the crowd continued to ebb and flow in and around the TRG pits. I realized that we were now the top positioned car of all the TRG entries, noting that the top team car driven by Andy Lally and Kevin Buckler had had a mishap in the middle of the night and had fallen well back of the leaders. During one of our pit stops, Mike Johnson, our crew chief from 2006 who was now a Speed Channel announcer, noted that the #64 JLowe Racing car was "carrying the flag" for TRG and was doing an admirable job of running with the big boys. Not long after that, Andrew Marriott, one of the Speed Channel reporters, interviewed Jim Pace when he got out of the car after his stint. JP noted that we were running particularly well at that point, but he also sounded a cautionary note. "A lot can happen between now and the end of the race—a lot will happen—and if we're there to

A crowd awaits the #64 Porsche in the Daytona pits

take advantage of it it'll be great for us and if not, well, it was somebody else's turn to get lucky."

As I watched the race wind down, I realized that we were still going to need a big dose of luck in order to make any progress on the top three spots. We were two laps down on the #85 Farnbacher Loles car of Dirk Werner and Leh Keen; one lap behind them were the #22 Alegra Porsche and then the #07 Pontiac of Kelly Collins, Paul Edwards, and Andy Pilgrim. The #85 car had been pretty much the strongest car of the GT field for most of the race, if not for the month of January, and there seemed little likelihood of us keeping pace, let alone overtaking any of the top three runners at that point. We had gone approximately 530 laps, and were running a lap or so in front of the next closest car in 5th place and relatively settled in our position. As JP noted, it was going to take some luck, on somebody's part, for things to change at that point.

From my position on the top of the box, I was able to watch as cars zipped on by down the front straight down into the Turn 1 braking zone. While I was busy watching the various Prototype and GT drivers find their deepest brake points, I felt another elbow in the ribs from Thomas. Once he got my attention, he pointed up at the Speed TV monitor. The camera was focused for some reason on the #85 Porsche, and we watched as it made its way through the infield. Dirk Werner was at the wheel, and each time he went deep into a turn on the brakes, you could see a puff of smoke come out from the rear end of the car. At first, I thought there was merely some rear brake lockup. I raised an eyebrow to Thomas, who smiled as he assured me, "She's been smoking for a couple laps now." I turned around and looked down from the pit box to find twenty or thirty people crowded behind me, looking at the same monitor, all of them with varying degrees of smiles on their faces.

"How much time left in the race?"

Thomas smiled. "It's just before noon; we have about ninety minutes or so to go. Enough time for them to blow that thing up."

"Well, that would be nice, but nobody around here better be counting any chickens…"

I tried my best to act casual and settle into my perch on the top of the pit box in front of the monitor. However, I kept scanning back and forth from the TV feed to the timing and scoring readout. We were now one lap behind the top three runners, and Johannes was running some of the fastest laps of the race. And, every so often, the Speed TV guys showed an updated photo of the Farnbacher Loles car, with that lovely tell-tale puff of smoke coming out of its back end.

While I was watching this drama unfold, Brian Till, another of the Speed Channel commentator crew, wandered up to our pit stall, trailed by a cameraman and a sound man. He caught my attention and gestured for me to come down from the box to have a chat with him. I did what I hoped was a comical double take, looking behind me to make sure he was speaking to me, and then dismounted the pit box. I approached Brian on the other side of the pit wall, and took a minute to see whether or not I could possibly make myself presentable for a brief TV appearance. Abandoning any semblance of trying to look human after a full day of driving, sweating, and barely sleeping, I gave up and smiled for the camera. The red light went on, and Brian opened with a fairly generous question. "I'm here with Dr. Jim Lowe, a neurosurgeon, and driver of the #64 car, which currently is running in fourth place in the GT class. Dr. Lowe, can you tell us whether or not you're surprised at being in this position this late in the race?"

At that point, while I primarily wanted to not look like too much of a dumbass, I was also mindful of trying to appear like I was familiar with the whole interview process (which I decidedly was not). I couldn't think of anything witty or otherwise memorable, so I resorted to cliché-speak, just like Crash Davis advised: "Well, we came here to be competitive, and we put together this team in order to try and be competitive, and this is where we had hoped to be come Sunday morning. Hopefully we'll keep running strong and have the finish that we were looking for." Brian was polite with my rather lame answer, but did manage to get in one quick zinger before he signed off. "Well guys, down here in the TRG pits, what's rather obvious is that, actually, it does take a brain surgeon." I smiled even wider as several guests around me shared a good laugh with Brian before he made his way on down the pit lane. I then crawled back up onto the box and resumed my perch, waiting anxiously to see how this marathon was going to turn out.

I've done quite a few lengthy surgeries in my career, including one particularly memorable brain tumor removal case that lasted almost thirty-six hours. (For that one, I at least got in breakfast and bathroom breaks along the way.) A common question asked of me is whether endurance racing has any similarities to long days in the OR; I've always struggled to find a good comparison that might make sense to those who haven't tried both. Simply put, while surgery is a contest—to finish the case safely and well—that requires the surgeon to move along expediently, and have the stamina to stand and focus, without mistake, for long periods, the similarities probably end there. No one is chasing after me as I work in the OR, personal risk is (mostly) non-existent, and surely no one would pay to watch a surgeon at work. And certainly, surgeons don't need to be conditioned athletes who can work for sustained periods with heart rates that rival Tour de France racers. But the biggest departure, for me, is this: I'm relaxed and comfortable in the OR, confident of the abilities my training and experience have served to develop. In the race car, so many variables are uncontrollable, and so much depends on split-second, instinctual responses, that the intensity of the event starts long before the green flag waves, and lasts until well after the lights are turned off. Even when I'm not in the car, I can't fully relax during our races—there's just too much that can go wrong, and will go wrong, in the blink of an eye. With rare exceptions, things always seem to happen very quickly out on the track.

What was happening that Sunday at Daytona was one of those exceptions.

On approximately the 585th GT lap, the Farnbacher Loles #85 car came into the pits. It was smoking heavily, and at that point the entire pit lane had its full attention. Here was the lead car, struggling mightily, with just over an hour to go in the twenty-four hour race. Faster by quite a bit than every other GT car on the track, it nonetheless was faltering at the final hour. We all craned our necks down pit lane as the rear deck lid was thrust open and oil added to the Porsche while it sat idling under the watchful eye of a Grand-Am official and the Speed Channel crew. It pulled out of pit lane smoking heavily the whole way down. Roger, Thomas, JP, and Ralf all stood around me in a tight circle as if we could collectively somehow will the car to give up the ghost.

We stood there side by side, chatting and generally trying to distract ourselves from the drama taking place out on the track. While we kept watch on the struggling front-runner, Johannes ran hard, fast, clean laps, trying to doing anything to catch up to the drivers just one lap ahead. At that point, we were one lap behind the #07 and the #22 cars, who were both gradually reeling in the Farnbacher Porsche.

What happened next could only best be described as the most obvious expression of Lady Luck smiling upon me in the best possible way. Hands patted me on the shoulders and elbowed poked me in the ribs as I witnessed the #85 car steaming down pit lane, beautifully belching hideous black smoke from its rear end. I couldn't have been more pleased than if I had opened the door and found Ed McMahon standing on the front porch bearing an oversized check. We all crowded the pit wall and looked to our left towards the Farnbacher pits, where mechanics furiously poured water on the engine and attempted to put out a small oil fire. It was clear at that point that their silver Porsche had given up the ghost. A cheer erupted from our pits as the Grand-Am official waved his hand, palm down, across his throat in the "turn her off" sign, signifying the end of the race for the Farnbacher car. Several of the crew and a few of my friends and coworkers joined me in jumping up and down as our #64 Porsche vaulted into third place. I grinned widely and accepted a few spirited high fives from several guests now crowded elbow to elbow into our pit tent area.

JP put an arm around my shoulder and said in that classic Mississippi drawl, "Well now, Dr. Lowe, we still got a little bit of racing to go." Ginny had been relatively silent, standing on my left side, until that moment.

"How much more time 'til this thing is over?" Clearly, she wasn't complaining; I could spot her anxiety being expressed as pleading aggravation, and recognized it for what it was.

"Don't worry, Honey, we're in the twenty-fourth hour now. Just have to stay clean and bring it home, and we've got Johannes behind the wheel."

Ginny looked at me with pleading eyes. "I think I'm gonna go take a walk. There's no way I can just stand here for the next 45 minutes waiting for this to end." With that, she started out of the tent, with a couple of our guests in tow. I knew she'd be back shortly, but given the fact that I felt like taking a similar walk, I understood completely. Instead however, I made my way back up to the top of the pit cart and once again assumed a watchful position. I fidgeted and watched helplessly as the laps ticked by while I kept an eye on the clock, which was absolutely crawling its way to the 1:30 p.m finish.

As I was holding vigil, now ignorant of the swelling crowd in our pit tent, an old acquaintance from Skip Barber approached me from behind the pit box and tapped me on the shoulder. The assailant, who will remain unnamed here, was someone I remembered from various Skip Barber events as being not particularly friendly or easy, both on and off-track. However, he was smiling broadly as he gestured to me for my attention. I leaned over the back rail of the seat and cocked an ear in his direction so that I could hear him over the noise.

"I just wanted to be the first to congratulate you on winning a podium at Daytona." As he said this his grin quickly faded as he saw the look on my face. I stared, mouth open in disbelief at such a flagrant malocchio, not able to understand why somebody would wish me such ill in that fashion. Superstitious or not, I couldn't fathom how anyone could think that this was a reasonable thing to say with a whole bunch of laps yet to be completed. I started icily for another moment or two and seriously considered whether I could just cold-cock him right there in the pits. Instead, I took a different tack.

"Thanks for mentioning it. You know this thing's not over yet, right?" I then gestured to JP and Ralf, who were chatting next to the pit box. When they approached to within quiet conversational distance, I told them both "Keep that guy away from me until this thing is over." Recognizing my distress, they both laughed as I turned back to re-glue my eyes to the monitor.

The last minutes of the race were a stressful eternity. Each time my car appeared at the tri-oval, I breathed a sigh of relief as it went by at full blast. We were clearly not going to be able to catch the #22 and #07 cars in front of us, and we were a full lap ahead of our next closest pursuer. At this rate, all we needed was a couple clean laps, and we would have our podium. With each circuit completed by Johannes, we crawled one lap closer to a finish that had been unthinkable only a few hours before. As the clock ticked nearer 1:30 p.m., I crawled down from the pit stand and made my way to the pit wall. Ginny elbowed her way through the crowd and slipped an arm around my waist, while JP stood to my right. I looked around and realized that it was standing room only underneath the canopy. Roger and Thomas stood off to one side, with Sebastien and Ralf behind them, and the remainder of the TRG crew, including Kevin Buckler, filling out the available wall space in support of our car.

First across the line taking the checkered flag for the DP class and overall win was Scott Pruett in the Ganassi car, followed shortly after by Ryan Dalziel in the SAMAX Pontiac and Max Angelelli in the Wayne Taylor Racing Pontiac. I had to wait another minute to see the Alegra Porsche take the win for the GT class, followed by Kelly Collins in the #07 Pontiac in second place. Once they passed by, I knew that Johannes couldn't be far behind. I stepped out from between JP and Ginny and stood up on the pit wall. Our white and red Porsche appeared in the distance, exiting the banking of NASCAR's Turn 4 and flying down the front straight at full speed.

Johannes wasn't bothering with a photo-op. He was all business as our car crossed the stripe, the checkered flag waving furiously overhead. I thrust both hands, fists clenched, high in the air, and let out a scream as I jumped over the wall. Despite the engine noise from cars finishing the race, I could hear the cheers erupting from the TRG pits. Arms still outstretched, I felt

#64 crosses the finish line at Daytona, 2007

Jim, Ginny and JP start the celebration in the Daytona pits, 2007

the surge of adrenaline and the thrill of the moment as I turned around and embraced first Ginny, and then Jim Pace, and then the both of them together. Over the next several minutes, I hugged everyone in sight, exchanged high fives, handshakes, and all manner of celebratory gestures with anybody within reach, narrowly avoiding accidentally kissing Jim Pace as I tried to reach out to Ginny a second time.

As the celebration slowed down slightly, I had the opportunity to turn and say a heartfelt thanks to Kevin Buckler and several of the crew guys, including Thomas, Roger, and Sebastien. JP, Ralf, and I stood together, with Ginny in between, as guests made their way forward to the pit wall to congratulate us. In something resembling a calm moment, I realized that I wasn't sure what was next. I turned to JP, and asked him quite innocently "Where do we go now?" In one of the weekend's more memorable moments, JP returned a classically understated response.

"Dr. Lowe, we're going to Victory Lane!"

Once the TRG tent had cleared some more, I was able to collect my gear, my wife, and my teammates, and start the walk towards Victory Lane. Ginny at my side, with helmet in hand, we made our way to the fenced entry of the Victory Lane area. Amazingly, there was already a fairly large crowed accumulated inside the bleacher area. The Ganassi Prototype had been parked front and center in anticipation of the coming celebration, and Pruett, Juan Pablo Montoya, and Salvador Duran were standing on the car and wildly waving their respective countries' flags. The four of us approached the entry gate, which was being guarded by Daytona security. However, when we arrived at the check point, the guard spotted us and waved us around the side so that we could make our way to the podium steps. JP, Ralf, and I stood there patiently, waiting for the podium ceremony to be completed for the Daytona Prototype guys. I watched as the prototype drivers did their celebration thing, enjoying the fact that I was very shortly going to be sharing a podium with a couple of guys named Gordon, Carpentier, and Montoya. As we stood there, Johannes finally joined us, still a little on the sweaty side after finally delivering the Porsche to the garage. This new arrival was cause for celebration all over again as we exchanged hugs and congratulations.

Moments later the podium cleared, and it was the GT drivers' turn. I waited patiently, heart racing, as the four Alegra drivers made their way to the well deserved top step, accepting the GT first place trophy, followed then by Kelly, Paul, and Andy from the #07 car on the second step. When our turn came, I habitually stepped back in order to allow my teammates to mount the steps first. However, JP was behind me and gave me a bit of a shove in the back. "Oh no, Dr. Lowe, this is your deal, you go up first." He smiled and gave me one additional reassuring shove as I hesitated for only a moment.

Swallowing hard, and choking back some tears, I remembered my dad's advice during high school football days about scoring touchdowns: "When you get in the end zone try and act like you've been there before." I hopped onto the stage and somehow maintained composure while giving a subtle fist pump as I made my way over towards the far end of the platform. My trip was interrupted by, of all people, Richard Petty, who held out his hand in congratulations. I was so intent on making the trip uneventfully that I almost ran by him, but I did manage to stop briefly and silently shake the King's hand, having nothing to say that was better than that. When I got to the end of the stage, I was greeted by Mark Lewis, the guest services coordinator from Daytona. He grabbed my hand and said the magical words: "Welcome to Victory Lane, Jim!" I almost asked him to say it again, not quite believing him the first time.

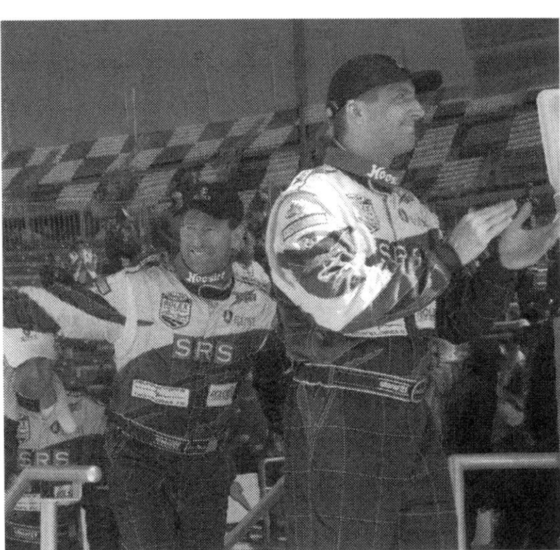

Jim and JP climb the podium steps, Daytona, 2007

I hopped up on the third step and was joined seconds later by JP, Ralf, and Johannes. We were handed white Rolex Daytona 24 Hours podium caps and purple neck bands embossed with tire maker Hoosier's name. We were then presented with the third place GT trophy, which was clearly the single biggest piece of hardware (literally and figuratively) ever handed to me. As I grabbed it on one side, JP grabbed the other. He looked at me and whispered, "When we hold it up tilt it down a little bit so they don't see the bottom in the photographs." Damn, was there any detail this guy didn't think of?

Podium smiles, 24 Hours of Daytona, 2007

JP and I simultaneously thrust the trophy overhead, and I thrilled to the cheers coming from the stands. The energy I felt at that point was simply amazing, the ultimate reward for all the work, all the trouble, all the effort, and all the time spent. Validation. Every bit of effort, every drop of sweat, every lap run, and every tear shed, they all led to that point. I had decided to get off the porch and tried my best to run with the big dogs. And, in that germ of an idea, I had made it all the way from first laps in a Jim Russell school car in Sonoma, California, to the podium at Daytona. Marvelously fulfilling and overwhelming all at once.

I looked over to the floor of the stage on my left and was excited to see four champagne bottles sitting ready for our celebration. After years of watching guys spray champagne on TV, I couldn't believe that I was actually going to have the thrill of doing the deed myself. After the trophies had been awarded, the presenters cleared the stage, knowing that it was going to get wet very quickly. With that silent signal, all eleven drivers simultaneously jumped down, grabbed the champagne bottles, and started celebrating. I grabbed my bottle, and shook it wildly as I managed somehow to get the cork to properly eject. The spray of champagne was wonderful as I shot it into the air, out towards the crowd, and then aimed it towards my three teammates. I turned in circles, spraying anybody in range, and stopped once or twice to turn the bottle upside down over my open mouth. I looked skyward and let out an unrestrained roar as I felt the electricity of

Spraying champagne

the adrenaline surge through me once again.

This was simply an amazing feeling, walking in circles around the Daytona podium in a shower of champagne, exchanging hugs with my teammates. I managed to stop for a moment, look out into the crowd, and take a scanning mental image of my surroundings. The track was visible over the pit lane fencing, the grandstands were right there looming behind it, and the Rolex 24 Hours at Daytona insignia was on the wall right behind me. I closed my eyes and immediately thought about my dad. I thought about how he always seemed excited to have some time to watch the Indy 500 with me and how my love of motorsports came directly from him. How he had stood there and witnessed my few successes to date and nearly all of my failures, all with continued and unrelenting encouragement. And here I was, getting sprayed with champagne and thinking that such a big part of this success was his success, his accomplishment, too.

I opened my eyes, and found my beautiful wife standing next to me. She had Jim Pace's champagne bottle in her hand and was enjoying a sip or two herself. She wrapped her arms around my neck, nearly concussing me with the champagne bottle, and planted a rather large kiss on my cheek. "Congratulations honey. What a great race! This is really wonderful!" My grin widened, and I either shouted or whispered, I'm not sure which, "I love you. Thank you Baby!" I turned with my arm around my wife's waist, and we picked the trophy up together, turning towards the crowd. Several of our guests were taking photos, and JP quickly joined us for what would turn out to be one of my favorite shots of the weekend. The three of us, holding the trophy high, as Gin and I kissed once again.

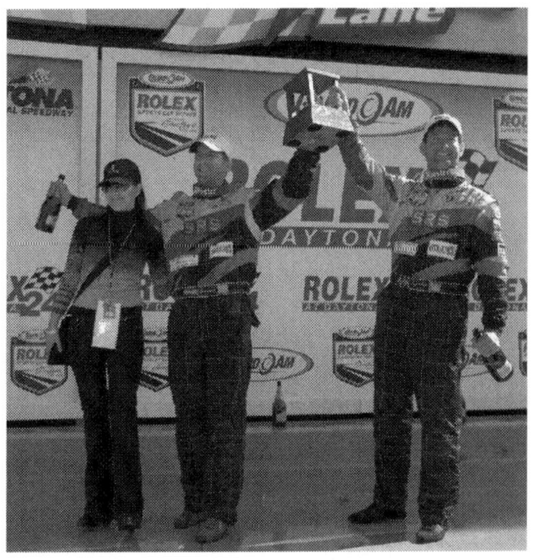

Jim, Gin and JP celebrate, Daytona, 2007

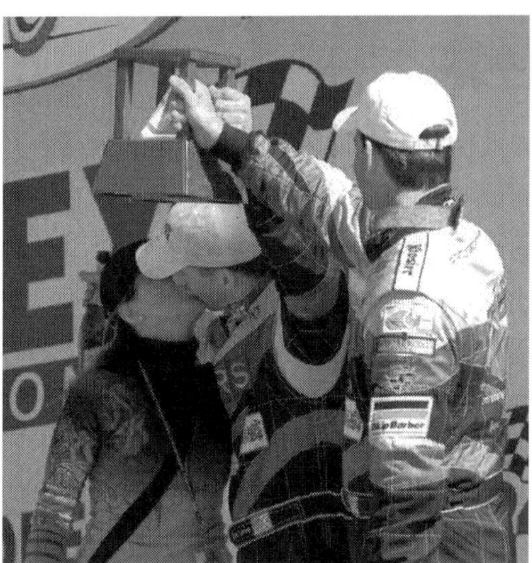

A podium kiss for Jim and Ginny

Once the celebration had wound down, I remembered to grab my empty champagne bottle and replaced my soaked podium hat on my wet head. Jim, Johannes, Ralf, and I made our way down to the front of the stage where we proceeded to pose for multiple pictures with the TRG mechanics, Thomas, Roger, Sebastien, Ashlei, Ginny, and Kevin Buckler. After a seemingly endless stream of photos, the crowd dispersed and one by one the team members broke off to return to their various stations. JP grabbed me and reminded me that there was now a press conference to go to. I gave Gin one big last hug,

Kevin Buckler celebrates with the drivers of the #64 Porsche, Daytona, 2007

handed off the trophy to Thomas and Roger, and followed after JP on the way to the Daytona press building.

As we walked, I had a moment to reflect on what we had accomplished over the last twenty-four hours. We had finished the race ahead of drivers such as Jimmie Johnson, Eddie Cheever, Christian Fittipaldi, Dan Wheldon, Ryan Hunter-Reay, and AJ Allmendinger. Infinitely more impressive was what we had accomplished in the last year. It had turned out to be a pretty long and interesting trip, all the way from the wreckage of '06 to a Daytona podium.

Once inside the press conference area, I again had to wait for the DP guys to finish their time on stage. Jeff Gordon, Juan Pablo Montoya, and Scott Pruett attracted an appropriate amount of attention and certainly took their time politely answering seemingly endless questions. After that, our turn came, and JP and I took the stage to represent the #64 car, along with most of the drivers from the top two GT cars. By the time the writers got around to addressing the third place GT car, I hoped only that someone would ask me something, anything, so that I would not be embarrassed, having shown up at a press conference where I clearly wasn't needed.

Finally, one of the writers asked me for a comment about my experience on the podium, noting that it was my first Grand-Am podium finish. I don't recall my exact remarks, but only that I mentioned that this had quite a different feeling about it compared to my debut race, noting that I managed to ball up a perfectly good Porsche in my first stint one year prior. Seemingly satisfied by that answer, they moved on to addressing the future of Jim Pace and his co-driver in Grand-Am. JP doled out a satisfactory sound bite, announcing that we had "unfinished business," surprising no one more than me when he stated that we would be back next year gunning for the top step. I stifled an enlarging grin as I realized that I had a committed teammate in Jim Pace and that there was no reason to suspect that we would do anything more than keep running Grand-Am races.

As JP spoke, I made a quick mental note to delay any mention of future racing plans to my wife, realizing that Ginny would probably hope that this success would be enough for me. We'd just have to sort that one out later, after the buzz wore off and I was back on planet earth.

After returning to the garage area and spending over an hour thanking our guests, signing various pieces of memorabilia, and posing for yet more photos, it was time to pack up and move on. I grabbed the trophy off the hood of the #64 car and collected my wife and a few bits of clothing as we headed back to the RV. Once there, there was another round of congratulations and goodbyes to make before we could head towards the airport. I stuffed my soggy suit in a bag, but made sure that the trophy and empty champagne bottle didn't leave my sight.

I met several of my friends at the airport, along with a few members of Ginny's family who had made the trip down with us. We boarded the plane together, and took off into the darkening sky. The pilot made a rather deliberate loop around the giant track before heading north, giving me one last glimpse at the still-intimidating structure that had become such an intimate part of my dreams.

***

We arrived home early enough in the evening that my son was still awake. As I pulled into the driveway and started unloading the car, Aidan appeared in the back doorway. Before I had a chance to turn around, he was heading my way.

"Congratulations Daddy, I heard you did really good!"

I turned around to Aidan, squatted down, and gave him a big hug and kiss. "Did you watch the race on TV?"

"Well, Grandma and Pop-pop and I watched a little bit, but mostly we just played Legos." I think he realized then that maybe that might be the wrong answer so he reassured me, "But we did save it on DVR so maybe you and I could watch the race later. But do you think maybe we could play some Legos tonight?"

I smiled at the wisdom of this, and proposed an alternate solution. "Well I'm not so sure I have enough energy for Legos tonight, Bubba, but could you maybe help me carry this into the house?" I handed him the trophy, exaggerating its weight as I held it out to him. "Be careful, it's really heavy!" Aidan grabbed it with both hands and clutched it close to his chest. "I got it Dad. Let's go." With that, my son disappeared into the house, clutching my trophy for third place in the 2007 Rolex 24 Hours of Daytona.

Chapter Twenty-Seven

"You drive like a maniac!"

Murray Marden doubled over in laughter as I stood next to my open car door in my driveway, while Paul Tracy yelled at me.

"If you drive like that tomorrow, we're gonna win the race!"

I struggled to explain myself to my driving partner. "I—I—shit, I was just trying to stay in front of you. I thought I'd piss you off if I didn't haul ass."

PT smiled at me as he slammed the door to his rental SUV, shaking his head. "Jimmy Smooth, I saw you make some moves in traffic just now that I've never seen you make on a race track. Why don't you drive like that when it matters?!"

By this time, Murray who had first endured a white knuckle ride from the race track back to my house, and now was enduring Tracy's hilarious commentary, was finally starting to recover. "I told you you were going too fast. Honestly Paul, I don't know what got into him."

I defended myself, "You know exactly what got into me. I kept telling you that it's Paul F'in Tracy behind me. I can't drive like some idiot, or he'll run me over. Jeez, I was only trying to make my partner happy and now both you guys are giving me a raft of shit."

PT and Murray were now both grinning at me. Paul shook his head. "Like I said, just drive like that tomorrow."

With that we headed into the house to get washed up before our scheduled meet-and-greet at the local McLaren Auto dealership. We were running behind schedule, given the late testing and long debrief at the track that afternoon, in anticipation of the next day's Grand-Am race at the

NJ Motorsports Park. However, I had made a commitment to long-time sponsor Bob DiStanislao and had arranged to bring Paul Tracy over to the dealership to sign some autographs and shake some hands.

I steered Paul and Murray to rooms where they could shower and clean up for the afternoon's event; I, too, got a quick cleanup and donned a fresh black JLowe Racing shirt.

When I made my way back down to my kitchen, I found PT sitting on a stool at the countertop, eating an ice cream sandwich. He looked up when I walked in, "What took you so long? You obviously don't shower as fast as you drive."

Murray walked in, and I was able to push both guys towards the door. "Come on, we're gonna be late. Bring your ice cream with you. And Paul, could you try and not look so scary?"

***

For me, it had certainly been a long strange trip that ultimately led to me teaming up with Paul Tracy in a Daytona Prototype car in 2012. The process seems like one continuous growth curve, but in reality there had been fairly significant and dramatic highlights and stumbles along the way.

Following our podium success at the 24 Hours that January, Jim Pace and I joined up for five additional races in 2007. We became an accepted and established driver pairing in the series and had some continued success, relatively speaking, in the GT class. Although we were unable to crack the top ten later in the season, we had some classic races, including repeat efforts at VIR, the 6 Hours of Watkins Glen, Laguna Seca, and the summer Daytona race.

During my first five years as a Grand-Am driver, I competed in twenty races, with my schedule limited by sparse sponsorship and the simultaneous demands of running a busy neurosurgical practice. During that time, I had the great privilege of driving alongside many truly gifted drivers and teaming with several who ultimately became mentors and friends. I also remained attached to Roger Reis, who crewed my cars, spent endless hours plotting next races with me, and even allowed me to toast him and his bride Crystal at their wedding. My circle of racing friends became wider, and I ultimately realized that many of them, like Murray Marden, had become true friends—on the track or off, racing or not. And together, we made three more attempts at winning the GT class at the Rolex 24 Hours of Daytona, coming no closer than fourth place in 2008.

Despite steeply accelerating expenses for the JLowe Racing team, and more recognition within the series, and maybe even within the racing community itself, we didn't seem to be making progress on the business side of the deal. Ultimately, when I was able to step back and took a look at the sums of money being expended and the daily effort required to support a GT class racing program, it just did not seem to make sense. And despite all of those efforts, I realized also that I had drifted far away from my original intent when I got into racing. The business of racing, and the time drain required to sustain it, simply weren't part of the original dream. Driving a race car was.

With that in mind, I decided to transition into a program where I was primarily responsible for driving the car, rather than worrying about team-related details. I simply wanted—needed—to get back behind the wheel and do it with the least amount of aggravation possible. So, in the end of 2010, when the opportunity presented itself for me to drive in a Daytona Prototype in the Rolex 24 Hours in 2011, I jumped at the chance.

Although I had never been in a Prototype before, at that point I felt confident enough in my basic driving ability to believe that I could pull it off, and reasonably well. With the assistance of Murray, we arranged to do some testing with the Starworks Motorsports Team, based out of Florida. This team was an emerging force in Grand-Am, and would later (without yours truly) go on to be a championship-level team. But at just the right time, there was one open seat in their DP effort offered to me for the upcoming 2011 Daytona race.

We tested first at Palm Beach International Raceway, formally known as Moroso Motorsports Park, which was familiar to me from my Skip Barber days. While Murray looked on, I got an orientation to the car from Daytona- and Le Mans-winning driver Ryan Dalziel. With Ryan's help, I had a full day getting acclimated to the different speed, sensation, and handling of the Prototype car. It was immediately obvious that this car was much more drivable than a GT car, especially at speed; with increased downforce and left foot braking, I quickly gained an overall sense of confidence. Once we transitioned to driving back at Daytona in January, I felt even more comfortable, especially given the fact that I certainly knew the track layout well. And, in every fashion, the Prototype delivered just so much more performance than the GT car. The top speed attained by the car was also much more interesting; at full song on the front straight of Daytona, we were touching just under 200 mph. And while that was happening, because of the high downforce and stability of the car, the ride felt exceptionally more relaxed than that of the GT car I was used to.

For the 2011 race, I was teamed not only with Ryan, but also with pro drivers Colin Braun, and Tomas Enge. Along with those three was Mike Foster, who had driven the car for the last year with Ryan in the Grand-Am series. Working hard with the four of them, I finally came up to a reasonable and comfortable pace in the Prototype, despite my relative inexperience in that machine.

When race time came for the 2011 Rolex 24, my role on the team was somewhat diminished, unfortunately. I did, however, drive several stints, including a hard-to-forget, two and a half hour stint under yellow in the middle of the night while the track was fogged out. The most unique part of that forced march was realizing that I was actually struggling to stay awake behind the wheel; getting nap jerks while I was trying to steer a Daytona Prototype around Daytona's infield and banking was quite a distressing sensation.

Mur and Jim at Daytona

The 2011 race ended poorly for us, however, when an oil leak signified an impending engine failure, and the car was retired late Sunday morning. Despite the poor outcome, and the not-so-special experience with the Starworks team itself, getting a legitimate Prototype drive

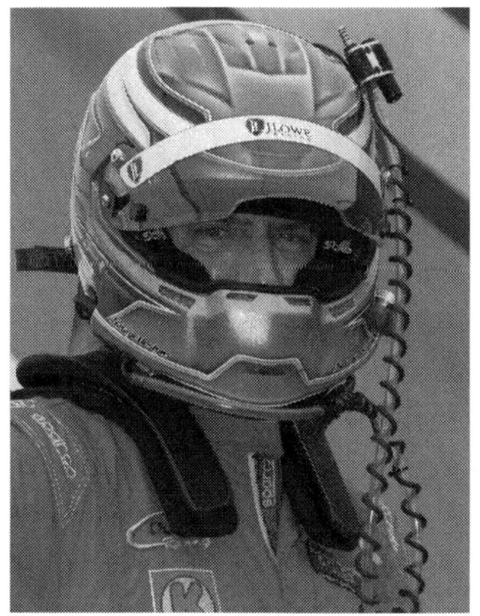

Jim ready for his next stint, 2012

under my belt and onto the résumé was invaluable, as was the experience and knowledge gained by teaming with Colin, Ryan, Tomas and Mike.

For the remainder of 2011, I strayed further from the racetrack, with the exception of occasional days karting with Aidan. My surgical practice needed my full attention, and the pleasant demands of family life where too rewarding to sacrifice more time away. I still worked at getting sponsor support for racing, but my efforts started to focus more on 2012 and beyond, as I searched for the right team and car combination for my future. Finally, I caught a big break: late in the year, having missed the rest of the Grand-Am season, I received an offer to drive with a team out of Ohio by the name of Doran Racing. Given the strong history of the team, which had been well established as a winning constructor and entrant over the last twenty years, I didn't hesitate to sign up. I was offered one of the four seats available in their Dallara Daytona Prototype, which would be co-driven by brothers Burt and Brian Frisselle, and some guy named Paul Tracy.

For the 2012 event, which was the fiftieth running of the Rolex 24 Hours at Daytona, we had a fairly strong showing. My co-drivers were great coaches, helping me again get up to speed after having been away from the track for the last year. The Doran organization definitely had its act together, and I immediately enjoyed the experience of working with Kevin and his crew. I also enjoyed the unusually large crowd that turned out for the fiftieth anniversary event—including that year's Grand Marshall, Jackie Stewart.

Accustomed to seeing racing stars and other celebs around the track at bigger events, I usually didn't bother trying to say hello or otherwise get involved in that sort of fan activity. But when I noticed Jackie taking a garage tour with his entourage, I couldn't pass up the opportunity to meet one of my childhood heroes. Wearing a race suit, I thankfully wasn't held back by the security guards as I pushed my way through the crowd around the little Scott.

I held out my hand. "Sir Jackie!"

He stopped and looked at my outstretched hand, and then seemed to relax a bit when he saw my fire suit. He extended his hand, and grasped mine firmly.

"Yes, hello, pleased to meet you." There was that familiar voice, that strange accent I first heard when I was just a boy. Goosebumps.

"Jackie, I'm Jim Lowe, one of the drivers, and I just wanted to say hello. I'm also a neurosurgeon, and I promised myself, if I ever, if…" I started to stutter and silently cursed the fact. But, instead of moving off, Jackie stayed patient, and waited for my tongue to untie itself.

"If I ever got to meet you, I promised I'd thank you personally for making racing safer for all of us. You deserve our gratitude."

Jackie acknowledged with his thanks, and then something amazing happened.

"What car are you driving?"

"I, uh, I'm, uh, the #77 car,"—I pointed behind me—"one of the Daytona Prototypes." Holy shit. Jackie Stewart just asked me about my race car.

"Well, how's she running for you?" This was not happening. I was talking racing with a living legend, and he was treating me like—like some sort of colleague. Like a fellow racer. Oh my God.

"We're a bit off pace, but we'll be there when the sun rises." I hoped that sounded OK, maybe even convincing.

One of his escorts then started to steer Jackie back on-course. "Good luck to you this weekend, Jim."

I waved as he turned away. "Thanks again, Jackie."

Unfortunately, the #77 car was a second generation Prototype, in a field filled with predominately newer and faster third generation cars. We calculated ultimately that we were two or three seconds off the potential race pace of the "Gen 3" car, thus realizing early on that we were unlikely to be competitive in terms of an overall win or podium. Nonetheless, we also knew that consistency and driving without getting into trouble could certainly make up for flaws in top end speed and performance. With that in mind, we put forth a professional and ultimately successful effort, backed by the Mars company (proudly sporting the "Combos" logo). When the dust settled, we finished in seventh place overall, only a handful of laps behind the winning Shank Racing DP driven by John Pew, Oz Negri, AJ Allmendinger, and Justin Wilson. For that crew, it was a popular win overall, and I was especially pleased to see friend and former Skip Barber driver Pew take home the winning trophy and a brand new Rolex Daytona watch. For my part, I was beyond satisfied to have driven well at a competitive pace and finish for the first time in the top ten of the overall standings. I had driven nose-to-tail with Dario Franchitti and Allan McNish down Daytona's front straight and held my own throughout the experience. And perhaps best of all, I knew that I was already contracted with Kevin Doran's team to run several more races during the year.

***

The Grand-Am race event at NJ Motorsports Park in May 2012 was turning out to be a pretty big deal for me. Given the fact that it had a bit of a home crowd feel to it, I always enjoyed any opportunity to run at the relatively new track laid down in the middle of Millville, NJ. In addition, there was more than the usual amount of press and attention generated in my direction, mainly because of the fact that I was now driving in the Prototype class and was still partnered with PT. Having a former champion, and the winningest open-wheel driver in North America as your teammate, certainly ups the ante when you're already a little tight about driving in front of the home crowd. But to his eternal credit, Paul gener-

Paul Tracy

ously put up with his slower teammate and seemed in fact to enjoy the experience of sharing a car with someone who had just so much to learn.

Aidan

As I had gotten to know Paul better, I found that I really enjoyed his company. His tough guy outer shell, complete with tattoos and a shaved head, didn't carry over to the way he treated me on or off the track. In fact, PT turned out to be a pretty sweet guy, who was generous with his time and always patient with me as I watched and studied his behavior on and off the track. After all, the guy was a living legend, and there was certainly no mandate requiring Paul to take care of his older and slower pupil. Nonetheless, PT not only treated me like a teammate, he did so with great irreverence—a true sign of having earned another guy's respect.

One such example of this came during the process of pouring new seats for the #77 Dallara Prototype just before the practice for the NJMP race began. Since Paul was shaped quite a bit differently than me in the torso, a different seat insert would be required for me to comfortably fit in the shell of the DP's main seat. The process of pouring a new seat includes sitting on a plastic bag filled with quickly solidifying liquid, all the while trying to obtain the ideal position and angle of your torso in the car. Once that was done, the rough edges of the seat would be cut off, and any other hard points smoothed down in order to provide the best in comfort. As I was going through this process, getting in and out of the car repeatedly while the new seat was tweaked, Tracy looked on, initially quietly. When I had made the fifth or sixth request to smooth out a few of the small left over bumps on the back of my seat, Tracy finally couldn't contain himself anymore.

"Jesus Christ Jimmy, you're like the Princess and the Pea".

I showed mock offense. "Are you kidding me? I can't drive with that knot sticking in my back."

"There's no knot there, you're just super sensitive. You're a Prima Donna—just like Dario was when he and I were teammates."

I smiled at any comparison, even negatively, with one of the world's great drivers, Dario Franchitti.

Tracy continued. "You need to just get into the car and just drive the thing. It doesn't matter what you feel back there. I'll drive that thing, I don't care what's going on. You can put any bump you want in that car seat and I'll still be able to drive it!"

"Well, that's just because you got a bigger ass than me."

PT laughed out loud with the rest of the crew. "Well, get your skinny ass out of there so we can get moving. We got some practicing to do."

Two days of practice went very well, and ultimately I qualified the car last in the Prototype division (no real surprise there, given that we were the only team still running the older generation-two version of the Prototype). It appeared we were several seconds off the pace of the generation-three Prototype drivers, even with PT behind the wheel. Nonetheless, I had managed to slowly bring my times up in the direction of where Paul's were, and I was relieved to have kept the car in one shiny piece, all the way through the practice testing and qualifying sessions.

Jim and Mur chat with Patrick Dempsey, Watkins Glen, 2012

When race day came, I proudly followed Paul around the paddock from meeting to debriefing to garage; on our way, I introduced him to several of my friends and co-workers who had made the short trip to the track to watch the race that day. The Grand-Am PR people also were interested in the story of the "Champ and the Chump" and gave us a fair amount of camera interview time. After fifteen minutes of listening to Paul answer questions about what it was like to be running in Grand-Am after so many successful years in open wheel racing, it was then my turn. I seized upon the opportunity and interrupted the interviewer to ask me my own question.

I grabbed the microphone and hammed it up for the camera. "So Dr. Lowe, tell us what it's like to be hanging out with Paul Tracy."

I deadpanned the answer. "Well, he's a bit of a pain in the ass, actually… and he kinda scares me, a little."

Murray, Paul, and I had a good laugh at that one, especially since the interviewer wasn't quite sure if I was being serious at first. Ultimately, that little bit of footage ended up on the cutting room floor, I think.

Racing around the NJ track in a Daytona Prototype was great fun and a big thrill as expected. I loved the intensity of the race start, the feeling of the huge surge of power pushing me along by the backside as we all accelerated down into the first turn. Knowing that I was going to be a few seconds off the pace of the front runners, I calmly slotted into the caboose position on the train and tried to stay on the bumper of the guy in front of me. Once again, I was surprised at the frantic pace of the first lap, as cars diced side by side and fought over apices, from turn to turn. Eventually we settled into a sort of resigned rhythm for each lap. For a while I could still see the front end of the pack when I made my way onto the front straight each time around, but try as I might, giving that I was lapping two to three seconds a lap slower than the lead cars, eventually I fell further back. With each successive lap, I worked on my own game; trying to brake later, rolling speed through the entire turn, and getting back to power as soon as I dared.

Jim takes the Doran DP #77 into turn one at New jersey Motorsports Park, 2012

The challenge became a personal one and I was more or less ignorant of the rest of the race for a prolonged period. Ultimately, I caught up to the back of the GT pack and started picking my way through the slower GT cars. One or two at a time, I made passes where I could take advantage of my extra down-force and increased horsepower. I even successfully passed one of the Mazda drivers under braking down through Turn 1—a particularly challenging move for me at that part of the track.

Before I knew it, Kevin was on the radio calling me in. My race was going to be over momentarily, and I had once again done my job. Remembering to savor my last lap, I brought the car back to the pit in one piece and delivered it in running condition to Paul.

As I cooled off underneath the shade of the pit awning, and Ginny tried to help me get rehydrated, I started to pick up the calls from PT over the radio. It was clear that Paul's cool suit wasn't working, and he was quickly getting overheated. Initially the crew decided to bring him in for a quick check to see if they could fix the system in the car. At that point, we all knew it was going to be impossible for him to keep running without a repair (given the external temps hovering at 100 degrees and the cockpit temps hovering at closer to 140).

After a brief stop and an attempt to fix the cool suit mechanism, PT was back on the track and trying to make up lap time. However, the radio told a story quite different from the timesheets: as Paul made better and better time, he began to complain more and more of the heat. Finally, he said that he was going to have to come in and take the cool suit off and attempt to drive without the shirt (which was quite a warm garment when it was malfunctioning). Sensing that the trouble would be a bit worse than that, and given Paul's complaints, I sought out my helmet and gloves, and prepared to get back in the car if necessary.

Moments after I had buckled up my chin strap and donned my gloves, Paul pulled into the pits in a screech. He tumbled out of the car and was obviously completely overheated. A crew member poured water over his steaming head as another pulled at the cool shirt, trying to peel it off him. It was pretty clear at that point that PT was in no condition to get right back behind the wheel. I looked over at Kevin who quickly pointed at me and gestured toward the car. I jumped over the wall, made my way to the gull-wing door, and gently tried to push Paul over toward the pit wall. His face was beet red, and he clearly had suffered significant overheating inside the boiling cockpit.

Once I was back behind the wheel of the Prototype, I managed to get it down pit lane while I was simultaneously tightening all the safety belts and checking on the radio connection. I called into Kevin to ask him for a review of the situation.

"Not to worry, go out and just do your laps. We're a couple of laps behind the closest car, and nobody in the DP class is behind us just now. You're currently running P10. Take your time, get some good laps in, and enjoy the rest of the ride."

"Copy that." The radio fell silent once again, and I was on my own.

I continued running hard laps, staying flat through the last-turn entry onto the front straight and generally trying to channel the voice of Jim Pace into my ears. Breathe, wiggle your fingers and toes, hard on the brakes, back to power. GT or DP car, it didn't matter—the principle was the same, and I had been taught by a master.

On the penultimate lap of the race, the leading cars of Alex Gurney and Scott Pruett collided, taking each other out and clearing the way for the SunTrust Racing Prototype of Max Angelelli and Ricky Taylor for the win. It also had the effect of vaulting our #77 Doran Dallara Prototype into eighth place, where I dutifully finished moments later.

In the post-race debrief, I noted that my fastest lap times of the race were four-tenths of a second behind Paul's. Much of this might be accounted for by the heat exhaustion from which he was suffering in the cockpit with the malfunctioning cool suit; some of it was also that we were simply both bumping up against the mechanical potential of the somewhat slower generation-two car. Either

Jim and Aidan relaxing at Watkins Glen, 2012

way, I was as proud of that particular number as I was of just about any other objective measure of my ability as a racer. In addition, I had put up a good fight and picked up the colors when Paul became a victim of the cool-suit malfunction. I was able to get back in the car and complete a second, unplanned stint, thankful all the time that I had been religious about my conditioning program. And, in spite of our eventual finish well out of the podium range, Paul and I had notched another top-ten in the Prototype class.

On the ride home, I drove in a much more relaxed fashion given that Paul was sitting in the seat behind me, and not tailing me in a rental car. It was my last job of the weekend to drop PT off at the airport hotel on the way back to my house. With Ginny at my side and Aidan and Murray in the backseat, I savored my situation with an immense degree of enjoyment. I was in the middle of a busy season, sharing a race car with Paul Tracy, and sharing the whole experience with my wonderful wife, amazing son, and good friends. I had once again survived a great battle on the track, running with the pros and doing an unexpectedly generous amount of driving, and I had come through in one piece. No, better than that; I had stepped up and done a job worthy of my position. I felt I had finally earned the right to drive the car, and drive the car in this particular group, against these drivers. Yes, I realized that none of them were ever going to lose sleep over my lap times, but at this point I finally belonged. Belonged on the track, belonged in this group, belonged wearing their uniform.

As we made our way through the traffic home, Paul and Aidan got into a very animated discussion about playing guitar and the various merits of Metallica versus Led Zeppelin. Aidan was genuinely pleased that someone was talking about something other than racing, and Paul and Murray appeared to be genuinely interested in what he had to say.

As I drove, I savored the emotion of the day. I had enjoyed great fun with friends, old and new, and family. I had left everything I had out on the track and couldn't have been more pleased with the results. Not the timesheet results, but the other results, the ones I could feel so intensely in my head and in my satisfied heart. I was at peace—I had met my personal version of a challenge I so desperately needed in my life and was the better man for it. The fulfillment was total – I had found my own zen-like experience that amplified the enjoyment of every other aspect of my life. My work was more rewarding, my relationship with my wife was loving and solid, and I cherished every moment with my son. Surely more challenges loomed in the future, but for now, I truly was at peace.

While the guys in the backseat chatted on, I turned and tapped Ginny on the hand.

"Remind me to call my dad when I get home, OK?"

Chapter Twenty-Eight

Checking the local South Jersey weather report once again, I inwardly groaned as I saw a low pressure system headed our way. After enduring record-high temps for the better part of July we were due for a break in the pattern. Lower temps would still be fine for outdoor activities, and more mild weather was almost always welcome. However, sandwiched between the official test days and the inaugural Grand-Am race at Indianapolis later in the month was a full week of scheduled ER and trauma service call for Joe and me. Normally, summer on-call days and nights were busy enough, especially with the population explosion created by vacationers, but the arrival of a low-pressure system upped the ante significantly. With low barometric pressure often came much larger waves, and with larger waves came more broken necks and spinal cord injuries.

A seemingly benign activity, body surfing is fun, easy, and available to anyone with swim trunks and a day off to spend at the beach. Unfortunately, the activity can also be deceptively dangerous, and in fact it's the mechanism by which I have met many of my more seriously injured patients. Riding a wave shoreward without the benefit of a board is pretty basic. In one variation of the technique, the body surfer places arms alongside the body, in order to streamline the surfer and allow one's head to stick out in front of the wave. I'm guilty of having done it myself—before I learned of the dangers of that particular method. A wave breaks when it encounters a sudden change in the bottom contour, such as when hitting a reef or, in the case of the Jersey shoreline, an angled sand bottom as the water gets shallow. Unfortunately, the combination of a rider with his head sticking out of the front of the wave and the force of a wave breaking with the surfer caught in the lip is often sufficient to create the terribly perfect circumstances for broken vertebrae, damaged disks, and injured spinal cords. Add to that the complete lack of awareness of the body surfer to the inherent danger (almost every patient has said to me, in one form or another, "I didn't realize you could get hurt doing that."), and you get an unfortunately frequent and awful occurrence of catastrophic, life-changing injury just because the weather changes.

Our week on call kept to the script, with the first 24 hours yielding two cases of spinal cord injuries from body surfers; both patients were partially paralyzed but without significant bony damage, so surgery was not immediately in order. Both Joe and I rounded daily on these patients, conferred with the trauma surgeons, and met with families to discuss current and future issues of care and expectations. All of that was routine and unfortunately familiar for us, and simply one small but significant part of each day on call. During the early part of the week, three additional patients arrived with various degrees of fracture and neurologic impairment, again with little to be offered in the way of immediate surgical care. For my part, I continued to slog my way through the rounding routine, counting down the days before I left for Indianapolis on Thursday for the Friday Grand-Am Brickyard Grand Prix. I was foolishly expecting the week's damage to be limited to the non-surgical kind, right up to the point where my trip to the racing mecca that was Indy was only one day away. However, the last trauma patient of the week, admitted on our last day of call, was a completely different clinical situation that demanded prompt attention and expedited surgery and, as it turned out, ultimately demanded all of my experience, skill, and compassion before the day was out.

Mary Sellars was visiting the Jersey Shore with her in-laws, husband, and two kids—one four years old, the other two. On an otherwise beautiful day, she joined her family for some innocuous fun in the unusually large surf at Sea Isle City, just a few islands south of the Atlantic City trauma center. Bodysurfing a wave toward the shore, Mary later recalled little about the forceful impact of her forehead against the sandy ocean floor, but she certainly realized that she had a serious problem when she emerged from the surf unable to feel her arms and unable to stand upright without assistance. After a quick triage by the local EMTs, Mary was rushed to our trauma center where she underwent numerous tests, trauma team admission, and a STAT consult by Joe.

Joe had done a neurological exam which revealed focal but significant areas of spinal cord damage; he then focused on the abnormal MRI findings as he relayed to me the details of the case by phone.

"She's got a massive herniation at C45, looks like her cord is getting squashed on the left side." (We use highly technical terms like "squashed" and "all messed up" all the time.)

I stared at the desktop screen at home, scrolling through the gray and white images of the scan completed only a few minutes prior to our call. "I'm on my way down; if you call the OR, I'll call the monitoring guys and Kurt."

We quickly moved into all-hands mode, mobilizing the troops for an emergent surgery which required several different participants. The sales rep Kurt would be present to make sure all of the necessary tools, equipment, and implants were on hand and properly sorted; the monitoring technician would be at the bedside to attach wires to the patient to continuously stream data on the electrical health of the spinal cord as we worked—a real-time virtual safety net for the team. All members of the team needed to be ready and sharp, so prepared for just such an emergency as to make it seem routine. Unlike the more dramatic TV and movie versions depicting emergency surgery and trauma care, in our world, things actually slow down a bit as the team gets ready to work. No nurses flailing about, no surgeons sprinting down the hall, nobody driving ninety miles an hour to the hospital. (OK, maybe that last part does happen, but I tend to drive that way every time I go to work.) The key is having a calm approach to the task at hand because that's what's required. We've all done this before, many times, and what's needed is a capable team that isn't in panic mode. Calm efficiency gets it done best, and that's what I found when I arrived at the hospital.

Standing next to the stretcher in the holding area was the understandably anxious husband, who offered his handshake in a hopeful fashion, no doubt sizing up the guy who was about to perform a very unexpected operation on his wife.

"I'm Dr. Lowe, Dr. Zerbo's partner. I'm sure he told you I'd be here; sorry to meet you under these circumstances." As I shook his hand I looked directly at his wife, who was lying flat in the stretcher wearing a neck brace and the requisite hospital gown, and looking terrified. If you've ever been in that situation, you know just how dehumanizing it is to meet someone and then talk with them while they tower over you above a bed or gurney. Mindful of that, I tried not to crowd myself over the patient and instead directed my attention to her as if we could have a polite moment to talk about her problem calmly.

"I know this isn't what you had planned for today, but let's talk about what happened to your neck and what we are going to do to fix it, OK?"

Mary nodded reflexively, wincing as she did from the pain of moving her neck even slightly.

"I heard all about how you were hurt; unfortunately, we see a lot of this sort of thing. Fortunately for you, you're much better off in terms of nerve function than many of our patients are."

I tried to be solid and confident with both the patient and her husband, balancing the desire to appear capable and experienced without seeming arrogant. It's generally tough to pull off, and I'm sure I've failed on many occasions, but usually I approach this as an opportunity to begin helping the family and the patient by putting them at ease. From there, it's all about finding the quickest way to educate everyone involved so that they can make some important decisions with some semblance of understanding some very complex concepts.

Having already heard the recommendation for surgery from my partner, Mr. Sellars spoke up. "Is surgery the only choice here, Doctor? We're from Canada, we obviously weren't quite ready for this today, and even the kids don't know we're here. They're back on the beach right now with my folks."

With that, Mary started crying—not a lot, just enough that the tears wet the sides of her face as she lay there. "Please, whatever you have to do, whatever I need to do, just do it soon. I can't stand the burning in my hands any more. Please tell me you can make it stop."

As the nurse placed EKG leads on her chest and various team members checked the chart and moved around the stretcher while performing the preparatory tasks of the impending surgery, I moved in closer. I needed those last few moments to connect with the husband and his distressed wife. "I know you've been told already, but I don't have any good or reasonable way to treat you without an operation. Your spinal cord is being severely pinched by the ruptured disc, and that's what's causing your pain and weakness. You have what we call a "Central Cord Syndrome"; it's one type of significant injury that we see when the disc is damaged and the cord gets compressed. If we don't go in now and get the pressure off of the spinal cord, the weakness and burning will probably stay the same, and the damage could get worse."

Realizing that they were finally accepting of the fact that emergent surgery was necessary, I knew what was coming next.

"Havc you done a lot of these?"

At this point, I again wanted to inspire confidence without appearing cocky, but I also needed to emphasize the gravity of the situation without scaring the shit out of them at a highly vulnerable time.

"On the good side, this is probably the most common operation that we do—that spinal surgeons worldwide do—I've done over three thousand of these—but for sure, there are risks that I know Dr. Zerbo already told you about. We're working right up against the spinal cord, and also around some very delicate structures, so there's always a chance of damage occurring every time we do this. But if you forget everything else, try to focus on this: the chance of damage with surgery is miniscule compared to the damage that is occurring while we stand here talking."

Mary looked at me, with drier but wider eyes now. "Doctor, I'm scared. My kids…" she trailed off and looked away.

"Look, I know it's a big deal for you, and I respect that, but this is routine and common for us, just the way you'd want it to be. In two hours you'll be awake in the recovery room, your hands will feel better, and your kids will still be enjoying the beach."

Mr. Sellars wrestled my attention away from the patient. "Doc, please take good care of my wife. Please."

"We're going to get started right away. I'll take good care and talk to you in a couple of hours when we're all done and it's over with."

With that, I left the holding area and went into the OR to do a procedure I had done literally thousands of times before.

Mary went to sleep routinely, with the anesthetist expertly inserting the breathing tube over a flexible lit tube, which allowed placement properly without moving the patient's damaged neck. The endotracheal tube was taped in place, IVs and arterial monitoring lines were inserted, and wires with needles on the ends placed through the skin into her scalp, arms, and legs. Each of the tubes and lines had immediate import: recording valuable blood pressure numbers, filling Mary's veins with saline, or checking electrical impulses travelling through the spinal cord as we worked against that fragile tissue. Each step was choreographed through countless repetitions until the movements were rote, ingrained, and reproducible without further thought. I helped Joe and the circulating nurse position the patient on the table, taking care to place yellow foam pads wherever the hard edges of the table contacted skin, and proceeded to drape out the surgical field—the area where the incision would be—with sterile blue paper sheets.

The first, and really most routine, part of the operation is one that seems to scare people the most. We make a cut in the skin of the front of the neck, and then work our way gently down to the front of the spine, moving our fingers back and forth to separate the tissue around the esophagus, the trachea, and the main blood vessels of the neck: the carotid artery and jugular vein. Despite the importance of these structures, they're quite easy to dissect and protect, and usually the front of the spine—bone and shock-absorber discs in between—is exposed within minutes of cutting skin. Petite and thin, Mary's neck was no exception, and I quickly identified the ruptured disc, confirmed it on X-Ray, and placed retractors in the area to maintain exposure while I began to work. Joe stood on the opposite side of the table, holding a suction tube in his left hand and picking out pieces of dissected disc with the forceps in his right.

On either side of the front of the spine, two paired muscles run lengthwise along the edges of the exposed areas of this surgery. These longus coli muscles have many small blood vessels at their edges and underneath the muscle belly; those vessels are a source of frequent but thankfully mild bleeding during this surgery. The careful surgeon touches each bleeding point with a bovie, an electric cautery blade, which typically stops the bleeding instantly. However, as the sparking blade hovers around the bleeding areas, the surgeon must keep in mind what lies not far underneath that area: the vertebral artery, which is the main source of blood supply to the brainstem. Each vertebral artery traverses the bone on either side of the neck, uniquely ending up in the part of the brain responsible for rudimentary and subconscious activity: breathing, swallowing, eye movements, and even staying awake. Injury to the vertebral artery can cause a severe and devastating stroke or death. Although it is not as well recognized as its cousin the carotid artery, the vertebral artery is even more important to your level of consciousness—how awake one is—than perhaps any other structure. Damage to that vessel is rarely benign and often has grave consequences. Fortunately, such an injury from surgery is exceedingly rare, as the artery is mostly protected by bone and rarely in the field of dissection in these routine operations.

As Joe tugged gently at a small fragment of disc material, I spotted a small area of bleeding just under the edge of the longus coli muscle on the left side of the surgical field. While Joe worked, I grabbed the bovie and routinely buzzed the edge of the muscle with the flat edge of the cauterizing blade. Since I was working under operating loupes attached to my glasses that magnified the view three times, the focus was narrowed and the details quite enlarged. As I worked the blade under the edge of the muscle, a sudden spray of blood shot out from the tip and my field of vision turned instantly and completely red. The blood shot forcibly out of the wound, and as I reflexively reached for a sponge to temporarily cover the area of bleeding, I was splattered with red across the front of my gown and mask.

With a typical episode of "routine" bleeding, the surgeons attack the problem by first regaining visibility: suctions are directed at the area of bleeding, and the offending vessel—the "bleeder"—is cauterized or tied off. Often this takes multiple tries, but the key is the ability to clear the field of blood with suction, so that the surgeon can clearly see the bleeding area. In this case, however, the bleeding was so rapid and forceful that both of the suctions used by Joe and me were overwhelmed by the sheer volume of blood. Classic surgical teaching now dictated we move to plan B—applying pressure to the bleeding area to limit the blood loss and regain control of the situation. Reaching blindly into the wound, I pushed a surgical sponge through the pumping stream of blood and placed it against the area where the bleeding had originated. On top of the first sponge, Joe immediately placed a second sponge, adding bulk to the tamponade against the muscle and the bleeder underneath. That maneuver helped slow the bleeding temporarily, but as soon as I relaxed my pressure against the sponge, the field filled with more blood.

We reloaded the sponges, and after a few tries, Joe and I were able to stop the active bleeding with pressure over the bleeder. I stood there, finger in the proverbial dike, finally ready to take a calmer assessment of the situation.

I turned to the anesthesiologist, who was peering somewhat anxiously over the drapes. "What's our pressure looking like, Mark? Are you guys stable up there?"

"All good on this side," Mark replied, "she's holding steady as a rock at a systolic of 105, and her heart rate hasn't budged."

I was happy to hear that, given what I was heard as I turned next to the cell-saver technician. "What'you got Steve?" Perched on a stool over the suction canisters and the machine that recycled the blood coursing through the suction tubes, Steve Lipsky was working furiously to clear the plumbing. "I've got 900 cc's already, Dr. Lowe." Given that the typical overall blood loss for this surgery was usually about 50 cc, and that the patient probably had a total blood volume of about 4 liters, this was alarming. Not quite believing the data, I stepped back from the table to turn my attention to Steve. "Really? You're not kidding—" My question was interrupted abruptly as I slid a bit in a puddle on the floor. I looked down to see red splatter on the floor along with a sizeable collection of thick blood. My clogs were covered with red, and blood covered most of my scrub pant legs visible below my gown.

No longer in need of any confirmation about the extent of the hemorrhage, I turned back to the field. I was pushing the sponge into the wound pretty firmly and was well aware that that pressure was a double-edged sword. In the area of exposure was the carotid artery, and continued pressure against the wound might also compress that artery.

"Tom? I'm not hearing anything from you, right?"

Tom Neill, the neuromonitoring technician, sat on the opposite side of the room, staring intently at this laptop screen. "I'm fine over here. Her corticals are steady, and there's no blip in the tracings from either side."

"I could be applying some compression to the carotid here, so keep an eye on it, and shout at the first sign of anything going the wrong way, OK?"

"You got it. She's hasn't budged from her baselines." Tom continued staring at the squiggly lines on his screen as the normal patterns confirmed absence of any serious change in the electrical activity of the brain and spinal cord.

Joe and I stared at each other over our loupes. “It can’t be the vertebral artery, can it? I mean, I was superficial—not anywhere near the artery with the bovie.”

“It’s sure not bleeding like a vein. I’ve never seen that before. Ever seen a vert injury?”

“Never. But if I had to imagine what one would look like, this would be it.” I gestured down at my blood-soaked gown and the red puddle in front of me.

“Tom, are you running brainstem responses?” I asked about the specific monitoring signals that could potentially show us whether or not there was damage from decreased vertebral artery blood flow to the base of the brain. Any suspicious deviation from the normal pattern could be a harbinger of brain malfunction—the occurrence of which, in the brainstem area, could result in a vegetative state or even brain death.

“Sorry Dr. Lowe, we don’t usually run those for these routine cervicals. I can get some leads in there now if you’d like.” Tom got to work under the drapes as Joe and I talked over the possibilities and what to do next.

“They describe aberrant vertebral arteries, but I’ve never really heard of one in this superficial location. I wasn’t deep enough for that, I think.” The last part was more question than statement.

Joe was quiet for a moment as I stood there, holding pressure with my fingers in Mary’s neck.

“It couldn’t be the carotid, could it?”

“You mean the left one?”

“I guess so, but is that even possible from this approach?” The typical exposure had the surgeon working near only one set of vessels, in this case the right carotid artery and jugular vein.

Given that I was already well down a road less travelled, I opined that at this point, we should be considering just about any possibility.

“Let’s try to get some better control over the bleeder, whatever it is, and then see if we can stop it all together.” I waited a moment for Joe to pick up his sucker, and then gently tugged at the sponges in the wound. As soon as I did, the wound filled again with bright red blood. I reacted by pure instinct, bred from twenty-five years of training and practice—that's why they call it "practice," by the way—while my mind was rapidly cycling through the possibilities.

"Shit! Sponges, quick now!"

I once again packed everything off, and got the bleeding back under control.

We had an unquestionably bad situation here—bleeding far worse than typical, source unknown right at that moment, and some very bad possible explanations looming. When strange things happen during surgery, and experienced surgeons get surprised, it's time to consider a different plan, a different thought process. What's the real problem? Is there an explanation that helps us then figure a way to fix the problem? And perhaps most of all, can we fix the problem and get back on track with little or no ultimate harm to the patient?

"Plan B??" I questioned Joe, who was already signaling for the charge nurse to come help.

"Let's get Pete Thompson in here. He might be able to help get control of the bleeder more proximally." Pete was a trauma surgeon originally trained as a vascular surgeon and certainly adept at handling both carotid and vertebral vessel problems. At that point, I figured we would need some way of determining if there was enough of an injury that we would have to open the neck lower down to get control—identify and put a clamp or suture around—the offending vessel.

Fortunately, Pete was on-call for trauma and was in-between cases just a few steps away from our room. When he arrived, I quickly gave him a synopsis of the case and voiced my concerns. I unnecessarily reminded him that although we shouldn't have encountered a major vessel in this exact location, there were reports in the Spine literature about arteries, especially vertebral arteries, running odd courses in unusual locations. These wayward arteries, called "aberrant," significantly increased the chance of the patient sustaining a vascular injury when the unsuspecting surgeon encountered them during the course of otherwise routine dissection.

"I'll wash my hands and look in there with you," Pete offered as Joe and I gave him the "hurry-up" look without calling too much attention to the fact that things were getting extreme.

When Pete returned and gowned up, I stepped to the side, still keeping a finger on the sponges in the wound. "Let me know when you're ready, and I'll get out of the way."

As Pete nodded, I pulled out the sponges and was again greeted with a hole rapidly filling with blood. Pete worked in the wound for a moment, calling for sponges and suction as necessary while attempting to identify the source of bleeding.

After a few minutes, Pete stuffed some sponges back in the wound and lookup up at me. "This thing is bleeding pretty good under the muscle. I can't even isolate the vessel. I don't think I can help you here. But I think you ought to give a call to Dr. Jamoona. He's right next door finishing a case. He might be able to do an angio and help out with a coil or something."

Dr. Amrith Jamoona was one of the hospital's newer neurosurgeons with specific expertise in treating blood vessels in and around the brain through endovascular techniques—working with catheters, injecting dye to examine the blood vessels, and stopping bleeding or obliterating aneurysms by injecting coils or glue. We hadn't had an opportunity to work together before this, but he responded quickly to the nurse's request and scrubbed in to help.

I described the problem to Amrith, who seemed a bit puzzled at first. "You can't control the bleeding? She's been stable, right?'

I explained the unusual situation. "We've got the active hemorrhage stopped, but each time we let up with the pressure, she bleeds more. It's not as bad as when it started, but the real issue is whether or not we have a major vessel injury. I know it sounds unlikely, given where we are in there, but I'm really concerned about a vertebral injury. Thankfully, her signals have remained OK, and her vitals are still fine, despite the blood loss."

Dr. Jamoona took another look and quickly confirmed what I was worried about. "It's certainly not typical for a venous bleed."

I wasn't offended by his statement of the obvious but did want to clarify that I understood the gravity of the situation, preferably without sounding too testy. "I understand that. I've done a few thousand of these and haven't seen anything that looks quite like this. I've heard about aberrant vertebral arteries before but haven't heard of one in quite this location."

Amrith offered a thought: "We could take her downstairs to the vascular suite, do an angio, and I could try to coil anything that's bleeding right there."

"I like the angiogram idea—I really think we need to see if there's a vessel injury—but I really don't want her to go downstairs. What if she starts bleeding in the elevator? We'd lose her right then and there."

We talked some more about options, and then Dr. Jamoona offered the solution: "I could call in the angio team and do one right here in the OR. I should be able to look at all four vessels, and we'd at least know if there's an injury or not. It'll take about twenty minutes for the team to get here, and we could start then."

Thankfully, the moments in my medical career where I have experienced a distinct feeling of dread have been few and far between. That sense of impending (or ongoing, as the case may be) disaster, and the feeling that irreversible harm has been done, is a surgical nightmare and the cause of stress, ulcers, depression, and more than a few early retirements in my field. I hadn't been there often, but I knew the sensation well enough when it occurred. And I knew then that this was rapidly becoming one of those. There was an accumulating heaviness in the pit of my stomach as I worked out the scenario in my head, considering all of the possible outcomes. Most of the endpoints I came up with were not good.

I looked at Joe, and back at Jamoona. "OK, let's do it that way. Joe, you better stay here to keep on the sponges and deal with any more bleeding. I'm going to go talk to the husband. I think we ought to tell him exactly what's up here." I stepped away from the table, pulling off my gloves and gown.

"Doctor, you'd better change your scrubs before you go out there." The circulating nurse pointed at my bloody green scrub pants. "And maybe wash your clogs a bit, huh?" I looked down at my yellow-white rubber clogs, cracked in several places after twenty-plus years of hard living. My bare feet inside were mostly red and I could feel the slippery sensation of the blood between my toes as I headed for the scrub sink.

Suitably cleaned up, I approached the husband in the surgical waiting area. He was sitting with legs up on a coffee table, head back, and eyes closed. “Mr. Sellars?”

He jumped to attention as I spoke, looking up at me with bright anticipation on his face. That look instantly turned dark when he saw my face and my look of concern.

“Is something wrong?” He was bolt upright as I pulled a chair next to him.

“She’s stable and still under anesthesia at the moment, but we’ve got a problem.”

I’ve said many times before that I’ve unfortunately met some of my patients and their families on the worst day of their lives. Whether the introduction is made over a CT scan while trying to convey some difficult concepts to a panicked patient or in the waiting room, where stunned family members are just beginning to understand the gravity of a loved one’s condition, I’ve been the bearer of bad news almost as often as I’ve been on the upside. The nature of our business includes managing and treating some very significant and occasionally deadly diagnoses, and from the beginning of our training, we have to learn how to best convey information, and occasionally condolences, in times of extreme emotion.

Although some of my colleagues might be criticized for their poor communication skills, most of the neurosurgeons I’ve worked with have an ability, innate or acquired I’m not sure, to talk about serious issues with patients and families. While many think that bedside manner is mostly demonstrated by physicians being talkative and outgoing with their patients, I feel that the real talent is exposed only when the interaction demands sensitivity and empathy in the extreme. Discussing overeating habits with a diabetic patient is one thing; telling a husband that the blood clot on his wife’s brain is a fatal occurrence is quite another. The demand is for the physician to have somehow acquired the skill required to speak gently, carefully, and clearly under stressful circumstances; the patient and/or family is dependent fully upon the ability of the doctor to educate them and help them make emotional decisions in what is often a frightening and foreign environment. I do take pride in my ability to talk with patients and families under these circumstances, but each event is a new and difficult experience all its own.

"We're experiencing unusual bleeding, and think there might be an injury to what's called the vertebral artery," I started out explaining to the husband. "Although there's no indication of damage on the electrical signals, and her blood pressure is fine, I'm concerned that the artery might be damaged, and that could cause significant problems."

"I don't understand, you don't know if there's a problem?"

I did my best to explain the issue to Mr. Sellars, trying to help him understand something I was not too sure of myself. "I've never seen this type of bleeding before, but the risk here is that she had an unusual variant of the artery's location, and it was damaged early in the case."

"You mean the surgery's not over yet?"

"Unfortunately, we'd only just gotten started with taking out the disc when the bleeding started. The rest of the disc removal and fusion hasn't been done yet; we're focused now on identifying the source of the bleeding and fixing it if possible."

The meat of the discussion was now at hand. "Doctor, is she going to be OK?"

I maintained eye contact with Mr. Sellars and replied, "I'm not sure yet. We need to get more information about the extent of the injury, but if the vertebral artery is damaged, it can have a wide range of effects."

"Like…?"

This was not a time to be reassuring, unfortunately. "Anything from no damage to significant stroke has been reported. I've had some experience with this type of injury in other cases—not like this one—where the outcome has been pretty bad."

The husband asked me to help him understand more. I offered some more detail, without adding too much confusing medical-ese. "If there's a stroke in this area, it could have very significant results—she might not wake up, she could die from this, there're too many possibilities to predict right at this moment."

Mr. Sellars fiddled with his phone, unconsciously twisting it from hand to hand, as he grimaced and fought the emotion of the moment. "She might not make it? Our kids don't even know we're here! My parents are with them…what will I tell them…Doctor, this can't be happening."

I was gentle but specific. "Look, we don't know everything I need to know to give you more information and advice just yet. I'm going back in there to see what the blood vessel test shows, and I'll be right out to let you know as soon as I know anything more. I promise you, we're doing all we can and everyone's in there doing their best." I stood up to leave.

"Please doctor…"

"I'll be back as soon as possible." I turned on my heel and left the waiting area, still very aware of the growing heaviness in my gut.

I tied on a new mask as I walked back into the OR. Joe was standing at the table, but he was no longer applying pressure in the wound, which I took as an encouraging sign. "No further bleeding since you left. She's been stable and there's been no change on Tom's end."

I went to the head of the table, peering over the edge of the drape as Dr. Jamoona was placing the catheter in Mary's groin. "We'll have a picture for you in just a moment. I have to get the catheter up to the arch, and then we'll start with the arteries, one by one."

I stood next to the anesthesiologist, helplessly watching the monitor screen as the ghostly image of the catheter snaked its way up through the aorta and up to the beginning of the carotid artery. I could feel my heart accelerate, and the gnawing sensation in my stomach intensified. Although the room was now crowded with at least twelve or thirteen people, I felt utterly alone. The beeps of the anesthesia machines, the soft instructions from Dr. Jamoona to the tech, all background noise faded out to an unconscious level. I looked down at my clogs once again, absentmindedly realizing that I had missed a few spots of blood when I had cleaned my feet earlier. Mary's blood. What would I tell the husband if we couldn't get her off the table? Jesus, her kids were playing unaware on the beach somewhere, while their mom was in a life-or-death fight in the OR. How would they deal with a brainstem stroke, with damage and impairment of almost unimaginable magnitude? I tried to switch my mind off that channel and refocused on Mary's most immediate needs. I knew I couldn't help her if I let myself become overwhelmed by the emotion of the situation.

"We're going to do the first run of the left carotid now," Amrith announced. Feeling more than a bit nauseated from the adrenaline, I watched as the dye spread seemingly magically out of the tip of the catheter and up through the artery. The pattern looked OK to me, but I waited for Amrith's opinion. "That's good, no problem there. Let's get the vert next." Although that was good news, I wasn't really as worried about the carotid on that side—it wasn't likely involved, given the anatomy and location of the bleeding. The vertebral artery was the issue, of course. I was fully aware of that and knew I might be about to see evidence, one way or another, of potentially the worst complication of my career. An injury would be there for all to see: the big blooming cloud of dye coming out of the hole in the artery would be easy to spot and obvious to anyone looking at the angiogram.

Swallowing hard, pulse pounding in my ears, I forced myself to watch the monitor as Dr. Jamoona steered the tip of the catheter into the opening of the vertebral artery.

"Here we go, image on continuous please."

The dye filled the artery, dark against the gray screen. Clean, smooth outlines of the artery's walls snaked upward, rapidly mapping the course of a normal, uninjured artery as it coursed towards Mary's brainstem. No cloud, no bloom of dye, just normal anatomy.

"That's a normal artery right there. No injury," pronounced Amrith.

I could feel, more than hear, Joe exhale as he looked in my direction. I started to hear the ambient noise in the OR again as I processed the information. "All good, right? I don't see anything consistent with an injury, right?"

As he started to maneuver the catheter into the right-sided vessels, Dr. Jamoona confirmed the good news. "It's normal anatomy here in all of the left sided vessels. I'm going to shoot the right side now, but I doubt there're any issues there."

As Amrith shot the rest of the dye study, demonstrating normal anatomy of the right carotid and vertebral, I moved closer to Joe to discuss next steps. "Best possible news, of course, but we need to decide what to do next. She might start bleeding again, but at least we know it's not from the vert, and we can control it better knowing that. Obviously, the small blood vessels under the muscle were what gave us fits, but we can deal with that now that things have quieted down, thank God. But if we quit now, we'll just have to come back later to get that disc out—I'd rather finish it off now."

Joe nodded in agreement, but warned, "That thing might bleed as soon as we put the retractor back in. We'd be working right there."

I looked over the drape at Mark. He didn't wait for my question. "She's been stable here. Pressures are fine, heart rate's fine, no resistance from up here."

"I'll go talk to the husband, and give him the news. I'll give him some options, but I think we should finish this up here."

Mr. Sellars was talking on his mobile as I turned the corner into the waiting room. "I'll call you back. The doctor's here." He looked at me, the stress evident in his eyes. I gave him a thumbs-up, and he brightened immediately.

"The dye study was negative—there's no artery injury, and she's stopped bleeding for a while now"

"Is she going to be alright? She's OK, right?"

I don't love the expression, but I said it anyway. "She's not out of the woods just yet, but the possibility of significant damage seems to be ruled out. Right now, she's stable in terms of blood pressure, her signals are fine, and we're considering proceeding with the surgery. But you have to know that there's a possibility she'll start bleeding again—after all, we don't know exactly why she bled so much in the first place."

I explained that we needed to get a retractor back in place, and that it would be right at the area of the bleeding; I also discussed the option of closing up and coming back another day. After answering his questions, I told Mr. Sellars my opinion that we should proceed, and he expressed understanding, and more importantly, trust.

"Please finish up as best you can, doctor. I don't think any of us can make it through another day of this—let's be done with it, but please get her out alright, OK?"

For the third time that day, I left the room after promising to take good care of his wife.

I reentered the operating room, where the air was somehow now more breathable than just a few moments before. I resumed my normal station at the side of the table, pausing only a moment to notice that the blood on the floor had been cleaned up in my absence.

"Retractor, please," I said, simultaneously gently pulling sponges out of the wound. "Let's get this back in there, but I want everyone heads-up right now. If she's going to bleed again, it will be now, as I stretch out the tissue over that area."

Whether it was moments before the gun at the start of a mile-relay race, trying to go deeper into the braking zone in Turn 1 at Daytona, or applying gentle force to a retractor in a patient's neck, I was familiar with that elevation in stress and focus demanded on occasions of routine but intense circumstances. Perhaps familiarity added to the possibility of success; perhaps the recognition of familiar sensations allowed the experienced runner/driver/surgeon to meet and beat the challenge. Maybe even luck had to factor in there somehow—helping explain why so many of my colleagues and fellow competitors are superstitious. More than likely, there is an inestimable and changing combination of factors that have to combine properly to allow one to move through, and on past, those moments of intense and otherwise insurmountable challenge.

I opened the retractor, ratcheting it wider click by click, intently watching for any sign of bleeding. Nothing. Dry as a bone, now.

"OK, we're good. Let's get this disc out and finish up the fusion before she changes her mind."

As we finished up the rest of the procedure without further problems, I continuously ran over in my mind what had just happened and why. Having eliminated all of the scariest and most significant possibilities, I was left with the rarest of explanations—that of an extreme amount of bleeding from a common source, presenting in a fashion so atypical as to derail an otherwise routine operation. I silently shook my head as I worked, wondering again at the amazing things I've encountered during my career. Neither Joe nor anyone else in the operating room with me had to question why I was muttering and shaking my head; I may as well have been thinking out loud.

***

The next morning, before I got on the plane to Indianapolis, I touched base with Joe. He had finished rounds a few moments before and updated me on Mary's condition.

He sounded pretty upbeat for a guy who had gotten so beat up the day before. "She's doing fine, like nothing ever happened. She walked this morning and told me her hands feel a whole lot better."

"What's her hemoglobin?"

"8.9 this morning, down just a bit from last night after she's gotten more IV fluid in her on the last shift."

"That's great!" I said, somewhat unnecessarily. "Her strength any better?"

"She's improved quite a bit at the shoulder. But here hands are still weak. Maybe a bit better than pre-op."

"Well, they know she is going to require a lot of time before the spinal cord function improves. It all sounds pretty encouraging though. How's the husband?"

Joe had talked to him after seeing Mary on rounds. "He's still pretty dazed by everything that went on, but he's busy making preparations for her to go to rehab in Canada as soon as possible. She's probably doing better than he is right now."

I thanked my partner for doing all the grunt work while I went off to play race car driver for another weekend. "Thanks for holding down the fort while I'm in Indy. I'll be near the phone if anything changes, but don't call at four tomorrow. I'll probably be busy right about then."

***

Friday morning, I was lying stretched out on the floor of the Doran Racing hauler, resting my head on a helmet bag, when Paul Tracy arrived for the morning warm-up. I wasn't suited up yet since the Grand-Am practice session wasn't scheduled to start for another hour. I opened one eye as PT came up the steps and took in his co-driver's not-so-animated form. "Yo Yo Jimmy Lowe, ready to run Indy, buddy?" Tracy exclaimed, stopping short as I rolled up on one elbow and looked at him. "Whoa JLowe, you look like shit, man. You stressed out or something?"

I plopped my head back down onto the bulky helmet bag. "Hey PT, you don't look so hot yourself, dude, but at least I can look good sometimes."

Tracy ignored my lame attempt at humor as he stepped over me and hung up his gear. "Drivers meeting in thirty minutes man. Anybody seen Kevin? Who's going first for practice? Wow, this is a super laid back deal here." Paul laughed as I sat up, stretched briefly, and then decided I was better off lying down.

I didn't pass on the opportunity to tease PT, one of the planet's most laid-back humans (when he's not behind the wheel of a race car, that is). "Dude, you're going to have to relax a bit. You're way too high-strung for me."

"Man, with Indy car teams I've been with, every minute is scheduled. It's way more intense. Here nobody even knows when they're driving or when we're meeting for strategy."

I reminded Paul that the strategy was for me to start, survive the stint, and then for him to take over and win the whole damn race all by himself. He chuckled again, more to himself. "OK then, I'll take the next few hours off."

Although we had had two full days of testing in early July for drivers and teams to get familiar with Indy's F1 road-course track layout and surfaces, the Doran car hadn't run a single lap in the rain. In fact, the four events that Paul and I had run together so far, including all of the 24 Hours of Daytona, had been in entirely dry conditions. I fully expected that streak to hold up at Indy, where there had been drought conditions for over a month and where the early forecast mentioned nothing about rain.

The morning practice on race day was limited to one hour, split between both drivers, immediately prior to a fifteen minute qualifying session. Both sessions were run on a dry track, despite that fact that unscheduled rain clouds threatened overhead. In the practice hour, Paul and I ran well, with both of us showing times that suggested the car was handling the variable grip of the Indy surfaces even better than during the test days. I drove the Dallara DP, newly painted yellow with M&M's Snack Mix sponsorship, as hard as I dared without risking taking it off the track. There would be no time to repair a banged up race car with the compressed schedule calling for a race start barely a few hours after the morning practice.

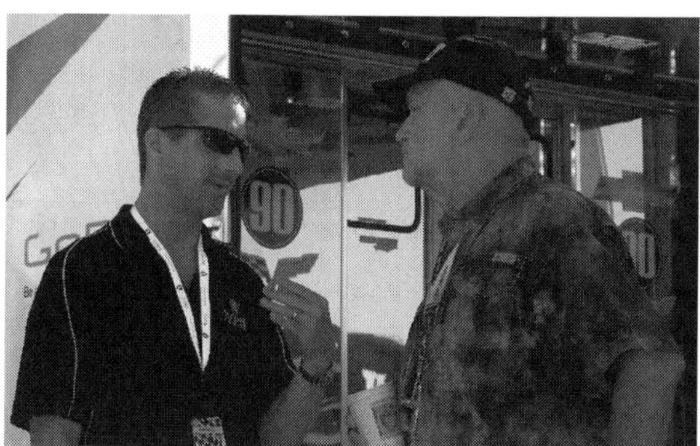

Jim chats with Ford's D.C. Williams

After completing the second part of the session with the prototype still a bright and dent-free shiny yellow, I took a five-minute breather outside the car. As the crew changed tires, refueled, and fiddled with suspension settings ideal for the coming qualifying attempt, I sat on the pit wall to catch my breath. A quick drink and a short stretch was in order, as I was still sweaty from the warm-up laps. Ignoring my rising heart rate and trying to steady my breathing, I put my balaclava on and donned my helmet. A moment later I fired up the engine, rolled past the elevated Indianapolis podium and the sign for Gasoline Alley, and headed out to join the other ten cars lined up at pit-out. I took my place at the end of the line, selecting neutral and rolling to a stop with one eye on the gauges and one on the starter standing in front of the lead car.

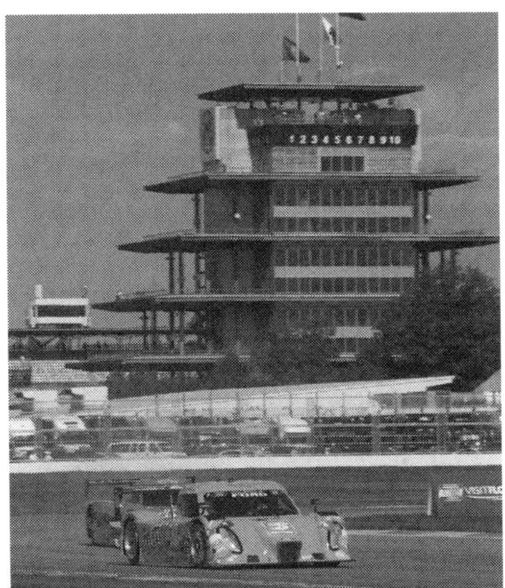

The Doran #77 DP on-track at Indianapolis, 2012

A moment later, the pit lane official dropped his black flag, exchanging it for a green one which he waved to signal the start of the session. One by one, each driver selected first gear, and spun the tires in a cloud of white smoke as we all struggled to put some instant heat into the rubber on the way out.

Having been on track only a few minutes before, I didn't really need a whole lot of reconnaissance on my out-lap. I did hazard a look around on my first trip around the Indy circuit, taking in the big crowd and enjoying for one last moment the look of the famous track from the best seat in the house. However, once I exited the infield's last turn, sliding out onto the banked surface of the oval, it was all focus, full-on attention to the task at hand.

I ran hard and as close to the edge as I could muster, still mindful of the need to bring the car back injury-free. For a lap or two I felt quite good, feeling stable and comfortable in both the heavy braking zones of Turns 1 and 8, and also the quick corners of Turns 5 and 12. Towards the middle of the session, I had managed to better my personal best time by nearly a second, right before I got a punctured left front tire. I didn't have enough time to become aware of the loss of tire pressure before the car lost grip in the braking zone of Turn 4. I spun off into the kitty litter, beaching the car with no hope of an easy exit. The session was checkered early when I couldn't get out of the gravel trap, no doubt short-changing several drivers setting up for one last final flying hot lap. While the spin and aborted session didn't ultimately affect my starting position, it would have been nice to get one last, incident-free lap into my brain right before the race started.

I returned to the hauler, planning to grab a bite to eat with the crew before retreating to the front office. Outside, there was the usual gaggle of media types around Paul, who was standing in front of the hauler doors, politely answering questions and signing autographs. I took a few moments to speak with a few of the reporters and answered some of the now-obligatory ques-

PT giving yet another autograph to a fan

tions about "What's it like to have Paul Tracy as your teammate?" and "How is it trying to perform alongside a racing legend?" I signed a few photos and hero cards from fans who were polite enough to include me when PT was around and then slipped away to put my feet up before race time.

Staking out prime couch space for a quick nap, I realized that I was very fatigued—and more than a little overwhelmed. I closed my eyes, listening to the sounds of the Continental Tires series support race starting up, letting my thoughts drift away from the increasingly raucous activity in the hauler. I'd be taking the green flag at Indianapolis, the track of my boyhood dreams, in just a few hours. But first, I had to get my head right and ready myself to switch into another gear altogether. Quiet meditation was in order.

PT stumbled in, followed by Murray. I barely acknowledged them, covering my eyes with a balaclava. "Nap time," Paul announced. He hit the floor, right next to Mur who set up under the desk. "Somebody wake me up when it's time to drive."

"I'm thinking I'll be a little busy around then," I answered, "Where's your handler? Can't he do the dirty work?"

PT ignored me, rolled over, and I kid you not, started snoring about ten seconds later.

I lay silently, listening to the sounds of the racing outside and the snoring inside. I fell into a dreamless sleep, enjoying the rare ability to shut it all down so as to have better capacity for the violent activity waiting for me when I awoke.

Rather than engine noise or loud talking, the noise that woke me was rain. It took me a bit, but I gradually became aware of the sound of hard raindrops beating on the roof of the hauler. It took a full minute more before I realized that it was indeed pouring outside, just in time for the beginning of our race. PT stirred a few moments later, lifted his head to listen, and summed up my concern.

"Dude, you ever driven a DP in the rain before?"

I shook my head, grimacing at the thought. "It can't be all that hard, right?"

"I couldn't tell you," PT smiled as he replied, "I've never driven one of these things in the rain either."

"Oh, that's just great," I said. "The blind leading the blind."

Mur had awakened, and joined in the conversation. "Well, look on the bright side. At least your blind guy is really fast."

My brain was now fully awake. OK, this rain wasn't on the agenda for my racing plans, but no one else seemed to care what I had in mind anyway. Like it or not, it looked like I'd be doing some wet running, in the rain, on TV, at Indy. Like beginning a routine surgery and ending up in the midst of an unanticipated complication, I was going to have to adapt, deal with the issue, and get through it safely if I wanted to come out the other side better off than when I started. Bear down, buddy, because you're here and this is how it's going to go. Like it or not.

Thirty minutes later I was strapped in to the yellow Dallara DP, doing the radio check and fiddling with gauges as the crew steered me out onto the tarmac. I hit the master control button, toggled the switches into the up position, and hit the start button to fire up the Ford engine. A satisfying roar filled my ears, and the vibration settled through my torso instantly. A few seconds later, the chill of the cold water circulating through my cool shirt presented itself, and the radio crackled to life.

"OK Jim, go on out through pit lane for the recon lap, and come back onto the front straight to your starting position. You're P10, on the left side. Look for Russ as you get there. Make sure you check for puddles on the recon."

"Thanks Kevin. Great to be racing Indy with you guys. I could've done without the rain though."

"Rain? What rain?" Rick had clicked onto the channel. I looked up as I started to pull out, seeing Rick standing next to the hauler in the downpour as if it were dry and sunny. He waved to me. "See you down there, Jim."

Minutes later I pulled the yellow prototype into position in my grid spot on the front straight of the Speedway, not too far away from the famous Yard of Bricks that was all that was left of the original Speedway surface. I sat belted into my seat as the crew opened the doors to get some air into the cockpit. The mix of hot air and rain felt nice, but the window started to fog almost immediately. I chatted a bit on the radio with Kevin and then stayed silent as they played the National Anthem. As Russ and Noah closed the doors of the DP, I saw the tail end of the flyover, knowing what was coming next.

Noah twirled his finger just in case I had missed it, but I heard the track announcer clearly enough over the Indianapolis PA system.

"Gentlemen, start your engines."

As I pushed the starter button, I again had that recurring anxiety sensation. I tried to embrace it, convincing myself that there was a feeling of enjoyment in there somewhere. I was about to start a race—at Indy, for chrissakes—whether I now thought it was a good idea or not. No going back now, showoff. And it's raining. Nice. So many thoughts jumbled together that it seemed like several people were all shouting at me at once.

I then realized Kevin's voice was in my ears. "There's going to be three pace laps, not two, because of the rain."

I snapped back to the task at hand. "Copy that," I replied, as I pulled off the line behind the blue and white prototype in front of me.

The column of eleven DP's snaked through the twelve turns of the first paced lap, sending up sprays of water here and there, weaving along behind the pace car as drivers sought to get heat into their grooved rain tires. As we came down the front straight for the second time, Kevin came back onto the radio.

"That's Scott Dixon behind you in the Ganassi prototype. Just wanted to let you know."

"Who?" I knew who Dixon was, of course, but wanted to bust balls a bit.

"Scott Dixon. You know, Indy 500 winner, Indy Car champ, famous fast guy."

"Never heard of him."

I chuckled as I bent the car down into Turn 1.

Kevin clicked back on a moment later. "Just thought you might like to know he's back there. You know, for when he passes you, I guess."

By this time we were on the back straight, heading for the last few turns before the front stretch and the green flag. "Well, I don't care if he's Mr. Famous Guy, tell him not to get too upset when he can't get past me." I could hear the crew laughing over the open mike as we made the turn onto the front straight. "Gotta go guys, see you in about an hour."

The line of cars slowed considerably as we approached the starter stand. The pace car had already pulled off into pit lane, leaving the pole sitter to control the speed of the start. I focused straight ahead, vaguely aware of the increasing spray coming off the tires of the car directly in front of me. Wipers going full speed, the sound of the engine straining at higher revs in first gear, all the senses on high alert now.

I thought then of the so absolutely cool concept of racing at Indy, of sitting in front of the black-and-white TV with my dad, listening to Jackie Stewart narrate another Indy 500, of landing face-down in fresh cut grass on some football field somewhere, of the long and beautiful trip to that moment when I somehow ended up here, at Indianapolis. All images, most minimally distorted, some more pleasant than others, all critical to the evolution of that moment.

I also thought for a moment about my patient back home, trying that day to walk again after nearly dying in my OR, her kids on the beach unaware of the drama their mother was fighting through, and reviewed for a moment the very recent good fortune that I had experienced and now embraced yet again. I had tackled the intensity of that OR, faced down the very real fear of having hurt one of my patients, and helped my patient (and me) survive the process by doing what I was meant to do—and doing it well. I was thankful that moment was safely past now, with life and the best living happening right in front of me, right now.

Despite the crescendo of noise all around me, I could easily hear Kevin's excited voice on the radio. "Green green GREEN!"

I pressed hard on the throttle as the whole straightaway seemingly exploded in a white cloud of spray. The car wiggled briefly as the wheels spun a bit and then lurched forward as they gained traction on the rough Indy track surface. I accelerated hard, eyes wide as I bit down harder on my drink tube nozzle, realizing that I couldn't see a thing out of the windscreen.

As the engine surged to full song, I remained wide-eyed with a too-firm grip on the Dallara's steering wheel. I was flying blind, much like a pilot's cockpit view in thick clouds. I had expected a tough time with visibility when the race went green, but this was ridiculous. I was sightless and slippery, blowing down Indy's front straight at a speed in excess of 180 mph. In front of me were nine other cars (until Dixon shot on by my right front fender, making it ten), all braking hard for Turn 1 on a slick track, with another thirty-five GT cars running up behind. Nowhere to go but into the slow-down zone, hoping to avoid the accordion effect of the cars bleeding off speed for the corner ahead while staying in front of the guys charging up in back of me.

Jim racing in the rain at Indy, 2012

I had noticed during the testing days and practice laps that there were two green lights spaced out high on the catch fencing to my left, positioned so the second light appeared just before the brake point of Turn 1. I hadn't realized it then, but now that I was racing hard in zero visibility, those lights were critical. Having nothing of interest to see through the white-out that was in front of me, I craned my neck, straining against the HANS device, and watched for the lights to appear. As the gray fence whizzed by, I saw the first green light, and then the second in rapid succession. On cue, I stomped down with my left foot, hitting the brake pedal just a bit softer than typical for dry conditions. I turned down early as the car slowed, heading for the inside line and hoping for better grip there. As the pack of cars slowed in seeming synchronized fashion, the spray died down and a fantastic view emerged through my windshield: Prototypes of all different colors surged through Turns 1, 2, and 3, door handle to door handle, bumping and rubbing as we all struggled for grip and tried to get our right feet flat to the floor. As the engine note intensified in my helmet, and the noise level rose exponentially, my view widened to take note of one car spinning off to my right and John Pew, directly in front of me, getting loose and nearly spinning out into Turn 3. I checked up in order to avoid contact and immediately lost my momentum going into the next sequence of turns. As I came alongside John, expecting to pass him, he suddenly recovered enough to resume his place in front of me. I tucked my nose right under the wide rear deck of his Riley DP and stayed with him until Turn 7. Exiting seven onto the inside straight at Indy was relatively mundane in dry conditions, but this wet running was a different deal altogether. I slid wide off the apex as I turned the corner, trying to put power down and avoid puddles at the same time. I watched as virtually every car in front of me wiggled its way down the straight, upshifting as I accelerated behind them.

The force of the gear change, automated as it was by pulling ever so gently on the right-sided paddle behind the steering wheel, caused instant wheelspin as I tried to point the car properly down the wide surface. As I did, the back end of the car swung out wildly as the rear wheels lost grip and spun freely. I reacted without thinking, sawing at the steering wheel until the nose returned to its original bearing and the rear of the car settled back down. Two further upshifts at full throttle on the inside straight resulted in the same sequence: wheels spin, car slides, adjust the steering input and catch the near-spin so that one might continue on in the correct direction. All while trying to keep on the tail of the car to your front, and remain in front of some very eager guys behind.

Moments later I was sliding the car back out onto the oval section of the track, briefly enjoying the enhanced grip of that surface before the higher speed made the lights go out again. The spray was everywhere, and the only way to improve things was to go slower, which was a poor option to embrace at that particular time. Instead I forced my right foot to push harder as I tried to stay on top of the car in front, watching again for the green beacons on the fence as I navigated the front straightaway at full speed. One light, two lights, !brake!, turn down and get back to power once the rear end settled. I ultimately settled into a rhythm, not quite as easily as when lapping in dry conditions, but a rhythm nonetheless, tiptoeing through the apex of each turn and catching the now-predictable slide of the car onto the banking each lap. As I did so, the race pace settled into a steady sequence, as cars generally lined up according to their pace and driver's ability to keep them facing forward. At one point, I passed a limping DP with front end damage, a sobering reminder of the need to stay clean and race clean until I handed the car off to Paul. Suitably reminded of my role, I raced hard but cautiously, not wanting to create a bigger gap to the front runners through a thoughtless mistake.

Wet laps at Indianapolis, 2012

Approximately thirty minutes into the race, the rain let up and the track started to dry rather quickly. Of all the possible combinations, the wet-to-dry progression of track conditions is one of the most challenging for the driver. Grip improves steadily, usually, but different sections of a track often dry at different paces. Hence the driver can't assume all turns are regaining grip at the same rate, risking calamity if a turn is attempted at "I've got faith and big balls" speed when the surface isn't quite up to par yet. It's a continuous learning process, all done while the driver desperately hopes he's learning faster than the other guy.

As the track dried, my confidence level rose, and I started to pick up the pace. Most of the racing line now appeared to be dry, although there were still puddles to be hit if you weren't paying attention. I gradually relaxed the tension in my shoulders, realizing that I had been straining at the bit and clenching my jaw for the last twenty laps or so. Kevin then clicked on to the radio, snapping me out of my calm happy place while negotiating Indy's Turn 1 flat out.

"You need to look for some wet spots and cool the tires, Jim."

Great. After struggling to find dry track and good grip, my soft rain tires were quickly going to pieces as the dry surface chewed up the pliable rubber. "Copy that Kevin, what's the window?" I wanted to know how much longer I was going to need to stay out on the rain tires.

"Just keep running, your pace is OK, but find some puddles for us, OK?"

I headed for each puddle that I could reasonably find without venturing too far off line, noticing that I was now getting lapped by several of the faster prototypes, all of whom seemed to have much better grip than my Dallara.

"Hey guys, I guess everybody's on slicks already?" I checked in with the crew once again. "I'm getting toasted out here, and the grip's gone away pretty badly."

"Stay out, stay out."

I ran several more laps, sliding more now than I remembered during the rain laps, feeling the tires literally melt under me as each corner went by. My braking became more of an adventure each time, and both the front and the rear of the car hunted for purchase on the dry surface as the tires died a slow ugly death.

Two laps later, my Indy adventure was over.

"Pit now, pit now. Driver change. Sticker tires."

"Copy that, pitting now. I'm on my way."

I pulled off to the right out of Turn 12, gliding the car onto pit road and hitting the pit lane speed limiter button just as I downshifted to first gear and passed the entrance cones. The 45 mph speed limit felt like a crawl as I loosened my belts, unplugged my cool suit hoses, and prepared for the driver change. On my way in, I chanced a look at the grandstands, taking in the big crowd, now sans umbrellas, and the freshly washed colors of pit lane. I was fully aware that I might not experience that particular view again anytime soon, or maybe ever. I sat there savoring the unique perspective of my personal front row seat at the world's most famous racetrack and had to purposefully keep up my speed all the way to our pit box, resisting the urge to stop, dismount, and do snow-angels right there on the tarmac.

I snaked my way out of the cockpit as Rick pulled at hoses and belts to clear a path for my exit and Paul's entrance. Steeping onto the asphalt, I spun to my left, cleared the back of the car, and hopped over the pit lane wall as the crew hefted fresh tires in the opposite direction.

I sat down with a heavy thud, pulling off gloves, helmet, and balaclava in seemingly one motion. I felt someone slap a wet towel onto the back of my neck, relieved at the cold wet sensation while feeling the heat inside me rise. I took slow, deep breaths, drank from a water bottle that appeared in front of me, and closed my eyes as the buzzing rose in my ears.

Cold, hot, wet, sweaty, exhausted, and exhilarated all at the same time, I let my own engine run down to idle as I sat in the pits at Indy. I felt a tug at my elbow and opened one eye suspiciously. I wasn't expecting kudos after the way I just drove—getting lapped, sliding all over the track, not passing anyone in my class. I grimaced as Kevin appeared in front of me.

"Nice job out there," he smiled as he handed me another water. "Sorry we left you out there so long on the wets. Everybody else pitted early, but we wanted you to get more time out there."

"Sorry I did such a poor job, I felt so slow out there…"

"Hey, you did fine. Car's in great shape, and Paul will get us back on the lead lap here in a moment. You did fine. Now you can relax and watch the race."

Kevin returned to his post up on the pit cart, and I closed my eyes once again.

I slowed my random thoughts, focused in on the good words from Kevin, and channeled my teenage self. Gotta be at least a little proud of having survived that in one piece now, huh? You just played with the big dogs on the big stage—Indy!—and handed a good car over to Paul Tracy—PT for chrissakes!—to take it home. Now enjoy the success for what it is—very special—and cheer on your teammate.

Paul did a fine job with our Gen-2 prototype, running as high as fourth place, especially when the rain returned and intensified. However, a stuttering restart and subsequent penalty, followed by a puncture, essentially ended our chances of a miracle finish. Still, we had much to be proud about: we finished in P6, right behind Darren Law and Joao Barbosa, and two guys named Dixon and Montoya. Even better, there were quite a few recognizable names behind us: Donohue, Dalziel, Westbrook, Gavin, Fogarty, and Gurney. Some pretty fast company, I thought.

I called my dad later that evening, right before I boarded the plane for home.

"Hey dad, hope you saw at least some of that, I really had fun today. Just drove Indy. Pretty cool. Better than it ever looked on TV. Thought of you a lot."

As always, he didn't say much, but I knew he was proud and maybe even a little excited.

"That's pretty great, Jimmer" was about all he could say.

***

Just a day after my adventure in the rain at Indianapolis, I was back at work, rounding on patients in the Trauma ICU. After seeing a few patients who thankfully didn't need anything in the way of my surgical services, I stopped to check on Mary Sellars. She was sitting in a bedside chair, wearing civvies and apparently waiting for her ride to the airport. I felt an immediate sense of relief when I saw her relaxed posture.

"Hey, Dr. Lowe here. Just stopping in the say goodbye."

Mary seemed to remember me, despite the fact that many of my patients lose quite a bit of recall for the events immediately surrounding a traumatic episode. "Hi Doc, heard you were away for a bit. Thanks for coming in."

I enjoyed the smile on Mary's still somewhat pale face.

"Apparently I gave you guys a bit of a scare, huh?"

I didn't see any need to sugarcoat it at that point. "Yeah, you made us work pretty hard the other day. But looks like you're none the worse for the wear and tear."

"Yeah, and my arms feel alive again. Thanks to you and Dr. Zerbo."

I shook her hand, and figured that was a good high note to leave on. "Tell your husband I said hello, and be sure to call with any questions. Glad to see you're doing so well."

I exited the room and searched out her chart so that I could jot down a progress note. As I sat down with the chart and wrote my note, one of the ICU nurses stopped at the desk.

"Hey Dr. Lowe, I read about your racing in the paper. That sounds pretty cool. I didn't know you were still doing that."

I looked up to see Janice, one of the long-time and very experienced Intensive Care nurses. "Yep, we've had a pretty good season so far. Daytona again, a couple more races, and I just got back from Indianapolis. I'm having fun, for sure."

Janice smiled. "It must be good for you. You look more relaxed than I remember."

"Yep, a great way to relax." I smiled back.

"I keep meaning to ask you, ever since I read that article in The Press—how did you get started with all that racing?"

I shut the chart. "It's a bit of a long story, but if you have a minute, I'll give you the Reader's Digest version."

Getting Up To Speed
Glossary of common racing terms

ALMS: "American Le Mans Series", one of the competing professional Sports Car racing series in the US; merged with Grand-Am in 2013 to form United Sportscar Championship

Apex: The ideal point in the corner where the car comes closest to the inside edge of the road on the perfect racing line

Chicane: A quick combination of turns interrupting a straightaway, usually put in place to slow the cars, see also moving chicane

Cool suit: Driver underwear that has cooling tubes that circulate ice water around the torso

Data: Computer information from sensors on the car showing speed, brake pressure, throttle application, cornering force, steering wheel position, etc.

DFL: Dead Fucking Last

Downforce: Aerodynamic force, created through wings and other parts of the car's body that helps keep the car glued to the track

Esses: Any series of S-shaped turns

Fire suit: Racing suit, usually designed to protect drivers from fire

Flat, Flat-out: Going through a turn at full-throttle; 100% commitment

Formula One: Also called "F1," Open-wheel, single-seater international race series with the world's fastest race cars

GT car: Race car built based upon a marque's existing road car (e.g., Porsche, Ferrari, Pontiac, BMW, Mazda) but not street-legal

Grand-Am: One sanctioning-body for American professional Sportscar racing; owned by NASCAR; merged with ALMS in 2013 to form United Sportscar Championship

Hairpin: A sharp, 180-degree turn

HANS Device: Driver safety device attached to the helmet and held onto the shoulders by the safety belts; designed to limit head flexion in an impact

Line: Preferred path of the race car through the corner to maximize speed

Lock-up: Braking hard enough that the wheel stops turning entirely, resulting in a loss of traction

Loose: term also used for Oversteer

Moving chicane: A particularly slow driver, who forces other, faster cars to find a way around him

NASCAR: National Association for Stock Car Auto Racing, family-owned series focused on stock car racing; also, parent organization of Grand-Am

Nomex: Fire-resistant material from which most fire suits are made

Open-wheel car: Race car without fenders—where the wheels are exposed

Oversteer: Action of a car where, in a corner, the rear tires are at a greater slip angle that the front, resulting in the back end of the car sliding away from the direction in which the driver is turning.

Pole: Driver/car that qualified in first position

Prototype, Daytona Prototype (DP): Purpose-built race car, not based on existing road-going cars; usually fastest class of car in sports car racing

Qualifying: Pre-race event where driver's fastest times determine starting order for the race

Single-seater: Race car with only one, centrally positioned seat

Slicks: Smooth racing tires, made without grooves to maximize the contact area of the rubber

Sticker tires: New tires that still have the manufacturer's sticker on them

Testing: Racing's version of "practice," during which various car setups are "tested" for maximum lap speed

Throttle: Gas pedal

Understeer: Action of a car where, in a corner, the slip angle of the front tires is greater than the rear tires, resulting in the front end of the car not turning enough when the driver turns the steering wheel

Acknowledgements

I certainly could not have completed this memoir without the help and guidance of good people too numerous to count. And surely, there would be no beginning or middle either, without the friends, family and occasional innocent bystanders who, in one way or another, contributed to getting and keeping this project moving.

As I hope would be unequivocally clear from even a cursory reading of the book, all things that reflect love and my happiness in life ultimately include and reflect my wife, Ginny. Her unwavering demonstration of love and support is my daily fuel, without which I'd be wandering aimlessly, with the gage stuck on "E".

My partner, Dr. Joe Zerbo, has suffered without complaint my long absences from work while I indulged myself at the racetrack, and remains the best example of the "ideal partner" and friend that any surgeon might dare hope for.

Jim Pace still is the first name I think of when considering all of the drivers who have had some hand in helping me develop from a back-row moving chicane to a solid, if unspectacular, racer. Others, like Paul Tracy, Gerardo Bonilla, Ryan Dalziel, Johannes van Overbeek, and Tim Sugden became valued friends also as they tried to get me up to speed.

Many hands made for lighter work in getting my first book to the finish line: Roger Garbow was of great help in all aspects of the book: design, edits, vision, production, and marketing all point back in Roger's direction, and thankfully so. Lois de la Haba helped navigate my first attempts at getting a book published, and her guidance and careful recommendations were valuable in getting me back on track when I strayed off the paved surface. Murray Marden was always willing to talk, and was a constant reminder of the huge fun we had on and off the race track.

Friends and family remain so valuable to me, and I enjoyed the chance to tell a story that might entertain them, and maybe even result in a few more new friends along the way. Many thanks to you all, and apologies for failing to name the very large number of you who are still so important in my life.

Thanks to all who contributed photos to this book, including Jackie Buys, Sidell Tilghman, Sue Auriemma, Regis Lefebure, and "some guy named Denny" from my dad's WWII unit.

Teammates

Thomas Blam

Colin Braun

Kevin Buckler

Steve Bunkhall

Sebastien Constans

Ryan Dalziel

Kathy Dandurand

David Donohue

Kevin Doran

Tomas Enge

Mike Forrest

Brian Frisselle

Burt Frisselle

Roger Garbow

Revere Greist

Mike Johnson

Ralf Kelleners

Eric Lux

Murray Marden

Ashlei Newkirk

Jim Pace

John Potter

Roger Reis

Tim Sugden

Paul Tracy

RJ Valentine

Johannes van Overbeek

Barry Waddell

James Walker

Jim Lowe Race History

1999-2000 Jim Russell Racing School

2000 Formula Russell race series

2001 Skip Barber Racing School

2001-2005 Skip Barber Formula Dodge regional race series

2004-2006 Skip Barber Masters National racing series

2006 Grand-Am Road Racing, (TRG) GT Class:
5 starts, 3 top-ten finishes.

2007 Grand-Am Road Racing, (TRG) GT Class:
6 starts, 1 top-ten finish

2008 Grand-Am Road Racing, (TRG, JLowe Racing) GT Class:
6 starts, 1 top-ten finish

2009 Grand-Am Road Racing, (JLowe Racing), GT Class:
2 starts, 1 top-ten finish

2010 Grand-Am Road Racing, (JLowe Racing), GT Class:
1 start

2011 Grand-Am Road Racing, (Starworks Motorsport), DP Class:
1 start

2012 Grand-Am Road Racing, (Doran Racing), DP Class:
4 starts, 4 top-ten finishes

2013 Grand-Am Road Racing, (Doran Racing), DP Class:
1 start

Rolex 24 at Daytona history:
8 starts; 4 finishes; 3 top-tens; 1 podium

Made in the USA
Columbia, SC
26 March 2019